THE IMPACT OF WAR (IN UKRAINE) ON THE EU

This timely book astutely charts the transformative effect on the EU of war (in Ukraine) from an EU legal and EU policy perspective. The EU, itself a unique peace project born out of two world wars, consistently reacts to and grows from (security) crisis to (security) crisis. Departing from the usual broad sweep of deepening and widening, this book focuses on the constitutional and substantive impact on the EU of the recent war in Ukraine. More so than ever before, this particular war proves to be a truly pivotal moment for the EU. Drawing on expert contributions from both academia and the EU institutions, this book offers a masterful exploration of how the EU is being challenged to the core.

Volume 132 in the Series Modern Studies in European Law

Modern Studies in European Law

Recent titles in this series:

The Evolving Governance of EU Competition Law in a Time of Disruptions:
A Constitutional Perspective
Edited by Carlo Maria Colombo, Kathryn Wright and Mariolina Eliantonio

The European Integrated Border Management:
Frontex, Human Rights, and International Responsibility
Giulia Raimondo

Private Autonomy in EU Internal Market Law:
Parameters of its Protection and Limitation
Rufat Babayev

Free Movement and Welfare Access in the European Union:
Re-Balancing Conflicting Interests in Citizenship Jurisprudence
Victoria Hooton

EU Trade and Investment Treaty-Making Post-Lisbon:
Moving Beyond Mixity
Gesa Kübek

The Normative Foundations for EU Criminal Justice:
Powers, Limits and Justifications
Jacob Öberg

EU Neighbourhood Law:
Wider Europe and the Extended EU's Legal Space
Alessandro Petti

The Dynamics of Powers in the European Union
Edited by Christina Eckes, Päivi Leino-Sandberg and Anna W Ghavanin

The European Convention on Human Rights and Private Law:
Comparative Perspectives from South-Eastern Europe
Edited by Mateja Durovic and Cristina Poncibò

Judging Composite Decision-Making:
The Transformation of European Administrative Law
Filipe Brito Bastos

EU Diplomacy in Multilateral Fora
Edited by Christine Kaddous and Frank Hoffmeister

The Market Citizenship Illusion: Free Movement Rights for Atypical Workers
Alice Welsh

Actors and Roles in EU Disability Law
Edited by Delia Ferri and Eva S Krolla

The Impact of War (in Ukraine) on the EU
Edited by Inge Govaere, Sacha Garben and Eleanor Spaventa

For the complete list of titles in this series
see www.bloomsbury.com/uk/series/modern-studies-in-european-law/

HART PUBLISHING
Bloomsbury Publishing Plc
Kemp House, Chawley Park, Cumnor Hill, Oxford, OX2 9PH, UK
1385 Broadway, New York, NY 10018, USA
Bloomsbury Publishing Ireland Limited, 29 Earlsfort Terrace, Dublin 2, D02 AY28, Ireland

HART PUBLISHING, the Hart/Stag logo, BLOOMSBURY and the Diana logo are trademarks of Bloomsbury Publishing Plc

First published in Great Britain 2025

A catalogue record for this book is available from the British Library.

A catalogue record for this book is available from the Library of Congress.

Library of Congress Control Number: 2025930951

ISBN: HB: 978-1-50998-608-8
ePDF: 978-1-50998-610-1
ePub: 978-1-50998-609-5

Typeset by Compuscript Ltd, Shannon

For product safety related questions contact productsafety@bloomsbury.com

To find out more about our authors and books visit www.hartpublishing.co.uk. Here you will find extracts, author information, details of forthcoming events and the option to sign up for our newsletters.

The Impact of War (in Ukraine) on the EU

Edited by

Inge Govaere
Sacha Garben
and
Eleanor Spaventa

•HART•
OXFORD • LONDON • NEW YORK • NEW DELHI • SYDNEY

FOREWORD

«L'Europe se fera dans les crises et elle sera la somme des solutions apportées à ces crises». Never, as in these last two decades, has Jean Monnet been proven to be so right.

The European Union – sometimes as part of global trends and events, other times with its own specific dynamics – has experienced 20 years of multiple, consecutive and/or overlapping crises: from the financial one to the so-called 'refugees' crisis; from terrorist attacks on its soil to Brexit; from the COVID pandemic to the effects of climate change. Furthermore, it has seen wars, conflicts, crises and instability in neighbouring territories, from the Middle East and Libya, to the full-scale Russian invasion of Ukraine on 24 February 2022.

Over these two decades the resilience of the EU and its capacity to adapt political and legal frameworks in creative, sustainable manners has been surprisingly effective. Many predicted, during this time, 'the beginning of the end' for the EU. Instead, Jean Monnet's prediction has guided us, collectively, through these tough, challenging, dramatic times. The EU we live in today is exactly the result of its responses to these crises.

Even if the EU has always been shaped by crises, the European reality post-24 February 2022 is profoundly different to anything we have experienced before. The level, speed, unity and relevance of the reaction has been unprecedented. As this book analyses, both the methods and the spirit of the response has been drastically different to how previous challenges, threats and crises were dealt with. Here again, we can refer to Monnet's wisdom to understand the reasons for this: *«Les hommes n'acceptent le changement que dans la nécessité et ils ne voient la nécessité que dans la crise».*

This different level of crisis has accorded a different level of response, driven by the full and common awareness, among European leaders, decision-makers and public opinion, of the necessity for change.

To navigate the complex lands of the impact of crises and their multiple ramifications – and specifically of the war against Ukraine – on the EU, we need solid compasses. This volume provides us an extraordinarily valuable tool to decrypt (and in some cases predict) trends in the EU responses to crises, in an extremely comprehensive and original way.

I am particularly proud that this insightful book project is based on an academic conference organised by the European Legal Studies Department of the College [illegible]urope, held in Bruges in March 2023 – which I had the privilege and honour to [illegible]. The conference brought together renowned scholars of European integra-[illegible]hem numerous resident and visiting faculty members as well as academic [illegible]llege of Europe, whose contributions have been invaluable in under-[illegible]d impact of the Russian war against Ukraine on the EU.

The analyses in this volume cover a wide array of topics, from the deepening of EU integration in politically sensitive areas like defence and migration to paradigm shifts in energy policy and transport networks. These contributions not only highlight the immediate impacts but also forecast the mid- and long-term implications for the EU's legal and constitutional framework. They offer valuable perspectives on how crises can serve as catalysts for change, driving forward the EU's integration agenda and shaping its future trajectory. I would like to acknowledge the contributions of the various authors and conference participants who contributed to and inspired this volume. Their insights and analyses have been invaluable in understanding the profound and multifaceted impact of the war on the EU.

Continued academic and policy discussions are crucial as the EU navigates these transformative times. By fostering a deeper understanding of the way in which the EU has responded to crises, we can provide precious elements for the shaping of future decision-making on how to strengthen, deepen and broaden the EU, both at a political and institutional level.

Understanding and embracing the lessons learned from this crisis, and from the peculiar way the EU has reacted to it, will be vital in continuing the journey of our integration.

Federica Mogherini

CONTENTS

CONTRIBUTORS

Marta Arpio, Director, Secretariat-General, Council of the EU

Matej Avbelj, Professor of European Law, Jean Monnet Chair, New University, Slovenia

Chloé Brière, Professor of EU law, Université libre de Bruxelles

Daniel Calleja, Director-General of the Legal Service, European Commission

Margherita Corsaro, Ecommerce Europe, formerly working in the European Commission

Bruno De Witte, Emeritus Professor of European law, Maastricht University

Eugenia Dumitriu Segnana, Director, Directorate 4 of the Legal Service, Council of the EU

Federico Fabbrini, Full Professor of European Law at Dublin City University and Founding Director of the Dublin European Law Institute (DELI)

Sacha Garben, Professor of EU Law, College of Europe (Bruges)

Inge Govaere, Professor of European Law, Director, Ghent European Law Institute (GELI) at Ghent University and Director of the European Legal Studies Department at the College of Europe (Bruges)

Kees Groenendijk, Emeritus Professor of Sociology of Law, Radboud University, Nijmegen, the Netherlands

Elspeth Guild, Professor of Law, University of Liverpool and Visiting Professor, College of Europe (Bruges)

Erwan Lannon, Professor at Ghent University – Ghent European Law Institute (GELI) and Visiting Professor at the College of Europe (Bruges and Natolin)

Dzhuliia Lypalo, lawyer at the Brussels Bar; associate at Linklaters LLP

Antigoni Matthaiou, Associate at Van Bael & Bellis

Christian Mestre, Professor at the University of Wuhan, Institute of International Law and Visiting Professor at College of Europe (Bruges)

Pierpaolo Settembri, European Commission, College of Europe, Sciences Po Paris

Beate Sjåfjell, Professor, Faculty of Law, University of Oslo; Visiting Professor, European Legal Studies Department, College of Europe; Academic Chair, the European University Alliance Circle U

Iyiola Solanke, Jacques Delors Professor of European Union Law at the University of Oxford and a Fellow of Somerville College, and a Visiting Professor at College of Europe (Bruges)

Eleanor Spaventa, Professor of European Union law at the law department of Bocconi University (Milan), Director Bocconi Lab in European Law (BLEST), and Visiting Professor at College of Europe

Erriketi Tla da Silva, Senior Academic Assistant at the College of Europe (Bruges) and a PhD candidate at Universiteit Wageningen, the Netherlands

Isabelle Van Damme, Professor of International Economic Law and Director of Studies at the World Trade Institute and the University of Bern, of counsel at Van Bael & Bellis, and Visiting Professor at the College of Europe (Bruges)

Introduction: The Impact of War (in Ukraine) on the EU

INGE GOVAERE, SACHA GARBEN AND ELEANOR SPAVENTA*

1. The Deepening and Widening of EU Integration

The European Union (EU), in all its complexity, is a unique peace project born out of two World Wars. The occurrence of warfare on the European continent on the edges of the EU proved in the late 1980s to be a strong driver, spurring on both the deepening and widening of the EU integration process. This potentially highly transformational impact of warfare in Europe on the EU itself is once again palpable today and is the focus of this book. What are the legal conundrums and options for the future of the EU posed by the war in Ukraine? Rather than discussing the EU's response to the ongoing war in Ukraine as such, the purpose is to adopt an inward-looking approach and scrutinise the EU transformational process from different angles and legal disciplines.

At the time of writing, it is almost three years since Russia dramatically escalated its illegal aggression on the sovereign territory of the Ukraine, and the human cost has been unspeakable. Where in the early days of the war there was still hope for a quick resolution, there now no longer seems to be a clear end in sight. Internal USA politics and the outcome of the USA elections are casting a shadow over the Transatlantic coalition of support for Ukraine, as it does for future relations with the EU and its unwavering commitment to NATO. Nevertheless, the EU remains steadfast in its quest for peace on the European continent and its support of Ukraine. As the Presidents of the Council, Commission and Parliament confirmed in their joint statement on 23 February 2024:

> The European Union will continue its strong and unwavering political, military, financial, economic, diplomatic and humanitarian support to help Ukraine defend itself, protect its people, its cities and its critical infrastructure, restore its territorial integrity, bring back the thousands of deported children, and bring the war to an end.
>
> The European Union has decided to open accession negotiations with Ukraine and will help it on its path towards EU membership. The future of Ukraine lies in the European Union. The European Union will continue to provide Ukraine with regular and predictable financial support. The 50 billion euro financial assistance package for 2024–2027 will help Ukraine meet its immediate needs, rebuild its economy and society, modernise its institutions and consolidate democracy and the rule of law.

* We would like to warmly thank Gordon Abeiku Mensah for the excellent assistance on the editing of the book chapters.

As a corollary effect, the war in Ukraine has spurred on 'tectonic shifts'[1] within the EU, in both constitutional and material terms. It is these textural and substantive changes to the EU legal order that are the subject of this book, borne out of a conference organised by the European Legal Studies Department of the College of Europe, Bruges.[2] As the various contributions to this book set out in great detail, the war has had a transformative impact in the *deepening* of EU integration in several politically sensitive areas, such as in the Common Foreign and Security Policy (CFSP) and defence, energy, transport and migration, and moreover has had a paradigm-shifting impact on the *broadening* of the EU integration process, as after many years of 'enlargement fatigue'[3] there is suddenly a new zeal for enlargement in Brussels and the EU national capitals. As an eye-catching result, discussed in more detail by Erwan Lannon in chapter seven, Ukraine, Moldova, Georgia, and Bosnia and Herzegovina are now official candidates for EU membership. In his chapter, Lannon raises difficult questions. With the outcome of the war being unpredictable, 'can a country (even only technically) at war become a Member State of the EU?' And further: 'Where to stop EU's integration? And what alternative to offer to European countries that either cannot (yet) join the EU or are not willing to join the EU?' To this, it seems, there are no easy answers.

2. The Impact on Methods and Spirit

One thing becomes instantly clear when surveying the various chapters in this book: the EU's response to the war in Ukraine has been surprisingly cohesive, determined and convincing. This is related *to the way in which* the EU has responded, ie in terms of its methods. And it is the result, and expression, of *the mentality in which* it has acted, namely in a spirit of solidarity with, firstly, Ukraine, and secondly, with one another. Both present a marked change compared to the previous decades of European (dis?) integration.

2.1. Methods

Strikingly, with the EU's response to the war, we have seen a firm return of the Community method even in times of crisis. Building on the strengthened legal framework introduced by the Lisbon Treaty to manage emergencies and crisis,[4] and new-found confidence in the EU's use of 'regular' EU law provisions and procedures after its response to the COVID-19 pandemic, the various actions taken in the different areas

[1] Informal meeting of the Heads of State or Government Declaration, Versailles, 10 and 11 March 2022, point 6.

[2] We wish to warmly thank all the participants to the Conference for their valuable participation. A special thanks also to Valérie Hauspie, the team of Academic Assistants and the 'Flying Faculty' for their input and help in the organisation of the programme and the event itself.

[3] D Devrim and E Schulz, 'Enlargement Fatigue in the European Union: From Enlargement to Many Unions' Real Instituto Elcano (2009), available at www.realinstitutoelcano.org/en/work-document/enlargement-fatigue-in-the-european-union-from-enlargement-to-many-unions-wp.

[4] See I Govaere and S Poli (eds), *EU Management of Global Emergencies: Legal Framework for Combating Threats and Crises* (Leiden, Brill, 2014).

of EU law in response to the war have similarly been firmly grounded in the Treaties. This is a remarkable shift, in stark contrast with the handling of some previous crises the EU has faced, particularly in the economic and financial crisis and connected debt crises, as well as in the 2015 so-called 'migration crisis'. In those cases, it was, the Union method – touted by Angela Merkel in her Bruges speech at the College of Europe[5] – that was widely considered, even by its critics, as the only alternative. This 'bits-and-pieces'[6] method mixes soft law and intergovernmentalism with EU and international hard law, is operated by shapeshifting European institutions alternating or double-hatting between their formal EU capacity and as forums for, or agents of, (some) of the Member States, with the goal of doing 'whatever it takes' to get results.

Although arguably at odds with the various achievements of democratic and constitutional legitimacy of the EU,[7] the Court condoned this demise of the Community method. As noted by Lenaerts and Gutiérrez-Fons, with *Pringle*,[8] the Court did not 'base its reasoning on "constitutional policy", ie arguments which focus on the legitimacy of this new form of governance' as it was 'for the political process to determine whether the SCG and ESM Treaties constitute a positive way for European integration to move forward'.[9] The abdication of responsibility in a 'Community based on the rule of law'[10] symbolised the pervasive sense that we would simply have to resign ourselves to the *Real*-law that in crisis situations, in the enlarged EU, these was no time or place for constitutional and democratic niceties.[11] In some way, this was a condemnation both of enlargement and of the Community method.

How different is reality now. As our contributors to part three, 'Institutional Views', all underline, the EU's response largely consists of the adoption of new legal acts, making use of existing legal bases in the Treaties. Marta Arpio states in chapter sixteen:

> When speaking about the impact of the war (in Ukraine) in the EU Constitutional blueprint, the first thing to note is that the response of the EU to the war has demonstrated the capacity and flexibility of the EU Treaties to cope with new unexpected situations, as the Russian aggression against Ukraine was. On the basis of the EU Treaties, the EU has been able to adopt, in a very short timeframe, far-reaching actions and measures to face the situation, some of them previously unthinkable.

Daniel Calleja concurs, stating in chapter seventeen: 'these unprecedented challenges arising from the war have best demonstrated the ability of the Union to act legally'; and

[5] Speech by Federal Chancellor Angela Merkel at the opening ceremony of the 61st academic year of the College of Europe in Bruges on 2 November 2010, available at www.coleurope.eu/sites/default/files/speech-files/europakolleg_brugge_mitschrift_englisch_0.pdf.

[6] D Curtin, 'The Constitutional Structure of the Union: A Europe of Bits and Pieces' (1993) 1 *Common Market Law Review* 17. For a revisitation of the theme by the author, see D Curtin, 'From a Europe of Bits and Pieces to a Union of Variegated Differentiation' EUI working paper (2020) RSCAS 2020/37.

[7] See the various contributions to S Garben, I Govaere and P Nemitz (eds), *Critical Reflections on Constitutional Democracy in the EU* (Oxford, Hart Publishing, 2019).

[8] Case C-370/12, *Thomas Pringle v Government of Ireland and Others*, EU:C:2012:756.

[9] K Lenaerts and J Gutiérrez-Fons, 'A Constitutional Perspective' in R Schütze and T Tridimas, *Oxford Principles of European Union Law, Vol I: The European Union Legal Order* (Oxford University Press,m 2018) 131.

[10] Case 294/83, *Parti écologiste "Les Verts" v European Parliament*, EU:C:1986:166.

[11] The Court has somewhat mitigated this problem by holding that EU institutions remain bound by the EU Charter of Fundamental Rights also when acting outside the EU legal framework. Joined Cases C-8/15 P to C-10/15 P, *Ledra Advertising Ltd and Others v European Commission and European Central Bank (ECB)*, EU:C:2016:701.

'the Union has managed to deliver, using the law as its guiding principle and its most effective tool'. Although keen to contest the criticism of the previous 'intergovernmental' approach to the handling of crises, Eugenia Dumitriu Segnana in chapter fifteen also agrees that the EU's response to Ukraine confirms

> a renewed impetus for European integration after a period of fatigue, illustrated by increased recourse to European solutions, making full use of the Union institutions and the legal framework foreseen in the Treaties. Collective responses to common challenges are discussed within the Union, in line with the aim of the Union of creating 'a process of creating an ever-closer union among the people of Europe' (Article 1 TEU).

Sometimes, these actions have simply involved a scaling-up of the EU's previous activities. As Chloé Brière reports in chapter eleven on the EU's response to war crimes, 'the EU has mobilised the instruments it traditionally relies on for the pursuit of foreign policy objectives. These measures do not constitute a fundamental change, even though the scale of the EU's response is different'. For one, 'the financial resources made available are higher than ever before, and the restrictive measures have targeted a higher number of persons on a relatively short timeframe and prior to the issuance of arrest warrants against them.' Furthermore, institutionally, the main impact has been in 'the new tasks granted to Eurojust, whose role evolved substantially after February 2022, giving a new impetus to its operational activities and capacities', constituting a quantitative but not qualitative shift.

The fact that the (more) effective use of an already existing policy can in some situations amount to a qualitative shift is demonstrated by the first-ever activation of the Temporary Protection Directive, examined by Elspeth Guild, Kees Groenendijk and Dzhuliia Lypalo in chapter 8:

> The opening of a special protection scheme for Ukrainians and non-Ukrainians who were resident there on the date of the invasion and entered the EU thereafter, which includes extensive rights, has been one of the most immediate and far-reaching EU responses to the 24 February 2022 Russian invasion of Ukraine.[12] The legal basis of the scheme is a directive adopted in 2001 on Temporary Protection,[13] … which had been slated for repeal, although this had not happened at the date of the invasion and is now on hold. Since then, according to UNHCR, 5,977,800[14] Ukrainians (or persons who were resident in Ukraine at the relevant date) have been recorded across Europe.

Other times, much like during the COVID-19 pandemic, the EU's legal response has entailed a degree of 'creative engineering'.[15] Federico Fabbrini sets out in chapter nine how the Act in Support of Ammunition Production (ASAP) – a new regulation adopted by the European Parliament and the Council to boost the production and procurement of ammunition and missiles to support Ukraine in the war against Russia – has 'attributed to the Commission the authority to use resources from the EU budget to fund the

[12] All EU states are part of the scheme with the exception of Denmark, which, because of particularities in its constitutional position in the EU, opened a parallel national scheme rather than join the EU scheme.

[13] Council Directive 2001/55/EC of 20 July 2001 on minimum standards for giving temporary protection in the event of a mass influx of displaced persons and on measures promoting a balance of efforts between the Member States in receiving such persons and bearing the consequences thereof [2001] OJ L 212/12.

[14] data2.unhcr.org/en/situations/ukraine.

[15] B de Witte, 'The European Union's COVID-19 recovery plan: The legal engineering of an economic policy shift' (2021) 58 *Common Market Law Review* 635.

industrial production of ammunitions and missiles urgently needed by Ukraine, thus helping to strengthen the EU's role in developing common defence capabilities' through 'a constructive use of supranational legal bases in the Treaties', thereby pushing 'the EU into a new terrain; that of industrial defence policy'.

Various authors stress that these changes, although brought about in a specific crisis context, are likely to be permanent. Isabelle Van Damme and Antigoni Matthaiou describe, in chapter ten, the 'sanctions revolution':

> The EU sanctions against Russia[16] are unparalleled in terms of scope and impact,[17] marking a 'sanctions revolution'.[18] Their objectives are clear and remain strongly supported, including at the multilateral level. They are imposed against a (previously) close trading partner of the EU, which is not the case for many other EU sanctions. Moreover, their effects on the geopolitical framework within which trade and other commercial relations take place are expected to be lasting and transformative.

Similarly, in the entirely different area of transport, Pierpaolo Settembri and Margherita Corsaro in chapter fourteen argue that Russia's aggression in Ukraine has 'changed EU transport policy for good':

> Measures such as the Solidarity Lanes, which were taken as an emergency reaction to address a specific problem, have created new trade and transport routes that are today stable, essential and irreversible (and growing). The corridors of TEN-T network have been redesigned and extended to reflect this new reality and to accelerate the integration of Ukraine (and Moldova) into the EU. This effort has been matched by corresponding changes in the way EU infrastructure policy is funded, notably by extending CEF to Ukraine and Moldova, repurposing other EU funds and involving international financial institutions to mobilise up to €1 billion just to increase the capacity of the Solidarity Lanes. In turn, partnerships with other third countries have been deprioritised and alternative global routes are being reconsidered, with the consequence that the broader transport landscape is undergoing a major shake-up.

As crises tend to do, the war exposed previously existing vulnerabilities. Christian Mestre in chapter thirteen argues that the international food system has already been disturbed by the COVID pandemic, drought brought on by climate change and rises in food prices. '[T]he war has deepened [the] food vulnerabilities' that were already present, and provided a catalyst for the adoption for a range of measures by the EU institutions. As he states, these

> measures and actions taken since the beginning of the conflict aimed to ensure food security in a European and international framework and restore the EU's food independency. These challenges should fundamentally change the philosophy and purposes of the CAP, and restore

[16] Council Regulation (EU) 269/2014 of 17 March 2014 concerning restrictive measures in respect of actions undermining or threatening the territorial integrity, sovereignty and independence of Ukraine [2014] OJ L78/6 (Current consolidated version: 15/09/2023) and Council Regulation (EU) 833/2014 of 31 July 2014 concerning restrictive measures in view of Russia's actions destabilizing the situation in Ukraine [2014] OJ L229/1 (Current consolidated version: 01/10/2023). Sanctions against Russia have first been implemented through both Regulations in reaction to the 2014 illegal annexation of Crimea. Following February 2022 full-scale invasion of Ukraine, these legislations have been substantially expanded by twelve sanctions packages. These latest developments are the main subject of our analysis.

[17] A Carpile and A Delivorias, 'EU sanctions on Russia: Overview, impact, challenges' (2023) *European Parliamentary Research Service PE 739.366.*

[18] Council of the European Union, 'EU sanctions in response to Russia's invasion of Ukraine (2023), available at www.consilium.europa.eu/en/infographics/eu-sanctions-russia-ukraine-invasion.

the balance between the production of food commodities and the respect for environmental protection.

Structural changes are thus fundamentally affecting EU law and policy in a variety of policy areas. These evolutions are, for now, taking place within the current framework of the post-Lisbon Treaties. The closest we are coming to effective Treaty change is with the intention to use the *passerelle* clause to move from unanimity to qualified majority voting in the area of Common Foreign and Security Policy. That change would be symbolic for the Union's new communitarian élan, facilitating the use of the Community method in future foreign policy crises.

There is one important exception to this trend. The European Political Community (EPC) was established after Russia's invasion of Ukraine, as an intergovernmental forum of the 44 European Heads of State, including all EU Member States.[19] At the three EPC meetings to date, the President of the European Council, the President of the European Commission, the President of the European Parliament and the High Representative of the European Union for Foreign Affairs and Security Policy also joined. As Bruno De Witte examines in chapter six, the contours and authority of the EPC are somewhat unclear, and for now not very convincing. The European Political Community aims to 'foster political dialogue and cooperation to address issues of common interest' and to 'strengthen the security, stability and prosperity of the European continent', stressing that this 'platform for political coordination does not replace any existing organisation, structure or process, and does not aim to create new ones at this stage'. As de Witte points out:

> [I]t seems … likely that the EPC will continue its current twilight existence as a forum for political dialogue without any concrete legal existence … But, if the EPC remains merely a forum for political dialogue, it is difficult to see how it could fulfil the ambitious role envisaged by its promotors, of being a dynamic and effective cooperation scheme that can connect Ukraine (and other candidate states) to their European partner countries whilst they wait for the many hurdles in the EU accession process to be overcome.

For now, it seems that this forum is providing a harmless setting for pan-European discussion and possible some loose coordination on important geopolitical issues. It remains to be seen if it can walk the tightrope between being so benign that it will soon be obsolete, and so useful that it will soon become problematic.

2.2. Spirit

What has made this remarkably effective and smooth cooperation possible, ultimately, is solidarity: a realisation that we as Europeans are 'in this' together and that we *all depend on peace* for anything we may want to do or have or be in life. We have seen outpourings of solidarity in society, and we have seen it at the level of the European governments and in the EU institutions through common action. Indeed, as Daniel

[19] The other countries are: Albania, Andorra, Armenia, Bosnia and Herzegovina, Georgia, Iceland, Kosovo, Liechtenstein, Moldova, Monaco, Montenegro, North Macedonia, Norway, San Marino, Serbia, Switzerland, Ukraine and the United Kingdom.

Calleja states in chapter seventeen, 'Unity and solidarity are the two key principles at stake here'. Solidarity language now permeates the political narrative about the EU's response to the war in Ukraine. Such political narratives on values generally, and solidarity in particular, have real impact. 'Different justificatory arguments have different impacts on the solidarity structure of the Union as well as on what "point and purpose" the EU is perceived to have'.[20] Moreover, as Sacha Garben sets out in chapter three, solidarity can have a tangible legal impact. Shortly before Russia's full-scale invasion, in light of the already existing Russian territorial breaches of Ukraine, the Court of Justice had in its *OPAL* ruling given firmer legal teeth than expected to the principle of solidarity in energy.[21] This can now be seized on by the Commission to develop its common energy policies,[22] capitalising on the surge of public support for this in reaction to the war.[23] But *OPAL* is of general relevance, beyond the field of energy, as the Court deliberately broadens the reflection and confirms solidarity's foundational importance in the EU legal order. As a general principle of EU law, it produces 'binding legal effects on the Member States and institutions of the European Union'. In the case at hand, this translated in a standard for the legality review. But perhaps (even) more powerful could be its role in 'influencing judicial methodology',[24] across all areas of EU law.

Sacha Garben argues that the Court should anchor its interpretation of solidarity in the EU Charter of Fundamental Rights, where it states that 'the Union is founded on the indivisible, universal values of human dignity, freedom, equality and solidarity'.[25] This may, for one, allow a different angle to conceptualise what solidarity in the field of energy should be about. On the one hand, as the Court held in *OPAL*, it requires solidarity between Member States. On the other hand, we may note, that a reading of solidarity in light of the EU Charter of Fundamental Rights, and particularly its Solidarity Chapter, means that solidarity in energy is also to be extended to those in society who are less well off, and – crucially – to future generations. That latter requirement in particular has, arguably, been missing in the EU's recent energy reforms since the war. As Erriketi Tla da Silva shows in chapter twelve, although the REPowerEU plan[26] represents a big step towards energy transition and reducing dependency on Russian fossil fuels, some of the targeted amendments to existing energy and environment legislation and to the Recovery and Resilience Facility are a risk to environmental protection and may lead to environmental degradation. She warns that amendments to the Renewable Energy Directive are not temporary, and that even the changes introduced by the

[20] A Sangiovanni 'Solidarity in the European Union.' (2013) 33 *Oxford Journal of Legal Studies* 213; J Miro, 'Debating fiscal solidarity in the EU: interests, values and identities in the legitimation of the Next Generation EU plan' (2022) 44 *Journal of European Integration* 307.

[21] Case C-848/19 P, *OPAL*, ECLI:EU:C:2021:598.

[22] L Marin, 'The principle of energy solidarity at its first stress test: the mitigation of the energy crisis between national sovereignty and supranational integration' *Diritti Comparati* (30 November2022), available at www.diritticomparati.it/the-principle-of-energy-solidarity-at-its-first-stress-test-the-mitigation-of-the-energy-crisis-between-national-sovereignty-and-supranational-integration/.

[23] eupinions.eu/de/text/under-pressure.

[24] T Tridimas, 'The general principles of EU law and the Europeanisation of national laws' (2020) 13 *Review of European Administrative Law* 5.

[25] Preamble.

[26] Commission, Communication from the Commission to the European Parliament, the European Council, the Council, the European Economic and Social Committee and The Committee of the Regions, REPowerEU Plan [2022] COM(2022) 230 final.

'emergency' Regulation (EU) 2022/2577 amount to a partial deregulation of renewable energy projects, with long-lasting effects that extend beyond the duration of the adopted provisions. She states that 'the presumptions and the exemptions introduced by these legislative changes can be characterised as a reversal of environmental standards that would be prohibited under the principle of non-regression underscoring the EU Treaties' – and we may add that it could similarly be incompatible with the principle of solidarity when interpreted in an inter-generational way, as the Solidarity Chapter of the EU Charter of Fundamental Rights solicits.

Furthermore, a universal interpretation of the general principle of solidarity in EU law would be a step towards addressing the shortcomings in the EU's moral, social fabric, as discussed by Iyiola Solanke in chapter four. Therein, she examines how the European solidarity we have seen expressed in response to the war in Ukraine is a somewhat treacherous one, extended to white Ukrainians but not on an equal basis to any other person fleeing Ukraine with a different skin colour. Furthermore, the triggering of the Temporary Protection Directive for Ukrainians begged the question why this had not been done for other refugees of war, such as Syrians or North Africans after the Arab Spring. As Solanke states:

> It has been boldly asserted that the war in Ukraine has 'profoundly changed'[27] the EU. Yet it has also highlighted deep-seated shortcomings in racial solidarity in Europe, and the limits to which racialised persons – regardless of citizenship or legal status[28] – are seen as having a European identity. If the EU has found a new common sense of military purpose, it is to be hoped that this will be accompanied by a new sense of social justice.

Indeed, the conception of solidarity that underpins EU migration law in particular is not universal, but exclusionary. It requires solidarity between Member States of the EU that need to cooperate to share the *burden* of immigrants.[29] A paradigm-shift is sorely needed here,[30] and a universal reading of the general principle of solidarity by the Court can procure it.

That is not to say that there may not be special duties, special solidarity, in the face of special circumstances. The latter could perhaps be inferred from the fact that Ukraine in the Euro-maidan lived a true Ackerman-ian 'constitutional moment' of popular mobilisation in favour of closer ties with the EU rather than Russia, which connects the EU people and the Ukranians in a special way. But as the minimum standards of dignity and solidarity are lacking as regards other groups of migrants,[31] or even non-migrant national minorities, the contrast with the treatment of Ukrainians brings out some dangerous in-group out-groups sub-currents of non-universal identity-based solidarity that Europe knows all too well, and that the raison d'être of the EU is, or should be, to escape from.

[27] P Wintour, 'No turning back': how the Ukraine war has profoundly changed the EU' *The Guardian* (30 September 2023), available at /www.theguardian.com/world/2023/sep/30/ukraine-russia-war-changed-eu?utm_term=6517c778fcd3adb22de89f06840d131c&utm_campaign=GuardianTodayUK&utm_source=esp&utm_medium=Email&CMP=GTUK_email.

[28] J Silga, 'Migration, Asylum and EU Anti-Discrimination Law' in C O'Cinneide, J Ringelheim and I Solanke (eds), *Edward Elgar Research Handbook on European Anti-Discrimination Law* (forthcoming).

[29] Cases C-715/17, C-718/17 and C-719/17.

[30] V Mitsilegas, 'Solidarity and Trust in the Common European Asylum System' (2014) 2 *Comparative Migration Studies* 181.

[31] S Carrera and R Cortinovis, 'The declaration on a voluntary solidarity mechanism and EU asylum policy – One Step Forward, Three Steps Back on Equal Solidarity' CEPS (2022), available at www.ceps.eu/wp-content/uploads/2022/10/CEPS-In-depth-analysis-2022-04_Voluntary-Solidarity.pdf.

For indeed, the EU, at its core, is a peace-project. As Matej Avbelj sets out in chapter two, 'peace has been from the very outset – and enduringly – the main normative value of the integration process'. As he recalls, even the future European federation, intimated in the Schuman declaration, is not a goal in and of itself; rather it has been advanced as 'indispensable to the preservation of peace'.[32] Unpacking the very concept of peace and tracing its evolution throughout European integration, Avbelj states that peace is considered as just peace, whose content is determined with reference to fundamental values of the EU, which are 'part of our soul, part of what defines us today':[33]

> The war in Ukraine presents more than a credible threat to the internal peace in the EU and it certainly signifies a total absence of peace in external terms, both under its subjective and objective conception. The normative relevance of the value of peace in the EU today is at an all-time high and it can be expected, even if for purely utilitarian reasons, that it will provide a significant boost to the process of European integration, in its widening and deepening leg alike. Provided, of course, that Ukraine prevails. In the opposite scenario not only just peace in the EU, but its very survival might be at stake. It is for that reason that the strategy of achieving peace in the EU and beyond has undergone a complete transformation from economic, political and legal peace-building mechanisms to the more recent explicit investment in the military capacity of the EU and its Member States. Peace continues to remain an enduring source of legitimisation of European integration, but the means of achieving it have been altered beyond imagination.

In this respect, Inge Govaere points out in chapter one that the first and foremost express objective of the EU as listed in Article 3(1) TEU is 'to promote peace, its values and the well-being of its peoples'. Against this backdrop several 'existential' conundrums posed by the war (in Ukraine) are pinpointed. In particular it is discussed why war *necessarily* triggers a transformative process of the EU which may be considered as truly 'existential' in nature. Then the issue is addressed of the limits and challenges that are exposed by the war in Ukraine for the EU as a global actor, before more introspectively dwelling on the future of the EU integration model in terms of a peace project based on common values.

Concurring with the observations about peace, solidarity and the need for the EU to address its colonial history that were raised in the preceding chapters, Beate Sjåfjell in chapter five argues that:

> A different approach is needed in the EU institutions' implementation of Treaty duties, to achieve sustainability and lasting peace. Ensuring peace is more than the absence of war; it is about contributing to global social justice and the mitigation of pressures on the very basis of human existence. Prerequisites for the fundamental transformation needed are a deeper recognition of the Europe's colonial history and its current neocolonialism, and revitalisation of the EU Treaty concept of solidarity;[34] towards a humble solidarity, 'unbound' by geopolitical borders.[35]

[32] Schuman Declaration, May 1950.

[33] U von der Leyen, 'State of the Union Speech 2021', available at ec.europa.eu/commission/presscorner/detail/en/SPEECH_21_4701.

[34] Garben, ch 3 in this volume.

[35] T Novitz, 'Sustainability as Solidarity Unbound: Labour Rights and Collective Voice in the United Nations Sustainable Development Goals and the European Union' in J López López (ed), *Inscribing Solidarity: Debates in Labor Law and Beyond* (Cambridge University Press, 2022), available at www.cambridge.org/core/books/inscribing-solidarity/sustainability-as-solidarity-unbound/017122A8C9FA18647A476FE91DBC4266.

3. From the Ashes of War

From the ashes of war may rise, once again, a stronger and more united Europe. What began as Ukranian's Constitutional Moment in the Euro-maidan, may prove to have become a Constitutional Moment for the entire EU, leaving it forever more deeply and broadly transformed. Importantly, contrary to the previous crises that have marked Europe over the past 15 years, the present extreme and urgent situation is not leading the EU to dilute its commitment to the establishment of transnational Constitutional Democracy but rather to take its foundational values more seriously. It is heartening, in particular, to see a rediscovery by the EU institutions, including the Court of Justice, of peace and solidarity at the very core of this foundation. Should, as previous enlargements did, the pre-accession discussions and reflections lead to the undertaking of internal reform through Treaty change, it may be hoped that these will further solidify these positive developments.

PART I

Constitutional Impact

1

Transformative Impact on the European Union of War (in Ukraine): Existential Conundrums

INGE GOVAERE

1.1. Introduction

War and peace lie at the very core of the European integration process.[1] Born out of two World Wars causing major destruction and bloodshed on the European continent, the first (and foremost) express objective of the EU as listed in Article 3(1) TEU is 'to promote peace, its values and the well-being of its peoples'.[2]

In view of this clear peacekeeping objective, the outbreak of warfare, especially when it occurs on a large scale on the European continent, inevitably leads the EU and its Member States to question it and to be put under considerable pressure both from outside and within to find an adequate response. Yet what is 'adequate' and from what perspective should this be assessed? Intuitively one might be tempted to focus especially on the EU's capacity to impact the countries at war, in particular Ukraine and Russia. That is not the perspective of this chapter. Instead, its analysis is purposely introspective, first identifying what makes the EU this special kind of global actor so very different from states and other international organisations (eg NATO), in order to assess how the current war possibly erodes these unique core characteristics.

How can there be an absolute certainty that the current war in Ukraine will fundamentally impact the EU? The straightforward explanation is that the EU is inherently a peace project carried forward by a reactive integration process spurred on by war. The European integration process is born out of the two World Wars fought on the European continent. Furthermore, it was in the wake of renewed war and bloodshed just outside

[1] The very first sentence of the 1950 Schuman Declaration reads: 'World peace cannot be safeguarded without the making of creative efforts proportionate to the dangers which threaten it.' The full text can be consulted at european-union.europa.eu/principles-countries-history/history-eu/1945-59/schuman-declaration-may-1950_en.

[2] This primary objective of the EU has often been forgotten and is apparently understudied even among scholars of International Peace and Conflict Studies; see H Anastasiou, 'The EU as a Peace Building System: Deconstructing Nationalism in an Era of Globalization' (2007) 12 *International Journal of Peace Studies* 31.

its borders, triggered by the end of the Cold War, that the 'European Union' as such fully emerged in the Maastricht Treaty and matured into the global actor that it is today.

The fact that warfare necessarily has a transformative impact on the EU is thus not of itself problematic per se. The thesis put forward here is that this transformation process may however pose an existential threat for the EU when it disregards and potentially jeopardises the uniqueness of the EU's peace objective and peacekeeping method combined. The transformative impact of war thus raises truly existential conundrums for the EU whenever its identity as a global actor is no longer taken for granted, or is even openly questioned. Such is the risk currently.

The aim of this chapter is thus to point to existential conundrums which the EU reaction to the war in Ukraine poses for the very identity of the EU itself. This is systematically analysed on the basis of three different but related questions. Section 1.2 explores what constitutes the EU identity; in other words that makes the EU such an unique global actor in terms of its peace objective and peacekeeping method. This sets the theoretical benchmark for the further analysis throughout the chapter. Section 1.3 looks into why and how war always and necessarily triggers a transformative process for the EU which may be considered as truly 'existential' in nature. Next, section 1.4 pinpoints when this transformation may be considered problematic for the EU, in particular in the current day and age. The issue will be briefly addressed of the limits and challenges that are exposed by the war in Ukraine for the EU as a global actor. Section 1.5 then ponders two potentially existential shifts provoked by the current response to the war in Ukraine, namely the shift from a soft to a (semi-) hard power, and a shift from revising membership conditions to revisiting the finality of the EU as such.

Without pertaining to be exhaustive, the focus will consistently lay on pinpointing existential conundrums as posed by the war (in Ukraine) for the specificity of the EU integration process. In so doing, it thus seeks to identify some red lines or red flags in terms of preserving the EU's identity, rather than to formulate conclusive answers.

1.2. The EU Identity: A Peace Project with a Unique Peacekeeping Method

The EU is inherently, and above all, a peace project. It was put into place after the two World Wars as a special kind of international organisation with the express aim to promote peace, its values and the well-being of its peoples. The competences conferred by the EU Treaties serve this higher and noble peace objective and should facilitate the attainment thereof.[3]

[3] Article 5 TEU lays down the principle of conferral, which clearly distinguishes the EU from a state. For an analysis of the complexity of this principle post-Lisbon, see I Govaere, 'To Give or to Grab: The Principle of Full, Crippled and Split Conferral of Powers Post-Lisbon' in M Cremona (ed), *Structural Principles in EU External Relations Law* (Oxford, Hart Publishing, 2018) 71–91. See also M Cremona, 'External competences and the principle of conferral' in R Schutze and T Tridimas (eds), *Oxford principles of European Union law* (Oxford, Oxford University Press, 2018) 1110–40. For a discussion of the division of competences, see S Garben, 'Confronting the Competence Conundrum: Democratising the European Union through an Expansion of its Legislative Powers' (2015) 35 *Oxford Journal of Legal Studies* 55; see also the various contributions to S Garben and I Govaere (eds), *The Division of Competences between the European Union and its Member States: Reflections on the Past, Present and Future* (Oxford, Hart Publishing, 2017).

The specificity of the EU, however, lies in the outspoken and unique soft power method used to secure peace. Although increasingly confounded with a state,[4] it is this intrinsic soft power characteristic which distinguishes the EU from (its Member) States, as well as from other international organisations expressly endowed with military capacity and traditionally tasked with securing military deterrence in Europe, in particular NATO.[5]

The uniqueness of the EU peacekeeping method rests on two intertwined and unique features, namely forging strategic economic interdependence and respecting a common set of core values.

Firstly, instead of relying on hard power and military deterrence, as NATO does,[6] the EU most visibly seeks to avoid armed conflict between Member States by creating far-reaching economic interdependence and deep (common/internal) market integration, so that no Member States can afford to wage war against another.[7]

Strategically starting out with the crucial commodities needed to wage war in the last century, namely coal and steel,[8] quickly followed by nuclear energy,[9] today the internal market logic encompasses most aspects of the economy and is still growing.[10]

Secondly, the fundamental constitutional conditionality is the respect by all the Member States of the common values, listed in Article 2 TEU,[11] including democracy, the rule of law and human rights.[12]

[4] See for instance the analysis of how the EU moves away from being a specialised international organisation, in J Larik, 'Foreign Policy Objectives as Norms of EU Constitutional Law in J Larik, *Foreign Policy Objectives in European Constitutional Law* (Oxford, 2016; online edn, Oxford Academic, 23 June 2016), available at doi.org/10.1093/acprof:oso/9780198736394.003.0004.

[5] The key principle of collective defence is laid down in Art 5 of The North Atlantic Treaty of 4 April 1949: 'The Parties agree that an armed attack against one or more of them in Europe or North America shall be considered an attack against them all and consequently they agree that, if such an armed attack occurs, each of them, in exercise of the right of individual or collective self-defence recognised by Article 51 of the Charter of the United Nations, will assist the Party or Parties so attacked by taking forthwith, individually and in concert with the other Parties, such action as it deems necessary, including the use of armed force, to restore and maintain the security of the North Atlantic area.' Full Treaty text available at www.nato.int/cps/en/natohq/official_texts_17120.htm. On NATO, see for instance TD Grant, 'NATO' in A van Aaken et al (eds), *The Oxford Handbook of International Law in Europe*, online edn (Oxford Academic, 20 June 2023), available at doi.org/10.1093/oxfordhb/9780198865315.013.23.

[6] See for instance, B Simma, 'NATO, the UN and the use of force: legal aspects' (1999) 10 *European Journal of International Law* 1.

[7] The 1950 Schuman Declaration has historically worded it as follows: 'The pooling of coal and steel production should immediately provide for the setting up of common foundations for economic development as a first step in the federation of Europe and will change the destinies of those regions which have long been devoted to the manufacture of munitions of war, of which they have been the most constant victims. The solidarity in production thus established will make it plain that any war between France and Germany becomes not merely unthinkable, but materially impossible'. (See n 1.)

[8] The ECSC Treaty applied from 1952 until its expiry in 2002.

[9] On the Euratom Treaty and its evolution, see eg, A Södersten, 'Explaining continuity and change: The case of the Euratom Treaty' (2022) 20 *International Journal of Constitutional Law* 788.

[10] See further S Garben and I Govaere (eds), *Internal Market 2.0* (Oxford, Hart Publishing, 2020). The 2024 Letta report offers interesting new insights as to the future direction of the internal market, see E Letta, 'Much more than a market – Speed, Security, Solidarity Empowering the Single Market to deliver a sustainable future and prosperity for all EU Citizens' (April 2024), available at www.consilium.europa.eu/media/ny3j24sm/much-more-than-a-market-report-by-enrico-letta.pdf.

[11] Article 2 TEU reads: 'The Union is founded on the values of respect for human dignity, freedom, democracy, equality, the rule of law and respect for human rights, including the rights of persons belonging to minorities. These values are common to the Member States in a society in which pluralism, non-discrimination, tolerance, justice, solidarity and equality between women and men prevail.'

[12] See S Garben, I Govaere and P Nemitz(eds), *Critical Reflections on Constitutional Democracy in the European Union* (Oxford, Hart Publishing, 2019).

Those values, which form the very cement on which the European construction is built, are currently under pressure in several Member States. Whilst the EU political institutions are struggling to find effective ways to counter backsliding of Member States,[13] in particular on the rule of law,[14] the CJEU has firmly recalled that those values constitute the 'very identity of the European Union as a common legal order'.[15]

Looking only at the finality of securing peace through market integration and common values, the EU so far has been highly successful in securing its aim. A symbolically important external recognition came in the form of the Nobel Peace Prize 2012, which was awarded to the EU 'to help transform Europe from a continent of war to a continent of peace',[16] in particular for having 'over six decades contributed to the advancement of peace and reconciliation, democracy and human rights in Europe'.[17] Perhaps more counterintuitively, the cumbersome Brexit process also proves the success of the EU peacekeeping model as it illustrates how deep-rooted and difficult it is to quickly unentangle the intra-EU economic, legal and institutional ties.[18]

The caveat is, however, that the EU has so far only managed to keep peace between the EU Member States, thus falling short of a more ambitious objective to maintain peace and stability on the European continent. The fact that the success story appears to be territorially limited to the EU is not all that surprising as obviously this goes hand in hand with the specific peacekeeping method used, namely forging economic interdependence between the Member States through the establishment of the internal market combined with the common values which form the very identity of the EU as a common legal order. Neither of those two unique characteristics extend to the relations with third (European) countries, at least not to the same degree.[19]

1.3. The EU Transformation Process in Response to War

If the EU has not managed to prevent the outbreak of war on the European continent altogether, the occurrence of war has always had a major transformative impact on the EU. It should be recalled that the full-scale war waged by Russia against Ukraine since 2022 is not the first or only manifestation of war on the European continent since

[13] See for instance A von Bogdandy et al (eds) 'Defending Checks and Balances in EU Member States' in *Beiträge zum ausländischen öffentlichen Recht und Völkerrecht*, vol 298. (Berlin, Heidelberg, Springer, 2021)

[14] For a thorough analysis, see A Rosas, J Raitio and P Pohjankoski (eds), *The Rule of Law's Anatomy in the EU: Foundations and Protections* (Oxford, Hart Publishing, 2023); A Von Bogdandy et al, 'The rule of law in the EU: Crisis and Solutions' Swedish Institute for European Policy Studies (SIPES) (April 2023); W Schroeder, 'The Rule of Law As a Value in the Sense of Article 2 TEU: What Does It Mean and Imply?' in von Bogdandy et al (n 13).

[15] CJEU, Cases C-156/21 *Hungary v Parliament and Council* ECLI:EU:C:2022:97 and C-157/21 *Poland v Parliament and Council* ECLI:EU:C:2022:98, respectively at [127] and [145].

[16] Presentation Speech by Thorbjørn Jagland, Chairman of the Norwegian Nobel Committee, Oslo, 10 December 2012, available at www.nobelprize.org/prizes/peace/2012/ceremony-speech.

[17] 'The Nobel Peace Prize 2012' NobelPrize.org, available at www.nobelprize.org/prizes/peace/2012/summary.

[18] See for instance M Dougan (ed), *The UK after Brexit: Legal and Policy Challenges* (Cambridge, Intersentia, 2017); A Lazowski, 'Exercises in Legal Acrobatics: Brexit Transitional Arrangements' (2017) 2 *European Papers* 845.

[19] See section 1.4 below.

the conception of the EEC. Over the past decades, the changing geopolitical and security context had already necessitated the EU to adjust and (partly) reinvent itself on several occasions. Can valuable lessons or red lines be drawn from those past experiences and offer solutions for the future? In search of useful answers, three significant periods with different security challenges are hereunder discerned, namely the Cold War period, the 1990s Balkan War and the 2022 large-scale Russian invasion of Ukraine.

1.3.1. The Cold War

The early days of the EEC was marked by the specific Cold War context. This era of strained peace somewhat paradoxically provided stability on the European continent. As Europe was geopolitically split between the communist East under the umbrella of the Soviet Union and the democratic West turned towards USA influence, not least to provide military cooperation in the framework of NATO, the EEC was primarily tasked with peacekeeping in relation to Western European countries only.[20]

As such, whilst membership was gradually extended to include nine more Western European countries,[21] the focus was above all internal, aiming at establishing and deepening intra-EU economic ties and creating the internal market by 1992.[22]

1.3.2. The 1990s Balkan Wars

The first pivotal moment for the European integration process came at the end of the 1980s and early 1990s. The fall of the Berlin Wall and the dissolution of the Soviet Union also triggered the breakup of Yugoslavia, resulting in war and bloodshed on the European continent at the immediate borders of the EEC. Fragmentation ensued and the emergence of several new European nation states called for the European map to be fundamentally redrafted. Such a seismic geopolitical shift with ensuing instability on the European continent blatantly exposed the limits of the European peace construction. Although the EEC was still performing well from an internal policy and intra-Member States perspective, it obviously lacked conferred competence, in particular in the area of foreign and security policy, to be able to make a difference.

Against this complex backdrop the EEC fundamentally transformed in two distinct but stringently related directions: firstly, to radically revise the extent of conferral of competence to the EU; and, secondly, to considerably widen the reach of the EU peacekeeping model through a big-bang enlargement. As both of these 'old' solutions of

[20] It has been pointed out that during the Cold War the EC did not contribute much to peace outside of its borders; see KK Patel, 'Who was saving whom? The European Community and the Cold War, 1960s–1970s' (2017) 19 *The British Journal of Politics and International Relations* 29.

[21] Having started out with only six founding Member States (Belgium, France, Germany, Italy, Luxembourg and the Netherlands), there were four EU enlargement waves before the 2004 big-bang enlargement, gradually including Denmark, Ireland and the UK (1973), Greece (1981), Spain and Portugal (1986) and Austria, Finland and Sweden (1994).

[22] See the various contributions to J Schwarze et al (eds), *The 1992 Challenge at National level* (Baden-Baden, Nomos Verlagsgesellschaft, 1990); CD Ehlermann, 'The Internal Market following the Single European Act' (1987) 24 *Common Market Law Review* 361.

widening and deepening are currently on the table again as the double path forward, it is interesting to briefly recall what was achieved at the time.

It is in the wake of the end of the Cold War that the 'European Union' was born by the Maastricht Treaty, by adding two intergovernmental pillars, namely Common Foreign and Security Policy (CFSP) and Justice and Home Affairs'(JHA) to the first 'EC' pillar.[23] In spite of the formal abolishment of the pillar structure by the Lisbon Treaty, the CFSP, including a Common Security and Defence Policy (CSDP), has survived as a 'horizontal pillar' with its own and specific set of rules and procedures.[24] Although the creation of the EU to replace the EEC was considered a major breakthrough at the time, it equally confirmed the understanding that the EU is not a global actor similar to a state by jealously guarding the sensitivities and prerogatives of the Member States with respect to foreign policy, defence and security matters. This stands in sharp contrast to the expectations raised in the current context for the EU to quickly and adequately tackle the newly arisen security concerns as if it were itself a state.

Secondly, and probably more directly important from the perspective of securing peace and stability on the European continent at the time, the end of the Cold War led to the so-called 'Big Bang enlargement' in May 2004 whereby 10 new Member States joined the EU at once.[25] The EU peace project for the first time spanned East and West Europe, including eight post-communist countries, later to be followed by the accessions of Bulgaria, Romania and Croatia.[26] Such a major enlargement allowed for more European states to experience first-hand and to directly benefit from the unique and visible EU peacekeeping method which is the integration in the internal market. Conversely, the sheer number of Member States coupled with their different historical and economic backgrounds as well as cultural and political sensitivities, has put considerable strain on the very fundament of the EU integration model.

With several newly emerging and fragile democracies requesting a quick accession to the EU, but aware of the major challenges which the integration of post-Soviet states might pose for the EU, the European Council in Copenhagen of June 1993 decided to tighten the accession criteria. It formulated the so-called the 'Copenhagen Criteria', which are three-fold.[27] First of all, political criteria assessing the institutional stability to protect democracy, the rule of law, human rights and respect for and protection of minorities. Secondly, economic criteria to make sure new Member States would have effectively switched to a functioning market economy and have the capacity to cope with competition and market forces within the internal market. Thirdly, ensuring that

[23] On the Maastricht Treaty, which also introduced the EMU and EU citizenship, see T Christiansen, S Duke and E Kirchner, 'Understanding and Assessing the Maastricht Treaty' (2012) 34 *Journal of European Integration* 685. This was later refined by the Amsterdam Treaty, whilst the Nice Treaty mainly served to reinforce the EU institutional structure prior to the bigbang enlargement; see M Tønnesson Andenæs and J Usher, *The Treaty of Nice and Beyond: Enlargement and Constitutional Reform* (Oxford, Hart, 2003).

[24] Article 24 TEU. See I Govaere, 'Multi-faceted Single Legal Personality and a Hidden Horizontal Pillar: EU External Relations Post-Lisbon' (2010–11) 13 *Cambridge Yearbook of European Legal Studies* 87; P Van Elsuwege, 'EU External Action after the Collapse of the Pillar Structure: In search of a New Balance between Delimitation and Consistency' (2010) 47 *Common Market Law Review* 987.

[25] The new Member States were: Czech Republic, Estonia, Cyprus, Latvia, Lithuania, Hungary, Malta, Poland, Slovakia and Slovenia. For a legal analysis, see M Maresceau (ed), *Enlarging the European Union: relations between the EU and Central and Eastern Europe* (Harlow, Longman, 1997).

[26] Bulgaria and Romania joined the EU in 2007, Croatia in 2013.

[27] The European Council Conclusions, Copenhagen 21–22 June 1993, DOC/93/3, 22 June 1993.

the new Member States have the administrative and institutional capacity to effectively implement the acquis Communautaire as well as the ability to take on all other obligations of EU membership.

At the time of their accession the new Member States were reported by the Commission to fully meet all of those conditions. However, respect for the rule of law in particular has come under a lot of strain over the past decade with considerable backsliding in several Member States, not least Hungary and Poland, a situation with which the EU is struggling to cope.[28] The suspension clause of Article 7 TEU, which allows for the suspension of EU membership rights in case of a serious breach of the values listed in Article 2 TEU (and was largely modelled on the conditionality clauses already inserted in the bilateral Europe Agreements with the Central and Eastern European countries prior to their accession), so far has proven to miss the requisite deterrent effect to ensure an ongoing compliance with those criteria after having gained membership.[29]

1.3.3. The 2022 Large-scale Russian Invasion of Ukraine

The 2022 Russian large-scale invasion of Ukraine and the ongoing daily reporting of war and bloodshed marks the second pivotal moment for the EU sparked by the fundamentally changing geopolitical and security context.[30] For one, it is not clear what the precise intentions of Russia are with respect to other European countries, in particular those that previously belonged to its influence sphere. Added to this, political turmoil in the USA, and especially the Trump administration having called into question the USA's previously unwavering military support within NATO,[31] leads to a renewed questioning of how peace can be maintained in Europe and what role the EU should play in this respect. In other words, the issue is no longer only how well the EU performs according to its own stated objective as a soft power, but rather how it could potentially fill a security gap in case the military deterrent of the Member States and NATO were to be deficient for lack of USA backing.

[28] See section 1.2 above.

[29] See for instance W Sadurski, 'Adding a Bite to a Bark? A Story of Article 7, the EU Enlargement, and Jörg Haider' (2010) 16 *Columbia Journal of European Law* 385, 388–389. K Miklossy, 'Tackling EU conditionality with the Hungarian Legal Manoeuvres' in Rosas, Raito and Pohjankoski (n 14) 171–87. Instead of the more political sensitive Art 7 TEU, it is mainly to the CJEU that the Commission has turned for enforcing compliance with the rule of law, see eg CJ Moreiro González, 'Implementing the Rule of Law in the European Union: How Long Trapped in Penelope's Spinning Wheel from Article 2 of the TEU?' (2024) *Cambridge Yearbook of European Legal Studies* 1, doi:10.1017/cel.2023.17. For the wider EU rule of law toolkit, see eg G Halmai, 'The Alternatives to a Bite or a Bark: After Launching Article 7 TEU Against the Hungarian Government' in U Belavusau and A Gliszczyńska-Grabias (eds), *Constitutionalism under Stress* (Oxford, Oxford University Press, 2020) 63–78.

[30] See eg MA Orenstein, 'The European Union's transformation after Russia's attack on Ukraine' (2023) 45 *Journal of European Integration* 333; H Maurer, R G Whitman and N Wright, 'The EU and the invasion of Ukraine: a collective responsibility to act?' (2023) 99 *International Affairs* 219; L Lonardo, 'Weapons, Humanitarian Assistance, Sanctions: a Legal Analysis of the EU's Immediate Response to the Russian Invasion of Ukraine of 2022' (2022) *European Law Review* 410.

[31] See also J P Kaufman, 'The US perspective on NATO under Trump: lessons of the past and prospects for the future' (2017) 93 *International Affairs* 251.

It is against this fundamentally changed geopolitical context that the question is repeatedly and loudly raised why the EU is not acting more forcefully and efficiently to secure peace and stability on the European continent. Also now, the answer is quite simply because under the current Treaties it cannot, or at least it appears difficult to do so any time soon.

In line with the transformative impact of the first pivotal moment, the current security crisis has the very high potential to set in motion an existential transformation of the EU. An immediate reaction is to call for a revisiting of the currently limited conferral of competence in relation to security and defence matters, as well as to further enlarge the EU by quickly including new Member States – in the first instance, Ukraine.[32]

This may at first sight seem to be a 'natural' and straightforward response in continuum of the prior European integration process, but a closer look reveals a potential existential threat for the EU. Never before has the EU opened EU membership negotiations with a country at war. Never before was the EU at a more dangerously pivotal point between exporting peace and EU values, or importing war.[33]

The crux of the matter is that, previously, the widening and deepening of the EU served to reinforce its unique peacekeeping method to achieve its peace project. Current discussions radically shift the focus away from the EU's unique peacekeeping method to instead call for the EU to act more as a state. In so doing, it brings with it underexplored but potentially existential conundrums for the EU integration and peacekeeping model as such. Before identifying two such important ongoing transformations that will determine the future identity of the EU, the following section goes briefly in search of potential red lines for the EU's external relations.

1.4. The Transformative Impact on the EU as a Global Actor

What existential challenges could the war in Ukraine possibly pose for the EU as a global actor? In particular, an important question addressed here is whether there is some congruity with the internal peacekeeping method and current challenges the EU is facing.

As far as the peace objective is concerned, the answer is clear-cut. In the same vein as the overall peacekeeping objective expressed in Article 3(1) TEU, also Article 3(5) TEU unequivocally states that 'in its relations with the wider world, the Union shall contribute to peace and security, as well as the strict observance and the development of international law'. With respect to the method to achieve peace, contrary to NATO which was set up around the same time as the EEC precisely to safeguard military security in Europe, the EU is endowed with neither an army nor other deterrent hard power.[34] It is instead an outspoken soft power global actor.

[32] See section 1.5 below.

[33] See section 1.5 below.

[34] The EU does engage in peacekeeping missions, however; see F Naert, 'Legal Aspects of EU Military Operations' (2011) 15 *Journal of International Peacekeeping* 218; I Govaere and S Poli (eds), *EU management of global emergencies: legal framework for combating threats and crises*, Vol 8. (Leiden, Brill/Martinus Nijhoff Publishers, 2014).

By analogy to the internal peacekeeping method, also externally the EU mainly relies on forging economic ties and leveraging its trade weight to promote peace and stability abroad.[35] Such trade leveraging can be either positive (eg offering access to the internal market as an incentive) or negative (eg imposing economic sanctions), depending on the geopolitical context. With respect to Russia, there has been a clear shift from positive to negative trade leveraging between the first 2016[36] and the second 2022 large-scale invasions of Ukraine. Incremental EU sanctions packages have since the outbreak of the war been stacked one above the other, but so far without the hoped for effect of stopping the war.[37]

The impact the EU has on war is thus very different internally and externally. In terms of its peacekeeping method there are, however, three fundamental differences between the internal and external context that merit to be highlighted. They concern respectively the applicable legal order, the underlying values, as well as the nature of the trade rules in question.

First of all, in its relations with third countries it is of course public international law with its wide range of dispute settlement methods which applies and needs to be upheld.[38] In contrast, in the intra-EU context exclusively the autonomous EU legal order – with its own characteristics of direct effect and primacy and, very importantly, uniform interpretation by the CJEU –applies.[39] It is the latter in particular that provides the crucial legal cementing and foundation of the EU integration process.

Secondly, respect for the constitutional values listed in Article 2 TEU is an ongoing 'obligation as to result' for the Member States and the EU, as the CJEU has made clear in the financial conditionality judgments.[40] However, those values 'common to the EU Member States' are not necessarily shared by the third countries concerned. Pursuant

[35] The EU Action Plan on Human Rights and Democracy 2020–2024 stated that 'the EU will leverage the broad range of policies and tools at its disposal to promote and defend human rights, democracy and the rule of law'; see JOIN (2020) 5 final, 4. The most powerful tool at the disposal of the EU is trade, as is acknowledged in 'Trade Policy Review – An Open, Sustainable and Assertive Trade Policy' COM(2021) 66 final (18 February 2021). See also P Van Elsuwege, 'The nexus between the Common Commercial Policy and human rights: Implications of the Lisbon Treaty' in M Hahn and G Van der Loo, *Law and Practice of the Common Commercial Polic*, (Leiden, Brill Nijhoff, 2020) 416–33.

[36] In May 2021, less than one year before the 2020 large-scale invasion, the EU had assessed its five-principled response to the 2016 first, more limited, invasion of Ukraine territory by Russia positively in the following terms: 'To meet the strategic challenge posed by the Russian leadership, our collective implementation of the five principles has given the EU purpose and a principled approach to defending our interests and promoting our values'; see 'EU-Russia relations: Push back, constrain and engage' JOIN(2021) 20 final.

[37] For an updated list of the massive and unprecedented sanctions packages adopted by the EU against Russia since the invasion of Ukraine, see https://finance.ec.europa.eu/eu-and-world/sanctions-restrictive-measures/sanctions-adopted-following-russias-military-aggression-against-ukraine_en#timeline-measures. See also K Meissner and C Graziani, 'The transformation and design of EU restrictive measures against Russia' (2023) 45 *Journal of European Integration* 377.

[38] According to Art 34 of the Statute of the ICJ, 'Only states may be parties in cases before the Court', thus effectively excluding the EU from this particular form of international dispute settlement.

[39] For an analysis of the autonomous legal order and its interaction with public international law, see I Govaere, 'Interconnecting Legal Systems and the Autonomous EU Legal Order: a Balloon Dynamic in I Govaere and S Garben (eds), *The Interface Between EU and International Law: Contemporary Reflections* (Oxford, Hart Publishing, 2019) 19.

[40] CJEU, Cases C-156/21 *Hungary v Parliament and Council* and C-157/21 *Poland v Parliament and Council* (n 15).

to Article 3(5) TEU and Article 21(1) TEU the objective to promote liberal democracy beyond its borders is more softly formulated as an 'obligation as to means', albeit one which should be consistently pursued.[41] This may not come as a surprise considering that in 2023 less than eight per cent of the world population lived in a full democracy,[42] whereas the global figures also show a worrying trend of rule of law backsliding in many countries, including in most EU Member States.[43]

Thirdly, in relation to third countries, international/world trade rules apply which lead to trade liberalisation, but third countries do not share the internal market objective to melt the markets into one in order to achieve the noble higher objective, ie peace.[44] Moreover, since the COVID health crises, the USA political turmoil and the war in Ukraine exposed the vulnerabilities and dependency of the EU on third countries, sometimes with respect to crucial resources, the focus of the EU has shifted to pursue so-called 'open strategic autonomy'.[45] This translates into the slogan 'work together when we can, work alone if we must'.[46] In so doing, it drifts further away from the internal market peacekeeping method of creating and instrumentalising strategic economic interdependencies in order to secure lasting peace. Without due care, an 'open strategic autonomy paradox' could thus easily emerge, to the extent that the open strategic autonomy approach has the potential to erode future trade leveraging attempts by the EU.

1.5. Current Challenges and the Future Identity of the EU

It is the unique and inherent characteristics of the EU peacekeeping method, combining strategic economic independence and common constitutional values, that explain

[41] See further I Govaere, 'Promoting the Rule of Law in EU External Relations: a Conceptual Framework' in A Rosas, J Raitio and P Pohjankoski (eds), *The Rule of Law's Anatomy in the EU: Foundations and Protections* (Oxford, Hart Publishing, 2023) 189–206.

[42] EIU, Democracy Index 2023, available at www.eiu.com/n/campaigns/democracy-index-2023.

[43] World Justice Project, Rule of Law Index 2023, available at worldjusticeproject.org/rule-of-law-index/downloads/WJPIndex2023.pdf.

[44] The EEA Agreement functionally extends the internal market to Norway, Lichtenstein and Iceland (see [1994] OJ L1/3), but does not have the same objective as the EU Treaty and therefore similar provisions do not necessarily receive a similar interpretation; see CJEU Opinion 1/91, at pts 15 and 16, where the CJEU pointed out this difference: '(15) With regard to the comparison of the objectives of the provisions of the agreement and those of Community law, it must be observed that the agreement is concerned with the application of rules on free trade and competition in economic and commercial relations between the Contracting Parties. (16) In contrast, as far as the Community is concerned, the rules on free trade and competition, which the agreement seeks to extend to the whole territory of the Contracting Parties, have developed and form part of the Community legal order, the objectives of which go beyond that of the agreemen':, ECLI:EU:C:1991:490.

[45] Europe's moment: Repair and Prepare for the Next Generation, COM(2020) 456 final (27 May 2020), where it is explained in the wake of the COVID pandemic that 'Europe needs to be more resilient to prevent, protect and withstand future shocks. We will always be committed to open and fair trade but must be aware of the need to reduce dependency and strengthen security of supply, notably for things like pharmaceutical ingredients or raw materials.' See also J Borrell, 'Why European Strategic Autonomy Matters' European External Action Service (3 December 2020) 2021, available at www.eeas.europa.eu/eeas/why-european-strategic-autonomy-matters_en.

[46] See COM(2021) 66 final (18 February 20210: 'Trade Policy Review- An Open, Sustainable and Assertive EU Trade Policy', and the Questions and Answers thereto at ec.europa.eu/commission/presscorner/detail/en/qanda_21_645. See also F Hoffmeister, 'Strategic autonomy in the European Union's external relations law' (2023) 60 *Common Market Law Review* 667, available at kluwerlawonline.com/journalarticle/Common+Market+Law+Review/60.3/COLA2023048.

its success so far in keeping peace among the Member States. The other side of the coin is that it is precisely for the very same reason that the EU currently does not possess the capacity to maintain peace outside of its borders, not even on the sole European continent. The true conundrum posed by the 2022 Russian invasion of Ukraine is how to remedy the latter without jeopardising the former. That is where the red lines or red flags should firmly be drawn.

As mentioned above, the EU transformative process is again triggered at full force in the wake of the 2022 Russian invasion of Ukraine.[47] With various options on the table in terms of both deepening and widening, it is not always clear what benchmark, if any, is currently used in practice to guide this existential transformation process. Two important ongoing tendencies are highlighted in this section, in relation to deepening and widening whilst pondering their potential impact on the EU identity, respectively.

1.5.1. A Shift from Soft to (Semi-)Hard Power?

The current Article 24 TEU embryonically lays the basis for the EU to develop into a (semi-) hard power. It provides that

> the Union's competence in matters of common foreign and security policy shall cover all areas of foreign policy and all questions relating to the Union's security, including the progressive framing of a common defence policy that might lead to a common defence.[48]

This comes on top of the mutual assistance clause of Article 42(7) TEU, which at the level of the Member States provides that they all have 'an obligation of aid and assistance by all means in their power' in case one Member State 'is the victim of armed aggression on its territory'.[49]

The realisation that the European states can no longer blindly trust USA military backing in the NATO framework has sparked a renewed interest in having the EU fill this security gap. The concept of EU 'strategic autonomy' not surprisingly finds its origin in this new and uncomfortable geopolitical context.[50] Yet the pursuit of strategic autonomy is not necessarily tantamount to the transformation of the EU into a (semi-)hard power similar to NATO. To think that the EU could easily and quickly assemble a truly European army or make this shift rapidly is anyhow largely illusory.[51]

[47] See section 1.2 above.

[48] For an interesting analysis, see P Koutrakos, *The EU common security and defence policy* (Oxford, Oxford University Press, 2013).

[49] Article 42(7) TEU continues: 'This shall not prejudice the specific character of the security and defence policy of certain Member States. Commitments and cooperation in this area shall be consistent with commitments under the North Atlantic Treaty Organisation, which, for those States which are members of it, remains the foundation of their collective defence and the forum for its implementation.' This was so far only triggered once, by France at the time of the 2015 Paris terrorist attacks; see the CEPS Commentary of 20 November 2015 by C Hillion and S Blockmans, 'Europe's self-defence: Tous pour un et un pour tous?', available at cdn.ceps.eu/wp-content/uploads/2015/11/CH%20&%20SB%20Tous%20pour%20un%20CEPS%20Commentary_0.pdf. Another potentially important provision in this respect is the Solidarity Clause of Art 222 TFEU: 'The Union and its Member States shall act jointly in a spirit of solidarity if a Member State is the object of a terrorist attack or the victim of a natural or man-made disaster.'

[50] See eg D Zandee et al, *European strategic autonomy in security and defence* (The Hague, Clingendael, 2020).

[51] See eg B Vroege, 'Strategic Autonomy in Military Production: The EDF and the Constitutional Limits to EU Defence-Industrial Spending Power' (2023) 28 *European Foreign Affairs Review* 341; C Hoeffler, 'Beyond

A firm shift to hard power would fundamentally affect the very identity of the EU as an inherently soft power. But it is a matter of degree. For the EU to step up its coordination and supporting measures in the area of defence, as it did with the creation of the European Peace Facility in March 2021,[52] does not automatically cross red lines but may to the contrary serve to reinforce economic and strategic interdependence within the EU. The underlying idea is to purposely shift the current military dependence of Member States, inter alia as concerns arms and munition, away from the USA in favour of more intra-EU strategic interdependence, convergence and interoperability.

In so far as the current process of deepening goes, the disturbing uncertainties surrounding the lasting American commitment to NATO had already provoked the following European Council statement on 15 December 2021:

> In the face of increased global instability, growing strategic competition and complex security threats, the EU will take more responsibility for its own security and in the field of defence, pursue a strategic course of action and increase its capacity to act autonomously.[53]

Not surprisingly, the materialisation of a subsequent security threat posed by Russia has induced a strong push for the EU to quickly transform from the current 'military dwarf'[54] into a military giant.[55]

The Versailles Declaration of 10 and 11 March 2022, just two weeks after the invasion of Ukraine, identified as the first of three key dimensions for the EU to tackle 'bolstering the defence capabilities'.[56] It was however also stated that this should not replace but rather reinforce NATO, by underlining that: 'A stronger and more capable EU in the field of security and defence will contribute positively to global and transatlantic security and is complementary to NATO, which remains the foundation of collective defence for its members.'.[57] In terms of participation, both NATO and the EU were reinforced, respectively, by the NATO membership of Finland and Sweden,[58] and

the regulatory state? The European Defence Fund and national military capacities' (2023) 30 *Journal of European Public Policy* 1281.

[52] Council Decision (CFSP) 2021/509 of 22 March 2021 establishing a European Peace Facility, and repealing Decision (CFSP) 2015/528, [2021] OJ L102/14.

[53] European Council Conclusions, Brussels, 16 December 2021, EUCO 22/21, CO EUR 19 CONCL 6, at para 11.

[54] This widely cited expression was used in 1991 by the former Belgian Prime Minister Mark Eyskens, who referred to the EU as 'an economic giant, a political dwarf and a military worm'; see Mark Eyskens as quoted in CR Whitney, 'Gulf Fighting Shatters Europeans' Fragile Unity' *New York Times* (25 January 1991). Recently, he has given this quote perspective by stating that it was an exaggerated warning to caution about colossal challenges ahead; see M Eyskens, 'België in het het Europese Brandpunt' *Onder Professoren Jubel* (6 June 20240, available at www.jubel.be/belgie-in-het-europese-brandpunt.

[55] See Ó Fernández et al, 'The impact of Russia's 2022 invasion of Ukraine on public perceptions of EU security and defence integration: a big data analysis' (2023) 45 *Journal of European Integration* 463.

[56] The other two key dimensions were 'reducing energy dependencies' and 'building a more robust economic base'; see Versailles Declaration, Informal meeting of the Heads of State or Government, Versailles, 10–11 March 2022, at para 7ff, available at www.consilium.europa.eu/media/54773/20220311-versailles-declaration-en.pdf.

[57] Versailles Declaration (ibid) para 8.

[58] On 18 May 2022 they simultaneously handed in their official letters of application to join NATO; see www.nato.int/cps/en/natohq/news_195468.htm. Finland officially joined in 2023, Sweden in 2024. For a discussion, see A Michalski, D Brommesson and A M Ekengren, 'Small states and the dilemma of geopolitics: role change in Finland and Sweden' (2024) 100 *International Affairs* 139; A Vicente, M A Alkış and I Maksymenko, 'The Impact of Russia's War against Ukraine on Finland and Sweden's Decision to Join NATO:

the Danish referendum on 1 June 2022 which effectively ended its CSDP opt-out with effect on 1 July 2022.[59]

Over the past years, the Member States already started to allocate historically high budget lines to their national defence spending.[60] This may be due both to the pressure exerted by the USA to meet their NATO obligations,[61] as well as the growing awareness that they might have to rise to the occasion without the crucial support of the USA. The EU, for its part, adopted in 2022 the Strategic Compass for Security and Defence[62] and in March 2024 launched the European Defence Industrial Policy,[63] which should inter alia forge strategical defence capacity and related interdependence and interoperability between the Member States by 2035.

The existential question now is how far the EU can move in this direction. Of course, it is inarguable that Europe's security should be high on the political agenda and urgently needs to be safeguarded, but does this really only concern the current EU Member States? It seems a legitimate question to at least ponder whether the responsibility to step into NATO's shoes, should the USA falter, should rest solely on the EU. Other avenues so far seem largely underexplored, such as reforming NATO altogether[64] or rethinking novel forms of cooperation to secure the wider European defence. In particular, far too little attention is being paid to the fact that, for the EU, such a radical shift would come at a huge cost. Evolving from an outspoken soft power into a (semi-)hard power also means shedding the very identity of the EU and its unique peacekeeping model.

Effects on the Global Nuclear Order' in A Vicente, P Sinovets and J Theron (eds), *Russia's War on Ukraine. Contributions to Political Science* (Berlin, Heidelberg, Springer, 2023) 229–246.

[59] See eg M Migliorati, 'New Nordic pathways? Explaining Nordic countries' defence policy choices in the wake of the Ukrainian war' (2024) *Journal of European Public Policy* 1. For a legal analysis of the original Danish opt-out, see G Butler, 'The European Defence Union and Denmark's Defence Opt-out: A Legal Appraisal' (2020) 25 *European Foreign Affairs Review* 117.

[60] According to the European Defence Agency (EDA) annual Defence Data report for 2022, defence spending from all 27 EU Member States in 2022 was at a historic high of €240 billion, see eda.europa.eu/docs/default-source/brochures/2022-eda_defencedata_web.pdf. High Representative Joseph Borrell is reported to have stated: 'Our armed forces must be ready for a much more demanding era. Adjusting to these new realities first and foremost means investing more on defence. A record €240 billion underpins the commitment of Member States to bolster European defence. However, we have key capability gaps and continue to lag behind other global players in spending. This is why it's not just about spending more in defence, but also about spending better and together. We must find extra value in our ability to cooperate and seize the opportunities to strengthen our armed forces through common planning, shared projects and joint procurements': eda.europa.eu/news-and-events/news/2023/11/30/record-high-european-defence-spending-boosted-by-procurement-of-new-equipment.

[61] See eg J Becker et al, 'Transatlantic Shakedown: Presidential Shaming and NATO Burden Sharing' (2024) 68 *Journal of Conflict Resolution* 195.

[62] Council of the European Union, 'A Strategic Compass for Security and Defence – For a European Union that protects its citizens, values and interests and contributes to international peace and security' Brussels, 21 March 2022, 7371/22.

[63] Joint Communication to the European Parliament, the Council, the European Economic and Social Committee and the Committee of the Regions, 'A new European Defence Industrial Strategy: Achieving EU readiness through a responsive and resilient European Defence Industry' JOIN (2024) 10 final, Brussels, 5 March 2024.

[64] In the same sense, see for instance J Ringsmose and M Webber, 'Hedging their bets? The case for a European pillar in NATO' (2020) 20 *Defence Studies* 295.

1.5.2. A Shift from Revising Membership Conditions to Revisiting the Finality of the EU?

Just a couple of days after the large-scale invasion by Russia, on 28 February 2022, Ukraine officially submitted an application for EU membership. Given the geopolitical context coupled with the prevailing idea that Ukraine was possibly invaded because of its rapprochement to Western values, this was met with a fast and positive response from the European Council. Less than two weeks later, the Versailles Declaration unequivocally proclaimed: 'Ukraine belongs to our European family.'[65] It was also announced that the Commission had been invited to submit its opinion on Ukraine's application, as well as those of Moldova and Georgia.[66]

In order to secure the EU peace objective, the European integration process necessarily has to be inclusive and the EU (potentially) open to accession by all European states.[67] The rapidity of the commitment expressed by the European Council and the huge expectations it has created for Ukraine and its people, however, raise fundamental issues for the EU in terms of accession strategy, criteria and procedure.

In terms of accession strategy, the existential conundrum is whether accession of Ukraine implies exporting peace or importing war. The official position of the EU is to recall that 'the enlargement process is a geo-strategic investment in peace, security, stability and prosperity'.[68] But, importantly, for the very first time the EU has launched its accession procedure with respect to a country at war. At the time of the Versailles Declaration the expectation was that the war would be short-lived. But nearly two years later, on 14–15 December 2023, the European Council decided to open accession negotiations with Ukraine, whilst Ukraine was still at war.[69] Increasingly it is uncertain when and on what terms peace will come about. Considering the speed with which the accession procedure was set in motion and the high expectations created for Ukraine and its people, the question is to what extent peace will then ultimately prove to be a prerequisite for the closure of the accession negotiations, as is currently widely assumed.[70] A similar concern plays for Moldova (and Georgia), two countries firmly in Ukraine's accession slipstream. Enlarging the EU to a country at (risk of) war entails an enormous gamble for the EU and its Member States, not least when considering the above-mentioned mutual assistance clause of Article 42(7) TEU.[71]

Also the EU accession criteria and procedure have come under a lot of strain by the rapidity of the launch of the accession process with Ukraine. Instead of learning

[65] Versailles Declaration (n 56) pt 4.

[66] ibid pts 4–5.

[67] See Art 49 TEU.

[68] Ministerial meeting opening the Intergovernmental Conference on the Accession of Ukraine to the European Union (Luxembourg, 25 June 2024), AD 9/24 LIMITE, CONF-UA 2, Brussels, 21 June 2024, at pt 6.

[69] On the official decision to open accession negotiations with Ukraine and Moldova, see European Council meeting (14 and 15 December 2023) Conclusions, EUCO 20/23, CO EUR 16, CONCL 6 of 15 December 2023, at pt 15.

[70] See for instance R Petrov, 'Bumpy Road of Ukraine Towards the EU Membership in Time of War: "Accession Through War" v "Gradual Integration"' (2023) 8 *European Papers* 1057, 1060–62.

[71] See section 1.5.1 below.

lessons from the aftermath of the 2004 big-bang enlargement through revisiting and tightening the accession criteria, needed to ensure more lasting commitments to the EU values than just at the time of accession, it is rather a relaxing of the same pre-accession compliance scrutiny that seems to be taking place in practice. Article 49 TEU clearly provides that 'Any European State which respects the values referred to in Article 2 and is committed to promoting them may apply to become a member of the Union'. It is the task of the Commission prior to accession to assess whether the EU's values are respected in the candidate country, as well as the fulfilment of the above-mentioned 'Copenhagen' political, economic and administrative/institutional criteria, which were introduced at the time of the 2004 big-bang enlargement to the East.[72] This screening is not only important for the acceding country to be able to withstand the pressure of the internal market; it is indispensable for the smooth functioning of the EU internal market and, above all, combined with the common values, for the EU to be able to maintain peace among its Member States.

Several external reports, measuring respect for democracy and the rule of law globally, are rather reserved with respect to the performance of Ukraine.[73] Whereas NATO, having also declared that 'Ukraine's future is in NATO', seems hesitant to grant Ukraine membership any time soon.[74] The Commission, on the other hand, gave the green light for Ukraine's EU candidate country status already on June 2022, while listing seven issues of concern in relation to inter alia the rule of law, corruption, fraud, money laundering, media and protection of minorities.[75] Just over a year later, in November 2023, it

[72] See section 1.3.2 below.

[73] The EIU Democracy Index 2023 (n 42) states that 'Ukraine was classified as a "hybrid regime" before the war began, and the government was struggling to improve the state of democracy. Since the start of the war, power has become more concentrated in the hands of the president, Volodmir Zelenskiy, at the expense of the executive branch and the parliament. Corruption remains an issue and martial law has been exercised to the maximum, meaning that media and other democratic freedoms have been circumscribed. As a result, Ukraine's score fell from 5.42 in 2022 to 5.06 in 2023, and the country dropped four places in the global ranking, from 87th to 91st.' This is similar to the trend measured by the World Justice Project Rule of Law Index 2023 (n 43), specifically at 171. See also for instance Council of Europe, 'Ukraine – Joint Follow-up Opinion of the Venice Commission and the Directorate General of Human Rights and Rule of Law (DGI) of the Council of Europe to the joint opinion on the draft amendments to the Law "On the Judiciary and the Status of Judges" and Certain Laws on the Activities of the Supreme Court and Judicial Authorities (CDL-AD(2020)022)', adopted by the Venice Commission at its 136th Plenary Session (Venice, 6–7 October 2023), CDL-AD(2023)027; Council of Europe, European Commission For Democracy Through Law (Venice Commission), 'Ukraine Opinion On The Law "On The Prevention Of Threats To National Security Related To The Excessive Influence Of Persons With Significant Economic And Political Weight In Public Life (Oligarchs)"', adopted by the Venice Commission at its 135th Plenary Session (Venice, 9–10 June 2023), CDL-AD(2023)018.

[74] See Vilnius Summit Communiqué Issued by NATO Heads of State and Government participating in the meeting of the North Atlantic Council in Vilnius 11 July 2023, Press Release (2023) 00, at pt 11: 'We fully support Ukraine's right to choose its own security arrangements. Ukraine's future is in NATO. … In line with the 1997 Charter on a Distinctive Partnership between NATO and Ukraine and the 2009 Complement, Allies will continue to support and review Ukraine's progress on interoperability as well as additional democratic and security sector reforms that are required. NATO Foreign Ministers will regularly assess progress through the adapted Annual National Programme. The Alliance will support Ukraine in making these reforms on its path towards future membership. We will be in a position to extend an invitation to Ukraine to join the Alliance when Allies agree, and conditions are met.'

[75] 'Commission Opinion on Ukraine's application for membership of the European Union' COM (2022) 407 final (17 June 2022).

recommended opening accession negotiations with Ukraine (and Moldova), expressing satisfaction with the progress made on those issues.[76]

This screening performed against the specific geopolitical context marked by the application of Ukraine whilst at war with Russia has been labelled

> an act of moral support, to boost the country's resistance to the aggression and, perhaps more than ever in the history of EU enlargement, as a (geo)political decision rather than a scrupulous legal application of the conditions related to art. 49 TEU.[77]

Though on the face of it, and in formal discourse, the regular accession procedure and criteria are claimed to be met, in practice there does seem to be an important element of fast-tracking as well as downscaling of accession criteria and assurance of their effective compliance. This then also sets the standard for the other candidate countries, such as Moldova and Georgia, which are in the slipstream of the accession of Ukraine, but most likely also for other candidate countries such as Albania, Bosnia and Herzegovina, Montenegro, Serbia and of course still also Turkey.

The truly existential question for the survival of the EU peacekeeping model is whether the current process of so-called 'accession through war',[78] will cede in due course to an accession process based on, as a minimum, the more objective and regular Copenhagen accession criteria so as to ensure that all Member States share the same common values and capacities, at least at the time of their accession to the EU. If not, it is the internal EU peacekeeping method of combining economic interdependence with respect for the common values that may well be jeopardised in the long run.

1.6. A Concluding Call for Thorough Reflection

The war in Ukraine poses novel and existential conundrums for the EU which warrant serious and urgent reflection. The European Council of 24 June 2022 gave a double message. It firmly stated that the future of Ukraine, Moldova and Georgia lies within the EU. To continue that 'The progress of each country towards the European Union will depend on its own merit in meeting the Copenhagen criteria, taking into consideration the EU's capacity to absorb new members.'[79] Much attention has gone to how the EU

[76] '2023 Communication on EU Enlargement Policy' COM(2023) 690 final of 8.11.2023, 22–23, pt 14, for Moldova at pt 15. Georgia did receive a a positive recommendation for a conditional candidate country status, see pt 16.

[77] R Petrov, 'Bumpy Road of Ukraine Towards the EU Membership in Time of War: "Accession Through War" v "Gradual Integration"' (2023) 8 *European Papers* 1057, 1059. On the same page, he points out: 'The European Council's decision to grant candidate status to Ukraine would probably not have happened in pre-war circumstances. While the country's aspirations to join the EU have been clear for some time, formally applying for membership was not seriously contemplated in Kyiv before the Russian invasion. Russia's aggression thus paradoxically turned into reality Ukraine's ambition to engage on an EU membership course. To be sure, the Commission's annual reports on the implementation of the association agreement had never been overly positive. Even Ukraine's internal evaluation of the domestic implementation efforts was rather humbling.'

[78] The concept of '"Accession through war" entails that the war justifies the EU taking a different approach in its assessment of the applicant's ability to join the Union'; see R Petrov and C Hillion '"Accession through War" – Ukraine's Road to the EU' (2022) 59 *Common Market Law Review* 1289.

[79] European Council meeting (23 and 24 June 2022)– Conclusions, EUCO 24/22, CO EUR 21, CONCL 5 of 24 June 2022, respectively at pts 10 and 14.

and its enlargement process could be instrumentalised for geopolitical purposes. Far less consideration has been given so far to the double shift which this provokes and which potentially affects the very identity of the EU.

Moving from an outspoken soft power to a (semi-)hard power and revising EU membership conditions in practice, although not formally, equals revisiting the finality of the EU as a successful peace project with a truly unique peacekeeping method. That the EU necessarily transforms and grows out of every major war is a given. The challenge is to identify the red lines that should not be crossed in this transformative process so as to ensure that the EU does not end up losing itself.

2

The Enduring Legitimisation of European Integration by Reference to Peace?

MATEJ AVBELJ*

2.1. Disbelief, *Blitzkrieg* and a New Painful Reality

In February 2022 global newspapers started to trickle information that Russia was planning a full-scale attack on Ukraine. Almost everyone, from the national leaders, academics, media pundits to the ordinary citizens in the West, received this information in disbelief. However, Russia had already flagrantly violated the territorial integrity of Ukraine. It has illegally annexed Crimea.[1] It has stirred mutiny in the eastern regions of Ukraine: Donbas and Luhansk.[2] It has tried to meddle with the Ukrainian leadership. It has, more than likely, also been responsible for shooting down a civil passenger jet killing the 300 innocent civilians on board.[3] All of this came on top of poisoning of Russian dissidents and disobedient Ukrainian leaders abroad,[4] as well as a total crackdown on political opposition and suppression of critical media, and the killing of investigative journalists in Moscow and elsewhere.[5]

In other words, by the beginning of February 2022 it was common knowledge that Russia no longer pretended to be a democracy and was ready to go some length towards open violations of international law, and even conduct terrorist acts. Nevertheless, few believed that Russia would go as far as waging an open, deliberate, full-scale aggression against Ukraine, a sovereign and independent European country in the twenty-first

* The research for this chapter has benefited from the support of the Jean Monnet Chair on Pluralism in the EU co-funded by the EU, as well as by the research program P6-0380 Violations of human rights and fundamental freedoms on Slovenian territory in the 20th century.

[1] TD Grant, 'Annexation of Crimea' (2015) 109 *American Journal of International Law* 68.

[2] V Mykhnenko, 'Causes and Consequences of the War in Eastern Ukraine: An Economic Geography Perspective' (2020) 72 *Europe-Asia Studies* 528.

[3] Bellingcat Investigation Team, 'Identifying the Separatists Linked to the Downing of MH17', available at www.bellingcat.com/news/uk-and-europe/2019/06/19/identifying-the-separatists-linked-to-the-downing-of-mh17.

[4] K Dewey, 'Poisonous affairs: Russia's evolving use of poison in covert operations' (2023) 29 *The Non-proliferation Review* 1.

[5] A Arkhangelsky, 'Murder in Moscow: Anna's legacy Ten years after investigative reporter Anna Politkovskaya was killed, where is Russian journalism today?' (2016) 45 *Index on Censorship* 69.

century, when the prohibition of aggression is *ius cogens* under international law and its violation amounts to a crime under international and national laws alike.[6]

And yet, the aggression did take place. On 24 February 2022 Russian tanks rumbled into Ukraine, their fighter jets targeting both military and civilian infrastructure in a *Blitzkrieg* whose object and purpose were to topple the democratically elected Ukrainian leadership literally overnight. While the West was holding its breath, taken aback by the developments, the Ukrainian leadership, apparently aided by US intelligence, which took away Putin's capacity to surprise, fought back and prevented the fall of Kyiv. Putin's initial plan of taking Ukraine and formally converting it into a vassal state, part of the Russian Mir,[7] thus failed completely. The Russian forces were consequently compelled into a retreat during which they have committed unspeakable crimes against humanity in the suburbs of Kyiv.[8] By failing to take the capital of Ukraine, Russia lost its *Blitzkrieg*.

Consequently, Russia's special military operation, as it was intentionally dubbed at the outset,[9] shifted to the fronts in the east and the south of Ukraine. The degree of its hostility and destruction soon reached the proportions at which even Russia had to publicly agree to the obvious: the attack on 24 February 2022 marked the beginning of the biggest military conflict in Europe since the end of World War II. This was not just another special military operation, that could fly under the radar; rather, it was nothing else than a start of a cruel, bloody and long war directed at the Ukrainian military and civilian targets alike.

2.2. Peace as a Victim of its Own Success

It is against this historical backdrop that this chapter will reflect on the question of the enduring legitimisation of European integration by reference to peace. Raising the question of peace in a time of war is, of course, more than obvious. War is a negation of peace; it is its antipode. But first, we must take a step back. For those who are cognisant of the historical legal and political evolution of the EU, there is little doubt that peace has been from the very outset – and hence enduringly – the main normative value of the integration process. However, at the same time the real value of this normative value, its concrete relevance, has changed profoundly through time. The importance of peace and hence its normative value was at its peak in the years immediately after the end of the World War II. But, the more the memories of World War II have faded away, the less relevant peace has become as a normative value of European integration. As a result, from the Schuman declaration to the Russian aggression on Ukraine, the strength of the normative value of peace has been on a persistent decline. The reason for this lies

[6] S Sayapin, *The Crime of Aggression in International Criminal Law* (The Hague, Asser Press, Springer, 2014).

[7] A Meienberger, 'The concept of the "Russkiy Mir": History of the Concept and Ukraine' (2023) 13 *Euxeinos* 15.

[8] I Kozak-Balaniuk, 'Acts Committed by Russian Citizens in Ukraine after 24 February 2022 That May Constitute the Crime of Genocide' (2023) *Review of European and Comparative Law* 101.

[9] EA Vertlieb, 'The Cognitive-Strategic Meaning of the Special Military Operation in Ukraine' (2023) 8 *Global Security and Intelligence Studies* 179.

in the fact that the strength of the normative value of peace hinges on its actual practical relevance. The more stable and long-lasting peace is, the less relevant in practice it becomes, which in turn also detracts from its normative value as a factor of legitimisation of the EU.

To demonstrate this point, we might, for example, recall the public debates, both political and academic, in the lead-up to the eventually aborted Treaty Establishing a Constitution for Europe.[10] There, the most vocal as well as the brightest minds of Europe justified, inter alia, a process of documentary constitutionalisation of the EU by the fact that a new, autonomous source of political legitimacy is necessary for the viability and the longevity of the EU.[11] The argument went that in the founding phase of the integration, when not just the memory of a destructive World War II was fresh, but its impact – economic, social and political – was also more than visible even to the most sceptic observer, lasting peace was the most pressing normative objective.[12] It was the glue that would bring and hold together the integration.

However, 50 years on, the normative value of peace was not only exhausted. Peace as a normative value in and of itself, in any case, would not be sufficient to legitimise the Union after so many years of both deepening and, especially in 2004, widening. In the early 2000s, especially with the big-bang enlargement portrayed as a success, Europe seemed to be, eventually and definitely, 'whole, free and at peace with itself'.[13] The founding fathers' ambition to ensure through economic cooperation that any war between EU Member States would be not merely unthinkable, but materially impossible,[14] was fulfilled. Ever since then, peace in Europe – neglecting of course the 1990s genocidal Balkan wars – where history has ended too with the fall of the Berlin Wall,[15] has been taken for granted. Its practical normative legitimizing value for the integration expired, and it had to be supplemented by something else. Hence, a Constitution and explicit polity-building.[16]

Thus the normative value of peace is a reverse function of its success. The more successful peace is, the lesser its normative value for an integration process. While this might appear paradoxical, in reality it is not. It is part of human nature, an essential characteristic of human affairs. Humans tend to treat something of value only when that something is available to them in limited and lesser quantities. When humans get too much of something, they become spoiled and yearn for something else. This general rule of human nature apparently applies to peace too.

[10] P Norman, *The Accidental Constitution* (Brussels, EuroComment, 2003).

[11] N Walker, 'Europe's Constitutional Engagement' (2005) 18 *Ratio Juris* 387. J Habermas, 'Why Europe Needs a Constitution?' (2001) 11 *New Left Review* 5, 17.

[12] For a summary of these beliefs and debates, see, Habermas (ibid) 7. For a more recent discussion, see M Avbelj, 'Revitalisation of EU Constitutionalism' (2021) 46 *European Law Review* 1; M Avbelj (ed), *The Future of EU Constitutionalism* (Oxford, Hart, 2023).

[13] GHW Bush, 'A Whole Europe, A Free Europe' (31 May 1989), available at voicesofdemocracy.umd.edu/bush-a-whole-europe-speech-text.

[14] R Schuman, 'The Schuman Declaration (May 9, 1950)', available at european-union.europa.eu/principles-countries-history/history-eu/1945-59/schuman-declaration-may-1950_en.

[15] F Fukuyama, *The End of History and the Last Man* (New York, Free Press, 2006).

[16] See, eg, M. Avbelj, 'The Pitfalls of (Comparative) Constitutionalism for European Integration' (2008) Eric Stein Working Paper 2008/1, available at csesp.files.wordpress.com/2015/05/eswp-2008-01-avbelj.pdf.

2.3. The Meaning of Peace as a Concept *an sich*

As a result of the historical declining practical relevance of peace in the construction of European integration, the normative value of peace has, by and large, become only declaratory and its meaning has been taken at face value. While everyone agreed that peace is an enduring factor of legitimisation of the EU – its alfa and omega – very few students of European integration actually closely engaged theoretically with peace as a normative concept, shedding light not necessarily on its essentially contested character,[17] but at least on the different shades of meaning of peace as a concept *an sich*. To many, perhaps even to everyone, peace has meant peace.[18]

However, even under the same semantics very different meanings of peace can lurk. This has been proven by recent civic reactions to the ongoing war in Ukraine. These reactions are instructive since they also foreclose an easy theoretical escape concerning the meaning of peace by arguing that everyone agrees at least on the negative definition of peace, which is, of course, war. In this way, peace can be simply defined by the absence of war. However, this immediately raises the question of the meaning of war, which is, again in the concrete context of the Russian aggression on Ukraine, by no means unequivocal.

A quick glimpse at the aforementioned civic reactions to the war in Ukraine, taken from the Slovenian public sphere (but similar debates – eg the Habermas–Snyder exchange[19] – are taking place elsewhere) shall suffice to drive this point home. A group composed of two former presidents of the republic, mayors of the two most populous Slovenian cities, members of the Academy of Science, academics, journalists, totalling more than 80 influential public figures, called upon the governments of the EU Member States, NATO and the Russian Federation to immediately stop this 'proxy war' in Ukraine, where the latter is 'a victim of conflict between two nuclear powers for their respective spheres of influence'.[20]

This public letter received an unprecedented reaction on behalf of 16 ambassadors of EU Member States plus the UK who stated explicitly:

> [W]hen there is a choice between right and wrong, between the aggressor and the victim, we remain on the side of justice and on the side of the people. We will never accept the fact that in Europe, or anywhere else in the world, internationally recognized borders are changed by force and that millions of people are subject to unspeakable suffering. Ukraine fights for its sovereignty. Our desire for peace cannot be fulfilled at the expense of the Ukrainian people, its fundamental rights, indeed its very survival.[21]

[17] Which cannot be excluded either, as peace is a social concept too, and social concepts as social constructs are, typically, essentially contested; WB Gallie, 'Essentially Contested Concepts' (1955–56) 56 *Proceedings of the Aristotelian Society New Series* 167.

[18] This is not just a peculiarity of EU studies; as even the scholars of Peace Studies suggest that their own discipline failed to engage with sufficient theoretical rigour with the concept of peace, noting, for example, that 'philosophy of peace is still in its infancy'; see C Wabel, 'Introduction: Toward a Philosophy and Metapsychology of Peace' in C Webel and J Galtung (eds), *Handbook of Peace and Conflict Studies* (Abingdon, Routledge, 2007).

[19] J Habermas, 'War and Indignation. The West's Red Line Dilemma' (6 May 2022), available at www.resetdoc.org/story/jurgen-habermas-war-indignation-west-red-line-dilemma.

[20] M Kučan et al, 'Zaustavite vojno v Ukrajini' [Stop the War in Ukraine], available at siol.net/novice/slovenija/javno-pismo-kucana-in-sopodpisnikov-zaustavite-vojno-v-ukrajini-599536.

[21] The Ambassador of the Kingdom of Belgium et al, 'Podpiramo Ukrajino' [We support Ukraine], available at www.delo.si/mnenja/gostujoce-pero/podpiramo-ukrajino (translated by the author of this chapter).

If anything, this civic exchange has demonstrated that 'peace' and 'war', even in the same factual context, like the one in Ukraine, can mean different things to different people. It is for this reason that this chapter initially considers the meaning of peace *in abstracto*, situating it in the next step within the legal framework of the EU. On this basis, the chapter concludes by examining the evolving normative legitimating function of peace in the EU.

If the meaning of peace seems to be entirely clear and fully intelligible already on the level of human intuition, when engaged with scientifically the definition of 'peace' is much more elusive. So much so that it spurred the development of an independent academic discipline, Peace Studies. According to its founder, Johan Galtung, the meaning of peace in the broadest sense combines both its negative and positive aspects. Accordingly, 'peace studies is about the human condition in general, concerned with our fulfilment … as humans through positive peace, and the reduction of suffering through negative peace'.[22] 'Negative peace' is thus about the transformation of conflicts,[23] whereas 'positive peace' stands for peace-building through cooperation and harmony.[24] Galtung's definition is individual-centred, and rightly so, therefore it includes everything that might impair individual's internal and external harmony.[25] In this sense it is too broad for the purposes of this chapter, which will nevertheless draw on it, albeit concentrating on peace solely at the level of political communities and in the relationships between them.

Accordingly, this chapter defines peace in negative terms as a negation of war, as the most intense form of armed violence. However, other forms of armed violence (eg psychological) can threaten peace too, not necessarily wholly, and hence the existence of peace also presumes the absence of such types of conflicts that do not reach the intensity of war. While it is thus, more or less, clear what peace is not, it is more complicated to define peace in positive terms. A positive definition of peace namely entails spelling out the conditions, the quality of a particular state of social affairs on the basis of which these could be qualified as peaceful.

Various answers, simultaneously already responding to the question of what peace we are talking about, can be offered here. One could distinguish at least among the following conceptions of peace: peace at any price (defeated state); imposed peace (vassal state); *modus vivendi* or peace of tension (mutual assured destruction during the Cold War),[26] real and just peace,[27] also peace of trust.[28] These conceptions of peace can be theoretically best imagined and analysed on a continuum stretching

[22] J Galtung and D Fischer, 'Peace Studies and Conflict Resolution: The Need for Transdisciplinarity' in J Galtungm and D Fischer (eds), *Johan Galtung: Pioneer of Peace Research* (Heidelberg, Springer, 2013) 142.

[23] ibid 139.

[24] ibid.

[25] The distinction between internal and external harmony resulting from peace is, among some authors, reflected also in the so-called internal and external peace. See, eg, C Webel and M Kaba, 'Definitions of Peace' in R Edsforth (ed), *A Cultural History of Peace in the Modern Age*, vol 6 (London, Bloomsbury Academic, 2022) 21–40.

[26] Bush (n 13).

[27] The EU reiterated its readiness to support Ukraine's initiative for a just peace based on respect for Ukraine's sovereignty and territorial integrity; see www.consilium.europa.eu/en/press/press-releases/2023/02/03/joint-statement-following-the-24th-eu-ukraine-summit.

[28] Bush (n 13).

from the peace of the lowest quality on one end, to the peace of the highest quality on the other.[29]

The lowest quality peace is peace at any price. It describes a situation in which an attacked entity decides to surrender to the aggressor either to avoid its total annihilation or because it estimates that continuation of resistance comes at a cost much higher than the consequences of occupation, no matter how grave. Peace at any price hence amounts to a total defeat and complete submission to the attacker. It is a measure of a last resort whereby the choice is between annihilation and the existence under the total discretion of the invader. The only normative value of peace at any price thus boils down to the absolute minimum, which is a mere survival in an externally dictated, unvoluntary 'harmony'.

Moving on the scale away from peace of the lowest quality, we find imposed peace. This is also a result of a defeat of an attacked entity, which might be of a military or political cause, or both. That defeat, however, is not total and complete as under the scenario of peace at any price, since the state might formally preserve its independence, legal subjectivity under international law, but in practice its sovereignty is hollowed out for it is turned into a vassal state, which is essentially dependent on the goodwill of its conqueror. In this state of affairs, unlike in peace at any price, the survival of an entity is not in question, but the peaceful content of its internal affairs is fully dependent on the conditions set externally. The absence of conflicts and violence as a signature of peace is hence not autonomously determined; it is not a result of self-determination, but of imposition.

The next form of peace, and of a higher quality, is peace as *modus vivendi* or peace of tension.[30] It denotes a situation in which the belligerent sides are so strong that waging a war between the two would almost certainly result in either's destruction and/or even in the destruction of the humanity as a whole. Under this conception of peace, peace is not defined by the absence of hostility and conflicts, but by the necessity of avoiding an all-out conflict for the fear of its destructive consequences. This conception of peace has characterised the period of Cold War between the West and the Soviet Union where peace 'flourished' under the threat of a mutually assured destruction.[31] Similarly, some authors have claimed that even after the end of the Cold War, the existence of nuclear weapons, when symmetry between the states is assured, has led to more peaceful international relations.[32] Accordingly, this form of 'nuclear peace' has thus contributed to the decrease of violence since the end of the Cold War.[33]

The highest quality of peace is 'real' peace, also branded as 'just peace' or 'peace of trust'. While views differ on the exact contours of just peace and the requirements

[29] Here we rely on the theoretical approach by C Davenport, E Melander and PM Regan, *The Peace Continuum: What is it and How to Study it?* (Oxford, Oxford University Press, 2018).

[30] Bush (n 13).

[31] HD Sokolski, *Getting MAD: A Nuclear Mutual Assured Destruction, Its Origins and Practice* (Carlisle Barracks, PA, Strategic Studies Institute, US Army War College, 2004).

[32] See, for example, Webel and Kaba (n 25).

[33] See, V Asal and K Byrdsley, 'Proliferation and International Crisis Behaviour' (2007) 44 *Journal of Peace Research* 139, who have argued that 'using data from the International Crisis Behavior (ICB) project, the results demonstrate that crises involving nuclear actors are more likely to end without violence and, as the number of nuclear actors involved increases, the likelihood of war continues to fall.'

that this must meet,[34] it is generally accepted that real peace demands the absence of hostilities, a genuine commitment to prevention and avoidance of conflicts, whereby the terms of peace comply at least with the minimum requirements of international law (respect for sovereign equality, internationally recognised boundaries, territorial integrity, self-determination) and, eventually, go much further by increasingly living up to the prevailing standards of justice. It goes without saying that just peace is also a normative ideal of the EU. Its 'justness' is dependent on the actual fulfilment of values articulated in Article 2 TEU. Accordingly, just peace inside the EU must reflect

> the respect for human dignity, freedom, democracy, equality, the rule of law, as well as the respect for human rights, including the rights of persons belonging to minorities, in a society in which pluralism, non-discrimination, tolerance, justice, solidarity and equality between women and men prevail.[35]

However, referring to peace inside the EU brings us to the question of whose peace we are talking about, ie whose peace matters. The answer to this question is dictated by the principle of proximity,[36] following which the meaning and the normative requirements of peace change as we move from the people with whom we live side-by-side to those that are more territorially distant from us. On this basis, we can distinguish between internal peace, external peace and peace for everyone (*erga omnes*). Internal peace is peace inside the borders of our community, which matters because of us. External peace is peace that takes place beyond our borders and whose presence or absence matters mainly if it affects us. In contrast to this subjective conception of external peace, the latter in objective terms, as peace for everyone, matters because it is or it ought to be a property that each community, not just ours, should enjoy.

2.4. The Meaning of Peace in the Legal Framework of the EU

Peace as a legitimising value of the EU was initially conceived of principally as internal peace, ie peace between the founding EU Member States. The Schuman declaration made it clear that its main purpose was to eliminate all hostilities between France and Germany.[37] However, despite the original internal focus on peace, the reference to peace by the EU and its Member States has always been also externally oriented, both for subjective (selfish) reasons as well as for the objective importance of peace in cosmopolitan terms. Already the Schuman declaration saw the construction of European integration as facilitating the development of the African continent,[38] ensuring its stability and prosperity. The 1973 Declaration on European identity[39] made it even

[34] For a classical treatment, see F Przetacznik, 'The Concept of Genuine and Just Peace as a Basic Collective Human Right' (1989) 6 *New York Law School Journal of Human Rights* 237.

[35] TEU, Art 2.

[36] J Waldron, 'The Principle of Proximity' (2011) *NYU School of Law, Public Law Research Paper No 11-08*, available at ssrn.com/abstract=1742413.

[37] Schuman (n 14).

[38] ibid.

[39] Declaration on European Identity (Copenhagen, 14 December 1973), available at www.cvce.eu/content/publication/1999/1/1/02798dc9-9c69-4b7d-b2c9-f03a8db7da32/publishable_en.pdf.

clearer that Member States of the then European Communities comprehend peace in all three conceptions: internally[40] and externally in subjective[41] and objective terms.[42]

However, commitment to peace is not of the same strength in all of its conceptions. Fully in line with the principle of proximity, it wanes from our peace to their peace, which serves also us, to global peace as such. This can be again nicely illustrated with a quick glimpse at the 2007 Berlin[43] and the 2017 Rome Declaration.[44] The EU Member States are, accordingly, 'striving for peace' *inter se*; being aware of 'major challenges which do not stop at national borders', 'committed to the peaceful resolution of conflicts in the world and to ensuring that people do not become victims of war, terrorism and violence'.[45] 'A stronger Europe on the global scene'[46] is in service of these objectives, by 'further developing existing partnerships, building new ones and promoting stability and prosperity in its immediate neighbourhood to the east and south, but also in the Middle East and across Africa and globally'.[47]

The same approach can be also identified in the Preambles to the Treaty on the European Union[48] and the Treaty on the Functioning of the EU.[49] Similarly, Article 3 of the Treaty on the European Union explicitly proclaims that 'the Union's aim is to promote peace, its values and the well-being of its peoples',[50] which again confirms the EU's primary centredness on its own, internal peace. Nevertheless, again in line with the principle of proximity, the EU is normatively concerned also with external peace, both in its subjective[51] and objective leg.[52] In accordance with Article 21(2)(c), the EU in should in its external policies and actions

[40] ibid. 'The Nine, one of whose essential aims is to maintain peace, will never succeed in doing so if they neglect their own security.'

[41] ibid. 'The Nine intend to preserve their historical links with the countries of the Middle East and to co-operate over the establishment and maintenance of peace, stability and progress in the region.'

[42] ibid. 'There can be no real peace if the developed countries do not pay more heed to the less favoured nations. Convinced of this fact, and conscious of their responsibilities and particular obligations, the Nine attach very great importance to the struggle against under-development.'

[43] Declaration on the occasion of the 50th anniversary of the signature of the Treaties of Rome, available at europa.eu/50/docs/berlin_declaration_en.pdf.

[44] Rome Declaration of the Leaders of 27 Member States and of the European Council, the European Parliament and the European Commission, available at ec.europa.eu/commission/presscorner/detail/en/STATEMENT_17_767.

[45] Berlin Declaration (n 43).

[46] Rome Declaration (n 44).

[47] ibid.

[48] 'RESOLVED to implement a common foreign and security policy including the progressive framing of a common defence policy, which might lead to a common defence in accordance with the provisions of Article 42, thereby reinforcing the European identity and its independence in order to promote peace, security and progress in Europe and in the world.'

[49] 'RESOLVED by thus pooling their resources to preserve and strengthen peace and liberty, and calling upon the other peoples of Europe who share their ideal to join in their efforts.'

[50] TEU, Art 3(1).

[51] TEU, Art 8(1): 'The Union shall develop a special relationship with neighbouring countries, aiming to establish an area of prosperity and good neighbourliness, founded on the values of the Union and characterised by close and peaceful relations based on cooperation.'

[52] TEU, Art 3(5): 'In its relations with the wider world, the Union shall uphold and promote its values and interests and contribute to the protection of its citizens. It shall contribute to peace, security, the sustainable development of the Earth, solidarity and mutual respect among peoples, free and fair trade, eradication of poverty and the protection of human rights, in particular the rights of the child, as well as to the strict observance and the development of international law, including respect for the principles of the United Nations Charter.'; also TEU, Art 21(2)(a).

> work for a high degree of cooperation in all fields of international relations, in order to, [inter alia] preserve peace, prevent conflicts and strengthen international security, in accordance with the purposes and principles of the United Nations Charter, with the principles of the Helsinki Final Act and with the aims of the Charter of Paris, including those relating to external borders.[53]

Similarly, with regard to common security and defence policy, Article 42 TEU envisages that it should result in 'an operational capacity drawing on civilian and military assets', which the Union may use 'on missions outside the Union for peace-keeping, conflict prevention and strengthening international security in accordance with the principles of the United Nations Charter'.[54] In order to achieve both internal as well as external peace the Treaty envisages the emergence of a common Union defence policy, gradually leading to a common defence, 'when the European Council, acting unanimously, so decides'.[55]

If prior to the Russian aggression in Ukraine the establishment of an EU common defence still seemed temporally very remote, subsequent developments changed that significantly. And, as we shall see in the next section, this change of the perspective also reversed the role of peace as an enduring source of EU legitimacy. Since February 2022, the EU has been more concerned about averting the war by military means than investing into peace through strengthening the economic, political and legal interdependency in international relations as it has traditionally been the case.

2.5. Transformation of the EU's Path to Peace

Ever since the Schuman declaration, the normative agenda of European integration has consisted of investing into economic, political and legal strategies of increased cooperation which would ensure that 'any war … becomes not merely unthinkable, but materially impossible'.[56] Initially this strategy was directed at France and Germany, as well as all other Members States of the integration, but after the fall of the Berlin Wall it has been extended to include the European continent as a whole and, gradually, the rest of the globe. The EU and its Member States have thus invested heavily into the building of peace, but in doing so, as the Russian invasion in Ukraine reminded them bitterly, they discounted the importance of averting the war. In a way, the EU has fallen into a trap, nicely described by an inverted Latin maxim: *Para pacem, si vis bellum!* As a result, when war in Europe became not just conceivable, but a reality, the EU increasingly found itself materially unable to fight back.

Of course, this is not to argue that the EU was building peace because it wanted the war. No: it is to claim that since the EU, unlike its economic and political 'partners' in international relations, invested too much, or even exclusively, in non-military means of securing peace, it has made itself vulnerable and weak, but also complacent. For a long time, it seemed that the EU peace-maintaining strategy has worked. It has indeed,

[53] TEU, Art 21(2)(c).
[54] TEU, Art 41(1).
[55] TEU, Art 42(2).
[56] Schuman (n 14).

until it did not anymore. In hindsight, this European approach of increasing peace by decreasing its military capacity might have even 'invited' the war. The comparative data demonstrates that after the end of the Cold War all EU Member States slashed their military spending at least by one-third.

If in the 1960s, 1970s and 1980s most of the Member States spent around three per cent of their GDP for defence, in the 1990s this rate dropped below two per cent, and now averages between 1.3 and 1.5 per cent of GDP.[57] Most of European NATO Member States thus do not meet their commitments of spending two per cent of their national GDP for defence purposes. Furthermore, across Europe the system of conscription has been replaced by slimmed-down, professional, typically all-volunteer, armies.[58] When, added to this, the UK, boasting one of the most powerful European armed forces, decided to leave the Union, Russia clearly felt it had the upper hand. In contrast to the EU Member States, Russia has never dropped the mandatory military draft and has kept its military spending close or even above four per cent of GDP over the last two decades. In short, while Europe was preparing for peace, Russia has worked towards the war.

As indicated in the introduction of this chapter, Russia found the EU Member States not only militarily unprepared, but also wedded to a mindset and political practice that has for decades taken peace for granted. All of a sudden, out of an existential threat, because the Member States understood that the fate of Ukraine decides also the fate of the CEE Member States geographically closest to it, and with them of the EU as a whole, the EU abandoned *Para pacem, si vis bellum!* in favour of its original version: *si vis pacem, para bellum*. And indeed, the EU Member States collectively and on an individual, bilateral basis started the unthinkable. Sending arms to Ukraine, first from their warehouses, then from the military market in Europe and today even from the markets in the third countries.[59] The fact of empty military reserves prompted the leaders across EU Member States, for the first time in decades, to call for a wartime economy.[60] French President Macron openly denounced 'a self-satisfied numbness' of the past 'comfortable years'.[61] Even more strikingly, his German counterpart, Bundeskanzler Scholz, whose guilt-stricken country prided itself on its pacificist internal and external policies following World War II, urged his allies to step up the defence spending.[62] In a similar vein, the then outgoing European Commission President, Ursula von der Leyen, pledged that, should she assume the presidency of the Commission in the next term, she would create a new Defence Commissioner post.[63]

[57] Stockholm International Peace Research Institute (SIPRI), available at www.sipri.org/databases/milex.

[58] See, M Bieri, 'Military Conscription in Europe: New Relevance' (2015) 180 *CSS Analyses in Security Policy* 1, available at www.research-collection.ethz.ch/bitstream/handle/20.500.11850/118187/eth-49394-01.pdf.

[59] A Grey, 'EU aims to shift European arms industry to "war economy mode"' Reuters, available at www.reuters.com/world/europe/eu-aims-shift-european-arms-industry-war-economy-mode-2024-03-04.

[60] J-M Bezat, C Pietralunga and E Vincent, '"We are now in a wartime economy", says France's top military procurement official', available at www.lemonde.fr/en/international/article/2023/03/15/we-are-now-in-a-wartime-economy-says-france-s-top-military-procurement-official_6019480_4.html.

[61] News Wires, 'Macron urges French defence firms to boost production to support Ukraine', available at www.france24.com/en/europe/20240119-macron-urges-french-defence-firms-to-boost-production-to-support-ukraine.

[62] J Posaner, 'Germany's Scholz wants European allies to up defense spending', available at www.politico.eu/article/germany-olaf-scholz-wants-european-allies-to-up-defense-spending.

[63] A Roussi, J Posaner and J Cienski, 'Von der Leyen plans new defense commissioner post', available at www.politico.eu/article/von-der-leyen-plans-new-defense-commissioner-post.

However, the EU's newly discovered militarisation in function of peace did not stop there. Lending credence to the thought that history indeed repeats itself, but hopefully neither as tragedy nor as farce,[64] the notorious Draghi's 'whatever it takes to save the euro',[65] has also made inroads in the contemporary Ukraine war crisis. As with the existential threat created by the Greek monetary crisis, today too we hear that 'We will do whatever it takes to ensure that Russia cannot win this war',[66] which means that 'the EU must support Ukraine with whatever is needed for Kyiv to win its war against Russia'.[67] This, presumably, includes sending EU ground troops into Ukraine.[68] Thus have spoken, not some fringe politicians, but the Presidents of France and the European Parliament respectively. The Swedish civil and military authorities went a step further, directly warning their citizens 'to prepare for war'.[69]

This shift in EU political discourse and practice as a resulting of the Ukraine war, has not decreased the value of peace as a source of enduring legitimation of European integration. Quite the opposite. The currency of peace as a legitimating factor of the EU has been strengthened, but what has changed fundamentally is the overall strategy for ensuring and preserving peace in the longer run. From its inception, the EU has operated on the basis of economy as a means of pacification of international relations. This works as long as the other states – but especially the most powerful ones – play along. When they do not, power, in the form of brute military force, becomes relevant too. Ultimately, maintaining peace necessitates that the aggressor ceases their actions, achieved through military measures that restore order and act as a deterrence. The EU has long resisted speaking the language of force. This has been a privilege and a risk that since February 2022 the EU can no longer afford.

2.6. Conclusion

This chapter has demonstrated that peace has been the main legitimating source of European integration, which has entered the process of legitimisation as a factor of input, throughput and output legitimacy either momentarily (ad hoc) or on a permanent basis. To recall,[70] the input legitimacy consists of values that are set as a precondition for entering the integration process. They typically require certain qualities from the candidate states and their commitment to specific ideals that the integration shall personify.

[64] As per Karl Marx.

[65] M Draghi, www.youtube.com/watch?v=ItcqFRMF1Q0.

[66] C Calcutt, L Kayali and V Melkozerova, 'Macron doesn't rule out sending Western troops to Ukraine', available at www.politico.eu/article/emmanuel-macron-doesnt-rule-out-sending-troops-to-ukraine-ammo.

[67] European Parliament, 'Parliament calls on the EU to give Ukraine whatever it needs to defeat Russia', available at www.europarl.europa.eu/news/en/press-room/20240223IPR18097/parliament-calls-on-the-eu-to-give-ukraine-whatever-it-needs-to-defeat-russia.

[68] 'Macron tells party leaders France's support to Ukraine has "no limits"' Le Monde (7 March 2024), available at www.lemonde.fr/en/politics/article/2024/03/07/macron-tells-party-leaders-no-limits-to-france-s-ukraine-support_6595283_5.html.

[69] L Nordstrom, 'Sweden's call for population to prepare for war sparks panic and criticism', available at www.france24.com/en/europe/20240118-sweden-s-call-for-population-to-prepare-for-war-sparks-panic-and-criticism.

[70] See M Avbelj, 'Values, Constitutionalism and the Viability of European Integration' in M Avbelj, *The Future of EU Constitutionalism* (Oxford, Hart, 2023) ch 4.

The throughput values are the values that guide the EU decision-making process *lato sensu*. Finally, the output values are the goals and objectives for which the EU has been created and which ought to be maximised to the greatest possible extent.[71]

All the symbolic, profoundly normative and value-laden declarations of the EU and its Member States confirm that peace is an enduring input and output legitimating factor of integration. From the very beginning peace has been a self-standing value to which all other values and achievements of the integration have been instrumental. In fact, even the future European federation, intimated in the Schuman declaration, is not a goal in and of itself; rather, it has been advanced as 'indispensable to the preservation of peace'.[72] A state that seeks admission to the EU has to be peace-loving. Peace is considered as just peace, whose content is determined with reference to fundamental values of the EU, which are 'part of our soul, part of what defines us today'.[73] Just peace defined through Article 2 TEU, to only slightly paraphrase the CJEU, makes up 'the very identity of the European Union as a common legal order'.[74] As such, its value is inexhaustible,[75] while its relevance hinges on the real and perceived threat to peace.

The war in Ukraine presents more than a credible threat to the internal peace in the EU and it certainly signifies a total absence of peace in external terms, both under its subjective and objective conception. The normative relevance of the value of peace in the EU today is at an all-time high and it can be expected, even if for purely utilitarian reasons, that it will provide a significant boost to the process of European integration, in its widening and deepening leg alike. Provided, of course, that Ukraine prevails. In the opposite scenario, not only just peace in the EU, but its very survival, might be at stake. It is for that reason that the strategy of achieving peace in the EU and beyond has undergone a complete transformation from economic, political and legal peace-building mechanisms to the more recent explicit investment in the military capacity of the EU and its Member States. Peace continues to remain an enduring source of legitimisation of European integration, but the means of achieving it have been altered beyond imagination.

[71] ibid.
[72] Schuman (n 14).
[73] U von der Leyen, 'State of the Union Speech 2021', available at ec.europa.eu/commission/presscorner/detail/en/SPEECH_21_4701.
[74] Cases C-156/21, C-157/21 *Hungary v European Parliament and Council of the European Union*, [127].
[75] ibid, [126].

3

The Impact of the War in Ukraine on the (Slow) Redress of the 'Solidarity Deficit' in the EU

SACHA GARBEN

3.1. Introduction

This chapter argues that the EU's response to the war in Ukraine has to be seen in the context of a broader, profound development in the EU's recent functioning and mentality, which it will conceptualise as a shift in the EU's solidarity arrangement.[1] As was noted in the Introduction to this book, it instantly becomes clear when surveying the various chapters that the EU's response to the war in Ukraine has been surprisingly cohesive, determined, and convincing. This applies to the way in which the EU has responded, ie in terms of its methods, but also to the spirit in which it has acted, namely in *solidarity* with, firstly, Ukraine, and secondly, with one another. As this chapter will explore, this presents a marked change compared to the past decades in which the EU was plagued by a 'solidarity deficit'.[2] This deficit consists in that although solidarity is a

[1] Parts of this chapter are an adaptation of S Garben, 'The (Slow) Redress of the 'Solidarity Deficit' in the EU and the Emerging Principle of Solidarity in EU Law' (2024) *Maastricht Journal of European and Comparative Law* (forthcoming).

[2] J Van der Walt, 'Editor's Introduction: Constitutional Sovereignty and Social Solidarity in Europe' in J van der Walt and J Ellsworth (eds), *Constitutional Sovereignty and Social Solidarity in Europe* (Nomos, Baden Baden, 2015). There is a growing scholarship that considers that, despite solidarity's somewhat ethereal nature, it is not only a theoretically important tool to understand the EU and an element explaining political (and individual) behaviour in relation thereto, but an EU legal concept gaining importance – a general principle of EU law in the making. The leading philosophical account of solidarity and EU is developed by Jürgen Habermas. See *The Inclusion of the Other* (Cambridge, MA, MIT Press, 1998); 'The European nation-state and the pressures of globalisation' (1999) I *New Left Review* 46; *The Post-national Constellation* (Cambridge, Polity Press, 2001). For a discussion of this work, see M Murphy, 'Between facts, norms and a post-national constellation: Habermas, law and European Social Policy'(2005) 12 *Journal of European Public Policy* 143. For the political consequences of solidarity, see eg M Ferrera and C Burelli, 'Cross-National Solidarity and Political Sustainability in the EU after the Crisis' (2019) 57 *Journal of Common Market Studies* 94; F Visconti and A Kyriazi, 'A solidarity bias? Assessing the effects of individual transnationalism on redistributive solidarity in the EU' (2024) 31 *Journal of European Public Policy* 528. A selection of the rich literature on solidarity in the EU legal order: A Sangiovanni, 'Solidarity in the European Union' (2013) 33 *Oxford Journal of Legal Studies* 213; F de Witte, *Justice in the EU: the emergence of transnational solidarity* (Oxford, Oxford

fundamental value of the EU project, as stated in Article 2 TEU, and in the preamble of the EU Charter of Fundamental Rights (EUCFR) where it is placed alongside human dignity, freedom, equality as the four universal values on which the Union is founded, and although the Court of Justice has since long held that it 'underpins the entire legal system of the European Union'[3] constituting 'its very root',[4] solidarity is underdeveloped in concrete legal and political terms, and has insufficiently guided the actions of the EU institutions and EU Member States over the past decades. This chapter identifies a trend towards a certain – admittedly slow and still incomplete – redress of this solidarity deficit both in political and in legal terms. It flags the EU's response to the war in Ukraine as one of the four main developments of change, alongside the European Pillar of Social Rights, the NextGenEU recovery fund, and the CJEU's recent case law on solidarity.

The chapter will first provide a general exploration of the notion of solidarity to arrive at a workable understanding for our purposes (section 3.2). It will then survey, in an (admittedly broad stokes) overview, the varying significance given to solidarity in the EU project, marking as different phases: the early days of European integration (section 3.3.1), the post-Maastricht period (section 3.3.2), the crisis years (section 3.3.3), and the past decade (section 3.3.4). Having identified the various elements of a solidarity shift in the most recent period, it will then delve more deeply into one of these elements: the possible development of solidarity as a general principle of EU law in reference to the CJEU's *OPAL* judgment on energy solidarity, rendered in the context of Russia's earlier aggression in Ukraine, before the full-scale invasion (section 3.4). Flagging the fundamental relevance of this ruling for the EU legal order more generally, this chapter considers the potential interpretation that should be given to solidarity as a general principle of EU law, arguing that it should be anchored in its conceptualisation in the EUCFR as 'universal' and 'indivisible' from human dignity, freedom and equality. Such an approach may have concrete legal significance in many areas of the EU legal order, most notably migration and the internal market.

3.2. Preliminary Remarks: Solidarity as a Multilateral Take-and-Give in the Common Interest

On a theoretical level, there is a question of how solidarity is distinct from related 'other-regarding dispositions' that involve a measure of generosity, in that someone deliberately performs an action that is sub-optimal for them but for the benefit of another, such

University Press, 2015); A Biondi, E Dagilytė and E Küçük (eds), *Solidarity in EU Law* (Cheltenham, UK and Northampton, MA, USA, Edward Elgar, 2018); M Kohn, 'Solidarity and social rights'(2018) 21 *Critical Review of International Social and Political Philosophy* 616; J Czuzai, 'The Principle of Solidarity in the EU Legal Order – Some Practical Examples after Lisbon' in J Czuzai, *The EU as a Global Actor – Bridging Legal Theory and Practice* (Leiden, Brill, 2017); P Hilpold, 'Understanding Solidarity Within EU Law: An Analysis of the "Islands of Solidarity" With Particular Regard to Monetary Union' (2015) 34 *Yearbook of European Law* 25; PG Xuereb, 'The Future of Europe: Solidarity and Constitutionalism. Towards a Solidarity Model' (2002) 27 *European Law Rev* 643; I Domurath, 'The Three Dimensions of Solidarity in the EU Legal Order: Limits of the Judicial and Legal Approach' (2013) 35 *Journal of European Integration* 459.

[3] Case C-848/19 P, *OPAL*, ECLI:EU:C:2021:598.

[4] Case 128/78, *Commission v UK (Tachographs)*.

as altruism, sophisticated selfishness, team-reasoning and Kantian duty (goodwill). In philosophy it has been argued that solidarity motivates generosity independently (thus, even in the absence) of these other-regarding motivations, on the basis of 'an identification with the condition of a certain group of people' to whom one does not (directly) belong.[5] It would therefore be a self-standing notion. However, the lack of team spirit as motivation for the generous action in this narrow approach, as well as the required lack of self-interest, seems to be at odds with the common meaning of the term.[6] Manifestations of genuine out-of-group, non-reciprocal generosity are rare,[7] and the usefulness of the concept of solidarity to understand the functioning of societies would be drastically limited (or altogether excluded) if such a narrow definition were followed. It does not seem necessary or appropriate to take such a strict approach to solidarity that excludes the conceptual forms of 'other-regarding generosity' that somehow rely on team or group membership and a combination of self- and collective interest. For our purposes, its key features will be taken to be that a certain act is performed that is (perceived as) sub-optimal for the actor(s) at least in the short term for the benefit of (an)other(s) – or put differently, in which the immediate self-interest is ignored or put aside and instead the interest of/shared with another (which may be a member of the same group or not) is served. This thus includes actions that are expected to yield benefits for the actor in the long term (with the exception of guaranteed overall net benefits for the actor individually, which would simply make the action a rational investment).

But the key to understanding solidarity as a societal mechanism is not found in single actions, and instead lies in its recognition of the inter-dependence and inter-connectedness of (groups of) people and their (in-)actions, and the various duties and responsibilities that flow from that. It is not so much about one-off transactions from one to another as it about an entire social network of efforts, contributions, responsibilities and duties in the common endeavour of life. In Somek's words, 'solidarity as transcendence is concerned with realising the wealth of human potential. Societies as a "system of cooperation" are seen as serving this end'.[8] Similarly, Sangiovanni understands demands for social solidarity at all levels of governance as 'demands for a fair return in the mutual production of important collective goods'.[9] The idea is that in our societies,

> we depend on the joint contributions of myriad other citizens and residents for the ability not only to develop but also to act on a plan of life. Without the support those contributions provide for the political and legal authority of the state, we would lack the resources necessary to function as biological, social and political beings. … our abilities to develop and make use of our talents, as well as our ability to profit from them, depend on the survival and

[5] C Arnsperger and Y Varoufakis, 'Toward a theory of solidarity' (2003) 59 *Erkenntnis* 157.

[6] For instance, solidarity is classically associated with collective action undertaken by workers against an employer, where team-reasoning is likely to play a key part. See R Sugden, 'Thinking as a team: towards an explanation of nonselfish behavior' (1993) 10 *Social Philosophy and Policy* 69.

[7] One could think of, for example, the provision of humanitarian assistance to another group (country) in the case of a natural disaster, when it is provided without any reasonable expectation of receiving such assistance when disaster strikes the assisting group (country) at a later point.

[8] A Somek, 'Solidarity Decomposed – Being and time in European citizenship' (2007) *University of Iowa Legal Studies Research Paper* Number 07–13, 44.

[9] Sangiovanni (n 2).

> maintenance of the scheme; without it, we would soon lose everything that we have gained. Therefore, those who are better able to gain from the scheme owe those less able, but who have made their gains possible, a fair return for what they have received.[10]

We should be careful not to (mis)understand the idea of societal solidarity as requiring some kind of direct, one-on-one take-and-give-back. Firstly, the contributions that have made current 'wins' possible may be long in the past and the return may be designed to benefit people who have not yet been born. As Kohn argues, in line with the solidaristic tradition, a purely compensatory approach presents various problems, as we understand solidaristic measures as being not necessarily concordant with the actual contribution and need of the individuals concerned, and also to be forward-looking.[11] She says, 'the normative idea is not that we must give the individual what she is owed but that we must use social wealth to promote the flourishing of all members of society', remembering that all 'people are born vulnerable and dependent. Social ties sustain us, and therefore we should repair and strengthen them'.[12] The relationships of solidaristic taking-and-giving in this construction are multilateral and take place across time and place. They are both very concrete (as every single person will have actually, tangibly benefited from collective goods from the moment of their conception) and very abstract (as it requires a degree of imagination to understand the complexity of this societal scheme and one's place within it). This multilateral take-and-give in the common interest is a powerful tool for societal cohesion and progress, but in its reciprocity, complexity and abstraction lies also one of society's main vulnerabilities. If this reciprocal taking-and-giving(-and-taking-and-giving, etc) works well, it leads to a virtuous cycle, but if there is a breakdown it can spiral the other way in a vicious cycle that critically endangers the health of the polity.

Against this background I argue that both: (i) the participation in the maintenance and (future) survival of a common (societal) scheme or project of which one is not certain whether it will be to one's immediate benefit in addition to an expected common benefit; and (ii) a measure of 'redistribution' of the benefits yielded by the common scheme or project from those that have been able to collect more than those who have less, are – within this conception – to be qualified as acts of solidarity. These two acts of solidarity are reciprocal and circular, as a successful society requires that these acts *both* have to be continuously (re-)taken indefinitively. If the same actors (individuals, social groups, Member States) are consistently asked to perform the first act of solidarity, ie to participate in the scheme without guaranteed benefits, and it consistently turns out that the benefits that are generated do not fall to them, making them the 'losers' of the system, and if subsequently the 'winners' do not engage in the second act of solidarity (ie redistribution), then the losing group will at some point refuse to continue engaging in its first act of solidarity, and the project is likely to fail. Similarly, 'winners' are not likely to engage in the second act of redistributive solidarity if the 'losers' are seen as unwilling to meaningfully cooperate in the common project that generated the benefits in the first place. Indeed, in the former situation, the 'losers' are not asked to participate

[10] ibid, 217.
[11] Kohn (n 2).
[12] ibid.

in a common scheme where the individual yields will be uncertain, but instead in a framework where their personal loss is certain. And in the latter situation, winners are asked to provide charity. Such sustained generosity can only be expected when group ties are so strong that the gains and losses of another member of the group are vicariously felt, which rarely applies to modern societies as a whole.

As Habermas has pointed out,[13] trust is a necessary ingredient in this equation, as it bridges the gap between the 'sacrifice' required of the participant and the 'pay back' in terms of common net benefit or redistribution. A high degree of commonality, especially in terms of identity, seems conducive to high levels of trust.[14] But let us be careful not to misunderstand this as a need for (ethnic, cultural, linguistic) homogeneity in society as a necessary requirement for solidarity. Other factors can instil trust, and solidarity – even when based on team reasoning – is a universal value that can function in a multilevel (or perhaps rather concentric) way. I would argue that in less close-knit (larger, more diverse) settings, inter-personal trust can be replaced by the enforcement of the solidarity settlement through common institutions (rules, courts), as long as these institutions are trusted to ensure that all partners play their role in the common scheme. The more visible the common scheme is (made), the more broadly shared its understanding (in terms of common purpose and assigned roles), the more direct individuals' participation in the development of the project is, and the more easily they can (be made to) imagine its benefits, and the sacrifices of others for their benefit within this context, the more easily loyalty will be vested the scheme. This all makes law, democratic participation and policies such as citizenship education function as the oil in society's solidarity machinery.

3.3. Solidarity in the EU

3.3.1. The Early Days of Solidarity

The fact that solidarity can be expected to be stronger when the common (societal) scheme is more developed and visible, participation is more direct, and when participants feel more strongly attached to the identity of the underlying group, clearly implies some challenges for the existence of solidarity in a context that transcends one's primary community, which in the EU context is generally still the national level.[15] Nevertheless, the fact that there are challenges does not mean such solidarity cannot also be present in a transnational setting such as the EU, or even at global level.[16] It has already been

[13] www.socialeurope.eu/are-we-still-good-europeans.

[14] Robert Putnam's work is often cited as evidence of the opposite, ie that diversity decreases trust. R Putnam, 'E Pluribus Unum: Diversity and Community in the Twenty-first Century The 2006 Johan Skytte Prize Lecture' (2007) 30 *Scandinavian Political Studies* 137. Subsequent research however casts doubt on these pessimistic findings; see eg M Abascal and D Baldassarr, 'Love Thy Neighbor? Ethnoracial Diversity and Trust Reexamined'(2015) 121 *American Journal of Sociology* 722.

[15] T Risse, *A community of Europeans? Transnational identities and public spheres* (Ithaca, Cornell University Press, 2010).

[16] C Gould, 'Transnational solidarities' (2007) 38 *Journal of Social Philosophy* 148.

shown that identity can, and in a majority of cases does, exist at several levels, including the national and EU level.[17] And, while it may be less developed and visible to citizens, it is clear that the EU provides a kind of common scheme from which all Member States are expected to (have) benefit(ed) from. Moreover, as we noted, trust generated by strong collective identity may be partially replaced by trust in the enforcement of the solidarity settlement by common institutions (rules, courts).

This latter approach resonates with the Court of Justice's early case law on solidarity, where it invoked it to unequivocally require Member States to apply EU legislation even where they disagreed with it or pleaded internal difficulties to comply.[18] The Court stated:

> In permitting Member States to profit from the advantages of the Community, the Treaty imposes on them also the obligation to respect its rules.
>
> For a State unilaterally to break, according to its own conception of national interest, the equilibrium between advantages and obligations flowing from its adherence to the Community brings into question the equality of Member states before Community Law and creates discrimination at the expense of their nationals, and above all of the nationals of the state itself which places itself outside the Community rules.
>
> This failure in the duty of solidarity accepted by the Member states by the fact of their adherence to the Community strikes at the fundamental basis of the Community legal order.

Participation in the project is framed, by the Court, as an act of solidarity. And, in return, there may be redistribution, as the Court clarified in another early case:[19]

> The solidarity which is at the basis of these obligations as of the whole of the Community system in accordance with the undertaking for provided for in Article 5 (ie the principle of sincere cooperation) is continued for the benefit of the states in the procedure for mutual assistance provided for in Article 108 where a Member State is seriously threatened with difficulties as regards its balance of payments.

Member States need to not only follow the rules but facilitate the achievement of common aims, they need to assist the Union. And in return, they may be assisted.

Indeed, the original Treaties featured some instruments for such assistance and more generally the sharing of the expected gains of the common market, most notably the structural funds. But – at least initially – the socio-economic model of the common market was one where economic integration would lead to the 'growing of the pie', and where the distribution of the pie slices would fall to the Member States: the intention was not to create a European welfare state. Such a disconnect between the first and second steps of solidarity outlined in the previous section could be considered as precarious and inherently instable, especially in combination with the initial lack of direct political participation by citizens in the decision-making of the common EEC scheme and the judicial development of a strong legal hierarchy placing European-level economic authority and competition above national-level social competence and redistribution.[20]

[17] Risse (n 15).

[18] Case 39-72, *Commission v Italian Republic (Premiums for slaughtering cows)*.

[19] Case 6 and 11-69, *Com v France*.

[20] See S Garben, 'Competition, Cooperation, and Solidarity in EU law – a Federal Perspective' in P Chiocchetti and F Allemand (eds), *Competitiveness and solidarity in the European Union: interdisciplinary perspectives* (Abingdon, Routledge, 2018).

However, it may be posited that an important stabilising solidarity factor in those early years was a non-economic benefit perceived as directly related to the EEC/ECSC project: peace on the European continent.[21] Wartime sacrifice was still keenly and widely felt at the time, and the development of transnational schemes such as the EEC/ECSC was explicitly and deliberately presented as the solution. Although Weiler's account[22] of the EEC's post-war 'political messianism' and 'telos-legitimacy' of peace may be overstated,[23] it does seem likely that the commonly felt sacrifice of war and benefit of peace provided a social embedding of the EEC's economic cooperation and integration project, which was hoped by many to provide the concrete machinery for the incremental building of solidarity as a way out of Europe's warring state. Monnet's famous words in the 1950's Schumann Declaration that 'Europe will not be made all at once, or according to a single plan – it will be built through concrete achievements which first create a de facto solidarity' can be read as a recognition of the importance of solidarity not just as an intangible value but as humankind's most powerful dynamic and concrete arrangement to achieve and maintain peace and prosperity, requiring continuous collective work. Through concrete cooperation, in 'an organised and living Europe' growing a 'a wider and deeper community between countries long opposed to one another by sanguinary divisions', 'war'… 'becomes not merely unthinkable, but materially impossible'.[24]

3.3.2. Solidarity Waning

About two generations on, the fading of the memories of war perhaps inevitably eroded the 'buffering', imaginary role of peace as a main benefit to inspire citizens' loyalty to European union as a scheme. Economic integration *in se* seemed to be left to take over as the main *telos* and focus of the common scheme instead,[25] expressed in 'economic constitutionalism'[26] with a certain deregulatory and individualistic orientation, presenting a fundamental challenge to solidaristic approaches to society and the market's place therein,[27] and favouring freedom and equality over the dignity and solidarity value components of constitutionalism.[28] This was firmly embedded in the global zeitgeist[29]

[21] J Weiler, *The Constitution of Europe* (Cambridge, Cambridge University Press, 1999) 86 ('promised land'), 240–41.

[22] ibid.

[23] For a critique, A Somek and J Rendl, 'Messianism, Exodus, and the Empty Signifier of European Integration' in J Komárek (ed), *European Constitutional Imaginaries: Between Ideology and Utopia* (Oxford, 2023; online edn, Oxford Academic, 2023) 147–59.

[24] Schumann declaration.

[25] RO Keohane, and S Hoffmann, 'Institutional Change in Europe in the 1980s' in RO Keohane and S Hoffmann (eds), *The New European Community: Decision-Making and Institutional Change* (Boulder, CO, Westview Press, 1991).

[26] See recently G Grégoire and X Miny (eds), *The Idea of Economic Constitution in Europe – Genealogy and Overview* (Leiden, Brill, 2022).

[27] This producing a shift even within social discourse itself: see H Collins, 'Discrimination, Equality and Social Inclusion' (2003) 66 *Modern Law Review* 16.

[28] M Wilkinson, *Authoritarian Liberalism and the Transformation of Modern Europe* (Oxford, Oxford University Press, 2021).

[29] For an account of the neoliberal 'imaginary' and its impact on European (private) law at the time, see M Bartl, 'Socio-Economic Imaginaries and European Private Law' in P Kjaer (ed), *The Law of Political Economy: Transformation in the Function of Law* (Cambridge, Cambridge University Press, 2020) 228–53.

at the end of the Cold War, consisting in a firm belief in both the inevitability and desirability of liberal democracy and market economy as humankind's destiny.[30]

And so, towards the end of the 1980s, the Single European Act 'relaunched' the – by then perceived as stagnant – European integration process with the objective of the 'completion of the Single Market' by 1992, leading to the adoption of '282 laws to remove technical, legal and bureaucratic barriers that hindered free trade and movement'.[31] With the 1992 Treaty of Maastricht, the Economic and Monetary Union was launched, widely perceived as a neoliberal or ordoliberal construct.[32] A few years later, 10 post-Communist countries acceded to the EU. In preparation for accession, the EU forced these countries to conform to neo-liberal policies,[33] which they then adopted and carried forward 'fervently',[34] thereby injecting further market-related zeal into the entire EU undertaking. Meanwhile, the Union's powerful integrative legal mechanism, in the form of economic freedoms directly invokable by economic actors in national courts, created a social problem. To cite Weiler:

> The situation implicated in preliminary references always posits an individual vindicating a personal, private interest against the public good. Paradoxically, European rights, in some interesting way, become anticommunity rights. If the social reality of the European construct were stronger, this could be seen as mitigating such an effect. But the reality of the situation, from a social perspective, is that – for good legal reasons – the principal artifact of the rule of law in the thin political space constituted by Union places the individual at odds with his or her thicker political space. This is how it should be, legally. This is what creates the most effective compliance pull. But this is why it also contributes to the national social and political turn against the Union.[35]

The problem identified lies not so much in the enforcement of just any individual rights against collectively adopted policies and rules. Fundamental human rights are, in fact, important aspects of a solidarity arrangement. Fundamental social rights are classically conceived as providing the infrastructure for, as well as protection and expression of, solidarity, but the same could be said for all human rights. The enforcement of these rights against collective decision-making may – at times – create a societal tension,[36] and for that reason judicial review should be handled with extreme care, but overall the protection of these human rights should serve to foster a society's solidarity arrangement rather than to undermine it. The problem lies, rather, in the enforcement of

[30] As represented by Fukuyama's announcement of the 'End of History' (Summer 1989) *The National Interest* 3. See J Stiglitz, 'The end of neoliberalism and the rebirth of history' (2019), available at www.social-europe.eu/the-end-of-neoliberalism-and-the-rebirth-of-history.

[31] www.consilium.europa.eu/en/infographics/30-years-of-the-eu-single-market.

[32] See eg H Lokdam and M Wilkinson, 'The European Economic Constitution in Crisis: A Conservative Transformation?' in Grégoire and Miny (n 26). At the same time, of course, that Treaty also introduced more solidaristic provisions, such as the concept of EU citizenship and strengthening of the powers of the (by then already directly elected) European Parliament.

[33] M Hočevar, 'The EU's Promotion of Neoliberal Capitalism During EU Enlargement: The Dependent Integration of Post-socialist Countries in M Hočevar, T Rutar, and M Lovec, *The Neoliberal World Order in Crisis, and Beyond: An East European Perspective*, (Ljubljana, FDV, 2023) 89.

[34] H Appel and MA Orenstein, 'Why did Neoliberalism Triumph and Endure in the Post-Communist World?' (2016) 48 Comparative Politics 313.

[35] J Weiler, 'The political and legal culture of European integration: An exploratory essay' (2011) 9 *International Journal of Constitutional Law* 678.

[36] Leading Waldron to argue against it altogether: J Waldron, 'The Core of the Case against Judicial Review' (2006) 115 *The Yale Law Journal* 1346.

individual economic interest, especially by powerful economic actors,[37] against public interest. In the EU context it could be argued that the right to non-discrimination not just for workers and citizens but for companies serves to open up national economic arrangements precisely in a spirit of European-level cooperation (in itself an expression of solidarity, albeit somewhat contradictorily in terms of competition), but as is well known, these rights have been extended far beyond the elimination of discrimination and protectionism to the constitutionalisation of pure economic freedom,[38] which – problematically – may be well invoked against core solidaristic expression and rights, such as citizens demonstrating for a clean environment,[39] or workers organising against a social dumping. These interpretations of the Treaty have 'constitutional' value, and cannot be overruled by collective decision-making at either national or European level, presenting a social and democratic problem.[40]

To what extent is this counter-weighed by the introduction of the concept of EU citizenship in the Maastricht Treaty, which is widely considered to have bolstered the Court's already prosocial case law in the area of the free movement of persons in the internal market, requiring Member States to extend, in solidarity, certain aspects of their welfare systems to non-nationals?[41] Indeed, it is in this context where solidarity as a legal concept in EU law was most fully developed.[42] It has been suggested that it is the 'appropriation' by the EU of 'solidarity' (first conceived as separate and outside of EU law[43]) in precisely this citizenship case law, that has led to the 'proud' inclusion of solidarity in the Draft Constitutional Treaty.[44] The Court of Justice played, from the outset, an active role in the fundamentalisation of EU citizenship and the attenuation of its economic underpinnings,[45] at times challenging at the Member States' inclination to see non-economically active EU citizens as 'unreasonable' burdens (although thereby implicitly accepting the underlying premise that they are indeed burdens). EU citizenship law of the time was driven by a solidaristic interpretation of equality (social inclusion of EU migrants into the national welfare system), as well as freedom (of movement) and dignity. This therefore does provide a prominent counterpoint to the critique of a disembodied single market in the post-Maastricht legal and political order myopically pursuing individual, economic freedom. Yet, as many have pointed

[37] As Floris de Witte points out, this tension can also exist in relation to the 'aspirational' individual rights of EU citizens when they are 'pitted against' other individuals in society. de Witte (n 2).

[38] S Garben, 'The "Fundamental Freedoms" and (Other) Fundamental Rights: Towards an Integrated Democratic Interpretation Framework' in S Garben and I Govaere (eds), *The Internal Market 2.0* (Oxford, Hart Publishing, 2021) 335–70.

[39] Case C-112/00, *Schmidberger*, ECLI:EU:C:2002:437.

[40] F Scharpf, 'The asymmetry of European integration, or why the EU cannot be a "social market economy"' (2010) 8 *Socio-Economic Review* 211; D Grimm, *The Constitution of European Democracy* (Oxford, Oxford University Press, 2017); S Schmidt, *The European Court of Justice and the Policy Process – The Shadow of Case Law* (Oxford, Oxford University Press, 2018).

[41] eg Case C-184/99, *Rudy Grzelczyk v Centre Public d'Aide Social d'Ottignes-Louvain-la-Neuve (CPAS)* [2001] ECR I-6193 [44].

[42] C Barnard, 'EU Citizenship and the Principle of Solidarity' in E Spaventa and M Dougan (eds), *Social Welfare and EU Law* (Oxford, Hart Publishing, 2005) 157–60; T Hervey, 'Social Solidarity: A Buttress Against Internal Market Law' in J Shaw (ed), *Social Law and Policy in an Evolving European Union* (Oxford, Hart Publishing, 2000) 31–48; M Dougan and E Spaventa, '"Wish You Weren't Here …". New Models of Social Solidarity in the European Union' in Spaventa and Dougan (ibid) 179–218.

[43] Somek (n 8) 6.

[44] ibid.

[45] See eg Case C-456/02, *Michel Trojani v Centre public d'aide sociale de Bruxelles (CPAS)* [2004] I-757.

out, EU citizenship failed to become genuinely decommodified,[46] and contained and expressed ideals of 'market citizenship'[47] and 'market solidarity',[48] based on an understanding of welfare mechanisms as 'insurance' systems.[49] Moreover, for our purposes, although highly significant for EU law and its self-perception, at least in some circles, EU citizenship did not reach the masses and failed to genuinely change the overall EU project in both its functioning and its understanding.

Looking back, these circumstances must have played a role in the failure of the Constitutional Treaty. Perhaps even more important than the lack of a European identity, was the lacking solidarity basis that made the idea that citizens would endorse a European Constitution misguided (or mad[50]). But instead of reflecting on these foundational problems, and its social and economic causes, the Court of Justice doubled down on economic freedom in its own conception of the EU's 'Constitution'. Emblematic are the 2007 *Viking/Laval* judgments. The Court gave an extremely wide application to the market freedoms, applying them to trade unions in their exercise of fundamental social rights, and conceptualised these fundamental rights as (at least in *Laval*) unjustified restrictions. To this day, social actors feel deeply betrayed by this case law. It fundamentally changed the solidarity settlement, already precarious and instable, as discussed above, by undermining solidaristic structures in the name of European economic competition. Although it has sometimes been argued that this line of cases can be read as requiring the solidarity of workers of rich Member States to workers of less well-off Members States, more convincing empirical and conceptual analyses point to the fact that the effect of the case law has been to empower businesses across all Member States vis-à-vis workers (often in vulnerable situations) across all Member States.[51] It has fundamentally undermined both national and transnational solidarity among workers. At that point in time, partially due to the 'over-constitutionalisation' of the market freedoms,[52] and partially because of the political configuration of the enlarged EU, EU law systematically stimulated social deregulation at national level while finding it all but impossible to enact social protection measures on the European level.[53]

3.3.3. Solidarity in Crisis

With constitutional protection of social rights in the EU at their low point following *Viking/Laval*, the Union entered the 2007–08 financial crisis, resulting in the sovereign debt and Euro crisis, where solidarity in political and economic terms came close to

[46] I Solanke, *EU Law*, 2nd edn (Cambridge, Cambridge University Press, 2023) 389–410.

[47] M Everson, 'The legacy of the market citizen' in J Shaw and G More (eds), *New Legal Dynamics of European Union* (Oxford, Clarendon Press, 1995) 73–89.

[48] de Witte (n 2).

[49] Somek (n 8).

[50] G de Burca, 'The Drafting of a Constitution for the European Union: Europe's Madisonian Moment or a Moment of Madness?' (2004) 61 *Washington & Lee Law Review* 555.

[51] M Houwerzijl, 'A Hunters Game: How Policy Can Change to Spot and Sink Letterbox-Type Practices' (2015) *ETUC Report*; M Houwerzijl, 'Improving cross-border social security' in W Buelen, (ed), *Putting an end to cross-border social security fraud and abuse, European Federation of Building and Woodworkers* (Brussels, EFBWW, 2018).

[52] Grimm (n 40).

[53] Scharpf (n 40).

collapse. Yet, the story here is not a straightforward one. It should be acknowledged that the role of solidarity in the Euro crisis is contested and complex. On the one hand, a large amount of financial assistance was provided to Member States in grave financial difficulties. On some views, Member States even went above and beyond not only what the Treaty requires but even allows: Article 122 does not textually require assistance to be given and the no-bail out clause of Article 125 seems to prohibit unconditional assistance. So for the 'creditor states' to create the various facilities (ESF, ESM) and engage in wide-scale financial assistance packages, while facing consequences of the economic downturn themselves, does constitute in itself an act of solidarity. This also seems to be the conceptual approach of the Court of Justice in this regard, which in *Pringle* followed (implicitly) the Advocate General in the interpretation that Article 125 did not preclude the ESM, an interpretation that the Advocate General reached explicitly on the basis of solidarity.[54] The Advocate General considered that a broad interpretation of 125 would actually preclude financial assistance but that such would run counter the concept of solidarity. That concept on the other hand does not impose a duty to provide such assistance either.

Others have argued that the very conditionality logic does not reflect real solidarity. Lambasting the German Government's approach, Habermas has in this context stated:

> Solidarity is a term that describes the mutually trusting relationship between two actors who have become part of a joint political project of their own free will. Solidarity is not charity, and it certainly isn't a form of conditioning for the advantage of one of the actors. Those who engage in solidarity are willing to accept short-term disadvantage in the service of their long-term self-interest and in the knowledge that the other will behave the same way in a similar situation. Reciprocal trust – in our case, trust across national borders – is just as important a variable as long-term self-interest. Trust bridges the time span until a service in return is due, though it is unsure when or if it will ever come due. The compulsory, rigid conditions for so-called solidarity aid clearly exposes the lack of such a foundation of trust – and the hollowness of our self-image as good Europeans.[55]

Perhaps it is not conditionality as such, but the way this has been operationalised, that has been – as debtor states would argue – decidedly un-solidaristic. The conditionalities specified in the Memorandums of Understanding have not been drafted in a spirit of transnational solidarity and with due regard to national solidarity structures, but instead carry a punitive flavour and have contributed to a grave social crisis in the debtor countries through demanding unprecedented 'structural reforms' that, more as the rule than the exception, dismantled national welfare and social protections, making the vulnerable pay.

Ultimately, what emerged was a fundamental upset of the solidarity settlement underpinning the common EU project. A lack of trust, a disagreement (or misunderstanding) about who (is supposed to) contribute(s) what to the common project, and differing (ideological, economic) views about the causes of the crisis, were important factors. Creditor states felt they were handing out charity to resolve a self-inflicted

[54] View of AG Kokott, Case C-370/12, *Thomas Pringle v Government of Ireland, Ireland and the Attorney General*, ECLI:EU:C:2012:675.

[55] www.socialeurope.eu/are-we-still-good-europeans. See also: www.pro-europa.eu/europe/jurgen-habermas-democracy-solidarity-and-the-european-crisis/?print=print.

crisis of over-spending, while debtor states felt humiliated and underappreciated, both ultimately feeling short-changed – everybody losing. Political narratives have played a corrosive role in this regard. A lot is captured by Eurogroup chief Jeroen Dijsselbloem's remark that 'I can't spend all my money on drinks and women and then ask for help.'

Some of the solidarity failures in the handling of the Euro crisis may be uniquely tied to the specifics of that unprecedented, global, economic disaster, but it also laid bare the fact that the EU's solidarity basis had already been eroded, through the aforementioned waning of peace-inspired solidarity in the early 1980s and the (policies adopted in the name of the) dominant neoliberal zeitgeist of the time. Years of hardline austerity followed the crisis, compounded by the Court's 'economic constitutionalism', almost entirely dismantling certain key solidaristic structures such as collective bargaining.

Then, in 2015, just as the EU was slowly recovering, Europe was faced with a high number of both refugees and irregular migrants seeking entry. The political crisis this caused, again stingingly confirmed the by-now near-total lack of solidarity between Member States (as well as, even more worryingly, to refugees). When the Council adopted a provisional emergency relocation scheme (Council Decision (EU) 2015/1523 and Council Decision (EU) 2015/1601), Poland, Hungary and Czechia refused to comply with it. The Commission then referred these Member States to the Court of Justice, the latter having already rejected the challenges against the relocation system brought by Hungary and Slovakia, stressing the solidarity obligation that rests on the Member States in this area on the basis of Article 80 TFEU.[56] The Court upheld the Commission's action, making multiple references to the principle of solidarity underlying the Union's asylum policy.[57]

Indeed, a positive duty of cooperation in terms of Member State solidarity has been specified in the area of freedom, security and justice. Article 67(2) TFEU provides that the Union

> shall ensure the absence of internal border controls for persons and shall frame a common policy on asylum, immigration and external border control, based on solidarity between Member States, which is fair towards third-country nationals. For the purpose of this Title, stateless persons shall be treated as third-country nationals.

This is repeated in Article 80 TFEU, which states that

> the policies of the Union set out in this Chapter and their implementation shall be governed by the principle of solidarity and fair sharing of responsibility, including its financial implications, between the Member States. Whenever necessary, the Union acts adopted pursuant to this Chapter shall contain appropriate measures to give effect to this principle.

Advocate General's Sharpston's passionate Opinion in those cases is often cited and considered an inspiring commitment to solidarity in the Union:

> 253. Solidarity is the lifeblood of the European project. Through their participation in that project and their citizenship of European Union, Member States and their nationals have obligations as well as benefits, duties as well as rights. Sharing in the European 'demos' is not a matter of looking through the Treaties and the secondary legislation to see what one can

[56] Cases C-643/15 and C-647/15.
[57] Cases C-715/17, C-718/17 and C-719/17.

> claim. It also requires one to shoulder collective responsibilities and (yes) burdens to further the common good.
>
> 254. Respecting the 'rules of the club' and playing one's proper part in solidarity with fellow Europeans cannot be based on a penny-pinching cost-benefit analysis along the lines (familiar, alas, from Brexiteer rhetoric) of 'what precisely does the EU cost me per week and what exactly do I personally get out of it?' Such self-centredness is a betrayal of the founding fathers' vision for a peaceful and prosperous continent. It is the antithesis of being a loyal Member State and being worthy, as an individual, of shared European citizenship. If the European project is to prosper and go forward, we must all do better than that.

Yet, although on the one hand, the judgments and Opinion refer to the principle of solidarity in asylum policy, on the other hand, the added value of these references in the judgments, and thus the notion, is not entirely clear. Ultimately, as Mitsilegas points out,[58] the conceptualisation of solidarity in this area – even in the lauded Opinion of the Advocate General – is about burden-sharing and state-centered, it is exclusionary as it does not extend solidarity towards the migrants themselves (rather systematically seeing them as undesirables), and as such hardly lives up to the foundational universal value of solidarity on which the Union is founded according to the Charter's preamble – nor for that matter the fundamental rights contained in that Charter.

3.3.4. Solidarity Shifting

Tragically and symbolically, 'the end of solidarity' in the EU may – from a UK perspective – be well represented by the Brexit vote in 2016 and the UK's subsequent withdrawal from the EU. Yet, for the EU, it was an opportunity for a reboot. Most notably, in November 2017, the European Commission, Parliament and Council signed a 'solemn' Inter-Institutional Proclamation on the European Pillar of Social Rights.[59] This was a remarkably swift follow-up from the Commission's own, unilateral 'launch' of the Pillar in April 2017,[60] itself the speedy outcome of a preparatory phase lasting only a year.[61] The Pillar signalled a profound change in political direction after the crisis years in which the EU's social dimension was put under significant pressure. The Pillar entailed first and foremost a high-profile political reaffirmation of a set of 20 social rights and principles, and signalled an intention to adopt concrete legal measures and policies in order to give further effect to these rights and principles. Since its adoption, the Pillar's 'implementation' has entailed – as foreseen – the deployment of the full array of EU governance instruments: regulations and directives,[62] recommendations and communications,[63]

[58] V Mitsilegas, 'Solidarity and Trust in the Common European Asylum System' (2014) 2 *Comparative Migration Studies* 181.

[59] [2017] OJ C428/10.

[60] European Commission, Proposal for a Interinstitutional Proclamation on the European Pillar of Social Rights, COM(2017) 251 final.

[61] European Commission, Communication of 8 March 2016 launching a consultation on a European Pillar of Social Rights, COM(2016)0127.

[62] Directive 2019/1152 on transparent and predictable working conditions, Work-Life Balance Directive 2019/1158, the EU minimum wage directive, the Pay Transparency Directive.

[63] eg, Council Recommendation of 8 November 2019 on access to social protection for workers and the self-employed [2019] OJ C 387, 1–8.

the creation of new institutions,[64] funding, and country-specific recommendations.[65] As such, the Pillar has followed in the footsteps of the 1989 Community Charter on the Fundamental Social Rights of Workers with its accompanying Action Programme, on the basis of which an important part of the EU social *acquis* was progressively adopted. The Pillar led to a renaissance of Social Europe, with new, high-profile solidarity flagships, including a minimum wage directive. It reflects, at least in the EU's political institution, a rejection of austerity and neoliberalism, and a political vision much more in line with the EU's foundational values.

Just as the first measures adopted under the Pillar were entering into force, the COVID-19 pandemic struck in early 2020. Authors such as Beaucillon[66] and Kurczewska[67] have pointed out that the initial response to the COVID-19 crisis was not in a spirit of solidarity, with Member States shamefully refusing to provide material assistance to Italy in the early days of the outbreak, and the well-worn struggles between 'Northern' and 'Southern' approaches to the EU budget flaring up initially. In a comprehensive study of political discourse on COVID-19 fiscal solidarity, Miro furthermore finds that 'during the COVID-19 crisis management debate, diverging visions on what is the EU and why should EU solidarity be embraced developed along the Northern–Southern interstate cleavage'.[68] Yet, EU leaders appealed for solidarity,[69] with success. It needs to be acknowledged that the EU has risen to this solidarity challenge. In particular, the 750 billion NextGenEU recovery fund, allowing the Commission to raise funds by issuing common debts, transferring this to the Member States in grants and loans, constitutes a decisive break with the previous non-solidaristic approach. While there remains a conditionality logic in place, it is a mirror image of the austerity conditionality we saw before.

Crucially, the COVID crisis measures SURE and NextGen provided the framework for financial assistance to Ukraine with the European Peace Facility and the MFA+. The MFA+ entails once again common borrowing and spending, which suggests a trend towards consolidating a centralised fiscal capacity at the EU level. Furthermore, as Guild et al write in chapter eight of this book, 'one of the most immediate and dramatic reactions of the EU was to open a special protection scheme for Ukrainians and non-Ukrainians who were resident in the country on the date of the invasion to enter the EU and remain with extensive rights' on the basis of the 2001 Temporary Protection Directive – before unused and slated for repeal. This means that in the two areas where solidarity was at a nadir only a few years ago, the EU 'found back its mojo' as one

[64] Regulation 2019/1149, adopted on the basis of Articles 46 and 48 TFEU on the free movement of workers, establishes the European Labour Authority.

[65] There are now systematic references to assessment of national systems (and currently the national recovery and resilience plans) with the European Pillar of Social Rights.

[66] C Beaucillon, 'European Solidarity in Times of Emergency: An Introduction to the Special Focus on COVID-19 and the EU' (2020) *European Papers*, available at www.europeanpapers.eu/en/europeanforum/european-solidarity-in-times-of-emergency-introduction-special-focus-covid-19#.

[67] U Kurczewska, 'European solidarity and its limitations during the Covid-19 pandemic' (2021) 17 *European Journal of Science and Theology* 1.

[68] J Miro, 'Debating fiscal solidarity in the EU: interests, values and identities in the legitimation of the Next Generation EU plan' (2022) 44 *Journal of European Integration* 307.

[69] See eg the speech of High Representative Borrell: 'Solidarity is essential in the face of an unprecedented global crisis', available at www.eeas.europa.eu/eeas/solidarity-essential-face-unprecedented-global-crisis_en.

newspaper put it.[70] Thirdly, the war is deepening EU integration in energy and defence. In energy, the war is driving EU energy autonomy, with the plan for REPowerEU seeking to 'to build an integrated energy market that secures supply in a spirit of solidarity'.[71] Highly noteworthy is that shortly before Russia's invasion of Ukraine, the Court of Justice in *OPAL* had already – in light of the already existing Russian territorial breaches of Ukraine – confirmed the relevance of the principle of solidarity in energy, giving it firmer legal teeth than expected,[72] as we will discuss below. This can now be seized on by the Commission to develop its common energy policies,[73] capitalising on the surge of public support for this in reaction to the war.[74]

As can be seen throughout this book, the war in Ukraine is driving integration in a range of areas. Solidarity language now permeates the political narrative.[75] In some areas, it is even used to 'label' political initiatives, such as the 'solidarity lanes' discussed in chapter fourteen by Settembri and Corsaro. As a response to Russia's blockade of Black Sea ports, which primarily hampered agricultural exports from Ukraine, the European Commission and bordering EU Member States established the 'solidarity lanes'[76] in May 2022 to enable such exports through alternative routes using all other available transport modes (rail, road and inland waterways). Political narratives on values generally, and solidarity in particular, have real impact. 'Different justificatory arguments have different impacts on the solidarity structure of the Union as well as on what "point and purpose" the EU is perceived to have'.[77] Of course, the question is whether this will be followed through in all respects. For one, the indisputable moral claim of the Ukrainian people, their courage and European-ness, and the fight for our values they are fighting, makes extension of solidarity towards them – apparently – easier than to other groups of migrants.[78] In this regard, Ursula von der Leyen has insisted, we need a permanent and legally binding mechanism for migration that ensures solidarity – and not just between Member States, but all migrants.[79]

[70] M Matthijs, 'How Europe Got Its Mojo Back – The EU Has Deftly Managed Inflation and the War in Ukraine', available at www.foreignaffairs.com/europe/how-europe-got-its-mojo-back.

[71] COM(2022) 230 final.

[72] Case C-848/19 P, *OPAL*, ECLI:EU:C:2021:598.

[73] L Marin, 'The principle of energy solidarity at its first stress test: the mitigation of the energy crisis between national sovereignty and supranational integration' (30 November 2022), available at www.diritticomparati.it/the-principle-of-energy-solidarity-at-its-first-stress-test-the-mitigation-of-the-energy-crisis-between-national-sovereignty-and-supranational-integration.

[74] eupinions.eu/de/text/under-pressure.

[75] For instance, the Council website features as one of the four main segments on the EU's response to the war in Ukraine, entitled 'EU solidaritt with Ukraine', available at www.consilium.europa.eu/en/policies/eu-response-ukraine-invasion/eu-solidarity-ukraine. The Commission presents 'solidarity with the Ukraine' as one of the 'main stories of the von der Leyen Commission': commission.europa.eu/strategy-and-policy/priorities-2019-2024/story-von-der-leyen-commission/solidarity-ukraine_en. The European Parliament has organised Ukraine 'solidarity days': www.europarl.europa.eu/news/en/press-room/20220321IPR25910/parliament-organises-the-ukraine-solidarity-days.

[76] 'An action plan for EU-Ukraine Solidarity Lanes to facilitate Ukraine's agricultural export and bilateral trade with the EU', COM(2022)217 (12 May 2022).

[77] Sangiovanni (n 2); Miro (n 68).

[78] S Carrera and R Cortinovis, 'The Declaration on a Voluntary Solidarity £Mechanism and EU Asylum policy – One Step Forward, Three Steps Back on Equal Solidarity' CEPS (2022), available at www.ceps.eu/wp-content/uploads/2022/10/CEPS-In-depth-analysis-2022-04_Voluntary-Solidarity.pdf.

[79] U von der Leyen, State of the Union Address, 14 September 2022.

3.4. Solidarity as a General Principle of Law

3.4.1. *Lex Lata*: Solidarity in the *OPAL* Ruling

The aforementioned judgment in *OPAL*, although rendered in the context of energy policy,[80] is of general relevance for solidarity, as the Court deliberately broadens the reflection and confirms its general relevance in the EU legal order. A number of things are striking in these relevant passages from the judgment.[81] First, the Court having to reach all the way back to the 1970s to find a precedent for its grand (re)discovery that solidarity 'underpins the entire legal system of the European Union' is symbolic, and telling in underlining for how long this foundational principle has been forgotten. By the same token, it shows how deliberately the Court is using the opportunity of this judgment to uncover it, signaling a potentially fundamental change in the direction of its case law.

Secondly, in terms of the concrete legal significance of this rediscovery, the judgment declares that 'the principle of solidarity … is itself one of the fundamental principles of EU law'. This is an important judicial development. Although the terminology is not entirely elucidating, as a general principles come in various shapes and sizes and, in the words of Takis Tridimas, their role is 'obfuscated' by the Court's 'diverse and often bewildering terminology', the importance of general principles is indisputable and profound as general principles 'do not apply only in specific areas of law but permeate the EU and the national legal systems and provide standards for determining the legality not only of public action but also private conduct', and moreover, 'through influencing judicial methodology, they may affect the national legal system as a whole'.[82] The Court confirms explicitly in the ruling that the principle of solidarity can produce 'binding legal effects on the Member States and institutions of the European Union'. In the case at hand, this translates in a standard for the legality review. But perhaps (even) more powerful could be its role in 'influencing judicial methodology'.

Thirdly, the judgment provides indications as to how the Court conceptualises solidarity. In this respect, what is *not* said and referred to is perhaps more important than what it: in the 'comprehensive' treatment of solidarity in EU law (at [39] and [40] of the judgment), the Court strikingly omits the reference in the EU Charter of Fundamental Rights, which states that 'the Union is founded on the indivisible, universal values of human dignity, freedom, equality and solidarity'. To list all the iterations of solidarity in the Treaties, while ignoring the EU Charter altogether, is curious. This may partially be explained because the Court is reluctant to refer to a preamble. The Court only started referring to 'ever closer union' after this seminal phrase had been moved from its original place in the preamble, to Article 1 EU Treaty. According to established case law, the

[80] TFEU, Art 194.

[81] [38]–[44].

[82] T Tridimas, 'The general principles of EU law and the Europeanisation of national laws' (2020) 2 *Review of European Administrative Law* 5. See generally T Tridimas, *The General Principles of EU Law* (Oxford, Oxford University Press, 2007).

Preamble to an EU act has no binding legal force and cannot be relied on either as a ground for derogating from the actual provisions of an act or for interpreting them in a manner which is clearly contrary to their wording. However, to refer to this Preamble's statement that the Union is founded on the indivisible, universal values of human dignity, freedom, equality and solidarity would not derogate from anything or lead to a *contra legem* interpretation. It would instead provide useful context, for which preambles are suitable.

3.4.2. *Lex Ferenda*: The Meaning of Solidarity as a General Principle

In seeking a possible source to interpret what solidarity should mean, recourse is often had to Article 2 TEU. This chapter argues that in considering what meaning should be given to solidarity as a general principle of EU law, the Charter's Preamble statement, that 'the Union is founded on the indivisible, universal values of human dignity, freedom, equality and solidarity' should be taken as a main anchor, as it provides us with a convincing and sophisticated understanding, as well as useful concrete indications, concerning the place of solidarity in the EU 'constitution', and the place of EU law in relation to solidarity. It does in no way contradict, but provides more meaning than, Article 2 TEU.

3.4.2.1. Universality

The Charter tells us, unequivocally, that the solidarity on which the EU is founded is *universal* (as is human dignity, freedom and equality). This means that there is no justification for an exclusionary interpretation of these principles and the rights that emanate from them; they belong to all human beings. The principle of universality is the cornerstone of international human rights law, and means that all people are equally entitled to human rights, regardless of where they come from and live, and that it is not up to any state or other authority to decide who has rights and who does not, that they do not depend on citizenship of nationality, as they are something we have, simply by virtue of being human. It is especially in relation to the value of solidarity that such universality is important, because of solidarity's team-reasoning component. The universality requirement prohibits us from falling into the trap of treacherous in-group, out-group dynamics, of generating in-group solidarity by explicit juxtaposition with others.[83] It reminds us that ultimately we are all part of same group and that we are

[83] Neuroscientific research shows both the importance, and the limits, of humans' neurobiological capabilities enabling us to empathise with others. Those limits are found mainly in, on the one hand, a self/other divide and in, on the other hand, one's definition of 'in-group' and 'out-group'. These limits are at least partially malleable, through socialisation. See eg HJ Ferguson and L Wimmer, 'A psychological exploration of empathy' in F Mezzenzana and D Peluso, *Conversations on Empathy: Interdisciplinary Perspectives on Imagination and Radical Othering* (Abingdon, Routledge, 2023).

all inter-connected and inter-dependent in various ways. While in a concentric circle approach, we are of course entitled to belong to various (closer-knit) sub-groups, in which deeper ties result in more extensive mutual rights and obligations, these should be peacefully embedded in one another, and not be at the cost of others. In the global scheme, we are all somehow, more directly or indirectly, indebted by human achievement, sacrifice and care by humans from all over the world, and from a long way back.[84] In accordance with universal solidarity, we owe a universal prosocial commitment as payback, and we should seek to pay it forward to future generations.

This may sound idealistic and abstract, but with some effort can be made more intelligible and concrete. Law cannot do this alone, but it can play a role. And in this, the Court of Justice could take responsibility for moral leadership. More specifically, it could ensure that in all the various iterations of solidarity in the Treaties, a *universalistic* reading is adopted. This could make a real difference, for instance in migration/asylum law where we see a myopic invocation of the solidarity principle as a duty on Member States to 'share' migrants as 'burdens', rather than with a spirit of solidarity towards the migrants themselves. The Court could in this area play an important role to protect the dignity of migrants and the equality of human beings. For one thing, this would cast an entirely different light on the Court's mutual trust case law in the area of asylum: instead of requiring us to 'trust' that authorities of EU Member States will not infringe the human rights of migrants (in the face of overwhelming evidence that they do and will), it would at least allow but arguably require, in a spirit of universal solidarity, all Member States to take responsibility for the human rights protection of migrants, and thus for instance to prevent their return to the Member State of first entry under the Dublin system if there is a reasonable ground to believe that their human rights will not be respected there.

3.4.2.2. Indivisibility

The second indication that we can derive from the Charter's Preamble, is that the founding values of dignity, freedom, equality and solidarity are indivisible. Much like the specification of universality, this too provides fertile conceptual ground, and allows us to understand certain (well-known) legitimacy shortcomings of European law specifically from a solidarity perspective. What is indivisibility to mean? Apart from the fact that the Union's actions have to be guided by all four values (and thus that all the rights contained in all four chapters of the Charter have to be respected and realised), it can be taken to mean that these four values have to inform each other's content. This in turn means that their relationship needs to be thoroughly theorised in order to interpret/apply each of these concepts, and the rest of the primary and secondary norms in the EU legal order. The stakes and potential are thus significant. This section will offer some tentative elements that may inform such a reflection.

Firstly, dignity- and freedom-based solidarity suggests that individuals should have some ownership over their participation in the common project and its modalities, for

[84] There is a clear link here to studies into the decolonialisation of EU law: I Solanke, 'Rethinking the Introduction to EU Law – Towards a De-Colonial Approach' guest lecture at the College of Europe, 15 March 2024.

otherwise it could undermine an important part of citizens' democratic agency and thereby their collective and individual freedom and dignity. Secondly, this also means that any redistribution of the gains of the project should carefully respect the recipients' dignity and not undermine their freedom. Crucially, redistributive measures should not take the form of a pedantic benefit that could be felt as a 'hand-out', and should instead seek to make a concrete contribution to the individual's meaningful employment or individual agency in a different way (empowering) without being condescending, punitive, shaming, captive or mistrustful (as unfortunately certain aspects of many Western welfare states have become). As a concrete example, retraining and lifelong learning are important policies, but if such policies are not carefully designed from a dignity- and freedom perspective, they may still lack effect or become counter-productive (for instance if the training does not at all correspond to the level and interest of the individual, and/or is compulsory to receive benefits). Similarly, at country level, financial assistance is a crucial part of the solidarity settlement, but from a dignity- and freedom perspective it may not be used to completely disempower (and punish) the recipient country, as for instance happened with the programme countries during the Euro crisis in an offence of their collective dignity.

Further potential lies in teasing out a dialectic relationship between the two values that are perhaps not natural allies: freedom and solidarity. We already indicated that solidarity should respect – and ideally bolster –freedom, but the same applies the other way around. The implications thereof are intuitive and perhaps not surprising: it means that economic freedoms should be read in a way that respects and bolsters solidarity, and not to undermine or dismantle it. This exposes the value problem in the well-known case law prioritising (and fundamentalising) corporations' economic rights (derived by the Court from Article 16 EU Charter on the freedom to conduct a business, and the freedom of establishment to provide services in the internal market) over fundamental social rights, such as to take collective action, to be protected against unjust dismissal, and not to be discriminated on grounds of religion, in cases such as *Viking, Laval, AGET, Alemmo-Herron* and *Achbita*.[85] Freedom would have to be read informed by solidarity, which would have led to fundamentally different outcomes in each of these cases.

3.5. Conclusion

This book explores the 'tectonic shifts'[86] within the EU caused or catalysed by the war in Ukraine, and the solidarity shift is certainly part of that. Solidarity's importance is pervasive and foundational, as rediscovered by the Court only much too recently in *OPAL* – a prescient judgment rendered in the context of Russia's earlier aggression in

[85] Case C-438/05, *Viking Line* EU:C:2007:772; Case C-341/05, *Laval un Partneri Ltd* EU:C:2007:809; Case C-426/11, *Alemo-Herron* EU:C:2013:521; Case C-201/15, *AGET Iraklis*, EU:C:2016:972; Case C-157/15, *Samira Achbita* EU:C:2017:203. See for discussion: S Garben, 'The Constitutional (Im)balance between "the Market" and "the Social" in the European Union' (2017) 13 *European Constitutional Law Review* 23; S Garben, 'European Social Union: Institutional Report' in A Kornezov (ed), *European Social Union*, Proceedings of the XXX FIDE Congress, Vol 3.

[86] Informal meeting of the Heads of State or Government Declaration, Versailles, 10 and 11 March 2022, pt 6.

Ukraine, pre-dating the full-scale invasion that would later catapult the language of solidarity to the very heart of the Union's current political narrative. Law is only one of the many relevant aspects for a well-functioning solidarity arrangement in a societal scheme, but it is an important one. This chapter has posited that there is significant potential for improvement of EU law if the general principle of solidarity were indeed to be given the more prominent and forceful application that the Court has signalled in *OPAL*. To do justice to solidarity, would be to anchor it in the conceptual framing as declared on behalf of the peoples of Europe in the preamble of the EU Charter of Fundamental Rights: recognising it to be universal and indivisible from dignity, freedom and equality and together constituting the Union's very foundation.

4

War, Xenophobia and the EU's Social Fabric

IYIOLA SOLANKE

4.1. Introduction

Xenophobia is a term used to describe hatred or fear of the 'Other'. Xenophobia is linked to many feelings and forms of behaviour that are damaging for interpersonal relations and dangerous for society – prejudice, animosity, fear and racism. When xenophobia is mentioned in relation to war, we are most likely to think of Rwanda or Bosnia and the horrific ethnic cleansing seen in those places.

However, xenophobia has also reared its ugly head in relation to the conflict in the Ukraine: on the same day that Russia invaded Ukraine stories of racism began to emerge, not only at the border as people tried to leave. but also at the borders while trying to enter neighbouring countries, as well as in refugee camps providing shelter.

War in Ukraine has demonstrated that something is rotten is the EU's social fabric: it is riven with racism at the environmental, institutional and individual level. From the time of the Russian invasion, students from Africa and Asia fleeing Ukraine have suffered discrimination as they tried to leave the country, seek refuge in other countries and continue with their studies. ODI Global has called this a 'racialised refugee hierarchy'.[1]

The question arises as to why, in the twenty-first century, in a European Union that professes to protect human rights, this vulnerable group was cast out from the right to regard granted all human beings in international law, not least the United Nations (UN) Human Rights Declaration of 1948 and the EU Charter of Fundamental Rights of 2000. At the UN press conference on the invasion, UN HR Commissioner for Refugees Grandi told reporters that the racism experienced at the borders was not 'a product of state policies'.[2] In this chapter, I argue that, on the contrary, this racism is the product of three connected state policies.

[1] C Kumar, A Knoll and P Vernon, 'How the war in Ukraine is impacting Africa-Europe relations and the migration dialogue', available at odi.org/en/insights/how-the-war-in-ukraine-is-impacting-africa-europe-relations-and-the-migration-dialogue.

[2] media.un.org/en/asset/k14/k14dezco4m.

The first is historical – policies of imperialism that informed the colonisation of countries in Africa, Asia and Latin America.[3] The latter two are current: first, the omission of teaching on colonialism from the curriculum in European schools and universities; and second, the continued animosity shown to migrants arriving in Europe from across the Global South. By obliterating the role played by colonised people in European wars and economic reconstruction, the EU and its Member States create an environment of ignorance within which the racism seen at the borders of Ukraine and elsewhere can flourish in institutions and between individuals.

Racism in a time of war negates human rights in the EU – this discrimination has damaged social relations within the EU and undermined confidence in its commitment to racial justice and human rights, which is increasingly seen as nothing more than 'lip service'. This has consequences for trade and security – plans for a Green transition in Europe rely upon access to natural resources in the Global South yet the influence of militia groups such as Wagner will only increase across the Global South as confidence in the sincerity of European solidarity wanes. The increase in price for uranium from Niger from 80c/kg to €200 is an example of this. There may also be consequences for migration cooperation.[4]

Section 4.2 of this chapter is descriptive and highlights the experiences of African and Asian students as they left Ukraine and tried to enter other countries. Section 4.3 seeks to explain these experiences by highlighting omissions in formal education across Europe in relation to the role of colonial troops in European wars and the absence of colonial history from the curriculum. Section 4.4 offers suggestions for a decolonial approach to asylum and migration in the EU.

4.2. War and Xenophobia

At the time of the invasion, there were over 76,000 students from 155 countries studying in the Ukraine. The largest number came from India, with Morocco and Nigeria not far behind.[5] Countries across Africa and Asia had students enrolled in institutions across the Ukraine – around 400 students came from Ghana, 500 from Ivory Coast, 200 from Kenya and around 100 Ugandans.[6]

While countries like Jamaica, Nigeria and Somalia evacuated their nationals home immediately, large numbers of Moroccans, Algerians, Cameroonians, Ivorians and Guineans remained in Europe.[7] Not knowing how long the war would last, these countries relied upon their diplomatic missions in Europe to support the students – for

[3] This applies to Western European countries such as France, Germany and Italy. Eastern European countries such as the Ukraine and Poland were not colonial powers.

[4] A Knoll, 'What the EU's asylum response to the war in Ukraine means for Africa-Europe relations', available at ecdpm.org/work/what-eu-asylum-response-war-ukraine-means-africa-europe-relations.

[5] studyinukraine.gov.ua/en/life-in-ukraine/international-students-in-ukraine.

[6] W Sawahel et al, 'Evacuation of Africa's students from Ukraine continues' University World News (3 March 2022), available at www.universityworldnews.com/post.php?story=20220303061012858.

[7] 'One year later, the shattered dreams of young Africans who fled Ukraine for France' *Le Monde* (25 February 2023), available at www.lemonde.fr/en/le-monde-africa/article/2023/02/25/one-year-later-the-shattered-dreams-of-young-africans-who-fled-ukraine-for-france_6017283_124.html#.

example, Uganda and Morocco advised their students to do as the Ukrainians and make their way to consuls in neighbouring countries; 118 Zimbabwean students were evacuated to Eastern Europe with the help of the Zimbabwean embassies in Moscow and Berlin.[8]

However evacuation was not straightforward: at least two students: Mohammed Abdel Monaim Talbi from Tlemcen in Algeria, who studied aerospace engineering in Kiev, died when he was shot while attempting to flee the fighting.[9] Likewise Naveen Shekharappa from India, who studied medicine in Ukraine, died while he was trying to find his way out of Kharkiv.[10]

As put by the Ghanaian MP Okudzeto-Ablakwa, 'everyone was equally displaced but not everyone was equally received – despite it being a humanitarian tragedy, Africans were explicitly dehumanised'.[11]

4.2.1. Leaving Ukraine and Entering Neighbouring Countries

African and Asian students struggled to leave the Ukraine. Some of these students lacked the necessary documents to leave – around 300 Somali students were stranded at the border for this reason.[12] There were also stories of COVID-19 vaccines not being recognised by border authorities: an Indian student who had taken the Indian-made Covaxin vaccine was prevented from boarding a flight in Qatar.[13] Accessing transport was another issue: the African and Asian students were met with what was described as a 'Ukrainians First'[14] policy, which saw them denied opportunities to evacuate safely and unable to access support packages. A BBC journalist tweeted that:

> A Nigerian medical student at Poland/Ukraine border (Medyka-Shehyni) told me she has been waiting 7hrs to cross, she says border guards are stopping black people and sending them to the back of the queue, saying they have to let 'Ukrainians' through first.[15]

While Ukrainian refugees were provided with complimentary shuttles and taken as close to the border as possible, African students and residents had to pay to board the buses and were then dropped off far away from the border. Those taking taxis were charged exorbitant rates by the drivers.

However, those who made it onto the buses or found taxis were the fortunate ones – many had to walk for three or more hours in freezing temperatures, and there are stories

[8] www.universityworldnews.com/post.php?story=20220303061012858.

[9] www.youtube.com/watch?v=NpboH8qCX94; www.youtube.com/watch?v=BKDLLrh0FJI.

[10] 'Indian student killed in Ukraine amid criticism over evacuation' Al Jazeera (1 March 2022), available at www.aljazeera.com/news/2022/3/1/indian-student-killed-in-ukraine-amid-criticism-over-evacuation.

[11] www.theafricareport.com/190099/africans-face-europes-unfair-two-track-refugee-policy.

[12] O Nor, 'Somalis held in Ukraine no freed – statement', available at shabellemedia.com/somalis-held-in-ukraine-no-freed-statement.

[13] B Kuchay 'Tears, anger at airport as Indian students return from Ukraine', available at www.aljazeera.com/news/2022/3/3/tears-anger-as-indian-students-return-from-ukraine-delhi-airport.

[14] people.com/politics/african-students-fleeing-ukraine-prevented-crossing-border; ; www.aljazeera.com/news/2022/3/2/we-burned-our-clothes-to-stay-warm-somali-recounts-ukraine-war; ; www.aljazeera.com/news/2022/3/3/yemen-students-ukraine-russia-war.

[15] people.com/politics/african-students-fleeing-ukraine-prevented-crossing-border.

of Somali students burning their clothes to stay warm during their flight from war,[16] only to be told that there was no way out for them and they must return or to be further detained at the border for hours.

Exit was sorted not only along nationalist lines but also along racist lines: 'first to leave were Ukrainians and other white Europeans, followed by Turkish and East Asians, then South Asians and Arabs, and finally, Africans'.[17] Trying to leave Ukraine was compared to 'Squid Games' with Ukrainians and Europeans at the top of the hierarchy, people from India and the Middle East in the middle, and Africans at the bottom.[18] Even Black Ukrainians were treated as foreigners.[19]

There was also racism from other citizens such as train passengers: one video on Twitter (now X) shows locals circling a young student's car, attempting to stop her and other African students from crossing the border.[20] A video shows students being held at gunpoint at the border. Perhaps it is therefore not surprising that some students felt it was safer to stay in the Ukraine; Percy Ohene-Yeboah, an engineering student from Ghana, took refuge in the basement of a church.[21]

Entering another country was just as difficult as leaving the Ukraine.[22] Several of the bordering countries – Poland, Moldova, Romania,[23] Hungary and Slovakia – refused to accept Africans and only permitted entry after intervention from the UN and the African Union condemning this discrimination.[24] Filippo Grandi, the UN High Commissioner for Refugees, noted in his press statement the 'ugly reality, that some Black and Brown people fleeing Ukraine – and other wars and conflicts around the world – have not received the same treatment as Ukrainian refugees'. Condemning acts of discrimination, violence and racism as unacceptable, he committed use of UN channels and resources to ensure that 'all people are protected equally'. He appealed to those countries neighbouring Ukraine to allow entry to anyone fleeing the conflict 'without discrimination on grounds of race, colour, descent, or national or ethnic origin and regardless of their immigration status', and he declared that 'There should be absolutely no discrimination between Ukrainians and non-Ukrainians, Europeans and non-Europeans. Everybody is fleeing from the same risks.'[25]

In February 2022, the African Union publicly condemned the situation:

> The current Chair of the African Union and President of the Republic of Senegal, H.E. Macky Sall, and the Chairperson of the African Union Commission, H.E. Moussa Faki Mahamat, are following closely the developments in Ukraine and are particularly disturbed by reports that African citizens on the Ukrainian side of the border are being refused the right to cross the border to safety.

[16] www.aljazeera.com/news/2022/3/2/we-burned-our-clothes-to-stay-warm-somali-recounts-ukraine-war.

[17] www.theafricareport.com/190099/africans-face-europes-unfair-two-track-refugee-policy.

[18] www.brookings.edu/blog/how-we-rise/2022/03/03/the-russian-invasion-of-ukraine-shows-racism-has-no-boundaries.

[19] www.wilsoncenter.org/event/life-black-ukrainian-how-some-natives-are-treated-foreigners.

[20] newsone.com/4296556/african-students-flee-ukraine-spotlights-racial-bias-refugee-crisis; ; www.globalcitizen.org/en/content/korrine-sky-racism-in-ukraine.

[21] people.com/politics/african-students-fleeing-ukraine-prevented-crossing-border.

[22] www.nationalgeographic.co.uk/history-and-civilisation/2022/03/fleeing-war-facing-racism-refugees-from-ukraine-meet-challenges-at-europes-borders.

[23] diasporarelief.org.

[24] www.theafricareport.com/190099/africans-face-europes-unfair-two-track-refugee-policy.

[25] media.un.org/en/asset/k14/k14dezco4m.

> The two Chairpersons recall that all people have the right to cross international borders during conflict, and as such, should enjoy the same rights to cross to safety from the conflict in Ukraine, notwithstanding their nationality or racial identity. Reports that Africans are singled out for unacceptable dissimilar treatment would be shockingly racist and in breach international law.
>
> In this regard, The Chairpersons urge all countries to respect international law and show the same empathy and support to all people fleeing war notwithstanding their racial identity. The Chairpersons commend the efforts by African Union Member State countries and their embassies in neighbouring countries to receive and orientate African citizens and their families trying to cross the border from Ukraine to safety.[26]

An even stronger statement was released by the National Association for the Advancement of Colored People (NAACP):

> The NAACP is disheartened with the events surrounding the invasion of Ukraine by Russia. In these crisis moments choosing citizenship over humanity is an atrocity. Right now in Ukraine, Black families, immigrants from the African diaspora and other people of color – mothers, children, and students are not only facing challenges to evacuate a deadly warzone but are being pushed from trains and beaten by police officers. These callous acts are atrocious and reprehensible. As the world comes to the aid of the Ukraine and nations support the resettlement of people fleeing the nation, every individual must be treated with dignity and humanity.

After calling upon the Biden Administration and the UN to 'take every necessary action to protect the rights and to ensure the safe passage of all persons fleeing this blatant attack on a Nation's sovereignty', the NAACP confirmed that it would do 'everything in its power to fight racist, cruel acts such as these – no matter where they are happening'.[27]

The NAACP also brought together a coalition including the Lawyers' Committee for Civil Rights Under Law (LCCR), the National Action Network (NAN), the National Association for the Advancement of Colored People Legal Defense and Educational Fund, Inc (NAACPLDF), the National Coalition on Black Civic Participation / Black Women's Roundtable (NCBCP/BWR), the National Council of Negro Women, Inc (NCNW) and the National Urban League (NUL) to pen a letter of disgust to President Ursula von der Leyen:

> We write today with an urgent concern regarding reports that Black families, immigrants from the African diaspora, and other people of color who reside in Ukraine have been treated in a discriminatory manner as they flee the escalating war in Ukraine.
>
> Press reports and online video reflect the use of racial hierarchy, violence, and state action taken against refugees of color as they attempt to flee Ukraine and enter bordering states of the European Union. We appreciate the European Union's public rejection of discrimination. Even in the face of challenges and threats as serious as war, we must be vigilant in protecting the human rights of the most vulnerable populations from the worst forms of discrimination. As you are aware, the provision of humane treatment to refugees is embedded in sovereign

[26] 'Statement of the African Union on the reported ill treatment of Africans trying to leave Ukraine' (28 February 2022, Addis Ababa), available at au.int/sites/default/files/pressreleases/41534-pr-english.pdf.

[27] 'NAACP Releases Statement on the Treatment of Africans During Russia's Attack on Ukraine' Press Statement (28 February 2022), available at naacp.org/articles/naacp-releases-statement-treatment-africans-during-russias-attack-ukraine.

law, international treaties, and customary law. Parliamentarians have a critical role to ensure the implementation of policy through actual practice.

We understand the difficulty and fluidity of monitoring border agents across sovereign states. We urge swift and proactive action to ensure the fair and humane treatment of all refugees with special attention to nondiscrimination. Thank you for your continued commitment to secure the safe passage and humane treatment of displaced persons fleeing the attack on Ukraine's sovereignty.

We further request additional information on measures undertaken to ensure the safe passage of all refugees. We are united in our fight against all forms of racism and discrimination – no matter where it occurs.[28]

4.2.2. Refuge and Temporary Protection

In 2001, the EU adopted a Directive on temporary protection (TPD)[29] in response to the refugee crisis resulting from conflict around former Yugoslavia in the 1990s. This was the first instrument of the Common European Asylum System (CEAS).[30] Following the invasion, the EU immediately activated the TPD[31] to help those fleeing the Ukraine. This remains the main legal framework with which Member States organise national schemes.

The main aim of the TPD is establishment of minimum standards for providing temporary protection to displaced persons from third countries who are unable to return to their country of origin. In addition, it seeks to promote 'a balance of efforts between the Member States in receiving and bearing the consequences of receiving such persons'.[32] Those falling under its scope benefit from residency rights, immediate access to the labour market and education, as well as social welfare and medical assistance.[33]

Most EU Member States activated temporary protection under this regional framework in March 2022.[34] Care and welcome packages were created to support those fleeing war in Ukraine. This focused predominantly on Ukrainian nationals, and even people in this group have experienced difficulties with, for example, finding affordable accommodation.[35] However, the TPD does not cover African and Asian students fleeing

[28] naacp.org/articles/naacp-releases-statement-treatment-africans-during-russias-attack-ukraine.

[29] Directive 2001/55/EC on temporary protection (TPD).

[30] S Mantu, K Zwaan and T Strik (eds), *The Temporary Protection Directive: Central Themes, Problem Issues and implementation in selected member states* (Nijmegen, Centrum voor Migratierecht, Radboud Universiteit Nijmegen, 2023).

[31] COMMUNICATION FROM THE COMMISSION on Operational guidelines for the implementation of Council implementing Decision 2022/382 establishing the existence of a mass influx of displaced persons from Ukraine within the meaning of Article 5 of Directive 2001/55/EC, and having the effect of introducing temporary protection (2022/C 126 I/01); Operational Guidelines available at eur-lex.europa.eu/legal-content/EN/TXT/PDF/?uri=CELEX:52022XC0321(03)&from=EN; ec.europa.eu/migrant-integration/news/eu-invokes-temporary-protection-directive-help-those-fleeing-ukraine_en.

[32] ouclf.law.ox.ac.uk/extending-social-protection-for-migrants-under-the-european-unions-temporary-protection-directive-lessons-from-the-war-in-ukraine/.

[33] 'Infographic – EU temporary protection for displaced persons', available at www.consilium.europa.eu/en/infographics/temporary-protection-displaced-persons.

[34] 'Temporary protection for displaced persons from Ukraine', available at whoiswho.euaa.europa.eu/temporary-protection.

[35] ACAPS Analysis Hub, 'UKRAINE: Overview of the situation of refugees from Ukraine in six host countries' Thematic Report (September 2023), available at www.acaps.org/fileadmin/Data_Product/Main_media/20230905_ACAPS_Ukraine_analysis_hub_regional_overview_refugees_in_host_countries.pdf.

war in the Ukraine: under Article 1 the scope is described as permanent residents of Ukraine or

> Stateless persons, and nationals of third countries other than Ukraine, who benefitted from international protection or equivalent national protection in Ukraine before 24 February 2022 and who have been displaced from Ukraine on or after 24 February 2022, and their family members.[36]

It therefore only automatically protects those foreign citizens who had sought asylum in Ukraine before the invasion.

The EU did extend the scope of protection to cover two additional groups:

> Non-Ukrainian nationals with a permanent residence permit who cannot return to their country of origin in safe and durable conditions (adequate national protection can also apply); and
>
> Non-Ukrainian nationals with a non-permanent residence permit who cannot return to their countrv of origin in safe and durable conditions.[37]

There are, however, fundamental problems with this: first, it has been noted that 'Ukrainian permanent residence under general immigration rules is difficult to obtain, as the grounds to apply are restrictive and applications are subject to a quota.'[38] Permanent residency is largely only acquired after an asylum application process which, as elsewhere in Europe, is notoriously difficult. Second, some EU Member States, such as Bulgaria and Sweden, do not permit temporary protection applications from Ukrainian permanent residents.[39] Finally, it is unclear what factors would be accepted as proof of inability to return to the country of origin – would lack of funds suffice? Or indeed what qualifies as 'safe and durable conditions'? Despite encouragement from the EU that Member States should extend TPD protection to other groups, such as stranded TCN students, in the immediate aftermath of the invasion few chose to do so.[40]

Poland was one of the countries that did grant temporary protection to TCNs fleeing Ukraine, but only as long as they held a valid permanent residence permit in Ukraine and could not 'safely and permanently return to their country'. TCN spouses of a Ukrainian citizen could also access protection but only 'provided that he/she came to the territory of the Republic of Poland from the territory of Ukraine in connection with military operations conducted in the territory of that state'.[41] Family reunion was however explicitly excluded: protection given under the Polish Act on Assistance to Ukrainian Nationals does not apply to the non-Ukrainian children of a Ukrainian national (or his/her spouse) who were not born in Poland.[42]

[36] Council Directive 2001/55/EC, Art 1(2).

[37] www.consilium.europa.eu/en/infographics/temporary-protection-displaced-persons.

[38] J Antoons, AS Walsh and J Smallenburg 'EU/EEA Temporary Protection for Ukraine – Taking Stock', available at www.fragomen.com/insights/eueea-temporary-protection-for-ukraine-taking-stock.html.

[39] ibid.

[40] For an overview of the application of the TPD to non-Ukrainians see ecre.org/wp-content/uploads/2022/12/ECRE-Update-November-2022-Implementation-of-the-TPD.pdf; ; ouclf.law.ox.ac.uk/extending-social-protection-for-migrants-under-the-european-unions-temporary-protection-directive-lessons-from-the-war-in-ukraine; or fra.europa.eu/en/publication/2022/national-legislation-implementing-eu-temporary-protection-directive-selected-eu-0.

[41] ukraina.interwencjaprawna.pl/how-can-citizens-of-other-countries-non-ukrainians-enter-poland.

[42] M Łysienia, 'Following the EU Response to the Russian Invasion of Ukraine? The Implementation of the Temporary Protection Directive in Poland' (2023) 12 *Central and Eastern European Migration Review* 180, available at doi: 10.54667/ceemr.2023.14.

The Netherlands, Portugal and Spain[43] also offered temporary protection to non-Ukrainians with temporary residence permits – but again only if they were unable to safely return home. The Netherlands decided to withdraw this in July 2022. According to the Secretary of State for Justice and Security, Eric van der Burg, pressure on housing made it

> imperative that we offer protection to people who are not safe in their own country. At the same time, we don't want to overburden municipalities. This shift in policy enables us to focus on providing accommodation and services to the people who need them.[44]

Subsequently, third country nationals could no longer reside in the Netherlands and enjoy rights extended under the TPD: they would have to leave municipal housing, their jobs and studies, and even leave the Netherlands unless they fell under the under the EU Qualification Directive. The temporary protection already granted to 4,500 third-country nationals was to be terminated on March 2023, although temporary protection for other displaced persons from Ukraine was automatically extended until March 2024. However, implementation of this was then delayed until September 2023, and this has now been further postponed.[45]

Those who were able to navigate these contradictory rules then suffered discrimination in access to housing: owners of Airbnb apartments in Hungary refused to rent to them, and racism was experienced in refugee camps: a Ghanaian student told DW that he left the refugee camp in north-eastern Ukraine because of discrimination – apparently a Ukrainian man had complained to camp officials that sleeping beside a Black man was traumatising. The student was then moved to another space within the camp. To avoid such experiences, the African refugees also avoided the refugee camps.[46]

Some were even placed in EU detention centres – 'In a letter to a member of the EU Parliament, Poland's border police admitted that 52 third country nationals who had fled from Ukraine had been taken to closed detention centres in the first three weeks of the war.'[47] According to a story in *The Independent*, one young Nigerian man who had been studying trade and economics in Kharkov had his phone confiscated by Polish border guards and was given 'no option' but to sign a form he did not understand:

> 'It was written in Polish. I didn't know what I was signing. I said I wouldn't sign, but they insisted I signed it and that if not I would go to jail for five months,' he said in a recorded

[43] ecre.org/wp-content/uploads/2022/12/ECRE-Update-November-2022-Implementation-of-the-TPD.pdf, 118.

[44] www.government.nl/latest/news/2022/07/19/non-ukrainians-with-a-temporary-ukrainian-residence-permit-no-longer-eligible-for-municipal-accommodation-and-services.

[45] In February 2023, the Dutch Government extended non-Ukrainian temporary protection status holders' right to stay in the Netherlands until 4 September 2023 (see entry on 'Netherlands' at www.fragomen.com/insights/european-unionukraine-temporary-protection-status-country-specific-updates.html). A legal challenge was brought by IND, the Dutch Council for Refugees, to ascertain whether early termination of temporary protection was lawful. The Amsterdam court ruled that it unlawful on 1 September 2023. See www.everaert.nl/en/non-ukrainian-third-country-nationals-with-temporary-right-of-residence-retain-temporary-protection-for-now.On 2 September 2023 temporary protection was again extended pending a decision on appeal to the Council of State: www.government.nl/topics/reception-of-refugees-from-ukraine/third-country-nationals. On 25 April 2024, the Council of State decided to ask the Court of Justice of the European Union (CJEU) to give judgment on this matter. Temporary protection has been extended until the CJEU makes a decision.

[46] www.dw.com/en/ukraine-war-african-students-face-russian-missiles-and-racism/a-61356066.

[47] www.independent.co.uk/news/world/europe/ukraine-refugees-detention-international-students-b2041310.html.

conversation with a Nigerian activist. The student said he was then taken to court, where there was no interpreter to translate what was being said so that he could understand, and then taken to a detention centre in the small village of Lesznowola. 'It is a closed camp inside a forest,' said Gabriel, speaking from the facility. 'There's no freedom. Some people have been here more than nine months. Some have gone mad. I'm scared.'[48]

4.2.3. Welfare and Education

Member States have introduced further support for Ukrainian nationals. In France, Ukrainian nationals were given housing, vouchers for food or clothing, while Africans were given nothing.[49] In Denmark, housing from which 'non-Westerners' had been forcibly removed was made available to Ukrainian refugees.[50] Poland introduced legislation entitling Ukrainian refugees to an 18-month stay without a permit, with the possibility to apply for a three-year temporary residence permit after Month 9. They can work, receive a national identity number and access healthcare, education and other benefits. Each Ukrainian refugee receives a one-time payment of €63 ($69.65). Each person or organisation that provides them accommodation receives €8.45 per day. The UK created a scheme allowing any citizen to sponsor a Ukrainian refugee: each household providing accommodation for a Ukrainian refugee receives £350 ($459.74) tax-free per month.[51] African and Asian students from the Ukraine do not benefit from any of these schemes, even though for some Ukraine had become a place that they called home – some even had families.[52]

There is also a stark contrast in treatment relating to access to further study for those who have been able to navigate their way around the complex residency regulations. While some African and Asian students have now returned to their former institutions of study in the Ukraine and some attend online lectures offered by their universities in Ukraine,[53] others wish to study in the country that they have fled to. Scholarships offered to refugees of Ukrainian nationality are not extended to those from third nations. These students must therefore fight to keep studying or lose everything, including the time invested and money paid for tuition and fees in the Ukraine, which will not be reimbursed.[54]

However, there they face high fees charged to international students. Across the EU, many institutions have opened their doors to African students[55] but at a cost,[56] meaning

[48] www.independent.co.uk/news/world/europe/ukraine-refugees-detention-international-students-b2041310.html.

[49] www.globalcitizen.org/en/content/africans-in-ukraine-does-the-world-still-care.

[50] www.theguardian.com/world/2022/may/02/denmark-accused-racism-anti-ghetto-law-ukraine-refugees.

[51] www.gov.uk/register-interest-homes-ukraine. The UK also created the Ukraine Family Scheme allowing Ukrainian citizens and their immediate family, resident in Ukraine on or immediately before 1 January 2022, to join UK-based family members.

[52] www.theafricareport.com/190099/africans-face-europes-unfair-two-track-refugee-policy.

[53] www.dw.com/en/ukraine-war-african-students-face-russian-missiles-and-racism/a-61356066.

[54] V Pietromarchi 'Across Europe, African students fight to study after Ukraine exit', available at www.aljazeera.com/news/2022/5/13/african-students-who-fled-war-in-ukraine-fight-to-keep-studying; www.aljazeera.com/features/2022/3/17/broken-dreams-palestinian-students-who-escaped-the-ukraine-war.

[55] www.universityworldnews.com/post.php?story=20220315065736746.

[56] www.globalcitizen.org/en/content/africans-in-ukraine-does-the-world-still-care.

another set of international tuition fees would need to be found.[57] Bulgaria offered to enrol those African students who could afford to pay tuition fees again, allowing them to complete their courses. There are no funds extended to support their transition: 'There are no assistance packages, no financial inducements for citizens to offer housing or other care. It's the recipient countries that stand to gain financially.'[58] On the contrary, those who made it to France were sent deportation letters.[59]

Hungary did allow African students displaced from Ukraine to continue their university studies: Decree No 1186/2022 allocated funds for a 'Students at Risk' programme permitting Ukrainian nationals and certain TCNs (Stipendium Hungaricum partners) to study in Hungary. Under Decree No 1179/2022 beneficiaries of temporary protection also received €347 per month for education and training.[60] On the whole, the future is uncertain for these students.[61]

Only exceptionally therefore is protection under EU law extended to non-European refugees from the Ukraine. Under these rules, non-Ukrainians without a residency permit have between two weeks and three months to figure out what to do next,[62] but there are only two stark choices: regularise their situation or leave. Two years on, student refugees from Africa and Asia fleeing war in the Ukraine continue to live in precarious conditions and are still desperately seeking to complete their studies[63] and rebuild their careers and lives.[64]

There has been a marked absence of solidarity with African and Asian students – protection is patchy and, where is is accessible, minimal. Simply put, the organisation of protection has been discriminatory.[65] Such differential treatment demonstrates that the solidarity said to underpin the EU does not extend to fraternity with Africans and Asians in need. As Grandi pointed out, the 'ugly reality' is that people from Africa and Asia experienced racism instead of solidarity: 'some Black and Brown people fleeing Ukraine – and other wars and conflicts around the world – have not received the same treatment as Ukrainian refugees.'[66]

[57] www.reuters.com/article/ukraine-africa-students-idAFL3N2VO2DE.

[58] www.theafricareport.com/190099/africans-face-europes-unfair-two-track-refugee-policy.

[59] www.lemonde.fr/en/le-monde-africa/article/2023/02/25/one-year-later-the-shattered-dreams-of-young-africans-who-fled-ukraine-for-france_6017283_124.html#.

[60] ecre.org/wp-content/uploads/2022/12/ECRE-Update-November-2022-Implementation-of-the-TPD.pdf, 58.

[61] E Achiri and H Sandilya, 'What's next for African and Asian war refugees?' *IPS* (8 April 2022), available at www.ips-journal.eu/topics/democracy-and-society/whats-next-for-african-and-asian-student-refugees-fleeing-the-war-in-ukraine-5870.

[62] www.theafricareport.com/190099/africans-face-europes-unfair-two-track-refugee-policy.

[63] Some have resumed study in Georgia; see equaltimes.org/after-fleeing-war-in-ukraine-many?lang=en.

[64] C Kane, 'One year later, the shattered dreams of young Africans who fled Ukraine for France' *Le Monde* (25 February 2023), available at www.lemonde.fr/en/le-monde-africa/article/2023/02/25/one-year-later-the-shattered-dreams-of-young-africans-who-fled-ukraine-for-france_6017283_124.html#.

[65] J Kienast, N Feith Tan and J Vedsted-Hansen, 'Preferential, differential or discriminatory? EU protection arrangements for persons displaced from Ukraine' (2022) ASILE project, Aarhus University, available at www.asileproject.eu/aarhus-university-2.

[66] 'UNHCR chief condemns 'discrimination, violence and racism' against some fleeing Ukraine', available at news.un.org/en/story/2022/03/1114282.

4.3. Racism and the EU's Social Fabric

These stories confirm that something is rotten in the EU's social fabric – the EU is hostile to Black and Brown refugees. At the UN press conference, Grandi told reporters, that the racism experienced at the borders was not 'a product of state policies'.[67] This is disputable – one can argue like Grandi that this is racism by individual border authorities who are 'bad eggs', but this gives rise to the question of why these border guards chose to act as they did? Why did they not fear any reprimand? One explanation, from a historical perspective, might be that this racism should be understood as the product of three inter-linked state policies: European colonialism/imperialism in the nineteenth and twentieth centuries as well as European amnesia and hostility to Black and Brown migrants in the twenty-first century.[68] Put together, these state policies have erased the role played by colonised peoples in European wars and economic reconstruction. This obliteration creates an environment within which the racism seen at the borders of Ukraine and elsewhere can flourish in institutions and between individuals. I would therefore argue that the racism at the borders should be understood within the context of colonialism, which though no longer explicit is able to cast its shadow upon the contemporary European social fabric through silencing.

4.3.1. European Wars and Colonial Troops

At least one African has died in the current war between Russia and the Ukraine: Lemekhani Nathan Nyirenda, 23, from Zambia studied nuclear engineering at the Moscow Engineering Physics Institute (MEPhI). Imprisoned in April 2020, he was sent to fight for Russia and was killed in Ukraine in November 2022.[69]

The current contempt for African and Asian lives across the EU is to some extent mirrored in the way colonial powers historically used colonial troops in their wars.

By the end of the nineteenth century, the whole of Africa, except Ethiopia and Liberia, was under European rule: Great Britain and France controlled the two largest colonial empires.[70] It is hardly a surprise, then, that significant numbers of African men served in their armies, not only of Britain and France, but also Germany,[71] Italy and

[67] media.un.org/en/asset/k14/k14dezco4m.

[68] 'Morrocco/Spain: Horrific Migrant Deaths at Melilla Border: Investigate Fully, Preserve Evidence, Ensure Dignified Treatment of the Dead', available at www.hrw.org/news/2022/06/29/morocco/spain-horrific-migrant-deaths-melilla-border#:~:text=The%20borders%20around%20Ceuta%20and%20Melilla%2C%20Spain's%20two,channels%20and%20obstacles%20to%20reaching%20official%20border%20posts.

[69] 'Zambian officials say student killed on Russia-Ukraine front line', available at www.aljazeera.com/news/2022/11/14/zambian-student-killed-on-russia-ukraine-battle-front-line. Nyirenda was imprisoned on drug charges; hoping to reduce his sentence, he signed up to the Wagner Group to fight in Ukraine. K St Julian-Varnon, 'Russian hypocrisy and the death of a Zambian student in Ukraine' (2023), available at www.aljazeera.com/opinions/2023/1/3/is-russia-really-africas-friend.

[70] www.bl.uk/world-war-one/themes/race-empire-and-colonial-troops.

[71] T Bührer, *Die Kaiserliche Schutztruppe für Deutsch-Ostafrika. Koloniale Sicherheitspolitik und transkulturelle Kriegführung 1885 bis 1918* (De Gruyter Oldenbourg, Munich, 2011). (= *Beiträge zur Militärgeschichte*, Band 70).

Belgium.[72] In fact, the rank and file of troops fighting in Africa were 'non-European' men; for example, when the Maji Maji War began in 1905 in Tanzania (then known as 'German East Africa), 200 European officers led 1,700 Tanzanian men and a police force of another 700 Africans.[73] Thus, although troops led by Kitchener in Sudan in 1898 are described as 'Anglo-Egyptian'[74] it is probable that very few white Europeans actually fought in this army.

The absence of white soldiers has been described as a 'distinguishing feature'[75] of colonial troops. Colonised men were recruited for a number of reasons: they were cheaper to hire, cheaper to replace and, according to the racist theory of 'martial races',[76] were imagined to have a higher capacity to bear pain; for example, Nepalese Ghurkhas, were described as 'natural born soldiers'.[77] West Africans were described by French General Charles Mangin as 'natural warriors', 'primitives … whose young blood flows so ardently, as if avid to be shed'. Such men were lauded in France 'for their courage and loyalty' yet simultaneously denigrated for their 'primitive savagery and mental inferiority'.[78]

At the start of World War I, colonial European powers drew upon these populations. Mangin was one of the strongest advocates of this – he promoted recruitment 'from the vast 'reservoirs of men' in Africa to strengthen the French army in the face of a larger and more populous Germany. It has been estimated that over four million men from Africa and Asia were mobilised into the European and American armies during the War, in both combat and non-combat roles.[79]

From 1914, soldiers from North and West Africa, as well as Madagascar and Indochina, were brought to France for active fighting.[80] Between 1914 and 1918, France recruited nearly 500,000 colonial troops, including 166,000 West Africans, 46,000 Madagascans, 50,000 Indochinese, 140,000 Algerians, 47,000 Tunisians and 24,300 Moroccans. In Germany, this led to public complaints from the Kaiser that the Allies were introducing "uncivilized' warfare and racially inferior warriors into the conflict at home in Europe'.[81] Many more also served as labourers or carriers in Africa. In total, over two million Africans were involved in the conflict as soldiers or labourers. In addition, up to 140,000 Chinese workers who were hired by the British and French governments to clear WWI battlefields.

Xenophobia came to inform the use of colonial troops in Britain and France: despite acknowledging their utility, racism determined where these troops would be deployed. Fear emerged that if these troops were put into action fighting against white men, even

[72] D Killingray and M Plaut, *Fighting for Britain: African Soldiers in the Second World War* (Oxford, James Currey Publishers, 2010).

[73] encyclopedia.1914-1918-online.net/article/colonial_policy_colonial_conflicts_and_war_before_1914.

[74] ibid.

[75] ibid.

[76] encyclopedia.1914-1918-online.net/article/martial_races_theory_of. According to the concept of 'martial races', certain ethnic, religious, caste or social groups were regarded as possessing a more masculine character, as being loyal and therefore especially suited for military service.

[77] n 72.

[78] www.bl.uk/world-war-one/articles/race-racism-and-military-strategy.

[79] www.bl.uk/world-war-one/themes/race-empire-and-colonial-troops.

[80] n 77.

[81] R Fogarty, *Race and War in France: Colonial Subjects in the French Army, 1914–1918* (Baltimore, MD, Johns Hopkins University Press, 2008).

if these white men were the enemy, this might undermine the prevailing racial hierarchy. As a result of this fear, the British army removed the 140,000 Indians troops on the Western Front in 1914, putting them instead into action in the Middle East in 1915. Likewise, around 20,000 South Africans were sent to France as labourers rather than for armed combat.

Although never taught in European schools or universities, war has therefore played a large part in the EU's social fabric by bringing individuals and their families from Africa, Asia and the Caribbean to Europe, whether that be wars of colonial expansion or global war such as World Wars I and II. As Das notes,

> the lives of hundreds of thousands of women and children in villages across Asia and Africa who lost their husbands, brothers or fathers, and faced different kinds of hardships – remains one of the most silent and under-researched areas in First World War history.

4.3.2. The Absence of Colonial History from the EU Educational Curriculum

Can there be a link between these historical state policies and the discriminatory treatment meted out to students from these former colonies? It is pertinent to ask why border guards, who may never otherwise have come into contact with a person of colour, discriminate against them. Why were these desperate women and men, carrying all that they possessed and some also carrying babies, not seen as refugees in desperate need of access to safety and shelter in the same way as the white refugees? Why, in the glare of international media, did they think that they could do this? Could it be that some of the racist colonial tropes – of being immune to pain, natural warriors and uncivilised/ savage primitives – influenced their thinking?

It seems plausible that the shadow of colonialism is so powerful precisely because colonialism is not studied in European schools and universities. The omission not only impoverishes understanding of European history but also silences the significant contribution of peoples from the colonies to Europe, in its wars and in post-war reconstruction of the European economy. The absence of these stories creates an environment within which institutional and individual racism can flourish and be practiced with – as we see – impunity. Sadly, mainstream media reporting only exacerbates this problem.[82]

There is already recognition that racism in Europe can only be clearly understood when set in the context of past European treatment of colonised peoples. When Bruno Candé was shot and killed in broad daylight by a racist Portuguese man (ironically, a retired soldier active in the former Portuguese colony of Angola),[83] the Council of Europe noted that Portugal must do more to confront its past as a colonial power and its role in the transatlantic slave trade in order to help fight racism and discrimination

[82] www.theguardian.com/commentisfree/2022/mar/02/civilised-european-look-like-us-racist-coverage-ukraine.

[83] www.theguardian.com/world/2021/jun/28/white-portuguese-man-sentenced-to-22-years-for-of-black-actor.

in the country today.[84] The same applies across the EU as a whole: Europe has a responsibility to teach the past in order to understand the present.[85] Widespread knowledge of European colonial history might repair the rotten-ness of racism and xenophobia which continues to spread across the continent today. As stated by Shada Islam, decolonising minds is crucial for the EU as it seeks to move its peoples ever closer.[86]

It is ironic that Europeans express less sympathy and support for the lives of Black people here in Europe than Black people in the USA. When George Floyd was murdered, people all over Europe joined demonstrations and protests to defend the importance of the lives of Black people – in the USA. Yet, in relation to justice for Europe's own George Floyd – Oury Jalloh, an asylum-seeker who burnt to death in a police cell in Germany whilst handcuffed to a mattress – there is little interest. This is to be regretted given the contributions of Black and Brown people to European military and economic success. The same level of concern given to George Floyd is now needed to protect the lives of African and Asian refugees in Europe following the invasion of Ukraine – their lives matter too, while they are still alive to enjoy it.

4.4. Decolonising Europe

The evidence shows that there are indeed two tracks for asylum-seekers and refugees in Europe: one for those from Africa, Asia and the Caribbean; and a second for everyone else, with the former track including 'long waits, arbitrary detention, extra expenses, and dehumanizing treatment'.[87] As has been noted, the consequences for Europe as a whole are frightening if racial discrimination is allowed to fester and develop. It would also be a tragedy if an EU created to defeat racism and xenophobia became instead the willing perpetrator of such.

It is therefore important to reflect upon what can be done differently to rescue and repair the EU's social fabric from the xenophobia amplified by the outbreak of war in the Ukraine. As Jackson Sow argues:

> No legal system premised upon colonial or neocolonial oppression, and fueled by white supremacy, can effectuate a vision of justice that is anything other than a white supremacist imagination of a world order that guarantees legal formalism and economic liberalism for the express purpose of maintaining strict racialized geopolitical hegemony. If a legal regime designed to create a more just, anti-racist world order is actually desired, it will need to be created. And for such a regime to be effective, the existing regime must be dismantled. As with all enforceable agreements, the sociolegal agreement currently undergirding the laws of asylum and refuge must be dissolved before a new agreement can take force.[88]

[84] www.theguardian.com/world/2021/mar/24/portugal-must-do-more-to-confront-colonial-past-says-council-of-europe.

[85] picum.org/migration-anti-racism-policies-are-we-ready-for-racism-free-europe.

[86] euobserver.com/opinion/156341.

[87] blog.ucsusa.org/chanese-forte/anti-blackness-in-europe-creates-vulnerability-during-war.

[88] M Jackson Sow, 'Ukrainian Refugees, Race, and International Law's Choice Between Order and Justice' (2022) 116 *American Journal of International Law* 698, available at racism.org/articles/citizenship-rights/human-rights/10920-ukrainian-refugees.

This work of dismantling and recreating will need to be undertaken carefully and at multiple locations. It requires adoption of a decolonial approach to European integration. This approach requires a 'fundamental re-examination of prevailing practices, thinking in particular about how these might preserve a 'Europe-centred, colonial lens'.[89]

Proposals from the Platform for International Cooperation on Undocumented Migrants (PICUM)[90] go some way towards this. PICUM offers recommendations that could assist with this agenda, advocating for five measures: mainstreaming anti-discrimination in migration policies; tackling racial discrimination in policing; creating partnerships with the Global South that are as mutually beneficial as the partnerships within the EU; teaching Europeans about the historical roots of racism; and promoting narratives that protect the dignity of all.

These recommendations are interlinked; in particular, the last one plays an important role in relation to the first. The first relates directly to migration: PICUM recommends that the EU mainstreams anti-racism in all of its migration policies, so that racial equality is integrated 'throughout the legal and policy EU framework on migration'. It is indeed a strange anomaly that anti-discrimination law does not apply to immigration law.[91] Addressing this anomaly will enable the EU to investigate the myriad ways in which structural, institutional and individual racism is experienced by migrants in Europe, regardless of their legal status. Studies and investigations are a good start but not enough – Frontex continues with its so-called 'pushbacks' in the Mediterranean, despite the damning report by OLAF – so concrete measures are required to address this racism.

PICUM also recommends action in relation to racial discrimination in policing. Studies by the Fundamental Rights Agency (FRA)[92] and case law before the ECtHR provide ample evidence that racist policing does not only occur in the USA. Nor is police brutality limited to the borders of the Ukraine – it is also visible in the behaviour of civilian police. Whilst to date the only country in Europe to charge a police officer with murder is the UK[93] it cannot be excluded that murderous activities also take place in other countries on the continent. Although policing is not a direct competence of the EU, coordinated activity is organised via CEPOL, the EU Agency for Law Enforcement Training.[94] Training is offered to members of national police forces; whilst fundamental rights is offered, at present it is focused on data protection. A course on anti-racist policing would fit well within this area of activity and contribute to prevention of racist policing across the EU.

[89] www.londonmet.ac.uk/about/equity/centre-for-equity-and-inclusion/race/decolonising-academia/what-does-decolonising-mean.

[90] picum.org/migration-anti-racism-policies-are-we-ready-for-racism-free-europe.

[91] J Silga, 'Migration, Asylum and EU Anti-Discrimination Law' in C O'Cinneide, J Ringelheim and I Solanke (eds), *Edward Elgar Research Handbook on European Anti-Discrimination Law* (forthcoming).

[92] www.enar-eu.org/the-sharp-edge-of-violence-police-brutality-and-community-resistance-of-racialised-groups.

[93] Chris Kaba 'was struck by a single gunshot fired by a Met Police officer into the vehicle he was driving just before 23:00 BST and died in hospital in the early hours of the following morning, an inquest was told. The construction worker was months away from becoming a father when he was shot.' www.bbc.co.uk/news/uk-england-66865099.

[94] www.cepol.europa.eu/newsroom/news/our-cepol-training-catalogue-2023-now-available-online.

Improving relationships with the Global South is just as important as repairing the relationships amongst communities across multiracial Europe. The continent of Africa, at least three times the size of Europe, was incorporated into EU law as a passive recipient of European largesse, as a terrain where a unified European could maintain and manifest its development policies. In the original Schuman Declaration, Africa was seen as a target for development:[95]

> This production will be offered to the world as a whole without distinction or exception, with the aim of contributing to raising living standards and to promoting peaceful achievements. With increased resources Europe will be able to pursue the achievement of one of its essential tasks, namely, the development of the African continent. In this way, there will be realised simply and speedily that fusion of interest which is indispensable to the establishment of a common economic system; it may be the leaven from which may grow a wider and deeper community between countries long opposed to one another by sanguinary divisions.

However, there were probably no representatives from any African nation at the table during the negotiations which resulted in the Treaty of Rome.

This attitude to Africa is no longer credible or conducive to European goals. The idea of Africa as a 'jungle' waiting to be moulded into a European 'garden' reflects neo-imperialist fantasies[96] and have been criticised. Orbie et al, for example, argue that 'the EU should be more modest about its so-called civilizational achievements and acknowledge the long and dark shadow of its colonial past'.[97] This becomes ever more pressing as the EU seeks to fulfil its ambitions in relation to climate change, which is to a large extent dependent upon cheap access to raw materials abundant in the Global South. Advantages linked to continuing colonial relationships can easily be lost, as France discovered when subsequent to a coup the price to uranium in Niger[98] increased from €81/kilo to over €200/kilo.[99] Given this, the second recommendation from PICUM correctly states that:

> Moving forward, the EU's relationship with the global South cannot replicate the unequal arrangements rooted in past colonial ties to impose its own agenda and goals – an agenda that harms the very people concerned. To avoid perpetuating neo-colonial dominance, the EU

[95] old.robert-schuman.eu//en/doc/questions-d-europe/qe-204-en.pdf.

[96] European Diplomatic Academy: Opening Remarks by High Representative Josep Borrell at the Inauguration of the Pilot Programme' (European Union External Action Service, 2022), available at www.eeas.europa.eu/eeas/european-diplomatic-academy-opening-remarks-high-representative-josep-borrell-inauguration_en.

[97] J Orbie et al, 'Decolonizing Rather than Decentring "Europe"' (2023) 28 *European Foreign Affairs Review* 1.

[98] There was a coup in Niger in July 2023, two coups in Burkina Faso in 2022 and two in Mali since 2020. The latest coup on the continent took place in Gabon in August 2023.

[99] France retaliated by suspending student mobility with Niger, Mali and Burkina Faso: new students from these countries who were about to start studies in France and current scholarship students without valid visas are no longer able to travel to France. It is estimated that in the academic year 2022/23 there were 6,600 students in France from the three Sahelian countries: 2,900 from Mali, 2,500 from Burkina Faso and 1,200 from Niger, representing 7% of the total number of students from Sub-Saharan Africa. These students 'received emails from the French Foreign Affairs Ministry in August saying that their stay and financial support – air fares, grants and allowances, and health insurance – had been cancelled for the start of the university year because of "events that took place in Niamey [the military takeover in Niger] at the end of July", reported Le Monde'. See www.universityworldnews.com/post.php?story=20230921004148603&utm_source=newsletter&utm_medium=email&utm_campaign=AFNL0421.

> must mainstream anti-racism in its foreign policy (across all areas), instead of mainstreaming migration control, and work on global justice and reparation measures.[100]

This goal is linked to the next: correcting the miseducation of Europeans. PICUM focuses on the need for an acknowledgement of 'the historical roots of racism to foster a better understanding of migration in the present and counter ahistorical and race-blind approaches to migration policies'. Beyond this, however, is the need to excavate and disseminate the historical colonial relationships focused on extraction and exploitation common across Europe until the second half of the twentieth century. Creation of a multilingual library of anti-colonial materials would be a good place to start with this.[101]

Finally, the EU needs to focus on the development of positive narratives, consistent with its image as a promoter and defender of human rights. In order to protect the dignity of all, action is required to prevent and correct racist disinformation spread across social media. Hatred and harassment encouraged in political discourse must also be eradicated.[102] As PICUM states:

> In addition to combatting disinformation and racist and xenophobic messages in the media, EU institutions should promote the same regarding political discourse targeting migrant and racialised communities. This will help to fight against ethnonationalist rhetoric that fosters discrimination of such groups.

In particular, removal of this rhetoric will cleanse the toxic environment within which it becomes possible for border officials to hold at gunpoint African and Asian students fleeing war; the institution of positive narratives should be designed to replace it with an attitude of care for all fellow human beings, regardless of their skin colour.

4.5. Conclusion

In her 2023 State of the Union speech, Commission President Ursula von der Leyen announced that:

> It is the moment to show to the young generation that we can build a continent where you can be who you are, love who you want, and aim as high as you want. A continent reconciled with nature and leading the way on new technologies. A continent that is united in freedom and peace. This is Europe's moment to once again answer the call of history.

This is a laudable statement, but it must extend to all people in and of Europe regardless of the colour of their skin.

It has been boldly asserted that the war in Ukraine has 'profoundly changed'[103] the EU. Yet it has also highlighted deep-seated shortcomings in racial solidarity in

[100] See also further recommendations by ECRE at ecre.org/editorial-an-offer-you-cant-refuse-the-external-dimension.

[101] www.anticolonialresearchlibrary.org.

[102] Borell's speech on the 'jungles' outside of the EU was rightly condemned by academics.

[103] P Wintour, 'No turning back': how the Ukraine war has profoundly changed the EU' *The Guardian* (30 September 2023), available at www.theguardian.com/world/2023/sep/30/ukraine-russia-war-changed-eu?utm_term=6517c778fcd3adb22de89f06840d131c&utm_campaign=GuardianTodayUK&utm_source=esp&utm_medium=Email&CMP=GTUK_email.

Europe, and the limits to which racialised persons – regardless of citizenship or legal status[104] – are seen as having a European identity. If the EU has found a new common sense of military purpose, it is to be hoped that this will be accompanied by a new sense of social justice.

The UN celebrates the International Day of Democracy every year on 15 September and this day is a reminder that racialised refugee schemes are a threat to democracy around the world. If nothing is done, student refugees from Africa and Asia – future leaders in their home countries with whom the EU will want to do business – will inevitably hold on to the firm conclusion that European anti-racism action plans[105] and 'assurances of equality are nothing more than lip service'[106] and that 'Refugee law – like much of public international law – is a vehicle for the maintenance of a Euro-dominant world order instead of human rights-focused global justice.'[107] This would be regrettable – the human rights good that the EU does overseas, for example in places like Western Sahara,[108] should not be overshadowed by the human rights wrongs it allows to be perpetrated at home.

[104] Silga (n 91).

[105] commission.europa.eu/strategy-and-policy/policies/justice-and-fundamental-rights/combatting-discrimination/racism-and-xenophobia/eu-anti-racism-action-plan-2020-2025_en.

[106] www.theafricareport.com/190099/africans-face-europes-unfair-two-track-refugee-policy.

[107] M Jackson Sow, 'Ukrainian Refugees, Race and International Law's Choice Between Order and Justice' (2022) 116 *American Journal of International Law* 698.

[108] euobserver.com/opinion/156703?utm_source=euobs&utm_medium=email.

5

No Peace without Sustainability, No Sustainability without Peace: The Implementation of EU Treaty Goals

BEATE SJÅFJELL

5.1. Introduction

Russia's inexcusable and atrocious invasion of Ukraine – war in Europe again – brings home to Europe how much chaos and suffering war entails. Continued unsustainabilities will lead to other wars, to resource wars, to wars over water, to wars over fertile land, and to forced migration with climate refugees as but one category, on a level that cannot be stopped at Europe's borders except with the most draconian and inhumane measures. Also within Europe, the risk of conflict and of war increases with continued unsustainability. Peace is more than the absence of war – peace is an inextricably interconnected element of sustainability. Sustainability requires peace; peace requires sustainability.

Peace is the fundament of the European Union (EU). The European project now encompasses much of Europe, with 27 EU Member States and three non-voting half-members of the European Economic Area (EEA) agreement. The underlying motivation for these former wartime adversaries to enter into mutual commitments of this kind was peace[1] – the end to all wars. The EU shares roots with the other post-war European project, the Council of Europe and its defence of human rights, democracy and the rule of law.[2]

The fundamental role of peace is now expressed in the Treaty on European Union (TEU): 'The Union's aim is to promote peace, its values and the well-being of its peoples' (Article 3(1) TEU). The Union is founded on the values of

> respect for human dignity, freedom, democracy, equality, the rule of law and respect for human rights, including the rights of persons belonging to minorities. These values are common to the Member States in a society in which pluralism, non-discrimination, tolerance, justice, solidarity and equality between women and men prevail (Article 2 TEU).

[1] This was expressed in the Preamble of the 1957 Treaty: emphasising 'economic and social progress'; 'solidarity', and persevering and strengthening 'peace and liberty'. I draw here on my analysis of the historical Treaty objectives in B Sjåfjell, *Towards a Sustainable European Company Law: A Normative Analysis of the Objectives of EU Law* (Alphen an den Rijn, Kluwer Law International, 2009), available at ssrn.com/abstract=4011934.

[2] Which increasingly has become integrated also in EU law.

Economic integration between the Member States was central to the original Treaty, seen as essential for repairing the wounds left by the war, rebuilding Europe and making a new war impossible.[3] Common rules facilitating trade and economic development were to be instrumental in providing peace and prosperity for the peoples of the Member States. Economic integration remains a core element, with the current Treaty emphasis on the social market economy, full employment and social progress. As the current Treaties clearly express, sustainable development is fundamental to achieving the Union's goals and an overarching objective in its own rights.[4]

Predating the formation of what is now the EU, Europe has a history of colonisation, which influences the EU's ability to contribute to peace and to global sustainability.[5] Criticism of what is denoted 'neocolonialism' in EU's relation with low-income countries outside of the EU has repeatedly been raised.[6] In this chapter, my concern is the neocolonialism through the globalised activities of European businesses,[7] which undermines the possibilities for sustainable development. I analyse the EU's law and policy initiatives to regulate business for sustainability, in light of the EU's overarching Treaty goals of sustainability. This emphasis is chosen for three reasons: firstly, regulating business and finance for sustainability has been on the EU agenda since 2018 and continues to be strongly emphasised. Secondly, regulating for sustainability is crucial as business-as-usual is a key driver for the extreme unsustainabilities of our time. Thirdly and consequently, an analysis of the EU's efforts in this context can help us see whether the EU is securing a sustainable peace. With the backdrop of war in Europe, my question is accordingly whether these EU initiatives are sufficient to mitigate the extreme unsustainabilities of our time.[8]

Section 5.2 presents a research-based concept of sustainability and the EU Treaty law basis for setting sustainable development, or sustainability as it is often referred to today, as an overarching objective, and introduces the EU regulatory framework for operationalising this objective. Section 5.3 analyses the EU's regulation of business and finance as initiatives to implement sustainability as an overarching objective of EU Treaty Law. I concentrate on three EU policy initiatives: the Sustainable Finance

[3] See PJG Kapteyn and P Verloren van Themaat, I, 'The Genesis of the European Communities and the Accession of Other European Countries' in LW Gormley (ed), *Introduction to the Law of the European Communities*, 3rd edn (Alphen aan den Rijn, Kluwer Law International, 1998) 1–7, which also gives an overview of the international political background.

[4] See further section II.B below.

[5] eg, F Cameron and S Islam, 'History Matters for the EU's Geopolitical Ambitions' European Policy Centre: Commentary (15 July 2021), available at www.epc.eu/en/Publications/History-matters-for-the-EU s-geopolitical-ambitions~41181.

[6] Neocolonialism may be defined as 'the control of the economic and political system by foreign actors despite formal decolonization', A Ziai, 'Postcolonial Critique of Economic Development' in C Scherrer, A Garcia and J Wullweber (eds), *Handbook on Critical Political Economy and Public Policy* (Cheltenham, UK and Northampton, MA, USA, Edward Elgar Publishing, 2023) 380, available at www.elgaronline.com/edcollchap/book/9781800373785/book-part-9781800373785-39.xml. See also eg M Ferdinand, *Decolonial Ecology: Thinking from the Caribbean World* (Cambridge, Polity Press, 2022), available at www.wiley.com/en-dk/Decolonial+Ecology%3A+Thinking+from+the+Caribbean+World-p-9781509546220; E Njuguna and M Ozbayoglu, 'Africa-EU Summit: Neo-Colonialism or Justice?' www.euractiv.com (17 February 2022), available at www.euractiv.com/section/energy-environment/opinion/africa-eu-summit-neo-colonialism-or-justice.

[7] J Hickel, *The Divide: A Brief Guide to Global Inequality and Its Solutions* (London, William Heinemann, 2017).

[8] Other chapters in this volume discuss the impact of war in Ukraine on the EU's environmental policies and on migration; see E Tla da Silva, ch 11; E Guild, K Groenendijk and D Lypalo, ch 8.

initiative; the Sustainable Corporate Governance initiative; and the Circular Economy initiative. Regulating finance, corporate governance and products – including product design – all hold the possibility for transforming business towards sustainability. Section 5.4 presents concluding reflections.

5.2. Sustainability in EU Treaty Law

5.2.1. Sustainability and Peace as More than the Absence of War

Peace is integral to sustainability, in terms of both absence of war and social justice that makes peace more than an absence of war and reduces the likelihood of war. Sustainability is an inextricably interconnected concept. It is not possible to achieve sustainability without including all elements, and any successes concerning individual elements risk being undermined if achieved in isolation. For example, achieved poverty reduction may be undermined by climate change and biodiversity loss.

The interdisciplinary analysis in this chapter positions sustainability as an EU law concept within a research-based understanding of sustainability. Sustainability is understood as a safe and just space for humanity: mitigating pressures on planetary boundaries and securing social foundations for humanity now and for the future.[9] The *safe space* metaphor is based on the planetary boundaries framework, which sets out and visualises different Earth system processes to inform the world about the space for sustainable action within these boundaries.[10] The work reflects the growing scientific understanding that life and its physical environment coevolve. The planetary boundaries framework brought together evidence of rising and interconnected global risks in several different contexts where environmental processes are being changed by human activities. It presents policy-makers with a dashboard of issues which arise from the collective impacts of humanity, impacts that are changing the fundamental dynamics of the Earth system upon which humans rely for our lives and livelihoods.[11]

Sustainability also encompasses 'questions of justice and inequality relating to global patterns of consumption and production, resource allocation, benefit distribution, and so on'[12] – in other words, securing a *just* space for humanity. The inclusion of 'just' in the 'safe and just space' draws on Kate Raworth's conceptualisation, which places crucial

[9] This section draws on current work with Sarah Cornell, including B Sjåfjell and S Cornell, 'What the Actual …? Tensions in the Science-Business-Policy Interface for Global Sustainability', European Law Open, 2024, 1–32. https://doi.org/10.1017/elo.2024.34.

[10] J Rockström et al, 'A Safe Operating Space for Humanity' (2009) 461 *Nature* 472, available at www.nature.com/articles/461472a; W Steffen et al, 'Planetary Boundaries: Guiding Human Development on a Changing Planet' (2015) 347 *Science* 1259855, available at science.sciencemag.org/content/347/6223/1259855; L Persson et al, 'Outside the Safe Operating Space of the Planetary Boundary for Novel Entities' (2022) 56 *Environmental Science & Technology* 1510; K Richardson et al, 'Earth beyond Six of Nine Planetary Boundaries' (2023) 9 *Science Advances* eadh2458, available at www.science.org/doi/10.1126/sciadv.adh2458.

[11] SE Cornell, 'Planetary Boundaries and Business: Putting the Operating into the Safe Operating Space for Humanity' (2016, University of Oslo), draft paper on file with current authors.

[12] LJ Kotzé and RE Kim, 'Earth System Law: The Juridical Dimensions of Earth System Governance' (2019) 1 *Earth System Governance* 100003, 7–8, available at www.sciencedirect.com/science/article/pii/S2589811619300023.

social goals within the planetary boundaries visualisation.[13] While planetary boundaries draws on Earth system sciences, the basis for conceptualising social foundations is the political consensus on which aspects were important in the adoption of the United Nations (UN) Sustainable Development Goals (SDGs).[14] As Raworth also emphasises, the minimum requirement intrinsic in securing the social foundation of humanity now and in the future is that of ensuring the realization of basic human rights.[15]

Figure 5.1 The safe and just space for humanity

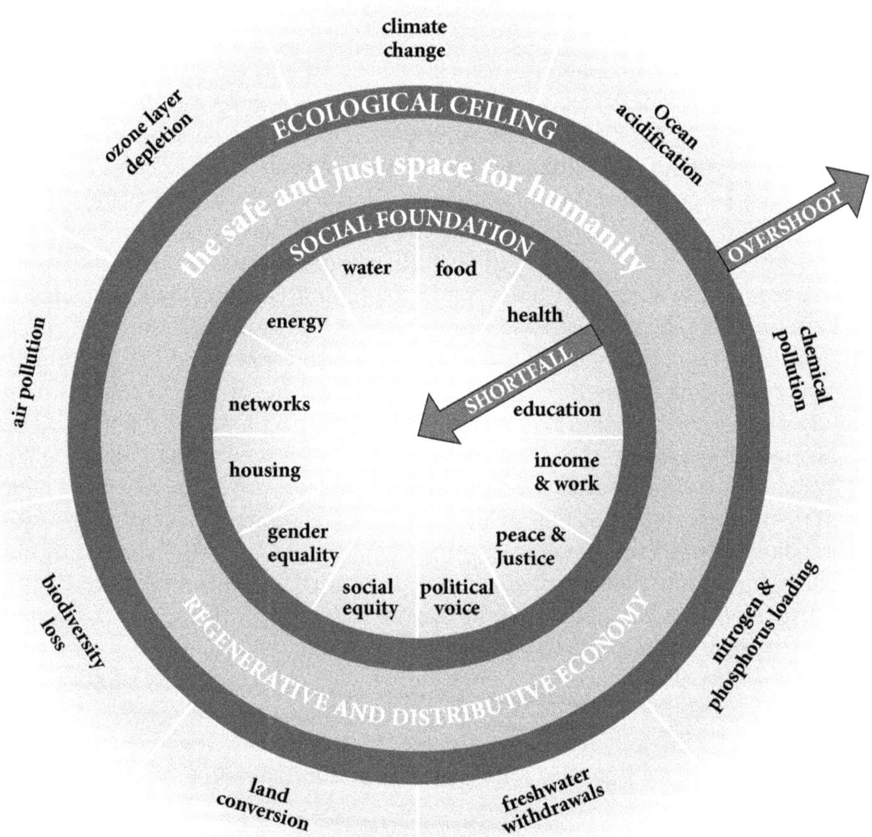

Source: Raworth 2017.[16]

[13] Sjåfjell and Cornell (n 9).

[14] United Nations General Assembly resolution 70/1, Transforming Our World: The 2030 Agenda for Sustainable Development, A/RES/70/1 (25 September 2015), available at www.undocs.org/A/RES/70/1; K Raworth, 'A Safe and Just Space for Humanity: Can We Live within the Doughnut' [2012] Oxfam Discussion Papers; M Leach, K Raworth and J Rockström, 'Between Social and Planetary Boundaries: Navigating Pathways in the Safe and Just Space for Humanity', World Social Science Report 2013 (Paris, OECD Publishing, 2013), available at steps-centre.org/blog/wssr.

[15] Raworth (n 14).

[16] K Raworth, *Doughnut Economics: Seven Ways to Think Like a 21st-Century Economist* (Chelsea, Vermont, USA, Chelsea Green Publishing, 2017).

5.2.2. Sustainability as an EU Treaty Objective, Principle and Rule

The EU's commitment to sustainability is anchored in the EU Treaties. Sustainability is an overarching objective of the EU and meant to be a guiding principle for its policies and activities within Europe, and in its relations with the rest of the world, to promote 'peace, its values and the wellbeing of its peoples'.[17] The internal founding values of the EU set out in the Treaty on the European Union (TEU) Article 3(3) and (5) are externalised in Article 21 TEU and reinforced in the EU's development cooperation with developing countries under Article 208 TFEU.

Article 11 of the Treaty on the Functioning of the European Union (TFEU) requires the implementation of environmental protection requirements in all EU policies with the aim of achieving sustainability.[18] A number of EU sources, including the values and aims expressed in Articles 2 and 3(5) TEU, the Charter of Fundamental Rights and the EU's own case law, provides further basis for the inclusion and promotion of fundamental human and social rights,[19] and Article 9 TFEU sets out the principle of social policy integration.[20] Policy coherence for development is set out as an EU legal norm in Article 208 TFEU, requiring that any area of EU law and policy must not work against developmental policies, also with the sustainability aim of 'leaving no-one behind'.[21]

Sustainability as an overarching EU Treaty law objective, principle and rule entails duties for the EU institutions,[22] and indirectly also obligations for the Member States.[23] The EU institutions' duty to promote the overarching objectives, interpreted in light of a research-based concept of sustainability, entails a duty to work towards sustainability, including promoting peace and mitigating the risks of war. Member States' obligation of loyalty and cooperation, Article 4(3) TEU, entails that Member States must ensure that they do not undermine the EU's promotion of EU Treaty objectives.[24] The loyalty of the

[17] TEU, Art 3(1), with the values set out in Art 2: 'respect for human dignity, freedom, democracy, equality, the rule of law and respect for human rights, including the rights of persons belonging to minorities'.

[18] J Nowag, *Environmental Integration in Competition and Free-Movement Laws* (Oxford, Oxford University Press, 2016); B Sjåfjell, 'The Environmental Integration Principle: A Necessary Step Towards Policy Coherence for Sustainability' in F Ippolito, ME Bartolino and M Condinanzi (eds), *The EU and the Proliferation of Integration Principles under the Lisbon Treaty* (Abingdon, Routledge, 2019), available at ssrn.com/abstract=3294910.

[19] For a discussion of the legal status of human rights protection after the Lisbon Treaty, which inter alia gives binding, primary law status to the Charter of Fundamental Rights, see S Douglas-Scott, 'The Court of Justice of the European Union and the European Court of Human Rights after the Treaty of Lisbon' in S Weatherill, S de Vries and U Bernitz (eds), *The Protection of Fundamental Rights in the EU after Lisbon* (London, Hart Publishing, 2013).

[20] Art 9 TFEU: 'In defining and implementing its policies and activities, the Union shall take into account requirements linked to the promotion of a high level of employment, the guarantee of adequate social protection, the fight against social exclusion, and a high level of education, training and protection of human health.'

[21] C Gammage, 'The EU's Evolving Commitment to Promoting Sustainability in its External Actions: Policy (In)Coherence for Development?' SMART working paper on file with current authors, University of Oslo (2020). See also UN General Assembly, General Assembly Resolution 70/1. Transforming Our World: the 2030 Agenda for Sustainable Development, A/RES/70/1 (25September 2015), available at www.undocs.org/A/RES/70/1.

[22] Sjåfjell (n 18). See also D Grimeaud, 'The integration of environmental concerns into EC policies: a genuine policy development?' (2000) 7 *European Energy and Environmental Law Review* 207; GM Durán and E Morgera, *Environmental Integration in the EU's External Relations: Beyond Multilateral Dimensions.* (London, Bloomsbury Publishing, 2012); J Solana, 'The Power of the Eurosystem to promote environmental protection' (2019) 30 *European Business Law Review* 547.

[23] Sjåfjell (n 18).

[24] J Temple Lang, 'Article 10 EC: The Most Important "General Principle" of Community Law' in U Bernitz, J Nergelius and C Cardner (eds), *General Principles of EC Law in a Process of Development* (Alphen aan den

Member States is owed to the EU Treaties and not to EU institutions or other Member States, in the sense that exceptionally EU Member States may be required to act where there is a clear scientific basis to do and where lack of action by the EU institutions poses risks to the EU's overarching objectives. And lack of action by one Member States cannot justify another Member State's inaction.[25]

Legal words on paper, including the EU Treaties, do not change anything if there is not a policy follow-up. The adoption of the UN SDGs in 2015,[26] together with the Paris Agreement on Climate Change in the same year,[27] have given a new impetus to the public discourse concerning EU laws and policies. The EU's commitment to implementing the SDGs is elaborated on in the European Commission's 2016 communication 'Next steps for a sustainable European future – European action for sustainability', and the EU's 2017 Consensus on Development.[28]

5.3. The EU's Sustainability Agenda: Business as Usual, Still?

This section analyses current policy developments in light of the above EU Treaty starting points.

5.3.1. Business as Usual, Sustainability and Peace

As Mark B Taylor shows in his analysis, war does not only involve state-funded armies and civil society caught between them. Elements of business are deeply implicated in war.[29] However, 'business as usual' has a broader significance for the undermining of peace and the risk of war, as a driver for the extreme unsustainabilities of our time. These unsustainabilities bring with them an increased risk of war, for historical reasons, currently, and for the future.

European prosperity is historically in part based on colonial exploitation, as Jason Hickel outlines.[30] Pressures on low-income countries to open up for foreign direct investments and facilitate global trade have contributed to making it difficult for these

Rijn, Kluwer Law International, 2008); see also M Klamert, 'Loyalty in the EU Treaties' in M Klamert (ed), *The Principle of Loyalty in EU Law* (Oxford, Oxford University Press, 2014), available at doi.org/10.1093/acprof:oso/9780199683123.003.0001.

[25] Temple Lang (n 24).

[26] General Assembly Resolution A/RES/70/1.

[27] The Paris Agreement, Paris, 12 December 2015, in force 4 November 2016, UN Doc FCCC/CP/2015/L.9/Rev/1.

[28] European Commission, 2019 EU Report on Policy Coherence for Development, SWD(2019) 20 Final, 28 January 2010. Joint Statement by the Council and the representatives of the governments of the Member States meeting within the Council, the European Parliament and the Commission, The new European Consensus on Development, Our World, Our Dignity, Our Future (2017/C 210/01), paras 9 and 10, available at op.europa.eu/s/n4Nh. The European Commission, *Next steps for a sustainable European future*, COM(2016) 739 final, 22 November 2016.

[29] MB Taylor, *War Economies and International Law: Regulating the Economic Activities of Violent Conflict* (Cambridge, Cambridge University Press, 2021), available at www.cambridge.org/core/books/war-economies-and-international-law/D941E61A6E84B557366EF216A5DD650E.

[30] J Hickel, *Less Is More* (Windmill Books, 2020), available at www.penguin.co.uk/books/441772/less-is-more-by-jason-hickel/9781786091215.

countries domestically to protect the environment and secure the welfare of their citizens.[31] European businesses and investors have seized opportunities to invest, expand and profit.[32] On an aggregate level, the harm for low-income countries may outweigh the benefits of creation of local jobs and transfer of technology. Through neocolonialism by multinational enterprises and their global value chains, people and communities are exploited, with human rights violations, land grabbing and pollution.[33] The destruction of local environment in low-income countries has direct negative effect for local population, and contributes to the continued transgression of planetary boundaries. Europe's improvements are to a great extent based on outsourcing of negative environmental impacts.[34] Business in aggregate is complicit in the interconnected undermining of economic and governance bases for well-functioning societies, through illicit financial flows and the use of tax havens.[35]

Continued destabilisation of the Earth system processes on which the relative safeness of this planet for humanity depends, will increase human suffering and may destabilise societies. Rising inequality within and between countries also undermines the possibility of stable peace. Business, and the regulation of business, are crucial if we are to be able to deal justly with the unsafe conditions of our time, and safely with the unjust ones.[36]

What will it take to transform business to business that is truly sustainable? Achieving such a transformation would not be the result of one initiative or reform. A whole jigsaw puzzle of sustainable business needs to be put into place, and a number of factors in the evolving regulatory framework have the potential to contribute to the necessary change. An important piece in this regulatory puzzle is the role of the board. Changing company law, the regulatory infrastructure for decision-making in this core legal form for doing business, can bring sustainability into the heart of corporate decision-making by reforming the duties of the board. The corporate board has a crucial role in determining the strategy and the direction of the corporation, and supervising how this plays out. Already in 2011, the Commission recognised that corporate boards have a 'vital part to play in the development of responsible companies'.[37]

Company law across jurisdictions gives corporate decision-makers room to make the decisions they see as best in the interests of the company, including shifting the

[31] ibid; J Dine, *Companies, International Trade and Human Rights* (Cambridge, Cambridge University Press, 2005), available at www.cambridge.org/core/books/companies-international-trade-and-human-rights/10D0BE5F31A38D34D55EBEC7633E27CA.

[32] Also Chinese and US businesses, for example, but the topic of this chapter is Europe.

[33] eg E Grant and O Das, 'Land Grabbing, Sustainable Development and Human Rights' (2015) 4 *Transnational Environmental Law* 289, available at www.cambridge.org/core/journals/transnational-environmental-law/article/land-grabbing-sustainable-development-and-human-rights/03793E858008583E95B419FD38DF4464.

[34] T Häyhä et al, 'Operationalizing the Concept of a Safe Operating Space at the EU Level – First Steps and Explorations' (Stockholm Resilience Centre, 2018) SRC Technical Report, available at www.stockholmresilience.org/publications/artiklar/2018-07-03-operationalizing-the-concept-of-a-safe-operating-space-at-the-eu-level---first-steps-and-explorations.html.

[35] Hickel (n 7); Global Witness, 'Out of Africa: British Tax Havens and Congo's Missing $1.5 Billion' (2016); V Galaz et al, 'Tax Havens and Global Environmental Degradation' (2018) 2 *Nature Ecology & Evolution* 1352, available at www.nature.com/articles/s41559-018-0497-3; Ziai (n 6) 381.

[36] Sjåfjell and Cornell (n 9).

[37] European Commission, Green paper. The EU corporate governance framework 2011, COM(2011) 164 final.

company onto a more sustainable path. However, this discretionary room is taken over by shareholder primacy, a social norm that dictates, contrary to company law, that boards are agents of shareholders and have a duty to maximise their returns. Shareholder primacy, which is a short form for the complex mix of perceived market signals and economic incentives, is a main barrier to more sustainable business.[38] Shareholder primacy is exacerbated in corporate groups and through contract-based global value chains.[39] Drawing on multijurisdictional comparative analyses, reforming company law rules on the key role of the corporate board is crucial to integrating sustainability into the governance of business.[40]

In previous work, I have, together with colleagues, suggested redefining corporate purpose and duties of the board (and by extension senior management), with research-based concepts of creating sustainable value and contributing to mitigating pressures on planetary boundaries as key elements.[41] Proposed duties of the board include sustainability assessment and due diligence across global value chains, with open, inclusive and participatory processes in affected communities.[42] In current work-in-progress, Sarah Cornell and I develop sustainable value creation as a dynamic, process-oriented concept, where economic value is created for business and for society in ways that are sustainable. This entails contributing to ensuring the resilience of the planetary ecosystems of which humanity is part, including by recognising the existence and complexity of ecological limits. It entails seeking to respond adaptively to changing hazards and working to mitigate pressures on planetary boundaries, as far as relevant and possible, depending on the sector, the size of the business and the possibilities for coordinated efforts. It also requires contributing to securing social foundations, including the achievement of human rights and other basic rights, and good governance locally, nationally, regionally

[38] CM Bruner and B Sjåfjell, 'Corporate Law, Corporate Governance and the Pursuit of Sustainability' in B Sjåfjell and CM Bruner (eds), *The Cambridge Handbook of Corporate Law, Corporate Governance and Sustainability* (Cambridge, Cambridge University Press, 2019), available at www.cambridge.org/core/product/identifier/9781108658386%23CN-bp-50/type/book_part; B Sjåfjell et al, 'Shareholder Primacy: The Main Barrier to Sustainable Companies' in B Sjåfjell and BJ Richardson (eds), *Company Law and Sustainability: Legal Barriers and Opportunities* (Cambridge, Cambridge University Press, 2015), available at ssrn.com/abstract=2664544; LA Stout, *The Shareholder Value Myth: How Putting Shareholders First Harms Investors, Corporations, and the Public* (Berrett-Koehler Publishers, 2012).

[39] L Anker-Sørensen, *Corporate Groups and Shadow Business Practices* (Cambridge, Cambridge University Press, 2022); J Salminen and M Rajavuori, 'Transnational Sustainability Laws and the Regulation of Global Value Chains: Comparison and a Framework for Analysis' (2019) 5 *Maastricht Journal of European and Comparative Law* 1023263X19871025, available at doi.org/10.1177/1023263X19871025.

[40] See eg B Sjåfjell, 'Realising the Potential of the Board for Corporate Sustainability' in B Sjåfjell and CM Bruner (n 38); Sjåfjell et al (n 38). See also LA Stout et al, 'The Modern Corporation Statement on Company Law' (Social Science Research Network 2016), available at ssrn.com/abstract=2848833; A Johnston et al, 'Corporate Governance for Sustainability' (Social Science Research Network, 2019) available at ssrn.com/abstract=3502101; CM Bruner, *The Corporation as Technology: Re-Calibrating Corporate Governance for a Sustainable Future* (Oxford, Oxford University Press, 2022); University of Cambridge Institute and for Sustainability Leadership, 'Future of Boards. Final Report: Summary and Synthesis (Phase 1, Part 4)' (2023).

[41] eg B Sjåfjell, 'A General Corporate Law Duty to Act Sustainably' in HS Birkmose, M Neville and K Engsig Sørensen (eds), *Instruments of EU Corporate Governance: Effecting Changes in the Management of Companies in a Changing World* (Alphen aan den Rijn, Kluwer Law International, 2023), available at ssrn.com/abstract=4224255.

[42] ibid; C Bright and K Buhmann, 'Risk-Based Due Diligence, Climate Change, Human Rights and the Just Transition' (2021) 13 *Sustainability* 10454, available at www.mdpi.com/2071–1050/13/18/10454.

and internationally.[43] Sustainable value creation entails moving away from linear, unsustainable business models towards more sustainable, more circular models.[44]

5.3.2. The EU's Sustainable Business Initiatives

Are the EU's efforts at regulating business for sustainability sufficient? Regulating business for sustainability has been high on the EU's agenda since 2018,[45] when the European Commission adopted its Action Plan on Financing Sustainable Growth, launching the EU's Sustainable Finance initiative.[46] The current Commission's flagship programme, the European Green Deal (2019),[47] emphasises its prioritisation of sustainability, with a 'just transition' that leaves 'nobody behind', refocusing the coordination of economic policies across the EU to integrate sustainability.[48] Executive Vice-President Frans Timmermans underlined at the time the need for an 'ambitious Green New Deal for Europe, which shapes the future for our children and ensures their health, prosperity and security on a green and thriving planet'.[49]

5.3.2.1. Finance for Sustainability – Or the 'Greening' of Finance as Usual?

The Sustainable Finance initiative demonstrates how quickly and decisively the EU legislator can act when it is perceived as important and urgent, with adoption of the first two regulations (the strongest form of secondary legislation, directly applicable in Member States) in 2019 and 2020. The aims of the Sustainable Finance initiative are to 'reorient capital flows towards sustainable investment in order to achieve sustainable

[43] Sjåfjell and Cornell (n 9), section 3(B).

[44] F Lüdeke-Freund et al, 'Sustainable Value Creation Through Business Models: The What, the Who and the How' (2020) 8 *Journal of Business Models* 62, available at journals.aau.dk/index.php/JOBM/article/view/6510; E Maitre-Ekern, 'Re-Thinking Producer Responsibility for a Sustainable Circular Economy from Extended Producer Responsibility to Pre-Market Producer Responsibility' (2021) 286 *Journal of Cleaner Production* 125454, available at www.sciencedirect.com/science/article/pii/S0959652620355001; D Monciardini et al, 'Circular Economy Regulation: An Emerging Research Agenda' in A Alexander, S Pascucci and F Charnley (eds), *Handbook of the Circular Economy: Transitions and Transformation* (Berlin, De Gruyter, 2023), available at www.degruyter.com/document/doi/10.1515/9783110723373-016/html.

[45] The paradigm shift in the Commission's approach to corporate social responsibility (CSR) predates this European Commission, 'A Renewed EU Strategy 2011-14 for Corporate Social Responsibility' (2011) COM/2011/0681 final. However, the revival of the now rather concept of CSR did not place sustainable business high on the EU's agenda.

[46] European Commission, 'Communication from the Commission to the European Parliament, the European Council, the Council, the European Economic and Social Committee and the Committee of the Regions. Action Plan on Financing Sustainable Growth' (2018)COM/2018/097 final, available at ec.europa.eu/info/publications/180308-action-plan-sustainable-growth_en.

[47] European Commission, 'Communication from the Commission to the European Parliament, the European Council, the Council, the European Economic and Social Committee and the Committee of the Regions. The European Green Deal. COM/2019/640 Final' (2019), available at eur-lex.europa.eu/legal-content/EN/TXT/?qid=1576150542719&uri=COM%3A2019%3A640%3AFIN.

[48] With reference to the UN SDGs, see U von der Leyen, 'A Union that strives for more. Political guidelines for the next European Commission 2019–2024' (16 July 20190, available at op.europa.eu/s/n4FS.

[49] European Commission (n 47). Quote from F Simon and S Morgan, 'Green Deal branded as 'hallmark' of new European Commission' *Euractiv* (11 September 2019), available at www.euractiv.com/section/energy-environment/news/green-deal-branded-as-hallmark-of-new-european-commission.

and inclusive growth'; 'manage financial risks stemming from climate change, resource depletion, environmental degradation and social issues'; and 'foster transparency and long-termism in financial and economic activity'.[50]

Informing the urgency and shaping the legislation is, above all, the emerging recognition of the financial risks of climate change. Sparking international and European discussion of how to deal with these financial risks were the recommendations presented by the Task Force on Climate-Related Financial Disclosures (TCFD) in 2017.[51] The TCFD was established by the Financial Stability Board, an international body endorsed by the G20 (a group of the world's major economies).[52] When analysed from a research-based sustainability perspective, the TCFD recommendations have shortcomings, beyond the obvious point that the report concentrates only on climate change. The TCFD's approach to physical risks is limited, and human and societal impacts are not included in its risk categories.[53]

Financial and corporate actors' recognition of the financial risks of climate change has recently been broadened to financial risks of biodiversity loss. The Task Force for Nature-Related Financial Disclosures (TNFD) presented the first version of recommendations in 2023, aiming for 'integrated approach to climate- and nature-related risks, scaling up finance for nature-based solutions'.[54] Critical voices have highlighted corporate capture of the process and the concurrent risk of continued greenwashing,[55] seeing the work as being 'shrouded in secrecy'.[56]

The lack of inclusion of human and societal impacts, and the pick-and-choose approach to environmental issues, is not in line with a research-based approach to sustainability. Yet, that is what is reflected in the EU's Sustainable Finance initiative, although the legislative initiatives under the Sustainable Finance initiative do take a somewhat broader approach. The strong emphasis on the financial business case for change constrains the EU's legislative initiatives in finance, and – as we will see below – more broadly in business law. The direct influence of the recommendations is traceable in the international and European reporting standards.[57]

[50] European Commission (n 46), section 1.

[51] TCFD, 'Final Report: Recommendations of the Task Force on Climate-Related Financial Disclosures' (2017), available at assets.bbhub.io/company/sites/60/2021/10/FINAL-2017-TCFD-Report.pdf.

[52] See www.fsb.org/about/history-of-the-fsb.

[53] B Sjåfjell, 'Taking Finance Seriously: Understanding the Financial Risks of Unsustainability' in K Alexander, M Gargantini and M Siri (eds), *The Cambridge Handbook of EU Sustainable Finance: Regulation, Supervision and Governance* (Cambridge, Cambridge University Press, in print 2024), preprint available at ssrn.com/abstract=4294693.

[54] TNFD, 'Taskforce on Nature-Related Financial Disclosures' Principle 6, available at tnfd.global.

[55] H Greep, 'Latest Draft Shows That TNFD's Reputation "as the next Frontier in Corporate Greenwashing on Nature" Remains Solidly Intact' *Banktrack* (7 November 2022), available at www.banktrack.org/article/latest_draft_shows_that_tnfd_s_reputation_as_the_next_frontier_in_corporate_greenwashing_on_nature_remains_solidly_intact.

[56] T Feitosa et al, 'Joint Open Letter to the TNFD: Your Work Is Undermining the Real Solutions to the Nature Crisis' Forests & Finance coalition (2023), available at forestsandfinance.org/wp-content/uploads/2023/08/Joint-CSO-letter-to-the-TNFD.pdf.

[57] The International Sustainability Standards Board has taken over the follow-up of the TCFD from 2024; IFRS, 'IFRS Foundation Welcomes Culmination of TCFD Work and Transfer of TCFD Monitoring Responsibilities to ISSB from 2024' (2023), available at www.ifrs.org/news-and-events/news/2023/07/foundation-welcomes-tcfd-responsibilities-from-2024. In the EU context, see, eg, EFRAG's conversion table between TCFD recommendations and draft European Sustainability Reporting Standards: www.efrag.org/Assets/Download?assetUrl=%2Fsites%2Fwebpublishing%2FSiteAssets%2FED_ESRS_AP4.pdf.

Much of the EU's legislative initiatives in this area are based on a belief in disclosure. With the Sustainable Finance Disclosure Regulation (2019), the Taxonomy Regulation (2020), the Corporate Sustainability Reporting Directive (2022) and its European Sustainability Reporting Standards (2023), the field of disclosure has taken a definitive step away from disclosure as voluntary wishy-washy. It is being firmed up and taken more seriously by financial and corporate actors. Yet, disclosure has its limitations, and does not mandate change.[58]

The approach to sustainability varies across the legislative initiatives. The Taxonomy Regulation, a classification system for economic activities to be characterised as environmentally sustainable, is 'a cornerstone of the EU's sustainable finance framework'.[59] To qualify as 'sustainable', according to the Taxonomy, the economic activity must contribute to at least one of six environmental objectives, and 'do no significant harm' to the others. The Taxonomy's concept of 'sustainable' is thereby limited to the mentioned six environmental objectives, two of them concerning climate.[60]

Social issues are included as 'minimum safeguards', requiring 'alignment' with the UN Guiding Principles on Business and Human Rights (UNGPs) and the OECD Guidelines for Multinational Enterprises for Responsible Business Conduct (OECD Guidelines), and international human rights and labour law instruments:

> The minimum safeguards … shall be procedures implemented by an undertaking that is carrying out an economic activity to ensure the alignment with the OECD Guidelines for Multinational Enterprises and the UN Guiding Principles on Business and Human Rights, including the principles and rights set out in the eight fundamental conventions identified in the Declaration of the International Labour Organisation on Fundamental Principles and Rights at Work and the International Bill of Human Rights.[61]

The Delegated Acts under the Taxonomy, gradually spelling out the six environmental objectives, do not go into the minimum safeguards.[62] A report from the Platform on Sustainable Finance,[63] advising on the application of the minimum safeguards, proposes several flags for non-alignment with the minimum safeguards: 'inadequate or non-existent corporate due diligence processes on human rights, including labour rights, bribery, taxation, and fair competition'; established 'liability of companies in respect for

[58] A Johnston and B Sjåfjell, 'The EU's Approach to Environmentally Sustainable Business: Can Disclosure Overcome the Failings of Shareholder Primacy?' in M Peters and M Eliantonio (eds), *Research Handbook on EU Environmental Law* (Cheltenham, UK and Northampton, MA, USA, Edward Elgar Publishing, 2020), available at www.elgaronline.com/view/edcoll/9781788970662/9781788970662.00036.xml.

[59] European Commission, 'EU Taxonomy for Sustainable Activities', available at finance.ec.europa.eu/sustainable-finance/tools-and-standards/eu-taxonomy-sustainable-activities_en.

[60] The other four concern 'water and marine resources', 'circular economy', 'pollution prevention and control' and 'protection and restoration of biodiversity and ecosystems': Art 3c of the Taxonomy.

[61] To qualify as an environmentally sustainable activity, the economic activity must be carried out 'carried out in compliance with the minimum safeguards': Arts 18, 3c of the Taxonomy.

[62] S Andreasen Lysgaard and J Grimheden, 'The EU Sustainable Finance Agenda: A Strengthened Case for Human Rights in Times of COVID-19' in G Oberleitner et al (eds), *European Yearbook on Human Rights 2021* (Cambridge, Intersentia, 2021) 198, available at www.cambridge.org/core/books/european-yearbook-on-human-rights-2021/eu-sustainable-finance-agenda-a-strengthened-case-for-human-rights-in-times-of-covid19/E75CA55057DF021A6AA00638F2F3AB9D.

[63] The Platform on Sustainable Finance is an advisory body established under Art 20 of the Taxonomy Regulation; see https://finance.ec.europa.eu/sustainable-finance/overview-sustainable-finance/platform-sustainable-finance_en#who.

breaches of any of these topics'; 'lack of collaboration with a National Contact Point' (under the OECD Guidelines) or 'an assessment of noncompliance with OECD guidelines', as well as a lack of response to 'allegations by the Business and Human Rights Resource Centre' (under the UNGPs).[64]

If followed up properly in practice – and that is indeed very uncertain – the 'minimum safeguards' requirements have the potential to reinforce these international norm sets.[65] However, it is a rather roundabout and very uncertain way of promoting social aspects of sustainability. The proposal for a social taxonomy to complement the environmentally focused Taxonomy Regulation has not been followed up since the Platform on Sustainable Finance presented its report in 2022.[66] There seems to be no interest in the Commission to move forward with such an idea.[67] That social issues are seen as being adequately dealt with by existing reporting rules[68] reflects the limited significance given to humans and society in the EU's Sustainable Finance initiative. This is insufficient in light of a research-based understanding of sustainability.[69]

5.3.2.2. Sustainable Business – Or Business as Usual?

EU company law, with secondary legislation developed since 1968, has never properly engaged with sustainability. EU company law case law has mainly concerned freedom of establishment and free movement of capital.[70] After the Commission's redefinition of corporate social responsibility in 2011 as 'the responsibility of enterprises for their impacts on society',[71] there was no action plan for sustainable business comparable to the action plan under the Sustainable Finance initiative (discussed above) or the Circular Economy initiative (see below). One outcome was the adoption of the so-called Non-Financial Reporting Directive, which was adopted in 2014 and reinvigorated a discussion on sustainability reporting. However, the 2014 Directive gave far

[64] Platform on Sustainable Finance, 'Final Report on Minimum Safeguards' (2022) 4–5.

[65] These are also referenced in the Sustainable Finance Disclosure Regulation, the Corporate Sustainability Reporting Directive, and the European Sustainability Reporting Standards.

[66] Platform on Sustainable Finance, 'Final Report on Social Taxonomy' (2022), available at commission.europa.eu/document/d07e1f1e-3a1f-4d55-add4-a130f26b33e3_en.

[67] Although some Member States and some investor groups hope that such rules will be possible in the future; G McNally and F Gambetta, 'French and German Investor Groups Continuing Work on Social Taxonomy' *Responsible Investor* (20 July 2023), available at www.responsible-investor.com/french-and-german-investor-groups-continuing-work-on-social-taxonomy; L Serenelli, 'Investors Call on European Commission to Outline Clear Social Impact Investment Rules' *IPE* (18 October 2023), available at www.ipe.com/news/investors-call-on-european-commission-to-outline-clear-social-impact-investment-rules/10069524.article.

[68] McNally and Gambetta (n 67), referring to statements by Martin Spolc, Head of Unit on sustainable finance in the Commission.

[69] eg H Ahlström and B Sjåfjell, 'Complexity and Uncertainty in Sustainable Finance: An Analysis of the EU Taxonomy' in T Cadman and T Sarker (eds), *De Gruyter Handbook of Sustainable Development and Finance* (Berlin, De Gruyter, 2022), available at doi.org/10.1515/9783110733488-002.

[70] S Grundmann and F Glasgow, *European Company Law: Organization, Finance and Capital Markets*, vol 1, 2nd edn (Cambridge, Intersentia, 2012).

[71] European Commission (n 45). This was a paradigm shift in comparison to the 2022 definition (more or less verbatim from Business Europe's input): 'CSR is a concept whereby companies integrate social and environmental concerns in their business operations and in their interaction with their stakeholders on a voluntary basis', European Commission, Communication from the Commission concerning Corporate Social Responsibility: A business contribution to Sustainable Development 2002 COM/2002/0347 final.

too much discretion to Member States and to businesses for these reporting rules to be able to have significant impact.[72] As a part of the Sustainable Finance initiative the Corporate Sustainability Reporting Directive was adopted in 2022, and the first set of European Sustainability Reporting Standards in 2023. As we saw above, the belief in disclosure remains strong. It is a compromise solution between those who do not wish to have rules that mandate change and those that promote such change. So far, requiring sustainability information has not been sufficient to close the gap between what boards and, by extension, senior executive management perceive as their duty (maximise returns for investors) and the sustainability aims intended promoted.[73]

The Sustainable Finance initiative did, however, also open up for regulating the corporate board, 'to promote corporate governance that is more conducive to sustainable investments'.[74] This made possible the Sustainable Corporate Governance initiative in 2020, which set out the aim of regulating company law and corporate governance for sustainability:

> This initiative aims to improve the EU regulatory framework on company law and corporate governance. It would enable companies to focus on long-term sustainable value creation rather than short-term benefits. It aims to better align the interests of companies, their shareholders, managers, stakeholders and society. It would help companies to better manage sustainability-related matters in their own operations and value chains as regards social and human rights, climate change, environment, etc.[75]

The Sustainable Corporate Governance initiative was in line with the increasing calls from academia to move beyond the reflexive theory ideas of disclosure, and integrate sustainability fully into corporate decision-making.[76] However, the launch of the initiative met extreme push-back, mainly by shareholder primacy proponents.[77] The Commission's proposal for a Directive under the Sustainable Corporate Governance initiative was stopped twice by the Regulatory Scrutiny Board, which had allowed itself

[72] Even measured by the number of companies that reported (without checking the reliability or relevance), the results were negative; see eg, Alliance for Corporate Transparency, 'The Alliance for Corporate Transparency Research Report 2019: An Analysis of the Sustainability Reports of 1000 Companies Pursuant to the EU Non-Financial Reporting Directive' (2019), available at www.allianceforcorporatetransparency.org/assets/2019_Research_Report%20_Alliance_for_Corporate_Transparency.pdf.

[73] D Monciardini, J Mähönen and G Tsagas, 'Rethinking Non-Financial Reporting: A Blueprint for Structural Regulatory Changes' (2020) 10 *Accounting, Economics, and Law: A Convivium*, available at www.degruyter.com/document/doi/10.1515/ael-2020–0092/html; J Mähönen, 'Comprehensive Approach to Relevant and Reliable Reporting in Europe: A Dream Impossible?' (2020) 12 *Sustainability* 5277, available at www.mdpi.com/2071–1050/12/13/5277.

[74] To assess '(i) the possible need to require corporate boards to develop and disclose a sustainability strategy, including appropriate due diligence throughout the supply chain, and measurable sustainability targets; and (ii) the possible need to clarify the rules according to which directors are expected to act in the company's long-term interest'; European Commission (n 46), Action Point 10(1).

[75] European Commission, 'Sustainable Corporate Governance Initiative' (2020), available at ec.europa.eu/info/law/better-regulation/have-your-say/initiatives/12548-Sustainable-corporate-governance_en.

[76] The calls from academics included research-based reform proposals from the Horizon 2020 funded research project Sustainable Market Actors for Responsible Trade (SMART, 2016–20); B Sjåfjell et al, 'Securing the Future of European Business: SMART Reform Proposals' (2020) SMART report; University of Oslo Faculty of Law Research Paper available at SSRN: https://ssrn.com/abstract=3595048.

[77] For an analysis of the debate, see B Sjåfjell and J Mähönen, 'Corporate Purpose and the Misleading Shareholder vs Stakeholder Dichotomy' (2024) 34 *Bond Law Review* 69, available at blr.scholasticahq.com/article/94050-corporate-purpose-and-the-misleading-shareholder-vs-stakeholder-dichotomy.

to be lobbied by business to the extent that the European Ombudsman later opened up an inquiry.[78]

The proposal that the Commission finally adopted in February 2022 was for a Corporate Sustainability Due Diligence Directive.[79] Such a proposal, concentrating on the due diligence element, had the support of the European Parliament,[80] which may be seen as informed by the UNGPs and the OECD Guidelines (including the OECD Guidance for Due Diligence). The proposal is very much on the defensive, with 'corporate sustainability' left undefined but in practice limited to those elements that can be traced back to international environmental and human rights legal instruments. It included a limited and flawed attempt at integrating sustainability issues into the role of the corporate board, but in the legislative negotiations concluded in December 2023, even this limited inclusion of core company law issues was taken out.[81]

In the first months of 2024, some Member States worked to undermine the political consensus achieved between the Parliament and the Council in December 2023. Despite civil society, academics and businesses themselves rallying around the Directive,[82] its fate seemed increasingly uncertain. The Council vote was postponed at least twice while the Belgian presidency sought to get an agreement into place. The result was a further weakening of the already reduced Directive.[83] Finally, on 15 March 2024, the Council agreed to adopt the Directive.[84] At the time of writing, the remaining hurdle now is for the European Parliament to adopt the Directive. Considering the Parliament's support in the process, this is expected to pass.

Despite its reduced scope and its weaknesses, getting the Corporate Sustainability Due Diligence Directive into place is significant. Corporate sustainability due diligence is a key tool for a corporate board. However, setting out due diligence rules without a

[78] European Ombudsman, 'The Composition of the European Commission's Regulatory Scrutiny Board and How It Interacts with Interest Representatives: Case Opened' (2023), available at www.ombudsman.europa.eu/en/opening-summary/en/168093.

[79] European Commission, 'Proposal for a Directive of the European Parliament and of the Council on Corporate Sustainability Due Diligence and Amending Directive (EU) 2019/1937' (2022), available at ec.europa.eu/info/publications/proposal-directive-corporate-sustainable-due-diligence-and-annex_en.

[80] European Parliament, 'MEPs: Companies Must No Longer Cause Harm to People and Planet with Impunity' (10 March 2021), available at www.europarl.europa.eu/news/en/press-room/20210304IPR99216/meps-companies-must-no-longer-cause-harm-to-people-and-planet-with-impunity.

[81] European Parliament, 'Corporate Due Diligence Rules Agreed to Safeguard Human Rights and Environment' (14 December 2023), available at www.europarl.europa.eu/news/en/press-room/20231205IPR15689/corporate-due-diligence-rules-agreed-to-safeguard-human-rights-and-environment.

[82] eg Business & Human Rights Resource Centre, 'Businesses Make Urgent Call for Support for EU Due Diligence Law Ahead of Council Vote' (27 February 2024), available at www.business-humanrights.org/en/latest-news/eu-csddd-company-statement; 'Joint Statement by UNDP, UNEP, UNICEF and OHCHR on the EU Corporate Sustainability Due Diligence Directive', available at www.unicef.org/eu/press-releases/joint-statement-undp-unep-unicef-and-ohchr-eu-corporate-sustainability-due-diligence.

[83] J Schickler, 'Exclusive: Governments Mull Stripped-down Sustainability Law' *euronews* (6 March 2024), available at www.euronews.com/my-europe/2024/03/06/exclusive-governments-mull-last-chance-bid-for-stripped-down-corporate-diligence-law; A Brunetti, 'Scope of EU Supply Chain Rules Cut by 70% Ahead of Key Friday Vote' *Euractiv* (11 March 2024), available at www.euractiv.com/section/economic-governance/news/scope-of-eu-supply-chain-rules-cut-by-70-ahead-of-key-friday-vote.

[84] M Segal, 'EU Council Approves Scaled-Back Environmental, Human Rights Sustainability Due Diligence Law' (15 March 2024) *ESG Today*, available at www.esgtoday.com/eu-council-approves-scaled-back-environmental-human-rights-sustainability-due-diligence-law.

corresponding duty for the board to ensure that the company's value creation is sustainable is insufficient for the transformation of business towards sustainability.[85]

Also, without company law reform, the evolving regulatory framework as a whole is changing gradually the role of the corporate board. But it is not doing that in a way that provides a level playing field for sustainability-oriented businesses, or that gives legal certainty to corporate decision-makers. They will continue to receive conflicting signals in the clash of norms; with the pressure, still, to maximise returns to investors according to the social norm of shareholder primacy; and the increasing pressure to be more sustainable in line with the evolving regulatory framework. A line of case law will be needed to reinforce sustainable corporate governance as the norm, which is a costly way of regulating and brings great uncertainty for all involved.[86] The current regulatory framework does not give legal certainty and the protection needed for those impacted by business as usual.

5.3.2.3. A More Resource-efficient, Green Circular Economy – And Somewhat Sustainable Products?

The EU's Circular Economy initiative is ambitious, with its Circular Economy Action Plan of 2020 aiming for 'sustainable products' as the norm.[87] The relative success of the Ecodesign Directive, giving Europeans more energy-efficient refrigerators and washing machines, has informed the Ecodesign for Sustainable Products Regulation.[88] Integrating sustainability into product design has a great potential to transform corporate decision-making in the real economy. Yet, social issues were not included in the proposal for the Ecodesign Regulation, referring to the then forthcoming Corporate Sustainability Due Diligence Directive as the place for social issues. In the adopted Regulation, the inclusion of social issues are pushed to a much later date, with the Commission to 'evaluate the potential benefits of the inclusion of social sustainability requirements' by 2028.[89]

[85] C Villiers, 'Global Supply Chains and Sustainability: The Role of Disclosure and Due Diligence Regulation' in B Sjåfjell and C M Bruner (eds), *The Cambridge Handbook of Corporate Law, Corporate Governance and Sustainability* (Cambridge, Cambridge University Press, 2019), available at www.cambridge.org/core/books/cambridge-handbook-of-corporate-law-corporate-governance-and-sustainability/global-supply-chains-and-sustainability/C5850FB1C813881C414670BE2BCB87A1; S Deva, 'Mandatory Human Rights Due Diligence Laws in Europe: A Mirage for Rightsholders?' (2023) *36 Leiden Journal of International Law* 389, available at www.cambridge.org/core/journals/leiden-journal-of-international-law/article/mandatory-human-rights-due-diligence-laws-in-europe-a-mirage-for-rightsholders/A826E647F5996B9D9EA331D0258129BB; S Deva and P Anand, 'A Global South Perspective on Labour Rights and Supply Chains for a Post-Growth World' (8 August 2023), available at ssrn.com/abstract=4534701; Sjåfjell (n 41).

[86] European Coalition for Corporate Justice, 'Suing Goliath: An Analysis of Civil Cases against EU Companies for Overseas Human Rights and Environmental Abuses' (2021), available at corporatejustice.org/publications/suing-goliath.

[87] European Commission, 'Communication from the Commission to the European Parliament, the Council, the European Economic and Social Committee and the Committee of the Regions. A New Circular Economy Action Plan For a Cleaner and More Competitive Europe' (2020)COM/2020/98 final, available at eur-lex.europa.eu/legal-content/EN/TXT/?qid=1583933814386&uri=COM:2020:98:FIN.

[88] Regulation (EU) 2024/1781 of the European Parliament and of the Council of 13 June 2024 establishing a framework for the setting of ecodesign requirements for sustainable products, amending Directive (EU) 2020/1828 and Regulation (EU) 2023/1542 and repealing Directive 2009/125/EC (Text with EEA relevance), available at data.europa.eu/eli/reg/2024/1781/oj/eng.

[89] ibid, Art 75(4).

The Ecodesign Regulation is to be followed up through sector-specific Delegated Acts, and textiles are a priority sector for the Commission.[90] The overproduction and overconsumption of 'fast fashion' are based on extreme environmental degradation and horrendous exploitation of workers across global value chains.[91] The Ecodesign Regulation does not deal with the latter, which is symptomatic of a deeper problem with the Circular Economy initiative. The emphasis in Circular Economy policy statements is often on how many jobs it will create. But to facilitate the transformation to sustainability, policy-makers must also deal with the job losses; not only in the EU, but, as is the case in the textile sector, across global value chains. The result of the Ecodesign Regulation cannot be simply to take away jobs from workers in the textile industry to green the economy and increase resource-efficiency. There has to be a process where the EU recognises its historic and current responsibility and follows up in a policy coherent manner.

Amongst the sector-specific product regulations already adopted, the Deforestation Regulation is an interesting example in our context. It prohibits access to markets for products that are not 'deforestation-free', mandates compliance with domestic legislation, and requires due diligence as a tool to ensure observance of the Regulation. Comparing this to the difficult process towards the Corporate Sustainability Due Diligence Directive raises questions of how it was possible to ensure adoption of this Regulation. One reason is probably that product-specific rules are easier to agree on, while broader conduct rules for companies on corporate sustainability due diligence, are perceived as more threatening. Further, with the EU being one of the world's largest 'importers of deforestation',[92] combating deforestation is key to reducing greenhouse gas emissions in line with the EU's Green Deal and the EU's internal and international obligations.[93] The deforestation that the Regulation in practice targets is mainly outside of the EU, which probably informed its adoption in the EU and is reflected in the protests against the Regulation in a number of former colonies of European countries, such as Malaysia and Indonesia.[94] Amongst the issues are concerns for smallholders who, while they may be working in sustainable and deforestation-free ways, do not have the capacity to substantiate this.[95] The controversy concerning these issues, as well as push-back

[90] European Commission, 'Circular Economy for Textiles: Taking Responsibility to Reduce, Reuse and Recycle Textile Waste and Boosting Markets for Used Textiles' (3 July 2023), available at ec.europa.eu/commission/presscorner/detail/en/ip_23_3635.

[91] S Butler and T Begum, 'Abuses "Still Rife": 10 Years on from Bangladesh's Rana Plaza Disaster' *The Guardian* (24 April 2023), available at www.theguardian.com/world/2023/apr/24/10-years-on-bangladesh-rana-plaza-disaster-safety-garment-workers-rights-pay; C Palm, SE Cornell and T Häyhä, 'Making Resilient Decisions for Sustainable Circularity of Fashion' (2021) 1 *Circular Economy and Sustainability* 651, available at link.springer.com/10.1007/s43615-021-00040-1.

[92] 'The EU is essentially the second-largest importer of deforestation in the world, second only to China, which has a much larger population', according to Michael Rice, Value Chains, Trade & Investment Lead at ClientEarth; N Oelsner and M Lecoq, 'Are Concerns about the EU's New Regulation on Deforestation Justified?' *euronews* (27 February 2024), available at www.euronews.com/green/2024/02/27/supply-chain-disruptions-are-concerns-about-the-eus-new-deforestation-regulation-justified.

[93] Regulation (EU) 2023/1115 of the European Parliament and of the Council of 31 May 2023 on the making available on the Union market and the export from the Union of certain commodities and products associated with deforestation and forest degradation and repealing Regulation (EU) No 995/2010 (Text with EEA relevance) 2023 (OJ L), Recital 13.

[94] MM Chu, 'EU Deforestation Law Risks Sidelining Small Farmers, Says Palm Oil Watchdog' Reuters (7 February 2023), available at www.reuters.com/business/environment/eu-deforestation-law-risks-sidelining-small-farmers-says-palm-oil-watchdog-2023-02-07; Oelsner and Lecoq (n 93).

[95] Chu (n 95); 'Malaysia Palm Oil, Rubber Farmers File EU Petition Opposing Deforestation Law' Reuters (15 March 2023), available at www.reuters.com/markets/commodities/malaysia-palm-oil-rubber-farmers-file-eu-petition-contesting-deforestation-law-2023-03-15.

from alleged pro-business groups, has led to much debate in the second half of 2024. The result at the time of writing is that the application date (which was December 2024) is postponed by 12 months, and proposed amendments are under discussion.[96]

There are also new product-specific legislative initiatives concerning social aspects. On 19 November 2024, the Council undertook the final adoption of the Forced Labour Regulation,[97] prohibiting access to market for product made by forced labour. This is a less strong compared to the Deforestation Regulation. The Forced Labour Regulation explicitly sets out that it does not impose new due diligence requirements,[98] reflecting, undoubtedly, the controversy concerning the Corporate Sustainability Due Diligence Directive. The Forced Labour Regulation's risk-based approach, to be followed up by the Commission and national competent authorities,[99] is a far cry from requiring that European companies ensure that workers across their global value chains are treated properly and fairly. Together with the lack of inclusion of social aspects in the Ecodesign Regulation (seen in light also of the resistance against the Corporate Sustainability Due Diligence Directive) the legislative developments indicate that humans, especially those outside of the EU, are not highly prioritised.

A Circular Economy initiative that does not fully engage with social justice is one that at best can make the European economy more resource-efficient in some shade of green.[100] It is not one that contributes to the fundamental transformation of business that is needed, in spite of the 2020 Circular Economy Action Plan's statement that the 'transition to the circular economy will be systemic, deep and transformative'.[101] Considering European countries historical responsibility for colonisation and the EU's current facilitation of the neo-colonisation by business, the EU has a responsibility to go beyond 'greening' at the cost of other countries' and communities' welfare. Already considering the EU's commitments to Policy Coherence for Development, the EU has a duty to ensure that its internal and external policies do not counteract each other's objectives.

5.3.3. Is the EU Facilitating Sustainable Business – Or 'Greening' Business as Usual?

Much of the EU's emphasis on how to achieve sustainability is concentrated on mitigating climate change, as we see in the slogan for the EU Green Deal with its aim of Europe being the 'first climate-neutral continent by 2050'. The EU Green Deal refers

[96] European Council, 'EU deforestation law: Council reconfirms its agreement to extend application timeline' press release, 20 November 2024, available at www.consilium.europa.eu/en/press/press-releases/2024/11/20/eu-deforestation-law-council-reconfirms-its-agreement-to-extend-application-timeline.

[97] European Council, 'Products made with forced labour: Council adopts ban', press release, 19 November 2024, available at www.consilium.europa.eu/en/press/press-releases/2024/11/19/products-made-with-forced-labour-council-adopts-ban.

[98] 'This Regulation does not create additional due diligence obligations for economic operators besides those already provided by Union or national law', final text of 6 November 2024 of the Regulation of the European Parliament and of the Council on prohibiting products made with forced labour on the Union market and amending Directive (EU) 2019/1937, Art 1(3), available at data.consilium.europa.eu/doc/document/PE-67-2024-INIT/en/pdf.

[99] Art 14 of the final text of 6 November 2024 (n 99).

[100] Maitre-Ekern (n 44).

[101] European Commission (n 87).

to key environmental reports,[102] and on its website presenting the Green Deal, the Commission states that 'Climate change and environmental degradation present an existential threat to Europe and the world'.[103] Yet, there is no reference in the Green Deal to the planetary boundaries (or ecological limits in other terminology), which it has in common with the Action Plan on Financing Sustainable Growth, and the Sustainable Corporate Governance initiative. The Circular Economy Action Plan references planetary boundaries, but it does so with a 'green growth' approach. The Earth system processes on which human prosperity relies are inextricably interconnected. Working towards sustainability means mitigating pressures on all planetary boundaries. There is very little research basis for assuming that infinite economic growth is compatible with sustainability.[104]

Further, sustainability as an overarching commitment of the EU encompasses the social dimension, including the protection of human rights, social policy, and policy coherence for development. As laid out above, this has a clear Treaty basis. Yet, in the Green Deal, the emphasis on creating a Just Transition and leaving nobody behind is limited to ensuring justice in the transition to sustainability within the EU Member States.[105] References to those 'most vulnerable' does not appear to encompass vulnerable people and communities outside of the EU.[106] As we have seen in this chapter, people are not a priority in the EU's initiatives for transforming business towards sustainability, and certainly not people across global value chains of European businesses.

The 'greening' of European finance, the belief in disclosure and limited due diligence rules for changing governance of business, and the emphasis on resource-efficiency in the Circular Economy initiative, all show that the EU is not doing enough. 'Greening' is not equivalent to a fundamental transformation in line with Treaty sustainability goals. The strictest rules, prohibiting access to market, seem to be applied to actors outside of the EU. True change requires a recognition of the EU Member States' colonial history and EU's facilitation of neocolonialism through European business.

5.4. Concluding Reflections

Business, including finance, is crucial to the achievement or the failure of achieving the EU's sustainability goals. Yet, in the EU's own assessment of its progress towards the SDGs, sustainable corporate governance appears to be a blind spot. Concerning EU progress towards SDG 12, Responsible Consumption and Production, the focus

[102] European Commission (n 47) fn 1.

[103] European Commission, 'The European Green Deal sets out how to make Europe the first climate-neutral continent by 2050, boosting the economy, improving people's health and quality of life, caring for nature, and leaving no one behind', 11 December 2019, available at ec.europa.eu/neighbourhood-enlargement/news_corner/news/european-green-deal-sets-out-how-make-europe-first-climate-neutral-continent-2050_en.

[104] eg T Parrique et al, 'Decoupling Debunked: Evidence and Arguments against Green Growth as a Sole Strategy for Sustainability' (2019) European *Environmental Bureau, available at* eeb.org/library/decoupling-debunked.

[105] European Commission (n 47), section 2.2.1.

[106] ibid.

is on 'developments in the areas of consumption patterns, the green economy, and waste generation and management'.[107] On the environmental issues, the report shows a 'mixed' picture, with 'consumption of hazardous chemicals' increasing, and with the 'circular use of materials … not growing fast enough to meet the target'.[108] There is a brief mention of the Circular Economy package of 2022, and its goal of making 'sustainable products the norm in the EU' and boosting 'circular business models'.[109] The Corporate Sustainability Due Diligence Directive is mentioned only once in the whole report, under 'International spillovers and policy relevance within the EU context', still as a proposal, and together with trade and the carbon border adjustment mechanism.[110] This is also the only mention of 'corporate sustainability'.

Business has very little agency in the EU's own assessment; people, especially outside of Europe, are not a matter of priority, while the belief in green growth remains strong. Within the EU, farmers protesting new rules opened the door to new negotiations.[111] There has been much less attention given to protests in former colonised countries against the Deforestation Regulation. What the protests have in common, though, is that they illustrate the need for a more inclusive, open and participatory process in EU's policy-making.[112]

Working to promote sustainability is not only a policy choice and a moral obligation; it is a legal duty under the EU Treaties, which the EU institutions and its Member States are violating. A different approach is needed in the EU institutions' implementation of Treaty duties, to achieve sustainability and lasting peace. Ensuring peace is more than the absence of war; it is about contributing to global social justice and the mitigation of pressures on the very basis of human existence. Prerequisites for the fundamental transformation needed are a deeper recognition of the Europe's colonial history and its current neocolonialism, and revitalisation of the EU Treaty concept of solidarity;[113] towards a humble solidarity, 'unbound' by geopolitical borders.[114]

[107] European Commission; Statistical Office of the European Union, Sustainable Development in the European Union: Monitoring Report on Progress towards the SDGs in an EU Context: 2024 Edition (2024) ch 12, available at ec.europa.eu/eurostat/documents/15234730/19397895/KS-05-24-071-EN-N.pdf.

[108] ibid.

[109] ibid.

[110] ibid, 334.

[111] J Henley, 'Farmers Clash with Riot Police in Brussels as EU Agriculture Leaders Meet' *The Guardian* (26 February 2024), available at www.theguardian.com/environment/2024/feb/26/farmers-protests-brussels-eu-agriculture-leaders-riot-police.

[112] eg CO Lichuma, '(Laws) Made in the "First World": A TWAIL Critique of the Use of Domestic Legislation to Extraterritorially Regulate Global Value Chains' (2021) 81 *Zeitschrift für ausländisches öffentliches Recht und Völkerrecht / Heidelberg Journal of International Law* 497, available at www.nomos-elibrary.de/10.17104/0044-2348-2021-2-497/laws-made-in-the-first-world-a-twail-critique-of-the-use-of-domestic-legislation-to-extraterritorially-regulate-global-value-chains-jahrgang-81-2021-heft-2?page=1; Deva and Anand (n 85).

[113] S Garben, ch 3 in this volume.

[114] T Novitz, 'Sustainability as Solidarity Unbound: Labour Rights and Collective Voice in the United Nations Sustainable Development Goals and the European Union' in J López López (ed), *Inscribing Solidarity: Debates in Labor Law and Beyond* (Cambridge, Cambridge University Press 2022), available at www.cambridge.org/core/books/inscribing-solidarity/sustainability-as-solidarity-unbound/017122A8C9FA18647A476FE91DBC4266.

6

The European Political Community and the Future of the EU

BRUNO DE WITTE

One of the political initiatives that emerged in response to the Russian aggression in Ukraine was the creation of a European Political Community (EPC) that aims to link together the EU, its Member States, Ukraine and other likeminded European countries. The idea of creating the EPC was first, but very briefly, mentioned by Emmanuel Macron in a speech at the European Parliament on 9 May 2022. The ideas in the speech were then articulated further in a one-page non-paper presented by the French Government at the European Council meeting of 23 and 24 June 2022.[1] The conclusions of that European Council gave cautious support to the idea, and on 6 October 2022 a meeting took place in Prague between the heads of state or government of 44 countries, presented in press releases as 'the inaugural meeting' of the EPC. The meeting did not adopt any formal written document apart from press releases by various participants,[2] nor did it create a secretariat or other organ for the EPC.

The EU Council made a revealing statement on its website after the meeting in Prague: 'this platform for political coordination does not replace any existing organization, structure or process, nor does it aim to create a new one at this stage.'[3] So, if we take this at face value, the EPC is not supposed to be an organisation, nor a structure, nor even a process. Therefore, the EPC is, so far, only a high-level political meeting place, allowing for bilateral deals to be made on the side, and nothing more. Although 44 states were represented at the highest political level, those states are not 'members' of anything and can stay away from further meetings if they wish. Since the Prague summit, this situation has not changed. More EPC meetings were held, in Chisinau (June 2023), Granada (October 2023), Woodstock (July 2024) and Budapest (November 2024), and there is a commitment to hold further summits in the coming years.

[1] The non-paper can be viewed at /www.rijksoverheid.nl/documenten/publicaties/2022/06/17/non-paper-european-political-community.

[2] For an account of what happened at the Prague meeting, see 'Outcome of the European Political Community and European Council meetings in Prague on 6–7 October 2022' Briefing note by the European Parliament Research Service, PE 734.671.

[3] www.consilium.europa.eu/en/meetings/international-summit/2022/10/06.

The modest reality of the EPC hardly justifies the use of the term 'Community'. Indeed, the term community has 'a strong resonance in EU circles, and may imply a preference for a real organization'.[4] The French Government's non-paper, mentioned above, had envisaged that the EPC 'would take the form of a light legal structure, with decision-making capacity, while respecting the decision-making autonomy of the European Union and of each of the States that make up this Community', but so far this has not happened.

In this chapter, I will address two main issues about the future of the EPC project: What could be its added political value compared to existing organisations and processes? And how could the 'light legal structure' envisaged by the French non-paper be constructed?

The basic, but rather vague, added value of the EPC is that nothing of the sort existed before. In the French non-paper, it was stated that 'today we have no non-specialized European forum to bring together all the members of the European family on an equal footing and in a spirit of unity of our continent'. This statement implicitly reduces the Council of Europe to a 'specialized' organisation. The Council of Europe, to which all 44 EPC participant countries except Kosovo belong, has itself started a relaunch following the war in Ukraine and the expulsion of Russia from the organisation. A High Level Reflection Group of the Council of Europe proposed that the Council of Europe should invest more in its core tasks of promoting human rights, democracy and the rule of law.[5]

On 16–17 May 2023, a summit meeting of the heads of state or government of the Council of Europe Member States was held in Reykjavik (for only the fourth time in the history of the Council of Europe). The Declaration adopted there confirms the resolve of the Member States to focus on the three core tasks.[6] This focus, if confirmed, would indeed justify the description of the Council of Europe as a specialised organisation, as well as the description (in the non-paper) of the EPC as a non-specialised forum dealing with a wider range of policy areas. The European Council's conclusions of June 2022 did not mention any particular areas for cooperation, but the French non-paper had listed a large number of them: foreign and security policy; climate change and the supply of energy and other raw materials; food security; infrastructure development and interconnection; mobility; migration; the fight against organised crime; and relations with other geopolitical actors.[7] Human rights, democracy and the rule of law are not mentioned and it may, indeed, seem better to leave those to the Council of Europe[8] (and to the EU, in both its internal and external relations).

Among the existing 'structures and processes' that deal with the potential subject matter of the EPC, the most important ones are the bilateral associations between the

[4] M Emerson and S Blockmans, 'The new agenda for the EU's enlargement and neighbourhood policies' (2022) *CEPS Policy Insight*, No 2022-20, 3.

[5] Report of the High Level Reflection Group of the Council of Europe (October 2022).

[6] United around our values, Reykjavik Declaration adopted by the 4th Summit of Heads of State and Government of the Council of Europe, 16–17 May 2023.

[7] For discussion of the areas of cooperation in which the EPC could play a useful role, see F Mayer, J Pisani-Ferry, D Schwarzer and S Vallée, 'Enlarging and deepening: giving substance to the European Political Community' *Bruegel Policy Contribution* no 15/22 (September 2022) and S Maillard et al, 'A European Political Community for a Geopolitical Era' (May 2023) *Institut Jacques Delors & Sciences Po*.

[8] See T Nguyen, 'European Political Community – From family photo to 'strategic intimacy'(8 November 2022), Hertie School Jacques Delors Centre – Policy Brief, 3.

EU and most of the non-EU countries that joined the EPC (including now also the UK). These associations are not fully fledged international organisations but they provide for regular 'meetings of the parties' in the form of association councils and association committees, and those organs have some modest decision-making powers. The substantive scope of the association agreements varies a lot, but the one with Ukraine certainly covers a large part of the Union *acquis*. However, it does not allow for autonomous policy-making and rule-making to develop the content of the association agreement, except for the possibility to amend the technical annexes. Furthermore, the associations connect the EU with single countries on a bilateral basis, creating in each case a strong dependency on the EU.

Exceptions to this bilateral model are the Energy Community and the Transport Community, both of which can be described in legal terms as international organisations.[9] Their members are the EU and six Balkan countries. They possess permanent organs (a Secretariat, a Ministerial Council and a Regional Steering Committee) entrusted with decision-making powers, even though the main object of those decisions is to extend the Union's *acquis* in the field of energy and transport to the non-EU countries involved. The use of the term 'Community' for the EPC somehow evokes those existing organisations, whilst ideally extending their scope to a wide (and as yet undelimited) range of policy fields. The similarity of the terms is, however, deceptive. So far, the EPC has no permanent organs and no autonomous decision-making powers whatsoever, and the 'Community' is one of political solidarity (hopefully, at least) rather than of policy-making.

Therefore, if a 'light legal structure' should be given to the EPC as well as a 'decision-making capacity', this would require an extra step, namely the conclusion of an international agreement establishing the EPC as an international organisation. Such a step would raise a number of legal issues of EU law: the question of the legal basis in the Treaties that should allow the Union to become a party to the agreement; the question whether the agreement should be mixed or EU-only; and the question whether the EPC could be entrusted with genuine decision-making powers, given the requirement, imposed by the case law of the Court of Justice, that the autonomy of the EU legal order must be preserved. These three issues will be briefly examined in the following paragraphs.

As for the legal basis, Article 8 TEU could be an obvious choice, as it enables the Union to conclude 'specific agreements' with its neighbouring countries, which 'may contain reciprocal rights and obligations as well as the possibility of undertaking activities jointly'. The final words are intriguing: do 'joint activities' include the possibility to equip the EPC with organs having decision-making powers? There is no firm answer to that question as Article 8 TEU has not, to date, been used as a legal basis for EU agreements. Instead, the Union has continued to rely on Article 217 TFEU as a basis for broad-ranging association agreements. That provision enables the conclusion of 'agreements establishing an association involving reciprocal rights and obligations, common action and special procedures'. The reference to 'common action' may seem to include the possibility to confer decision-making powers on association councils,

[9] The Energy Community Treaty, [2006] OJ L198/15; Treaty establishing the Transport Community [2017] OJ L278/3.

and the practice over the years has confirmed the possibility for association councils to take decisions amending and supplementing the agreement itself. So, Article 217 TFEU could well be used as the legal basis for concluding an EPC agreement, although it is worth keeping in mind that it requires a unanimous decision of the Council, unlike agreements based on Article 8 TEU.

Association agreements are usually concluded as mixed agreements, with the participation of both the EU and its Member States, but this is not required by the Treaty text. In fact, the Trade and Cooperation Agreement with the UK is an EU-only association agreement without the participation of the EU Member States. This precedent could be replicated for an EPC agreement on condition that the EPC's scope of activity would be entirely covered by the EU's exclusive or shared competences. However, given the 'high politics' character of some of the domains envisaged for the EPC, the EU Member States may well insist on being parties to the agreement, if only as a matter of so-called facultative mixity.[10]

Respect for the decision-making autonomy of the Union is a major constraint on granting a decisional capacity to the EPC. This constraint is mentioned both in the French non-paper and in the conclusions of the June 2022 European Council ('such a framework … will fully respect the European Union's decision-making autonomy'). It is certainly possible for the Union to conclude agreements creating international bodies with their own decision-making powers, as this has frequently happened in the past. But the Court of Justice has developed a doctrine whereby the transfer of powers to international institutions or bodies must respect the essential characteristics of the Union legal order. What that entails is not very clear.[11] It could, however, be taken to mean that the EU can only confer decision-making powers to an international body if it preserves a right to veto any of that body's decisions. Such a veto right is naturally present in association councils and committees, since they are bilateral, but if it were to be included in a future EPC agreement, the non-EU countries would naturally claim corresponding veto rights which, in view of the large membership of the EPC, would seriously reduce its decision-making capacity. In order to avoid this trap, one could envisage a flexibility mechanism whereby dissenting states can opt out from a decision rather than exercise their veto power. Alternatively, one could turn the EPC into a funding mechanism rather than a rule-making body, although its added value would then be limited, given that associated states already now participate in a number of EU funding programmes (and EU agencies).[12]

In view of the difficulties discussed above, it seems more likely that the EPC will continue its current twilight existence as a forum for political dialogue without any concrete legal existence. This may, in fact, correspond to the wishes of the EU institutions, so as to avoid the emergence of a new Europe-wide international organisation that might act as a rival to the EU, at least in some policy domains. Candidate countries

[10] On the notion of facultative mixity, see J Heliskoski and G Kübek, 'A Typology of EU Mixed Agreements Revisited' in N Levrat et al (eds), *The EU and its Member States' Joint Participation in International Agreements* (Oxford, Hart, 2022) 23, 31–33.

[11] See eg the discussion by N Nic Shuibhne, 'What is the Autonomy of EU Law, and Why Does That Matter?' (2019) 88 *Nordic Journal of International Law* 9.

[12] See the list in Emerson and Blockmans (n 4) 7.

might, correspondingly, wish to preserve the informal nature of the EPC so as to avoid it becoming an 'outer circle'[13] in which they would remain trapped instead of achieving their objective of full accession to the European Union. But, if the EPC remains merely a forum for political dialogue, it is difficult to see how it could fulfil the ambitious role envisaged by its promotors, of being a dynamic and effective cooperation scheme that can connect Ukraine (and other candidate states) to their European partner countries whilst they wait for the many hurdles in the EU accession process to be overcome.

[13] See the Franco-German paper on EU institutional reform that discusses the EPC as potentially developing into the outer tier of a future European integration landscape composed of four concentric tiers: Sailing on High Seas: Reforming and Enlarging the EU for the 21st Century, Report of the Franco-German working group on EU institutional reform (18 September 2023) 41.

PART II

Substantive Impact

7

The Impact of the War in Ukraine on European Neighbourhood Policy and the Enlargement Process: From Wider Europe to Wider Neighbourhood

ERWAN LANNON

7.1. Introduction: A Tectonic Shift in European History

The impact of the war in Ukraine on the European Neighbourhood Policy (ENP) and the Enlargement Process is profound. The EU Member States, gathered in Versailles on 11 March 2022, recognised that this war is a 'tectonic shift in European history'.[1]

To address the issue of the impact of the war in Ukraine on the ENP and the Enlargement Process more than a year and a half after the Russian invasion, launched on 24 February 2022, is rather premature as the war is not over. It is indeed a challenge as nobody is, for the time being, in a position to anticipate how the war will end. However, some of the major consequences of this war are already visible. The fact that since June 2022 Ukraine and Moldova are official candidates for EU membership is, in this regard, self-explanatory.

In section 7.2, I will evaluate the impact of the war on the legal frameworks and instruments of the ENP, especially the bilateral agreements and financial cooperation. I will also consider the issue of the relevance of the ENP in general and the Eastern partnership (EaP) in particular. In section 7.3, it is the impact on the legal framework, the criteria and the enlargement methodology at large that will be taken into consideration. Some issues linked to the future of EU integration and the widening-deepening nexus will also be addressed.

[1] Informal meeting of the Heads of State or Government Declaration, Versailles, 10 and 11 March 2022, pt 6.

7.2. The Impact of the War on the European Neighbourhood Policy

The impact of the war on the ENP is and will be major. In the longer term the relevance of the ENP, at least in its current state, is at stake.

7.2.1. The (Potential) Impact on the ENP Legal Frameworks and Instruments

The impact on the ENP legal frameworks and instruments, notably on the main agreements is rather limited in the short term, but the impact at financial level is already important and the Eastern Partnership is already being recalibrated.

7.2.1.1. A Short-term Limited Impact on the Main Bilateral Agreements

The Association Agreements including Deep and Comprehensive Free Trade Areas (AA-DCFTAs) concluded with Moldova, Georgia and Ukraine will be used in the pre-accession strategy. They have been mentioned in the applications[2] and systematically referred to in the opinions and analytical reports of the European Commission. For Ukraine, the Commission stressed, for example, that the 'opinion also takes into account Ukraine's efforts in implementing its obligations under' the AA-DCFTA.[3] With the granting of candidate status for EU membership, the implementation of the AA-DCFTAs is used as a key indicator to evaluate the progress of the latter on its way to the EU membership. The opinions of the European Commission already referred to the fact that the ability to 'assume the obligations of membership has been evaluated' on the basis of the 'following indicators:

- the commitments in the (AA-DCFTA) and their implementation;
- the level of adoption, implementation and enforcement of the *acquis* outside the AA-DCFTA.[4]

It has been emphasised that the AA-DCFTA 'captures a substantial part of the EU *acquis* with a detailed timetable of implementation varying from 3 to 7 years' for the

[2] In the Ukrainian application for EU membership there are two references to the AA-DCFTA. The first refers to the 'significant and dynamic progress made by Ukraine in the implementation of the Association Agreement between Ukraine and the EU and the regulatory approximation of Ukrainian legislation to the vast majority of EU legal norms'. The second to the 'tangible progress of the economic integration between Ukraine and the EU made possible by the Deep and Comprehensive Free Trade Area, and noting that the EU has been Ukraine's main trading partner for almost ten years, its share of the total trade of the state again reaching more than 40% in 2021'. EU Council, Application of Ukraine for membership of the European Union – Transmission to Member States' Parliaments, Joint Statement by the President of Ukraine Volodymyr Zelenskyy, the Chairman of the Verkhovna Rada of Ukraine Ruslan Stefanchuk and the Prime Minister of Ukraine Denys Shmyhal on Ukraine's application for membership of the European Union, Annex II (Brussels, 4 March 2022) 7–8.

[3] Commission Opinion on Ukraine's application for membership of the European Union, COM(2022) 407 final (Brussels, 17 June 2022) 2.

[4] ibid, 16.

regulatory alignment.[5] In other words, the AA-DCFTAs are appropriate legal instruments for the pre-accession[6] as they focus on legislative alignment and approximation as well as on normative and regulatory convergence. There is therefore no need to adopt new main agreements in this case. Updating bilateral relations by adding new protocols is possible given the existence of a solid institutional and decision-making framework.[7] Additional bilateral or regional sectoral agreements can also be concluded if required. During the 3 February 2023 EU–Ukraine summit, it was confirmed that for 2023–24 a 'revised Priority Action Plan for enhanced implementation of the DCFTA' is the 'roadmap outlining the next steps to ease Ukraine's access to EU's Internal Market'.[8]

On the other hand, a potential impact, linked to the war outcome and the difficult regional context, could consist of an upgrade of the current agreement with Armenia that is not an AA-DCFTA but a Comprehensive and Enhanced Partnership Agreement (CEPA).[9] The differences are limited to some specific aspects as the negotiations were originally conducted on the basis of a mandate for an AA-DCFTA and then amended to negotiate a CEPA when Armenia decided to join the Eurasian Economic Union (EAEU). In other words, this CEPA is an AA-DCFTA minus. Contrary to the three AA-DCFTAs, the CEPA does not include tariff liberalisation or mandatory technical regulatory alignment in the area of goods 'given the obligations arising from the Republic of Armenia's membership' of the EAEU. However, it has been notified by the parties to the WTO in August 2019 under Article V:7(a) of the General Agreement on Trade in Services (GATS) as it provides for the liberalisation of trade in services.[10] Thus, protocols containing the appropriate trade and customs tariff liberalisation and technical regulatory alignment in the area of goods and a notification under Article XXIV of the General Agreement. on Tariffs and Trade (GATT) could, with other technical amendments, enable the parties to upgrade the Armenian CEPA to get closer to a fully fledged AA-DCFTA. A change of the legal basis[11] (and title of the agreement) would

[5] Commission Opinion on the Republic of Moldova's application for membership of the European Union, COM(2022) 406 final (Brussels, 17 June 2022) 12–13.

[6] See P Van Elsuwege and G Van der Loo, 'The EU-Ukraine Association Agreement as a Stepping-Stone towards EU Membership?' EPC-Egmont Institute discussion paper (14 March 2022).

[7] The AA-DCFTAs' Association Councils can adopt legally binding decisions. In the case of Ukraine, the EU–Ukraine annual summits, the meetings of the Association Council, the Association Committee and the various thematic sub committees 'as well as six dedicated Cluster Sub-committees covering almost all chapters of the EU *acquis*' provide dialogue channels and are used to monitor the 'process of gradual approximation and implementation of Ukraine's legislation with the EU *acquis*'. Moreover, 'Ukraine's implementation of the EU *acquis* is documented in the EU's annual 'Association Implementation Reports' since 2016, Commission Opinion on Ukraine's application (n 3) 16.

[8] European Council, Joint statement following the 24th EU–Ukraine Summit, Press release 64/23, pt 7, available at www.consilium.europa.eu/en/meetings/international-summit/2023/02/03/.

[9] Comprehensive and enhanced Partnership Agreement between the European Union and the European Atomic Energy Community and their Member States, of the one part, and the Republic of Armenia, of the other part, [2018] OJ L 23/4.

[10] Note on the meeting of 20 September 2020, Chairman: Ambassador H.E. Mr. Mārtiņš Kreitus (Latvia), WTO, WT/REG405/M/1, 8 October 2020 (20-6923), Committee on Regional Trade Agreements Ninety-seventh Session, Comprehensive and Enhanced partnership Agreement between the European Union and the Republic of Armenia (Services), Geneva, available at docs.wto.org/dol2fe/Pages/SS/directdoc.aspx?filename=q:/WT/REG/405M1.pdf&Open=True.

[11] The CEPA is based on Arts 207 and 209 TFEU, reference being made to Art 37 TEU and Arts 91 and 100(2) TFEU. As association agreements, the AA-DCFTAs are based on Art 217 TFEU, reference being made to Arts 31(1) and 37 TEU.

however necessitate a new decision of the Council and imply an unpredictable ratification process.

At the level of the Mediterranean partners, it remains to be seen if the outcomes of the war could reinvigorate the – now frozen – negotiations of the DCFTAs with Morocco and Tunisia or initiate those with Egypt and Jordan, as envisaged in the mandate.[12] In the case of Tunisia, it should be noted that the EU and Tunisia made public the initial texts of the DCFTA 'presented to Tunisian experts during the preliminary discussions in Tunis in October 2015 and during the first round of negotiations from 18–21 April 2016'.[13] Since May 2019, the 'negotiations have been brough to a standstill'.[14] The negotiations with Morocco, which started in March 2013, were put on hold after four rounds of negotiations 'at the request of Morocco to carry out additional studies before continuing negotiations'.[15] Since then, the

> 'General entreprises of Morocco and BusinessEurope issued a joint statement for the modernisation of EU-Morocco trade and investment' and Moroccan authorities expressed, in May 2022, their 'interest in engaging into informal discussions on the possible strengthening of EU Morocco relations.[16]

It remains to be seen whether the outcomes of the war in Ukraine, and the one between Israel and Hamas will have an impact on a relaunch of negotiations with Tunisia and Morocco. At time of writing, it is, in both cases, more a modernisation of the current agreements that is envisaged instead of new fully fledged DCFTAs. In other words, if (potential) candidate countries can accept the delegation of sovereignty implied by a deep integration in the form of regulatory convergence and legislative alignment, it is not the case for non-European neighbours that tend to preserve their sovereignty and favour shallow economic integration within the framework of classic FTAs in line with Article XXIV of the GATT and Article V of the GATS.

7.2.1.2. An Important Impact on Financial Instruments and Cooperation

The impact of the war on financial instruments and cooperation was almost immediate on bilateral and sub-regional cooperation programmes involving Belarus and/or Russia. A medium-term impact is foreseen for the 2024 mid-term review of the Multi-annual Financial Framework (MFF), including the Neighbourhood, Development and International Cooperation Instrument[17] (NDICI) and the Instrument for Pre-Accession

[12] European Commission, Recommendation from the Commission to the Council authorizing the Commission to open bilateral negotiations with Egypt, Jordan, Morocco and Tunisia to upgrade the respective Euro-Mediterranean Association Agreements with a view to establish Deep and comprehensive Free Trade Areas, SEC(2011) 1191 final (Brussels, 14 October 2011) 2.

[13] European Commission, EU–Tunisia Deep and Comprehensive Free Trade Area: Documents, available at policy.trade.ec.europa.eu/eu-trade-relationships-country-and-region/countries-and-regions/tunisia/eu-tunisia-dcfta-documents_en.

[14] European Commission, Overview of ongoing bilateral and regional negotiations, consulted 15 October 2023, available at circabc.europa.eu/rest/download/a7aab8e0-085d-4e36-826f-cbe8e913cf13.

[15] ibid.

[16] ibid.

[17] Regulation (EU) 2021/947 of the European Parliament and of the Council of 9 June 2021 establishing the Neighbourhood, Development and International Cooperation Instrument – Global Europe, amending and repealing Decision No 466/2014/EU of the European Parliament and of the Council and repealing Regulation

assistance[18] (IPA III). The longer-term impact will be very important at financial and substantive levels, one of the most striking developments being the militarisation of the aid provided by the EU.

7.2.1.2.1. The Immediate and Medium-term Impacts

Ukraine and Moldova are among the beneficiaries of the NDICI, but as candidate countries should become beneficiaries of the IPA. Both regulations were introduced as part of the 2021–2027 MFF. However, the IPA III Regulation is one of the rare financial regulations that was not merged into the NDICI like many others, including the European Development Fund (EDF). One of the main issues is that IPA III was already, at least partly, programmed for the Western Balkans countries and Turkey. As underlined in 2022 by the European Commission, the IPA III Regulation was adopted in September 2021 and its 'programming framework' in December 2021 through 'annual and multi-annual financing decisions worth over EUR 4 billion', including the Economic and Investment Plan for the Western Balkans. Moreover, programming of IPA III also implied 'two high-level geopolitical dialogues' between the Commission and the European Parliament in 'October 2021 and May 2022 to discuss the general approach to the implementation of IPA III, its objectives and the programming of IPA funds'.[19]

A year and a half after the start of the war its impact is already very important on a number of programmes at bilateral and (sub-)regional levels. For example, the Northern dimension, a thematic cooperation platform between the EU, the Russian Federation, Norway and Iceland, was suspended in autumn 2022.[20] Every programme involving Russia and Belarus has been affected. In August 2023 the European Commission decided to 'transfer €135 million' of the NDICI 'originally planned for 2021–2027 Interreg NEXT programmes with Russia and Belarus, to other Interreg programmes with Ukraine and Moldova'. In fact, 'in line with the measures adopted by the EU, in March 2022', the European Commission had already 'suspended cooperation with Russia and its ally Belarus in Interreg programmes'. In concrete terms, €26 million were 'redistributed to support cooperation programmes with Ukraine and Moldova' and the 'remaining funding from the 2021–2027 period' were redistributed in the 'same manner'. To reallocate the funds, the European Commission decided that 'regions in Finland, Estonia, Latvia and Poland which were supposed to participate in cooperation programmes with Russia and Belarus may participate in other existing Interreg programmes'.[21] In March 2022 the European Commission then also 'suspended the cooperation with Russia and its ally

(EU) 2017/1601 of the European Parliament and of the Council and Council Regulation (EC, Euratom), [2021] OJ L 209/1.

[18] Regulation (EU) 2021/1529 of the European Parliament and of the Council of 15 September 2021 establishing the Instrument for Pre-Accession assistance (IPA III), [2021] OJ L 330/1.

[19] European Commission, 2022 Communication on EU Enlargement Policy, COM(2022) 528 final (Brussels, 12 October 2022) 5.

[20] See northerndimension.info.

[21] European Commission, Ukraine: €135 million initially planned for programmes with Russia and Belarus will be transferred to strengthen cooperation with Ukraine and Moldova (16 August 2023), available at neighbourhood-enlargement.ec.europa.eu/news/ukraine-eu135-million-initially-planned-programmes-russia-and-belarus-will-be-transferred-strengthen-2023-08-16_en.

Belarus' at the level of the Cross-Border Cooperation programmes (CBC).[22] As a result, four cross-border Interreg programmes,[23] as well as two transnational programmes (the Danube Transnational Programme and Interreg NEXT Black Sea Basin) benefited from '68% increased funding for the year 2022'.[24]

The Council had decided in October 2020 to review the EU's relations with Belarus given the deterioration of the political situation. Regarding the Eastern Partnership multilateral framework, and 'with the exception of institutions responsible for violations and abuses of human rights' the Council decided to 'maintain cooperation with Belarus at non-political level, and intensify cooperation with key non-state Belarusian stakeholders'.[25] Given Belarus's involvement in Russia's military invasion of Ukraine, more sanctions have been adopted and relations are on hold.[26]

These are just some illustrations of the immediate impact of the war on financial cooperation instruments in the framework of the ENP. For the medium term (2024–27) the European Commission proposed, in June 2023, to create the Ukraine Facility. This facility, financed by the EU budget but 'above the MFF ceilings', should be operational from the beginning of 2024.[27] The financial support will be 'in the form of non-repayable support (such as grants, guarantees, and interest subsidies) and highly concessional loans', the objective being to provide 'continuous support of up to €50 billion' until 2027. The EU's support will concentrate on its macro-financial stability, promoting recovery, and rebuilding and modernising the country, while also 'supporting reforms as part of its EU accession'.[28] The 2024 mid-term review of the MFF will allow for more reallocations

[22] See the two lists of Land-Border and Sea basin programmes at neighbourhood-enlargement.ec.europa.eu/european-neighbourhood-policy/cross-border-cooperation_en.

[23] Involving 'Ukraine and Moldova, Hungary/Slovakia/Romania/Ukraine, Poland/Ukraine, Romania/Moldova, Romania/Ukraine'.

[24] European Commission, Ukraine: €26.2 million initially planned for Russia and Belarus will be transferred to strengthen cooperation with Ukraine and Moldova, Daily news (3 June 2022), available at ec.europa.eu/commission/presscorner/detail/en/mex_22_3463; and Regulation (EU) 2022/2192 of the European Parliament and of the Council of 9 November 2022 laying down specific provisions for the 2014–2020 cooperation programmes supported by the European Neighbourhood Instrument and under the European territorial cooperation goal, following programme implementation disruption, [2022] OJ L 292/1.

[25] Pt d. The EU will also: 'a) Scale down bilateral cooperation with Belarusian authorities at central level and increase EU's support to the Belarusian people and civil society; Exclude from this cooperation institutions responsible for violations and abuses of human rights. b) Recalibrate bilateral financial EU assistance to Belarus in order to ensure it benefits the population at large notably by directing it to the maximum possible extent away from central authorities and towards non-state, local and regional actors, including through cross-border cooperation programmes. c) Continue engagement with Belarus on issues of interest to the EU and the Belarusian society.' Council conclusions on Belarus as adopted by the Council (Foreign Affairs) on 12 October 2020, pt 8, available at www.consilium.europa.eu/media/46076/council-conclusions-on-belarus.pdf.

[26] The Council stressed on its website that, in the case of the sanctions in response to the involvement in Russia's military invasion of Ukraine, the importance of: 'individual and economic sanctions targeting 22 people'; 'restrictions on trade'; 'a SWIFT ban for five Belarusian banks'; 'a prohibition on transactions with the Central Bank of Belarus'; 'limits on the financial inflows from Belarus to the EU'; and 'a prohibition on the provision of euro-denominated banknotes to Belarus'. EU Council, restrictive measures against Belarus, available at www.consilium.europa.eu/en/policies/sanctions/restrictive-measures-against-belarus.

[27] European Commission, Proposal for a Council Regulation amending Regulation (EU, Euratom) 2020/2093 laying down the multiannual financial framework for the years 2021 to 2027, COM(2023) 337 final (Brussels, 20 June 2023).

[28] European Court of Auditors, Opinion 03/2023, concerning the proposal for a Regulation of the European Parliament and of the Council on establishing the Ukraine Facility, 2023/0200(COD), Luxembourg

and reorientations. The war is promoting the creation of new cooperation instruments, such as the 2023 'New growth plan for the Western Balkans' (see below) and also new forms of financing, including the financing of lethal weapons.

7.2.1.2.2. The ENP–CFSP Nexus: The Militarisation of the Cooperation for ENP Countries

The longer-term impact of the war on cooperation is more difficult to apprehend, but what is obvious is that we are witnessing a militarisation of the cooperation. It is not ENP cooperation *stricto sensu*, as it is not financed through the NDICI, but designed and implemented according to the CFSP intergovernmental rules and procedures of the Treaty, including Article 21(2)(c) TEU stating that the EU shall 'define and pursue common policies and actions' in order to 'preserve peace, prevent conflicts and strengthen international security'.

The relations between the ENP and the CFSP including CSDP have evolved alongside the adoption of treaties and strategies, and because of external events. When it was designed by the European Commission between 2003 and 2006, CFSP was considered more as one of the pillars of the ENP. A couple of paragraphs were prepared by the Secretary-General/High-Representative' (SG/HR) services in the EU Council for the first ENP action plans, the European Commission remaining in charge of these specific ENP roadmaps, which included the main priorities of the cooperation. Also, an alignment on CFSP declarations and/or participation to CFSP missions and operations was proposed to the ENP countries. In 2006 the Commission recognised that the 'ENP has achieved little in supporting the resolution of frozen or open conflicts in the region, notwithstanding certain specific achievements)'.[29]

With the entry into force of the Treaty of Lisbon (ToL), the creation of the EEAS, the adoption of the EU Global Strategy (EUGS) in 2016 and the two reviews of the ENP in 2011 (with the Arab Spring'+[30]) and in 2015–17 (with the impact of the war in Syria and Iraq and the refugee crisis[31]), EU's security and migratory policies objectives have tended to prevail over some ENP objectives. The goal is to put forward the Member

(20 June 2023). European Commission, Proposal for a regulation if the European Parliament and the Council, on establishing the Ukraine Facility, COM(2023) 338 final (Brussels, 20 June 2023) Art 1.

[29] European Commission, Communication, Strengthening the European Neighborhood Policy, COM(2006)726 final (Brussels, 4 December 2006) 4.

[30] One of the five elements needed to build a 'deep and sustainable democracy' was: 'security and law enforcement sector reform (including the police) and the establishment of democratic control over armed and security forces'. See also at pt 1.3 the three priority actions for 'Intensifying our political and security co-operation': 'enhance EU involvement in solving protracted conflicts; make joined-up use of the Common Foreign and Security Policy and other EU instruments; promote joint action' in 'international fora on key security issues'. European Commission and High representative, Joint Communication, A new response to a changing Neighbourhood, COM(2011) 303 final (Brussels, 25 May 2011) 3 and 5–6.

[31] The Council invited the HR/VP and the Commission to 'develop a set of proposals on ensuring coherence of the Policy with the security and foreign policy dimensions of the EU's actions abroad' and stressed that the ENP 'should contribute to promoting stability in the neighbourhood in line with the comprehensive approach and the external dimension of other relevant EU policies such as the area of Freedom, Security and Justice'. Moreover, the 'ENP instruments should be used more widely to strengthen partners' capacity to address security threats, notably through security sector reforms'. Finally, the 'on-going ENP review should aim at closer coordination between ENP and wider CFSP/CSDP activities in a comprehensive manner'. EU Council, 3382nd Council meeting Foreign Affairs, Press 8084/15, Luxembourg (20 April 2015) 8, pt 8.

States' interests according to the EUGS 'principled pragmatism'[32] approach, but also to use the ToL as it provides the means for the EU to 'deliver coherent and consistent policies and programmes by bringing together strands of EU foreign and assistance policy that were previously run by different institutions'.[33] Within the ENP, the security sector reform (SSR) became an important priority from 2011 onwards. The three AA-DCFTAs also include a title devoted to political dialogue and 'convergence in the field of foreign and security policy' including the following issues: conflict prevention; crisis management and military-technological cooperation non-proliferation of weapons of mass destruction; disarmament; arms controls; arms export control; and the fight against illicit trafficking of arms and terrorism.[34]

With the war in Ukraine and its consequences, including in the Southern Caucasus, the CFSP/CSDP dimension is becoming even more important, with new or reinforced CSDP military and civilian missions for Ukraine,[35] but also for Armenia[36] and Moldova.[37]

The CFSP Council decision 2022/338/CFSP of 28 February 2022 for the 'supply of military equipment, and platforms, designed to deliver lethal force' to the Ukrainian Armed Forces (UAF) financed under the European Peace Facility (EPF), is considered a

[32] Council of the EU, A Global Strategy for the European Union's Foreign and Security Policy Shared Vision, Common Action: A Stronger Europe (Brussels, June 2016), available at www.eeas.europa.eu/sites/default/files/eugs_review_web_0.pdf.

[33] COM(2011) 303 final (n 30) 18.

[34] See Arts 7–13 of the Association Agreement between the European Union and its Member States, of the one part, and Ukraine, of the other part, [2014] OJ L 161/3.

[35] In 2014, the EU Advisory Mission for Civilian Security Sector Reform Ukraine (EUAM Ukraine) was created to 'assist Ukraine in the field of civilian security sector reform, including police and rule of law'. Art 1 of Council Decision 2014/486/CFSP of 22 July 2014 on the European Union Advisory Mission for Civilian Security Sector Reform Ukraine (EUAM Ukraine), [2014] OJ L 217/42. It has been amended twice since the Russian invasion. First with Council Decision (CFSP) 2022/452 of 18 March 2022 ([2022] OJ L92/3) to *provide* EUAM Ukraine with the 'temporary, additional task of advising Ukrainian authorities, in particular the Ukrainian Border Guards Service, Customs Service and local police forces, with the aim of facilitating the flow of refugees from Ukraine to Poland, Romania and Slovakia and the flow of humanitarian aid into Ukraine'. Second, with Council Decision (CFSP) 2022/638 of 13 April 2022 ([2022] OJ L117/38) designed to 'support to Ukrainian authorities to facilitate the investigation and prosecution of international crimes'. The support is in 'particular to the Office of the Prosecutor General, regional Public Prosecutor Offices and Law Enforcement Agencies' (Art 2a). The EU Military Assistance Mission in support of Ukraine (EUMAM Ukraine) was adopted, on 17 October 2022, as a direct response to Russian invasion. Its objective is to help to develop the "military capability of Ukraine's Armed Forces (UAF) to regenerate and to effectively conduct operations, in order to allow Ukraine to defend its territorial integrity within its internationally recognised borders' and to 'effectively exercise its sovereignty and protect the civilians in Ukraine'. Art 1(2) of Council Decision (CFSP) 2022/1968 of 17 October 2022, European Union Military Assistance Mission in support of Ukraine (EUMAM Ukraine), [2022] OJ L270/85.

[36] In January 2023 the EU Council adopted Decision 2023/162/CFSP of 23 January 2023 on a European Union mission in Armenia (EUMA). It is a civilian mission designed to 'contribute to decreasing the number of incidents in conflict-affected and border areas in Armenia', and to diminish the 'level of risks for the population living in such areas and thereby to contribute to the normalisation of relations between Armenia and Azerbaijan on the ground'. Art 2 of EU Council Decision 2023/162/CFSP of 23 January 2023 on a European Union mission in Armenia (EUMA), [2023] OJ L22/29.

[37] The EU Council adopted, in April 2023, the EU Partnership Mission in the Republic of Moldova. It is a civilian mission designed to 'contribute to enhancing the resilience of the security sector' in the 'areas of crisis management and hybrid threats, including cybersecurity and countering foreign information manipulation and interference (FIMI)'. Art 2(1) of Council Decision 2023/855/CFSP of 24 April 2023 on a European Union Partnership Mission in Moldova (EUPM Moldova), [2023] OJ L110/30.

gamechanger for the EU.[38] The EPF was established by Council Decision 2021/509/CFSP of 22 March 2021,[39] for the 'financing by Member States of Union actions' under the CFSP when 'pursuant to Article 41(2) TEU, the operating expenditure arising from those actions is not charged to the Union budget' (Article 1(1)). In other words, the EPF is financed outside of the EU general budget and its principles.[40] It has been operational since July 2021[41] and became of utmost importance for the EU to support Ukraine at military level. The adoption of Council decision 2022/338/CFSP aims at contributing to 'strengthening the capabilities and resilience of the Ukrainian Armed Forces' and to 'defend the territorial integrity and sovereignty of Ukraine and protect the civilian population against the ongoing military aggression' (Article 1). €450 million were budgeted for the first 24 months' duration of the assistance measure (Article 3). Since then, the EPF initial financial ceiling (€5.6 billion) was increased several times to a total of more than €12 billion in September 2023.[42] In fact, on 20 March 2023, the EU Council earmarked €1 billion from the EPF to 'partially reimburse Member States for deliveries of ammunition (and missiles if requested) to Ukraine from their stocks', as well as 'another €1 billion for the joint procurement of ammunition (and missiles if requested) from the EU and Norwegian defence industries'.[43]

A second Council decision (2022/339/CFSP of 28 February 2022) on an assistance measure under the EPF to support the UAF was adopted at the same time to 'finance the provision of equipment and supplies not designed to deliver lethal force, such as personal protective equipment, first aid kits and fuel' (Article 1(2) and (3)). Given the evolution of the situation on the ground it has also been amended several times.[44]

Many other internal and external budgetary lines are impacted, from emergency and humanitarian aid, civil protection support, macro-financial assistance, reception and temporary protection of refugees and trade liberalisation measures. In the meantime, the preliminary plans for the reconstruction of Ukraine have already been discussed at different levels. It is therefore not possible to detail the massive impact of the war on cooperation at large. What is obvious is that from the 2011 securitisation of the ENP cooperation to the militarisation of the aid with the financing of lethal

[38] Council Decision 2022/338/CFSP of 28 February 2022 on an assistance measure under the European Peace Facility for the supply to the Ukrainian Armed Forces of military equipment, and platforms, designed to deliver lethal force, [2022] OJ L60/1.

[39] Council Decision 2021/509/CFSP of 22 March 2021, establishing a European Peace Facility, and repealing Decision (CFSP) 2015/528, [2021] OJ L102/14.

[40] The EPF replaced and expanded on the former Athena Mechanism and the African Peace Facility.

[41] See B Bilquin, 'European Peace Facility: State of play as of 31 March 2023', European Parliament research Service (EPRS), European Parliament Briefing PE 747.089 (Brussels, April 2023), available at www.europarl.europa.eu/RegData/etudes/BRIE/2023/747089/EPRS_BRI(2023)747089_EN.pdf.

[42] See EU council, European Peace Facility, available at www.consilium.europa.eu/en/policies/european-peace-facility; and EU Council, Ukraine: Council agrees on further support under the European Peace Facility, Press release 708/22 (17 October 2022). In fact, 'the delivery of military assistance is carried out by the EU Member States; through the EPF, the EU can reimburse Member States for a part of their military deliveries. The EPF-funded military assistance to Ukraine has absorbed, in the first 12 months of the war, 60% of the initially planned financial ceiling of the EPF of €5 billion for 2021–2027'. Bilquin (n 41).

[43] Bilquin (n 41). See Regulation 2023/1525 of the European Parliament and of the Council of 20 July 2023, on supporting ammunition production (ASAP), [2023] OJ L185/7.

[44] Council Decision 2022/339/CFSP of 28 February 2022 on an assistance measure under the European Peace Facility to support the Ukrainian Armed Forces, [2022] OJ L/14.

equipment in 2023, there is a clear rise of intergovernmentalism and pragmatism in the EU approach, with all it entails.

7.2.2. Is the ENP Still Relevant? A Recurrent Question

Is the ENP still relevant? This question is not new. In the March 2015 Joint Consultation Paper entitled 'Towards a new European Neighbourhood Policy', the two first questions put forward by the European Commission and the High Representative were precisely: 'Should the ENP be maintained?' and 'Should a single framework continue to cover both East and South?'.[45] These questions are still valid. To answer them, it is necessary to briefly get back to the original objectives and ambitions of the ENP.

7.2.2.1. The 2002 ENP Initial Objectives and the Russia Factor in 2023

The conclusions of the December 2002 Copenhagen European Council included the main general objectives and beneficiaries of the ENP before the big-bang enlargement. It must be stressed that these conclusions were adopted before the 2004 and 2007 waves of enlargement and before the 2008 war in Georgia.

In 2002, the then 15 Member States stated that the EU remained 'determined to avoid new dividing lines in Europe and to promote stability and prosperity within and beyond the new borders of the Union' while underlining that 'enlargement will strengthen relations with Russia'.[46] The result might well be the exact opposite as new dividing lines have been created within Ukraine (in 2014 and since 2022) and in Georgia (2008). The Nagorno Karabakh – although located in Azerbaijan territory and internationally recognised as such, but previously beyond the control of its government – saw, in 2023, a massive exodus of ethnic Armenians. Belarus has been, at least strategically, absorbed by the Russian Federation with the comeback of nuclear tactical missiles[47] and as its territory is used for conducting military operations in Ukraine. The *Suwalki* Gap, a strategic corridor between Belarus, Lithuania, Poland and the Kaliningrad Russian enclave, is now considered as one of NATO's 'fragile hot spots'.

One should remember that if the 'Russia factor' was taken into consideration in drafting the ENP there was a clear lack of consensus among the 15 Member States and within EU institutions about how to address it in concrete terms. Christopher Patten and Javier Solana, respectively Commissioner for External Relations and SG/HR, while

[45] European Commission and High representative, Joint Consultation Paper, Towards a new European Neighbourhood Policy, JOIN(2015) 6 final (Brussels, 4 March 2015).

[46] European Council, Presidency Conclusions, Copenhagen, 12 and 13 December 2002, pt 24: 'The enlargement will strengthen relations with Russia. The European Union also wishes to enhance its relations with Ukraine, Moldova, Belarus and the southern Mediterranean countries based on a long-term approach promoting democratic and economic reforms, sustainable developments and trade and is developing new initiatives for this purpose. The European Council welcomes the intention of the Commission and the Secretary-General/High Representative to bring forward proposals to that end.'

[47] 'The deployment is Moscow's first move of such warheads – shorter-range less powerful nuclear weapons that could potentially be used on the battlefield – outside Russia since the fall of the Soviet Union'; Reuters Europe, 'Belarus starts taking delivery of Russian nuclear weapons' (14 June 2023), available at www.reuters.com/world/europe/belarus-has-started-taking-delivery-russian-tactical-nuclear-weapons-president-2023-06-14.

preparing the 2002 Copenhagen European Council meeting, wrote a joint letter in August 2002 in which they emphasised the need to 'consider how Russa might be linked to, or fall within a new neighbourhood policy'. They stressed that Russia being an 'indivisible part of the region', it was 'difficult to envisage strengthened regional co-operation without' this country.[48]

In the December 2002 European Council conclusions, after referring to the expected impact of the big-bang enlargement on EU–Russia relations, the Member States declared that the EU also 'wishes to enhance its relations with Ukraine, Moldova, Belarus and the southern Mediterranean countries' in order to promote 'democratic and economic reforms'.[49] The non-respect of alphabetical order indicated the ranking of EU's priorities.

Russia was next referred to the ENP countries in the first March 2003 Communication of the European Commission entitled: 'Wider Europe – Neighbourhood'.[50] The Commission proposed that

> Russia, the countries of the Western NIS and the Southern Mediterranean should be offered the prospect of a stake in the EU's Internal Market and further integration and liberalisation to promote the free movement of – persons, goods, services and capital (four freedoms).[51]

It also added that the 'new neighbourhood policy will only constitute one pillar of the overall EU/Russia strategic partnership'. In fact, Russia is mentioned 40 times in the March 2003 Communication (excluding annexes).

However, a year later, in its May 2004 Communication entitled 'European Neighbourhood Policy – Strategy Paper', the Commission acknowledged that Russia and the EU 'decided to develop' their strategic partnership outside the ENP 'through the creation of four common spaces, as defined' in St Petersburg in May 2003.[52] The Commission proposed simultaneously the 'inclusion of Armenia, Azerbaijan and Georgia within the scope of the ENP'.[53] This was another major geopolitical shift for the nascent ENP of a 'just enlarged EU'.

2007 saw Bulgaria and Romania adding an important share of the western shores of the Black Sea to EU waters, as well as the implementation of the first ENP financial instrument, the European Neighbourhood Partnership Instrument (ENPI), which included Russia among its beneficiaries. 2007 was also the year of Vladimir Putin's famous speech in Munich. On 10 February 2007 he stressed that he perceived NATO's expansion as a 'serious provocation', insisting that NATO members were 'trying to impose new dividing lines and walls' on Russia. He asked how 'many years and decades, as well as several generations of politicians' will be needed to 'dissemble and dismantle these new walls?'.[54] EU Enlargement and NATO enlargement cannot be disconnected

[48] EU Council, Chris Patten and Javier Solana, Wider Europe, Joint Letter (7 August 2002) 4.

[49] European Council, Presidency conclusions (12 and 13 December 2002) pts 22 and 24.

[50] European Commission, Communication, Wider Europe – Neighbourhood: A New Framework for Relations with our Eastern and Southern Neighbours', COM(2003) 104 final (Brussels, 11 March 2003).

[51] ibid, 4.

[52] European Commission, Communication, European Neighbourhood Policy – Strategy Paper (Brussels, 12 May 2004) COM(2004) 373, 4.

[53] ibid, 7.

[54] V Putin, Speech and the Following Discussion at the Munich Conference on Security Policy, Munich (10 February 2007), en.kremlin.ru/events/president/transcripts/24034.

as far as European neighbours are concerned.[55] In 2008 the war in Georgia redrew Eurasian borders. On 1 July 2013, Croatia's accession further enlarged the EU's territory in the Western Balkans and on the North-eastern shores of the Adriatic Sea. March 2014 saw the annexation by Russia of Crimea, followed by the creation of so-called 'people's republics' by Russia-backed rebellion in the Donetsk and Luhansk regions.

Today, there is more instability, insecurity and poverty in the EU's wider neighbourhood. Moreover, new dividing lines and even new frontlines have been created since 2002. The impact of the war on the entire area is reinforced by an already very difficult context at security, political and socio-economic levels. There is no 'deep and sustainable democracy' in the Southern neighbourhood, as promoted in 2011. Russia is at war with one candidate – Ukraine – while Moldova is facing the destabilisation factor of Transnistria, and to a lesser extent of the autonomous region of *Gagauzia*. Belarus has been implicated in Russia's military aggression against Ukraine and is facing heightened sanctions as a result, whereas Armenia is almost in a state of war with Azerbaijan. The immediate impact of this dramatic geostrategic situation was a recalibration of the Eastern Partnership after the Russian invasion.

7.2.2.2. The Eastern Partnership Recalibration

The impact of the war on the Eastern partnership is very important. For the short- to medium-term the Eastern Partnership' has been preserved but recalibrated. It was at the 12 December 2022 Eastern partnership Foreign Ministers Meeting, without Belarus, that the 'EU's commitment to the Eastern Partnership'[56] was reiterated. This was not so obvious as one-third of the Eastern partners started to move from the ENP to the 'accession track' when Moldova and Ukraine were granted candidate status for EU membership, Georgia being invited to follow the same path. The EaP was therefore recalibrated and should be used mainly for (intra-) regional cooperation. A lighter administrative machinery and refocused priorities have been put in place.

Is the EaP as such still relevant? For the time being it is. The EaP can help to maintain a multilateral/regional dimension for the cooperation that has been already severely affected, as analysed above. In time, it could also be used to relaunch cooperation, notably at the sectoral level. Beyond the EaP, the European Political Community (EPC) launched on 6 October 2022 in Prague, is now to be taken into consideration as a framework for political dialogue. However, the EPC geographical coverage is much broader than the EaP, and Belarus and Russia are, of course, not invited for the time being.[57]

[55] NATO's accessions since 1999: 12 March 1999: Czechia, Hungary and Poland; 29 March 2004: Bulgaria, Estonia, Latvia, Lithuania, Romania, Slovakia and Slovenia; 1 April 2009: Albania and Croatia; 5 June 2017: Montenegro; 27 March 2020: Republic of North Macedonia: 4 April 2023: Finland. NATO, 'Enlargement and Article 10', available at www.nato.int/cps/en/natohq/topics_49212.htm.

[56] EU Council, Eastern Partnership Foreign Ministers meeting, Eastern Partnership Foreign Ministers meeting, Main results (Brussels, 12 December 2022), available at www.consilium.europa.eu/en/meetings/international-ministerial-meetings/2022/12/12.

[57] The participants of the first EPC meeting were the '27 EU Member States; Albania; Armenia; Azerbaijan; Bosnia and Herzegovina; Georgia; Iceland; Kosovo; Liechtenstein; Moldova; Montenegro; North Macedonia; Norway; Serbia; Switzerland; Turkey; Ukraine; the United Kingdom; the President of the European Commission; the President of the European Council'. EU Council, Meeting of the European Political Community, Main results, Prague (6 October 2022), available at www.consilium.europa.eu/en/

The EPC follows a continental approach with more than 40 members, and this is an asset to tackle the major issues at stake. In fact, the two main issues addressed in Prague were 'peace and security, especially Russia's war in Ukraine' and the 'energy crisis'.[58] However, the Commission stressed that this framework 'will not replace existing EU policies and instruments, notably enlargement, and will fully respect the European Union's decision-making autonomy'.[59]

The European Parliament in its Resolution of 23 June 2022 on 'the candidate status of Ukraine, the Republic of Moldova and Georgia', called the Commission, the Member States and the HR/VP to 'update the Eastern Partnership policy in order to enable it to remain a transformative and meaningful instrument in the current context' that is also threatening the 'security of Ukraine's neighbouring countries' and affecting 'stability in the region'. The MEPs reiterated the 'need for regional cooperation between the Eastern Partnership countries'.[60] It remains to be seen if the EaP will be adapted or replaced by a new regional framework for cooperation.

7.3. The Impact of the War on the Enlargement Process

The impact of the war on enlargement will vary in time and depth. More than 18 months after the launch of the Russian invasion of Ukraine, the impact on the enlargement methodology is visible. For the application phase it is quite limited regarding the procedural aspects governed by Article 49 TEU, directly linked to the values referred to in Article 2 TEU. The specific context is nevertheless very unusual and the rapidity of the application phase is obvious.[61] For instance, Ukraine 'received questionnaires on 8 April 2022 on the political and economic criteria and on 13 April on the EU *acquis* chapters and provided its replies on 17 April and on 9 May respectively'.[62]

For the longer-term perspectives related to EU integration and notably its limits, the impact of the war will be crucial. The outcome of the war being unpredictable it triggers an immediate question: can a country (even only technically) at war become a Member State of the EU? The Cyprus issue comes immediately to mind even if it is obviously difficult to compare the two cases, notably given the scale of the current war, involving a nuclear power, one of the five permanent members of the UN Security Council.

meetings/international-summit/2022/10/06. In 2023, Monaco, San Marino and the president of the European Parliament were also present at the meeting. See EU Council, Meeting of the European Political Community, Main results, Bulboaca, Moldova (1 June 2023), available at www.consilium.europa.eu/en/meetings/international-summit/2023/06/01.

[58] 'The European Political Community aims to: foster political dialogue and cooperation to address issues of common interest; strengthen the security, stability and prosperity of the European continent. This does not replace any existing organisation, structure or process, nor does it aim to create a new one at this stage'. EU Council, Meeting of the European Political Community, Main results, Prague (6 October 2022).

[59] European Commission (n 19) 2.

[60] European Parliament Resolution of 23 June 2022 on the candidate status of Ukraine, the Republic of Moldova and Georgia (2022/2716(RSP) P9_TA(2022)0249), pt 12.

[61] For a comparison with the big bang enlargement see E Lannon, *Le Traité d'adhésion d'Athènes: Les négociations, les conditions de l'admission et les principales adaptations des traités résultant de l'élargissement de l'UE à vingt-cinq États membres* (2004) *Cahiers de Droit Européen* 15.

[62] European Commission, Commission Opinion on Ukraine's application (n 3) 2.

7.3.1. The Impact on the Current EU Enlargement Methodology

The applications for EU membership were submitted by Ukraine on 28 February 2022, followed by the Republic of Moldova and Georgia on 3 March. This is a first as Ukraine had been resisting Russian's invasion since 24 February 2022. Four days later, the President of Ukraine, Volodymyr Zelensky, submitted to Emmanuel Macron (head of state of the country in charge of the rotating presidency of the EU Council's configurations) the application of Ukraine in the form of a brief letter stating:

> Your Excellency, Ukraine herewith, as a European state respecting the values enshrined in the Article 2 of the Treaty on European Union, has the honour to apply, in accordance with the Article 49 of the Treaty on European Union, for membership of the European Union. A Joint Statement of the Ukrainian state authorities on the application of Ukraine for membership of the European Union is attached.[63]

This is in line with the procedure of Article 49 TEU stating that: 'any European State which respects the values referred to in Article 2 and is committed to promoting them may apply to become a member of the Union'. In order to do so the 'applicant State shall address its application to the Council'.[64] On 7 March 2022, the EU Council requested the Commission to submit its opinions following Article 49 TEU requirement, according to which the EU Council 'shall act unanimously after consulting the Commission'. In the meantime, at the 11 March 2022 Versailles informal meeting, the European Council acknowledged the three applications. The Member States insisted that the EU would deepen its support for Ukraine in 'pursuing its European path', while no specific comments were made for Moldova and Georgia.[65]

7.3.1.1. Moldova, Ukraine and Georgia as Candidate Countries: Article 49 TEU and the 2020 Revised Enlargement Methodology

The Commission stressed that the three opinions, published on 17 June 2022, are 'structural' assessments 'against established criteria'. It was emphasised that the Commission was 'following a methodology *similar* to that used in previous Commission Opinions'.[66] It is thus not identical, given notably the specific context and timing.

The Commission recommended granting Ukraine and Moldova a candidate status 'on the understanding that steps' are 'taken' in a number of areas (seven steps for Ukraine

[63] General Secretariat of the Council, Application of Ukraine for membership of the European Union – Transmission to Member States' Parliaments, Communication CM 2003/22 (Brussels, 4 March 2022).

[64] In this regard the 'Joint Statement by the President of Ukraine Volodymyr Zelenskyy, the Chairman of the Verkhovna Rada of Ukraine Ruslan Stefanchuk and the Prime Minister of Ukraine Denys Shmyhal on Ukraine's application for membership of the European Union' and annexed to Ukraine's application states that: 'We, representatives of the authorities in Ukraine, reaffirming that Ukraine is a European state that shares European democratic values, set out in Article 2 of the Treaty on European Union of 1992 and the Treaty on the Functioning of the EU of 1957, in particular respect for human dignity, freedom, democracy, equality, the rule of law and human rights, including the rights of persons belonging to minorities; having regard to Article 49 of the Treaty on European Union, according to which any European State which respects the said values may apply for membership of the Union.'

[65] Informal meeting of the Heads of State or Government Declaration, Versailles (10 and 11 March 2022), pt 4.

[66] Italics added.

and nine for Moldova). For Georgia, the Commission recommended granting 'candidate status, once [12] priorities will have been addressed'.[67] The vocabulary used is of importance as a distinction is made between Moldova and Ukraine, on the one hand and Georgia, on the other hand.

Still, according to Article 49 TEU, the 'European Parliament and national Parliaments shall be notified' of an application.[68] So, ahead of the meeting of the European Council of 23–24 June 2022 the European Parliament, having been notified of the three applications, adopted on 23 June 2022 a Resolution on the 'candidate status of Ukraine, the Republic of Moldova and Georgia'. The Resolution called the European Council to 'grant EU candidate status to Ukraine and the Republic of Moldova without delay, and to grant the same status to Georgia once its government has delivered on the indicated priorities in the Commission's opinion' (point 3). The Members of the Parliament (MEPs) underlined that 'accession to the EU must take place in accordance with Article 49 TEU, based on respect for the relevant procedures and conditional upon the fulfilment of the established criteria'. They stressed that accession 'remains a merit-based process that requires adoption and implementation of relevant reforms' and this 'notably in the areas of democracy, the rule of law, human rights, a market economy and implementation of the EU *acquis*' (point 7). Also of interest, with regard to the ENP, is the reference made to the 'need to take advantage of the experiences of Ukraine, the Republic of Moldova and Georgia with the implementation of their respective' AA-DCFTAs and this 'as a basis for the upcoming accession process, thus allowing the three countries to gradually integrate within the EU single market and enhance sectoral cooperation'. The MEPs also called the Commission and the Member States to 'prepare internal structures and provide additional resources, as well as increased technical assistance and political support' (point 9).[69] The resolution was adopted with '529 votes to 45 and 14 abstentions'.[70]

On 24 June 2022, the European Council recognised the 'European perspective of the three applicant countries' while 'granting the status of EU candidate country to Ukraine and Moldova' and inviting the Commission to 'report to the Council on the fulfilment of the conditions' specified in its opinions.[71] The European Council declared to be 'ready to grant the status of candidate country to Georgia once the priorities specified' in the Commission's opinion 'on Georgia's membership application have been addressed'.[72]

The three opinions referred to the usual legal framework within which the European Commission submits its opinion: Article 49 TEU linked to Article 2 TEU. This is very

[67] Commission Opinion on Moldova's application (n 5) 16–17. European Commission, Commission Opinion on Ukraine's application (n 3) 17–18.

[68] Art 49(2) TEU states that accession agreements 'shall be submitted for ratification by all the contracting States in accordance with their respective constitutional requirements'. In the case of France see the issue of a potential referendum in Art 88(5) of the French Constitution.

[69] European Parliament Resolution of 23 June 2022 (n 60).

[70] European Parliament, Grant EU candidate status to Ukraine and Moldova without delay, MEPs demand, Press release no 20220616IPR33216 (23 June 2022), available at www.europarl.europa.eu/pdfs/news/expert/2022/6/press_release/20220616IPR33216/20220616IPR33216_en.pdf.

[71] One should remember that the leaders of France, Germany, Italy and Romania went to Kyiv on 16 June 2022 to support the candidacy of Ukraine and Moldova. European Council, conclusions, 24 June 2022 (Brussels), EUCO 24/22, pt III Membership applications of Ukraine, The Republic of Moldova and Georgia pts 10–11.

[72] ibid, pt 13.

important as Article 2 TEU, in its Lisbon version, constitutionalised the specific right to protect minorities previously only mentioned in the Copenhagen criteria:

> The Union is founded on the values of respect for human dignity, freedom, democracy, equality, the rule of law and respect for human rights, including the rights of persons belonging to minorities. These values are common to the Member States in a society in which pluralism, non-discrimination, tolerance, justice, solidarity and equality between women and men prevail.[73]

It is worth citing also *in extenso* the conclusions of the 1993 European Council as they structure the Commission's opinions: 'accession will take place as soon as an associated country is able to assume the obligations of membership by satisfying the economic and political conditions required'. At political level, 'membership requires that the candidate country has achieved stability of institutions guaranteeing democracy, the rule of law, human rights and respect for and protection of minorities'. The economic conditions are 'the existence of a functioning market economy as well as the capacity to cope with competitive pressure and market forces within the Union'. Also, EU membership 'presupposes the candidate's ability to take on the obligations of membership including adherence to the aims of political, economic and monetary union'. In a separate paragraph it was also underlined that the EU's 'capacity to absorb new members, while maintaining the momentum of European integration, is also an important consideration in the general interest of both the Union and the candidate countries'.[74] The absorption capacity, meaning the capability of the EU to integrate new members while 'maintaining the momentum of European integration', echoes the debates linked to the widening-deepening nexus[75] that will grow with the negotiation phase.

The European Commission insists on the importance of the 'ability to take on and implement effectively the obligations of membership',[76] the 'effective implementation' being a recurrent keyword in its progress reports. The 24 June 2022 European Council Conclusions reiterated that the 'progress of each country' will 'depend on its own merit in meeting the Copenhagen criteria, taking into consideration the EU's capacity to absorb new members'.[77] Finally, it is important to underscore the specificity of the Western Balkans countries subject to additional conditions for membership in the framework of the Stabilisation and Association Process (SAP) and mainly related to regional cooperation and good neighbourly relations.[78]

The assessments of the applications in the three opinions and analytical reports were thus made on the usual set of criteria. As mentioned above: Articles 49 and 2 TEU, the Copenhagen criteria and also the 'subsequent' European Council conclusions. First, the 1995 Madrid European Council conclusions with the need 'to create the conditions for the gradual, harmonious integration' of the applicant countries, 'particularly

[73] Emphasis added.

[74] European Council, Conclusions of the Presidency, DOC/93/3 (Copenhagen, 21–22 June 1993) pt 7.

[75] Report of the Franco-German Working Group on EU institutional reform – Sailing on High Seas: Reforming and Enlarging the EU for the 21st Century, Paris-Berlin (18 September 2023), available at www.politico.eu/wp-content/uploads/2023/09/19/Paper-EU-reform.pdf. See also D Triantafyllou, *Révision des traités: l'Europe est-elle prête à un saut qualitatif?*, Schuman Paper no 725 (Paris, 6 November 2023).

[76] European Commission, Accession Criteria, available at neighbourhood-enlargement.ec.europa.eu/enlargement-policy/glossary/accession-criteria_en.

[77] European Council conclusions (n 71), pt 14.

[78] European Commission, Conditions for membership, available at neighbourhood-enlargement.ec.europa.eu/enlargement-policy/conditions-membership_en., On 'good neighbourly relations' and 'regional cooperation' as well as on the influence of Russia, China and Turkey in the Western Balkans, see P Mirel, 'European

through the development of the market economy, the adjustment of their administrative structures and the creation of a stable economic and monetary environment'. Second, the December 2006 European Council conclusions stating that the 'enlargement strategy based on consolidation, conditionality and communication, combined with the EU's capacity to integrate new members, forms the basis for a renewed consensus on enlargement'.[79] The opinions also take into account the 'efforts made' by the candidate in 'implementing its obligations' under the AA-DCFTAs, as a criterion to evaluate its ability to 'assume the obligations of membership'.[80]

It is the 2020 revised enlargement methodology that is taken into consideration.[81] For the purpose of the pre-accession, the EU *acquis* is therefore structured around six thematic clusters: i) Fundamentals; ii) Internal market; iii) Competitiveness & inclusive growth; iv) Green agenda & sustainable connectivity v) Resources, agriculture & cohesion; vi) External relations. The main elements of the revised enlargement methodology are that: i) negotiations on each cluster open as a whole (after the candidate fulfils the opening benchmarks); ii) each chapter is dealt with individually with respect to its provisional closure; iii) negotiations on the fundamentals' cluster open first and close last; iv) progress under the fundamentals' cluster determine the overall pace of negotiations; v) sufficient progress leads to 'closer integration' (accelerated integration and funding).[82] Moreover, the Member States can decide to put negotiations on hold in certain areas, or suspend them overall. According to the Commission the accession process had to become 'more predictable, more credible – based on objective criteria and rigorous positive and negative conditionality, and reversibility – more dynamic and subject to stronger political steering'.[83]

The key of the revised methodology is that a firm commitment to the 'fundamentals first' principle is essential. The 'fundamentals first' approach links the rule of law and fundamental rights with the two other key areas of the accession process: 'economic governance – strengthened focus on economic development and improved competitiveness – and the strengthening of democratic institutions and public administration reform'. Moreover, 'good neighbourly relations and regional cooperation are essential'.[84] The latter is to be underscored given the importance of the Russia factor.

7.3.1.2. The European Commission Opinion and Analytical Report on Moldova

In its Opinion of 17 June 2022, the European Commission assessed Moldova's application on the basis of its capacity to 'meet the criteria set by the European Council

Union-Western Balkans: for a revised membership negotiation framework', *European issues*, no 529, Robert Schuman Foundation (Paris, 30 September 2019).

[79] European Commission, Analytical Report following the Communication from the Commission to the European Parliament, the European Council and the Council: Commission Opinion on the Republic of Moldova's application for membership of the European Union, Commission Staff Working Document, SWD(2023) 32 final, (Brussels, 1 February 2023) 2.

[80] European Commission, Commission Opinion on Ukraine's application (n 3) 16.

[81] European Commission, Communication on Enhancing the accession process – A credible EU perspective for the Western Balkans, COM(2020) 57 final (Brussels, 5 February 2020).

[82] ibid 4–5.

[83] ibid, 1.

[84] IPA III (n 18) Preamble, pt 6.

in Copenhagen in 1993, as well as in Madrid in 1995, notably regarding the country's administrative capacity' taking into consideration Moldova's efforts in implementing the AA-DCFTA. Concerning the political criteria, the Commission evaluated that overall, 'Moldova has a solid foundation in place to reach the stability of institutions guaranteeing democracy, the rule of law, human rights and respect for and protection of minorities'. At the level of the economic criteria, Moldova 'has pursued reasonably sound macroeconomic policies, significantly strengthened financial sector stability, and improved the business environment'. For the capacity to fulfil the obligations of membership, Moldova 'has worked since 2016 on the implementation' of the AA-DCFTA and 'gradually taken up the alignment process across many chapters and has a satisfactory track record of implementation'. Therefore, 'overall, Moldova has established a solid basis for further alignment'.[85]

The Commission recommended that Moldova be granted candidate status, on the understanding that the nine steps summarised in Table 7.1 are taken.

Table 7.1 Nine steps identified by the European Commission in its Opinion on Moldova's application for membership

i)	'complete essential steps of the recently launched comprehensive **justice system reform** across all institutions in the justice and prosecution chains, to ensure their independence, integrity, efficiency, accountability and transparency, including through efficient use of asset verification and effective democratic oversight; in particular, fill all the remaining vacancies of the Supreme Council Magistracy and in its specialised bodies';
ii)	'across all these areas, address **shortcomings identified by OSCE/ODIHR and the Council of Europe/the Venice Commission**';
iii)	'deliver on the commitment to fight **corruption** at all levels by taking decisive steps towards proactive and efficient investigations, and a credible track record of prosecutions and convictions; substantially increase the take up of the recommendations of the National Anticorruption Centre';
iv)	'implement the commitment to "**de-oligarchisation**" by eliminating the excessive influence of vested interests in economic, political, and public life';
v)	'strengthen the fight against **organised crime**, based on detailed threat assessments, increased cooperation with regional, EU and international partners and better coordination of law enforcement agencies; in particular, put in place a legislative package on asset recovery and a comprehensive framework for the fight against **financial crime and money laundering**, ensuring that anti-money laundering legislation is in compliance with the standards of the Financial Action Task Force (FATF)';
vi)	'increase the capacity to deliver on reforms and provide quality public services including through stepping up implementation of public **administration reform**; assess and update the public administration reform strategy';
vii)	'complete the reform of **Public Financial Management** including improving **public procurement** at all levels of government';
viii)	'enhance the **involvement of civil society in decision-making** processes at all levels';
ix)	'strengthen the **protection of human rights**, particularly of **vulnerable groups**, and sustain its commitments to enhance **gender equality** and **fight violence against women**';

Source: Commission Opinion on the Republic of Moldova's application for membership of the European Union (see n 5) 16–17 (emphasis added).

[85] Commission Opinion on the Republic of Moldova's application (n 5) 15–16.

One should note the importance of the issue of 'corruption' and organised crime in general as mentioned in the three opinions, like the 'de-oligarchisation' that is very specific to these 'post-soviet space' eastern European countries.

Eight months later, on 1 February 2023, the three analytical reports that are 'structural assessments against the Copenhagen criteria and subsequent European Council conclusions',[86] were published simultaneously. They completed the Commission's opinions on the application for membership and assessed the countries 'overall capacity to uphold the obligations of membership, i.e., the full body of EU law as expressed in the Treaty, secondary legislation, and the EU's policies (*acquis* of the European Union)'. It focused on legislative alignment with the *acquis* 'in the 33 *acquis* chapters, except for areas that were covered in detail'[87] by the opinions. The assessment scale used by the European Commission to 'describe the state of play' is the following: 'early stage, some level of preparation, moderately prepared, good level of preparation and well advanced'. In Moldova's analytical report no area was assessed as being at a 'good level of preparation' or 'well advanced'.

In February 2023, Moldova was at an early stage of preparation in the areas of: public procurement; financial control; free movement of workers; company law; financial services; social policy and employment; fisheries policy; regional policy; and own resources. Moldova achieved some level of preparation to implement the EU *acquis* in the areas of justice, freedom and security; statistics; free movement of goods; right of establishment and freedom to provide services; intellectual property law; competition policy; consumer and health protection; digital transformation and media; economic and monetary policy; enterprise and industrial policy; education and culture; customs union; transport policy; energy policy; trans-European networks; environment and climate change; food safety, and veterinary and phytosanitary policy. Finally, Moldova is moderately prepared in the areas of: science and research; external relations; and foreign, security and defence policy. The last point is of importance, even if not included in the fundamentals. Moreover, it should be stressed that this analytical report 'does not address the situation of non-government-controlled areas of Moldova', meaning Transnistria.[88]

7.3.1.3. The European Commission Opinion and Analytical Report on Ukraine

In its Opinion, concerning the political criteria, the Commission evaluated on 17 June 2022 that overall, Ukraine was 'well advanced in reaching the stability of institutions guaranteeing democracy, the rule of law, human rights and respect for and protection of minorities'.[89] For the economic criteria, Ukraine has notably 'continued its strong macro-economic record, demonstrating a noteworthy resilience with macroeconomic and financial stability ensured also after Russia's invasion'. The 'need to continue'

[86] European Commission (n 79) 3.
[87] ibid.
[88] ibid, 3.
[89] European Commission, Commission Opinion on Ukraine's application (n 3) 20.

so-called 'ambitious structural reforms' in order to 'remove corruption, reduce the state footprint and the persistent influence of oligarchs' was also stressed. For the capacity to fulfil the obligations of membership, there has been since 2016 an 'overall satisfactory track record of implementation' of the AA-DFCTA.[90] The Commission recommended that Ukraine 'be granted candidate status, on the understanding that the following 7 Steps', summarised in Table 7.2 below, are taken.

Table 7.2 Seven steps identified by the European Commission in its Opinion on Ukraine's application for membership

i)	'enact and implement legislation on a selection procedure for judges of the **Constitutional Court of Ukraine,** including a pre-selection process based on evaluation of their integrity and professional skills, in line with Venice Commission recommendations';
ii)	'finalise the integrity vetting of the **candidates for the High Council of Justice members** by the Ethics Council and the selection of candidate to establish the **High Qualification Commission of Judges of Ukraine**';
iii)	'further strengthen the fight against **corruption**, in particular at high level, through proactive and efficient investigations, and a credible track record of prosecutions and convictions; complete the **appointment of a new head of the Specialised Anti-Corruption Prosecutor's Office** through certifying the identified winner of the competition and launch and complete the selection process and appointment for a new Director of the National Anti-Corruption Bureau of Ukraine';
iv)	'ensure that **anti-money laundering legislation** is in compliance with the standards of the Financial Action Task Force (FATF); adopt an overarching strategic plan for the reform of the entire law enforcement sector as part of Ukraine's security environment';
v)	'implement the **Anti-Oligarch law** to limit the excessive influence of oligarchs in economic, political, and public life; this should be done in a legally sound manner, taking into account the forthcoming opinion of the Venice Commission on the relevant legislation';
vi)	'tackle the influence of vested interests by adopting a **media law** that aligns Ukraine's legislation with the EU audio-visual media services directive and empowers the independent media regulator';
vii)	'finalise the reform of the legal framework for **national minorities** currently under preparation as recommended by the Venice Commission, and adopt immediate and **effective implementation mechanisms**';

Source: Commission Opinion on Ukraine's application for membership of the European Union (n 3) 20–21 (emphasis added).

The importance of the judicial dimension and of the legal framework for national minorities are of particular importance for Ukraine. It is also important to stress that Crimea is mentioned five times in the Opinion and only twice in the analytical report, mainly to describe the administrative organisation or lack of statistics. There is one exception in the Opinion where the Commission states that the elections for the 26 vacant seats in the *Verkhovna Rada* have not been held 'in the Autonomous Republic of Crimea and the

[90] ibid, 20.

City of Sevastopol (Crimea) illegally annexed by the Russian Federation and in the parts of Donetsk and Luhansk oblasts beyond the government's control'.[91]

The analytical report of Ukraine stated that overall, in February 2023, Ukraine was at an early stage of preparation for implementing the EU *acquis* and applying European financial control standards in the areas of: free movement of workers; intellectual property law; in the field of social policy and employment; in the area of environment and climate change; of agriculture and rural development; and in the area of fisheries and of own resources. Overall, Ukraine has some level of preparation to implement the EU *acquis* in the areas of: justice, freedom and security; public procurement; statistics; concerning the right of establishment and freedom to provide services; in terms of alignment with the EU requirements in the area of the free movement of capital; of company law; competition policy; financial services; in consumer and health protection; in the area of taxation; enterprise and industrial policy; in education and culture; in the area of transport policy; of Trans-European networks and regarding regional policy. Ukraine is moderately prepared in the areas of: free movement of goods; in the domain of digital transformation and media;[92] economic and monetary policy; science and research; food safety; veterinary and phytosanitary policy. Ukraine has a good level of preparation in the area of: the customs union; on external relations; and foreign, security and defence policy. No area was overall assessed as being 'well advanced'.

7.3.1.4. The European Commission Opinion and Analytical Report on Georgia: A Deferred Candidate Status

The Commission in its 17 June 2022 Opinion recommended that 'Georgia be granted candidate status' once the 12 'priorities', summarised in the Table 7.3 below, 'have been addressed'. In other words, unlike with Ukraine and Moldova, the granting of candidate status was deferred and linked to 'priorities' to be 'addressed', and not 'steps' to be 'taken'.[93]

As mentioned above, the June 2022 European Council declared itself to be 'ready to grant the status of candidate country to Georgia' only once the above-mentioned 12 priorities 'on Georgia's membership application have been addressed'.[94] The approach followed for Georgia was similar to the one chosen for Bosnia and Herzegovina, when the European Council stated it was ready to grant candidate country status once 14 key priorities of the Commission' opinion would be implemented, 'with special attention to the priorities that constitute a substantial set of reforms'.[95] Georgia's analytical report is more critical compared to the two others especially at the level of the functioning of state institutions and high-level corruption. The analytical report does not refer to

[91] European Commission, Commission Opinion on Ukraine's application (n 3) 5.
[92] But 'well advanced in providing digital services', ibid, 33.
[93] European Commission, Commission Opinion on Georgia's application for membership of the European Union (Brussels, 17 June 2022), COM(2022) 405 final, 17.
[94] European Council conclusions (n 71), pt 13.
[95] European Commission (n 19) 1–2.

Table 7.3 Georgia's 12 priorities identified by the European Commission in its Opinion on the application for membership

- 'address the issue of **political polarisation**, through ensuring cooperation across political parties …';
- 'guarantee the full **functioning of all state institutions**, strengthening their independent and effective accountability as well as their democratic oversight functions; further **improve the electoral framework**, addressing all **shortcomings identified by OSCE/ODIHR and the Council of Europe/Venice Commission** in these processes';
- 'adopt and implement a transparent and effective **judicial reform** strategy and action plan post-2021 based on a broad, inclusive and cross-party consultation process; ensure a **judiciary that is fully and truly independent**, accountable and impartial along the entire judicial institutional chain, also to **safeguard the separation of powers**; notably ensure the proper functioning and **integrity of all judicial and prosecutorial institutions, in particular the Supreme Court** and address any shortcomings identified including the **nomination of judges** at all levels and of the Prosecutor-General; undertake a thorough **reform of the High Council of Justice** and appoint the High Council's remaining members. … to be fully in line with European standards and the recommendations of the Venice Commission';
- 'strengthen the independence of its **Anti-Corruption Agency** bringing together all key anti-corruption functions, in particular to **rigorously address high-level corruption cases**; equip the new Special Investigative Service and Personal Data Protection Service with resources commensurate to their mandates and ensure their institutional independence';
- 'implement the commitment to '**de-oligarchisation**' by eliminating the excessive influence of vested interests in economic, political, and public life';
- 'strengthen the **fight against organised crime** based on detailed threat assessments, notably by ensuring rigorous investigations, prosecutions and a credible track record of prosecutions and convictions; **guarantee accountability and oversight of law enforcement agencies**';
- 'undertake stronger efforts to guarantee a free, professional, pluralistic and **independent media** environment, notably by ensuring that criminal procedures brought against media owners fulfil the highest legal standards, and by launching impartial, effective and timely investigations in cases of threats against safety of journalists and other media professionals';
- 'move swiftly to strengthen the **protection of human rights of vulnerable groups**, including by bringing perpetrators and instigators of violence to justice more effectively';
- 'notably consolidate efforts to enhance **gender equality and fight violence against women';**
- 'ensure the **involvement of civil society in decision-making** processes at all levels';
- 'adopt legislation so that Georgian courts proactively **take into account European Court of Human Rights judgments** in their deliberations';
- 'ensure that an independent person is given preference in the process of **nominating a new Public Defender** (Ombudsperson) and that this process is conducted in a transparent manner; ensure the Office's effective institutional independence'.

Source: Commission Opinion on Georgia's application for membership of the European Union (n 93) 17–18 (emphasis added).

Abkhazia or South Ossetia, but the Opinion does briefly, recalling that the Georgian Government 'does not exercise effective control over its regions of Abkhazia and South Ossetia', and that the EU 'has been engaged since 2008 in peaceful conflict resolution efforts'.[96]

On 1 February 2023 Georgia was at an early stage of preparation in the fields of: free movement of workers; competition policy; environment and climate change; agriculture and rural development; regional policy; and its own resources. It had some level of preparation to implement the *acquis* in the areas of: justice, freedom and security; public procurement; statistics; financial control; free movement of goods; company law; intellectual property rights; financial services; consumer protection; public health; information society and media; taxation; social policy; employment; transport policy; energy; trans-European networks; food safety, veterinary and phytosanitary policy; and fisheries. Georgia was moderately prepared regarding the right of establishment and freedom to provide services; in the area of free movement of capital; in economic and monetary policy; in the area of enterprise and industrial policy; of science and research; of education and culture; of external relations and in the area of Foreign, security and defence policy. No area was assessed as being at a 'good level of preparation' or 'well advanced'.[97]

An unusual 'oral update' of progress in fulfilling conditions to launch EU membership talks with the three applicants was broadcast on 22 June 2023 by Oliver Varhelyi, the Commissioner for Neighbourhood and Enlargement. He indicated that, in December 2022, 'there was a clear request from a number of Member States' to 'see how these countries are making progress with these priorities' and this 'resulted in an undertaking by the Commission to provide a so-called oral update'. He acknowledged that 'this is something that we never do because we have an annual regular reporting cycle that we don't like to break'. Therefore, it is 'on a truly exceptional basis' that the European Commission 'took the obligation to provide the Council with the oral update'.[98] The Commission indicated it 'will report on the fulfilment' of the steps/priorities specified in the opinions 'as part of its regular enlargement package, in which Ukraine, Moldova and Georgia will be included as of 2023'.[99] The three reports, not analysed here, were published on 8 November 2023 in order to allow the European Council to decide, in December 2023, whether to launch accession negotiations in 2024.[100]

The impact of the war on the current EU enlargement methodology has been relatively limited for the application phase of the process. However, the systemic use of AA-DCFTAs, the unusual oral interim report and the rapidity of the application phase

[96] European Commission, Commission Opinion on Georgia's application (n 93) 3.

[97] European Commission, Georgia Analytical Report, Commission Staff Working Document, SWD(2023) 31 final (Brussels, 1 February 2023).

[98] European Commission, Press remarks by Neighbourhood and Enlargement Commissioner Olivér Várhelyi, following the informal General Affairs Council, SPEECH/23/3458 (Stockholm, 22 June 2023).

[99] European Commission (n 19) 1.

[100] European Commission, Georgia 2023 Report, Commission Staff Working Document, SWD(2023) 697 final (Brussels, 8 November 2023). European Commission, Republic of Moldova 2023 Report, Commission Staff Working Document, SWD(2023) 698 final (Brussels, 8 November 2023). European Commission, Ukraine 2023 Report, Commission Staff Working Document, SWD(2023) 699 final (Brussels, 8 November 2023).

is striking, especially in the context of a high-intensity war. The negotiating phase might well see another methodological revision.

7.3.2. The Impact of the War on the Future and Possibly Definitive Limits of EU Integration

The impact of the war on the future and possibly definitive limits of EU integration is an issue emerging at geopolitical and legal levels. Where to stop EU's integration? And what alternative to offer to European countries that either cannot (yet) join the EU or are not willing to join the EU? These are questions yet to be answered. To answer the enlargement fatigue, the Commission proposed to accelerate the accession process in the Western Balkans.

7.3.2.1. The Southern Caucasus: Eurasia Getting Closer to the EU

The fact that the European Commission deferred but finally proposed to grant the candidate status to Georgia is of utmost importance as it gives the signal that at least parts of the Southern Caucasus could join the EU.[101] That does not mean that the Member States will agree immediately with this proposal, but this is a geopolitical shift in the making.

7.3.2.1.1. Armenia between a Rock and a Hard Place

As acknowledged by the spokesperson of the EEAS, a 'mass exodus of Karabakh Armenians' took place 'as a result of Azerbaijan's military operation of 19 and 20 September' 2023 'and of the previous months-long blockage of the Lachin corridor'.[102] This exodus, as well as Azerbaijan's ambition for a corridor through Armenia to its exclave of Nakhchivan, might well change Armenia–EU and Armenia–Russia relationships in the future.

As explained above, this could result in an upgrade of the current CEPA. If Georgia attained candidate status, the geopolitical position of Armenia would change accordingly – another domino effect, much feared by autocrats in the region, as the possibility would arise of having another candidate country in Eurasia implementing political reforms at their doorstep.

The outcome of the war in Ukraine is also key for Armenia–EU relations but, at the time of writing, the risk of another conflict between Armenia and Azerbaijan supported by Türkiye is very high. Armenia is between a rock and a hard place, and it is very difficult to anticipate whether it will remain in the Russian sphere of influence.

[101] 'In the light of the results achieved since June 2022, within the framework of the twelve priorities and beyond', the Commission recommended in November 2023 that the 'Council grants Georgia the status of a candidate country on the understanding that' nine steps are taken. European Commission, 2023 Communication on EU Enlargement Policy, COM(2023) 690 final (Brussels, 8 November 2023) 25–26.

[102] European External Action Service, Azerbaijan: Statement by the Spokesperson on the displacement of people from Nagorno-Karabakh, EEAS Press Team (Brussels, 29 September 2023).

7.3.2.1.2. Azerbaijan as an EU Gas Supplier and a Bridge Over the Caspian Sea

The impact of the war in Ukraine on Azerbaijan is also clear. Azerbaijan has a strategic importance given the fact that it is an EU energy supplier on the shores of the Caspian Sea and at a crossroads between Central Asia, Middle East and Europe. This has been reinforced with the war and its consequences notably in diversifying EU's gas suppliers. Energy security was a major reason in 2004 for welcoming Azerbaijan into the ENP. On 18 July 2022 a Memorandum of Understanding (MoU) on a Strategic Partnership in the Field of Energy was signed between the EU and Azerbaijan. Its main objective is to 'double the capacity of the Southern Gas Corridor to deliver at least 20 billion cubic meters to the EU annually by 2027' in order to 'contribute to the diversification objectives in the REPowerEU Plan and help Europe to end its dependency on Russian gas'.[103]

In a resolution adopted on 5 October 2023, the European Parliament called on the EU to 'reduce its dependency on Azeri gas imports' and 'in the event of military aggression or significant hybrid attacks against Armenia, for a full EU import stop of Azeri oil and gas', as well as for the MoU to be 'suspended'.[104] The negotiations that started in 2017 for a new comprehensive agreement to replace the 1999 Partnership and cooperation agreement, which were supposed to resume in 2021, might thus be affected.[105]

The European Political Community offers opportunities to pursue a political dialogue. However, some limits have already been reached. The empty chair policy, followed by Türkiye and Azerbaijan during the third meeting of the EPC, held in Granada on 5 October 2023,[106] highlighted the limits of this informal intergovernmental forum and the current difficult context.

7.3.3. An Acceleration of the Accession Process in the Western Balkans

A direct impact of granting candidate status to Ukraine and Moldova has been an acceleration of the accession process in the Western Balkans. The 'full and unequivocal commitment to EU membership perspective of the Western Balkans' was reconfirmed by EU leaders in June 2022. The European Council called for an 'acceleration of the accession process and for further advancement of the gradual integration between the EU and the Western Balkans' in a 'reversible and merit-based manner', on the basis of the revised methodology.[107] The European Council of June 2022 also insisted on the

[103] European Commission, EU and Azerbaijan enhance bilateral relations, including energy cooperation, Press release IP/22/4550 (Brussels, 18 July 2022).

[104] The resolution was adopted by 491 votes in favour, 9 against with 36 abstentions. European Parliament, Nagorno-Karabakh: MEPs demand review of EU relations with Azerbaijan, AFET Press Release, 20230929IPR06132 (Strasbourg, 5 October 2023), available at www.europarl.europa.eu/news/en/press-room/20230929IPR06132/nagorno-karabakh-meps-demand-review-of-eu-relations-with-azerbaijan.

[105] European Commission, Overview of FTA negotiations (September 2023), available at policy.trade.ec.europa.eu/eu-trade-relationships-country-and-region/negotiations-and-agreements_en.

[106] Spanish Presidency of the Council of the EU, Meeting of the European Political Community (5 October 2023), available at spanish-presidency.consilium.europa.eu/en/events/meeting-of-the-european-political-community.

[107] European Council conclusions (n 71), pts 15–16.

importance of the reforms in the 'area of rule of law and in particular in the independence and functioning of the judiciary and the fight against corruption'. The leaders also stressed the urgency to resolve 'outstanding bilateral and regional disputes, particularly the Belgrade-Pristina dialogue on normalisation of relations between Serbia and Kosovo'.[108]

On 19 July 2022 the first Intergovernmental conference (IGC) on accession negotiations took place with North Macedonia and Albania and the Commission 'immediately launched the analytical examination of the EU *acquis* (screening) process'.[109] Then, the 15 December 2022 European Council granted Bosnia and Herzegovina candidate status, another landmark decision.[110]

The Commission, in its 2022 Communication, insisted that the CFSP is 'an issue that has grown in importance in this new geopolitical context' and stressed that if Albania, Bosnia and Herzegovina, Kosovo, North Macedonia and Montenegro 'aligned with EU restrictive measures in response to Russia's war of aggression against Ukraine', Serbia and Türkiye 'have not done so to date'.[111]

In 2023 a brand-new financial instrument, designed to address weaknesses and offer a prospect of a faster accession process, was proposed by the European Commission: the New growth plan for the Western Balkans. The main idea of this was to 'boost socio-economic convergence and bring' EU's partners 'closer to the EU's single market in many areas, in addition to significant additional financial support'.[112] The pre-accession strategy in the Western Balkans is clearly becoming more pragmatic and based on the 'more for more' approach[113] also stimulating more competition among neighbours in the region.

7.3.4. Türkiye: Forever Candidate?

According to the European Commission, Türkiye remains 'a key partner for the European Union and a candidate country' even if the accession negotiations 'are at a standstill since 2018'. However, the 'continuing backsliding in the areas of fundamental rights, the independence of the judiciary, economic management, and the lack of reforms in some sectoral issues' has been acknowledged by the Commission.[114]

Not only is Türkiye moving away from the EU in terms of accession, but it has become a competitor in the Eastern Mediterranean. For instance, in June 2022, the European Council expressed 'deep concern about recent repeated actions and statements by Turkey' and stressed that the latter must not only 'respect the sovereignty and territorial integrity of all EU Member States', but also 'fully respect international law' and 'de-escalate tensions in the interest of regional stability in the Eastern Mediterranean'.[115]

[108] ibid, pt 19.
[109] European Commission (n 19) 6.
[110] European Council Conclusions (Brussels, 15 December 2022) pt 30.
[111] European Commission (n 19) 1–2.
[112] European Commission, New growth plan for the Western Balkans, COM(2023) 691 final (Brussels, 8 November 2023) 9.
[113] ibid, 2.
[114] European Commission (n 19) 2.
[115] European Council conclusions (n 71), pt 30.

The impact of the war in Ukraine on Türkiye is also very important. As a riparian state of the Black Sea having control on the Bosporus Strait, according to the 1936 Montreux Convention regarding the Regime of Straits,[116] and thus over the passage of Russian warships, it plays a fundamental role in this regard. Türkiye is also exporting weapons to Ukraine including the famous TB2 *Bayraktar* drones. These were a 'key factor in several Ukrainian military successes, including the halting of the Russian advance from Belorussia or the destruction of the Moskva cruiser'. They are also used by Azerbaijan in the conflict in Nagorno Karabakh.[117]

Some new proposals with regard to Türkiye are to be expected as the June 2023 European Council tasked the HR/VP and the Commission to submit a report 'on the state of play of EU-Türkiye relations, building on the instruments and options identified by the European Council, and with a view to proceeding in a strategic and forward-looking manner'.[118]

7.4. Conclusion

Nobody could have envisaged in 2021 that Ukraine and Moldova would be granted candidate status for EU membership in 2022, just after the start of the war, and be in a position to start accession negotiations in 2024. This is a major shift impacting both the ENP and the enlargement process as a whole.

The ENP was designed, from 2002, to anticipate the consequences of the 2004–07 big-bang enlargement. New borders implied new neighbours, a side-effect of EU enlargement. The potential limits of any further EU (and NATO) enlargement were, however, uncertain.

Russia is trying to redraw its territorial limits with a war that started in 2014 with the annexation of Crimea and the support of the pro-Russian rebellion in the Donetsk and Luhansk regions. The 2014 events together with the 'migratory crisis' generated by the Syria and Iraq wars already impacted the ENP, but the impact of the Russian aggression is of another scale.

The very existence of the Eastern partnership is at stake as two, possibly three, out of its six current members are progressively leaving the ENP framework for the pre-accession track, the three remaining Eastern partners being Armenia, Azerbaijan and in principle Belarus. For the time being, the EaP has been recalibrated, and new reorientations and reallocations of funds are expected for the 2024 mid-term-review of the MFF.

It remains to be seen whether the EPC, which 'extends from Reykjavik to Baku or Yerevan, from Oslo to Ankara',[119] will be complementary to the accession process, or

[116] Montreux Convention regarding the Regime of Straits concluded on 20 July 1936 and ratified by: 'Australia, Bulgaria, France, Greece, Japan, Romania, Turkey, Union of Soviet Socialist Republics, United Kingdom of Great Britain and Northern Ireland, Yugoslavia (Federal Republic of)': treaties.un.org/pages/showDetails.aspx?objid=0800000280166981.

[117] L Péria-Peigné, 'TB2 *Bayraktar*: Big Strategy for a Little Drone' *Briefings de l'Ifri* (17 April 2023), available at www.ifri.org/sites/default/files/atoms/files/peria-peigne_tb2_bayraktar_2023.pdf.

[118] European Council Conclusions (Brussels, 29–30 June 2023) pt 42.

[119] The idea of the EPC was put forward by Enrico Letta in April 2022: E Letta, Interview, *Les Echos* (24 April 2022), available at www.lesechos.fr/monde/europe/enrico-letta-il-faut-construire-une-confederation-

a sort of alternative to it. The first point of the Conclusion of the European Council of June 2022 was in fact devoted to 'Wider Europe', as the European Council held a 'strategic discussion on the European Union's relations with its partners in Europe' and discussed the 'proposal to launch a European political community'. The European Council stressed that the aim of the EPC is to 'offer a platform for political coordination for European countries across the continent'. It is designed for liked-minded partners, in other words, 'all European countries' within the EU have 'close relations', the objective being to 'foster political dialogue and cooperation to address issues of common interest so as to strengthen the security, stability and prosperity of the European continent'. Even if the Member States stressed that the EPC would 'not replace existing EU policies and instruments, notably enlargement', many questions are still to be answered.[120]

The Wider Europe of the 2002 Patten Solana led to the EU Wider Neighbourhood Policy in 2004, with the inclusion of the three Southern Caucasus countries into the ENP framework. Whether the Wider Europe of the June 2022 conclusions of the European Council is going to lead to a new 'enlarged neighbourhood policy', merging the patchwork of EU's proximity strategies and/or extending it to the neighbours of EU's neighbours,[121] remains to be seen.

The proper articulation of the widening and deepening processes will also be essential for the future of EU integration. Are we witnessing a change regarding the main elements of the revised enlargement methodology? For the time being, the 2020 revised methodology is being followed, with some differences and novelties like the unusual 'oral update' of candidate's progress and the systematic use of the AA-DCFTAs. The focus should remain, from the European Commission's perspective, 'full and effective implementation' of the *acquis*. The main question is how politicised will the evaluations and process be in an evolving geopolitical context. Will rational thinking prevail over emotional choices? Ideally, a balanced approach between technicalities and the geopolitical imperatives should prevail. However, some, like Charles Michel,[122] are in favour of a more 'gradual, phased integration', and others insist, like Pierre Mirel, on the need to revise deeply the financial incentives.[123]

Many obstacles will appear on the long and winding road to EU accession. The major issue is of course whether a country at war (Ukraine) or having no control over parts of its territory (Georgia, Moldova and Ukraine) can become an EU Member State.

europeenne-pour-accueillir-lukraine-1402563. It was mentioned by Emmanuel Macron in May 2022, at the closing of the Conference on the Future of Europe: E Macron, 'Discours à l'occasion de la Conférence sur l'avenir de l'Europe' (9 May 2022), available at www.elysee.fr/front/pdf/elysee-module-19590-fr.pdf. The European Geo-Political Community 'from Reykjavik to Ankara' is by Charles Michel: see EU council, Speech by President at the plenary session of the European Economic and Social Committee, SPEECH 465/22 (Brussels, 18 May 2022).

[120] European Council conclusions (n 71), pt 1.

[121] See E Lannon, 'The "neighbours of the EU's neighbours", the "EU's broader neighbourhood" and the "arc of crisis and strategic challenges" from the Sahel to Central Asia' in S Gstöhl and E Lannon (eds), *The Neighbours of the European Union's Neighbours – Diplomatic and Geopolitical Dimensions beyond the European Neighbourhood Policy* (Farnham, Ashgate, 2014) 1–25.

[122] Council of the EU, Charles Michel, Speech (465/22) by President at the plenary session of the European Economic and Social Committee (Brussels, 18 May 2022).

[123] P Mirel, 'Union européenne-Balkans occidentaux: les illusions perdues?' (2022) 4 *Politique étrangère* 11, 23–25.

Ukraine, Georgia and Moldova will not become NATO members, like Cyprus,[124] if there are Russian troops on their soil, because of the principle of collective defence of Article 5 of the North Atlantic Treaty.[125] Nor will Serbia join NATO in the near future. At the level of CFSP/CSDP, Article 42(7) TEU, the mutual assistance clause,[126] was triggered by France following the Paris terrorist attacks of 2015, is also to be kept in mind given the strategic context.

Thus, a differentiated and gradual accession seems to be the only way forward. What is nevertheless striking is to put to the side the major issues of Transnistria, the annexed territories of the Donbass, Crimea, but also for Georgia: South Ossetia and Abkhazia. The approach followed for Kosovo and Cyprus seems inappropriate for the next enlargement wave(s) as five EU Member States do not recognise Kosovo as a sovereign state,[127] whereas the Cyprus issue is still to be solved. One should therefore acknowledge that the challenges of enlargement ahead will be much more difficult to overcome, compared to the previous ones.[128] For the President of the European Council it is a 'geopolitical imperative'.[129]

[124] Cyprus is not a NATO member and 'remains the only European Union member who is not even a member of the Alliance's Partnership for Peace program, due entirely to the outstanding reunification problem. Immediate NATO membership for a reunified island, however, would automatically embed, and therefore replace, a joint Greek-Turkish-British security guarantee within an Alliance commitment to the entire island without any need for alternative mechanisms.' D Wilson, 'NATO membership for Cyprus. Yes, Cyprus' *New Atlanticist* (1 April 2019), available at www.atlanticcouncil.org/blogs/new-atlanticist/nato-membership-for-cyprus.

[125] The North Atlantic Treaty (Washington DC, 4 April 1949)., available at www.nato.int/cps/en/natohq/official_texts_17120.htm.

[126] It is in fact the remaining of the former Art V of the Brussels Treaty that established in March 1948 the Western (European) Union.

[127] Cyprus, Greece, Romania, Slovakia and Spain.

[128] See M Maresceau, *Élargissement, Abécédaire de Droit de l'Union Européenne: En l'honneur de Catherine Flaesch-Mougin* (Rennes, Presses Universitaires de Rennes, 2017) 173–86.

[129] European Council, op-ed article by President Charles Michel, 'The world is watching our European continent', Press release 712/23 (Brussels, 5 October 2023).

8

The Impact of War in Ukraine on EU Migration

ELSPETH GUILD, KEES GROENENDIJK AND DZHULIIA LYPALO

8.1. The Full Scale Invasion of Ukraine and the Opening of an EU Temporary Protection Scheme for those Fleeing

The opening of a special protection scheme for Ukrainians and non-Ukrainians who were resident there on the date of the invasion and entered the EU thereafter, which includes extensive rights, has been one of the most immediate and far-reaching EU responses to the 24 February 2022 Russian invasion of Ukraine.[1] The legal basis of the scheme is a directive adopted in 2001 on Temporary Protection (TP; the TP Directive),[2] which had been slated for repeal, although this had not happened at the date of the invasion and is now on hold. Since then, according to UNHCR, 5,977,800[3] Ukrainians (or persons who were resident in Ukraine at the relevant date) have been recorded across Europe. Most of these persons are registered under the TP scheme or parallel schemes in non-EU states. The largest numbers have been registered in Poland (approximately one million) and the Czech Republic (under half a million). The majority of these persons are women and children. Ukrainian President Zelensky, in a March 2022 tweet, thanked the EU[4] for opening the scheme to save his people.

Critical to EU arrivals of refugees from Ukraine has been the fact that the EU lifted the mandatory visa requirement in June 2017, thus their entry thereafter was not dependent on the possession of a valid visa (though this was a requirement for non-Ukrainians nationals of EU mandatory visa countries who were resident in that country). The reintroduction of a mandatory visa for Ukrainian nationals following the Russian invasion

[1] All EU states are part of the scheme with the exception of Denmark, which, because of particularities in its constitutional position in the EU, opened a parallel national scheme rather than join the EU scheme.

[2] Council Directive 2001/55/EC of 20 July 2001 on minimum standards for giving temporary protection in the event of a mass influx of displaced persons and on measures promoting a balance of efforts between the Member States in receiving such persons and bearing the consequences thereof, [2001] OJ L 212/12.

[3] data2.unhcr.org/en/situations/ukraine.

[4] twitter.com/ZelenskyyUa/status/1500222175944577028?cxt=HHwWiMC4lduH7tEpAAAA.

is politically unthinkable. For the same reason, introducing a mandatory visa requirement for these nationals at the end of the TP scheme would not be realistic.

The TP scheme, which is discussed below, provides those who come within its scope with immediate rights which are only evidenced by a state document (in most Member States, a residence permit, but in some, a provisional residence permission sticker) for a minimum of one year, which, at the time of writing, has been extended for a further year to March 2024. Some Member States have issued documents for more than one year.[5] There is no provision for renewal of the scheme beyond a maximum of three years.

The question we pose here, bearing in mind the current duration of the war in Ukraine, is whether the war will continue for more than three years and, regardless, what the correct EU response should be when the TP scheme ends as regards those displaced from Ukraine who still cannot go home. We will address this question from the perspective of the EU and international human rights law.

In order to understand the challenge that this war presents for the EU over time, we will examine the question as follows. In section 8.2, we set out the main features of the TP scheme as contained in the Directive and the measures taken around it. We will also set out its place in international law. In section 8.3, we examine the scheme, comparing the rights of TP beneficiaries with the Refugee Convention and other measures within the EU's Common European Asylum System (CEAS). In section 8.4, we address the options at the end of the maximum three-year period of TP if Ukraine is still not a safe country to return to, or to which the displaced persons have good reasons to not yet return. In section 8.5, we set out our conclusions from this investigation.

8.1.1. The Directive

The TP Directive has its roots in the civil war which took place in the former Yugoslavia from 1992 to 1995, and the war in Kosovo in 1998 to 1999. At that time, the EU had no competence to make binding EU rules for action in respect of asylum, migration or border control. The Council was unable to reach an agreement on two Commission proposals in 1997 and 1998 for 'joint action' under the Third Pillar of the EU concerning TP of displaced persons. Thus, the outflow of several million persons fleeing the conflict and their reception in EU states depended exclusively on national law implementing international commitments.[6] This resulted in very substantial differences in approaches and outcomes. The bombing of Serbia in 1999, in the context of the Kosovo crisis, once again led to a substantial displacement of people from the region, again without a common coordinated response to their reception by EU Member States. Thus, one of the first measures adopted when the EU was granted competence in the field was this Directive which bears the hallmarks of an EU response to the war in the region. It is the first measure adopted under the Common European Asylum System (CEAS) and, as such, the language used is often inconsistent with later directives under the CEAS. The other CEAS measures were subject to a full review and revision in 2011–13, but the TP Directive was left untouched.

[5] eg, Germany which has granted documents valid for two years.
[6] This competence was only accorded to the EU institutions in 1999 with the Amsterdam Treaty.

The Directive is designed to meet two objectives: first, it is a means to accommodate mass influxes of displaced persons (from outside the EU) unable to return to their country; second, it promotes a balance of efforts among Member States by establishing a minimum standard of treatment for such persons (Article 1). The assumption of the Directive is that TP beneficiaries will be prima facie refugees, and their access to protection should be based on a collective measure whereby everyone who comes within the scope of a TP scheme automatically obtains the rights set out in it. This assumption is founded on international law in that the treatment of TP beneficiaries must be consistent with Member States' obligations under instruments of international law to which they are parties and prohibit discrimination (Preamble 16). The main instruments of international law relevant to TP beneficiaries are the Refugee Convention,[7] the Convention against Torture, Inhuman and Degrading Treatment,[8] the Convention against Enforced Disappearances,[9] and the two International Covenants, one on Civil and Political Rights (ICCPR)[10] the other on Economic, Social and Cultural Rights (ICESCR).[11] The definition of a refugee is contained in the Refugee Convention while the obligations on non-refoulement are found in the Refugee Convention, the Convention against Torture and the Convention against Enforced Disappearances. The civil and economic rights of all persons are set out in the ICCPR and ICESCR, with the Refugee Convention rights being *lex specialis* in respect of refugees. The reference in the Directive to non-discrimination is directed at ensuring that TP beneficiaries, which are prima facie refugees (though they have not been through a refugee determination procedure), are entitled to almost the same rights as refugees who have been through a determination procedure. TP beneficiaries are specifically defined as including refugees under the Refugee Convention, but also persons who have fled armed conflict or endemic violence and those at serious risk of generalised violation of their human rights (engaging the Convention against Torture and the Convention against Enforced Disappearances). This is also the language which would later be used to describe refugees and other beneficiaries of international protection in the Qualification Directive adopted three years later. In European regional law, the relevant standards are found in the European Convention on Human Rights (ECHR) Article 3 and the EU Charter of Fundamental Rights (the Charter) Articles 3, 4, 18 and 19.

The opening of a TP scheme is based on the need to protect national asylum determination procedures from being overwhelmed by the arrival of mass numbers of refugees (Article 2(a)) and does not prejudice refugee status under the Refugee Convention, though it allows Member States to delay determination until the end of the scheme

[7] UN General Assembly, Convention Relating to the Status of Refugees, 28 July 1951, United Nations, Treaty Series, vol.189, 137, available at www.refworld.org/docid/3be01b964.html.

[8] UN General Assembly, Convention Against Torture and Other Cruel, Inhuman or Degrading Treatment or Punishment, 10 December 1984, United Nations, Treaty Series, vol 1465, 85, available at www.refworld.org/docid/3ae6b3a94.html (accessed 28 February 2023).

[9] UN General Assembly, International Convention for the Protection of All Persons from Enforced Disappearance, 20 December 2006, available at www.refworld.org/docid/47fdfaeb0.html.

[10] UN General Assembly, International Covenant on Civil and Political Rights, 16 December 1966, United Nations, Treaty Series, vol 999, 171, available at www.refworld.org/docid/3ae6b3aa0.html.

[11] UN General Assembly, International Covenant on Economic, Social and Cultural Rights, 16 December 1966, United Nations, Treaty Series, vol 993, 3, available at www.refworld.org/docid/3ae6b36c0.html.

(Articles 3, 21, 22 and 23 – see below). The opening of a scheme is subject to specific rules engaging all the actors of the EU legislator, but giving a special place to the Council (which represents the Member States' executives directly). The duration of a TP scheme is specified in Articles 6 and 7, which do not permit extension beyond three years. The Commission's original proposal that two years should be the maximum duration was met with opposition from several Member States preferring one year or 18 months. Only after strong pressure from Germany, which considered TP as an alternative rather than a short precursor to international protection, was the maximum extended to three years.[12]

Chapter III sets out the obligations of Member States towards TP beneficiaries. By designing the Directive in this manner and defining state obligations to beneficiaries, the legislator gives the beneficiaries rights, the acknowledgement of which by the national administrations is only declaratory of their existence and evidence of the state's duty to provide them to those beneficiaries. We set out the key rights in the next section together with the international refugee and human rights law source. The Directive sets out the relationship of TP with international protection in Articles 17–19). We explain these rules in section 8.3 below, in particular from the perspective of options available for the EU at the end of the TP scheme.

8.1.2. The Scheme

The Council adopted an implementing decision on 4 March 2022 in accordance with the Directive, opening a TP scheme for Ukraine.[13] After confirming the support of the EU for Ukraine and its disapproval of the Russian invasion, which it states seeks to undermine European and global security and stability (Preamble 3), the Decision notes that the conflict has implications for the EU, including a high likelihood of migratory pressure. It has regard to the exemption of Ukrainians from mandatory visa requirements,[14] and in light of the experience after the Russian annexation of Crimea, the numbers could be expected to be between 2.5 and 6.5 million persons (UNHCR estimated four million at the time). As a result of these forecasts, the Council found that the EU was facing a mass influx of displaced persons unable to return because of Russian military aggression (Preambles 6 and 7). The decision welcomes the favourable opinion of UNHCR to the opening of the scheme.[15] The scope of the TP scheme includes: (1) Ukrainian nationals residing in Ukraine before 24 February 2022; (2) stateless persons and third-country nationals with international protection in Ukraine before 24 February 2022; (3) family members of (1) and (2) (Article 1(a)–(c)); (4) third-country nationals with

[12] Council documents 5191/01 and 6914/01 of 15 January and 19 March 2001 and J.R. Durieux and A. Hurwitz, How Many is Too Many? African and European Legal Responses to Mass Influxes of Refugees, German Yearbook of International Law 2005 (47) 105–59.

[13] Council Implementing Decision (EU) 2022/382 of 4 March 2022 establishing the existence of a mass influx of displaced persons from Ukraine within the meaning of Article 5 of Directive 2001/55/EC and having the effect of introducing temporary protection ST/6846/2022/INIT, [2022] OJ L71/1.

[14] Annex II, Regulation 2018/1806.

[15] For a discussion on the concept of mass influx see N Arenas. 'The Concept of Mass Influx of Displaced Persons in the European Directive Establishing the Temporary' (2005) 7 *European Journal of Migration and Law* 435.

a valid permanent residence permit in Ukraine who are unable to return safely and in durable conditions to their country or region of origin (Article 2). Thereafter, Member States may apply the scheme to other persons, including third-country nationals who were residing legally in Ukraine at the relevant date and who are unable to return in safe and durable conditions to their country of origin (Article 2(3)).

In a declaration by the Member States issued with the Council Decision, the Member States undertook that they would not apply Article 11 of the Directive, which allocates TP beneficiaries to residence in specific states as determined by criteria set out therein.[16] The purpose of this non-application of the residence rules was to alleviate the pressure on the Member States experiencing mass arrivals by allowing TP beneficiaries to move to other Member States at will. We will examine the implications of this further in the next section.

8.1.3. The Border

As mentioned above, the EU lifted mandatory visa requirements for Ukrainians in June 2017 in response to Russia's annexation of Crimea. This meant that Ukrainian nationals are able to enter the EU with their (biometric) passports for short stays of 90 days out of every 180, provided they fulfilled the conditions of evidence of resources for their stay and legitimate interest (and do not constitute a danger to public policy, health or security). This 90-day rule is found in the Schengen Borders Code,[17] which applies to 27 states, excluding the EU states Bulgaria, Cyprus, Ireland and Romania, but including the non-EU states Iceland, Liechtenstein, Norway and Switzerland. Once within the Schengen area, anyone who has been admitted as a visitor under the Schengen rules is entitled to travel to any other Schengen state as part of the permitted 90 days. Thereafter and before the opening of the TP scheme, those Ukrainians who sought to stay longer and exercise economic activities had to seek residence permits mainly in accordance with national law. According to Eurostat, Ukrainians were issued first residence permits in the EU at the rate of about 750,000 in 2019, 600,000 in 2020 and almost 900,000 in 2021.[18] According to Eurostat, 1.57 million Ukrainians lived in the EU at the end of 2021.[19] The most important state issuing these residence permits was Poland, where, according to academic studies, they have had a very positive impact on the labour market.[20]

Thus, when the invasion took place, many Ukrainians were already residing in the EU, working and presumably with housing. This means that many of those who fled after the invasion may have someone they know or a family member already living in the EU.

[16] See recital 15 of the Council Implementing Decision of 4 March 2022.

[17] Regulation (EU) 2016/399 of the European Parliament and of the Council of 9 March 2016 on a Union Code on the rules governing the movement of persons across borders (Schengen Borders Code) (codification), [2016] OJ L77/1.

[18] ec.europa.eu/eurostat/statistics-explained/index.php?title=Residence_permits_-_statistics_on_first_permits_issued_during_the_year&oldid=584076#First_residence_permits_by_citizenship.

[19] ec.europa.eu/eurostat/statistics-explained/index.php?title=Ukrainian_citizens_in_the_EU#Ukrainian_citizens_authorised_to_stay_in_the_EU.

[20] P Strzelecki, J Growiec and R Wyszyński, 'The contribution of immigration from Ukraine to economic growth in Poland' (2022) 158 *Review of World Economics* 365.

While over 650,000 of these residents were living in Poland, Italy had over 230,000 residents and Portugal and Spain accounted for over 100,000.[21] UNHCR statistics indicate that many Ukrainians fleeing the invasion went to other countries in Europe where they had links.[22]

As mentioned above, the decision of the Member States not to apply restrictions on which Member State a TP beneficiary may live meant that once they entered the EU, they could choose where they wanted to go and could go there lawfully during their first 90 days within the Schengen area. As the rights under the Directive are declaratory, not constitutive, these people were (in law) entitled to those rights in every Member State through which they passed. However, according to the Commission's guidelines, TP beneficiaries need to notify the national authorities of their exercise of TP status on the national territory within that 90-day period. Many Member States simplified the task by making available specialised personnel with the requisite language skills to assist TP beneficiaries at railways stations and other entry points. Where a TP beneficiary notified his or her presence in one Member State but then decided to move to another, the only requirement was to deregister in the first Member State and register in the second or subsequent state. In this way, Ukrainians were given the right to what the EU calls secondary movement: to move from one Member State to another at will and take up residence there. They are the only group of third-country nationals (outside of family members of mobile EU citizens) with such a right. Bearing in mind the importance of secondary movement in the EU legislators' debates on the New Pact for Migration and Asylum,[23] an assessment of secondary movement in the TP Ukraine Scheme is of great importance before any new efforts to prevent secondary movement more generally among asylumseekers are adopted.

In order to assist Member State authorities in applying the TP scheme correctly, the Commission issued guidelines on external border management to facilitate EU–Ukraine border crossing two days before the Council Decision opening the scheme but in anticipation of it.[24] Later in March 2022, it issued operational guidelines for the implementation of the Scheme, seeking to answer the questions which were arising in practice for Member State authorities.[25] Wherever the Directive was unclear or left options open to the Member States, the Commission strongly recommended a generous exercise of discretion in favour of those claiming TP protection, for instance, calling on the Member States to include Ukrainians who may have fled before 24 February 2022 in the scheme.[26]

[21] ibid.

[22] data.unhcr.org/en/situations/Ukraine.

[23] G Elspeth. 'Promoting the European way of life: Migration and asylum in the EU.' (2020) 26 *European Law Journal* 355.

[24] C(2022) 1404 final, 2 March 2022.

[25] Communication from the Commission on Operational guidelines for the implementation of Council implementing Decision 2022/382 establishing the existence of a mass influx of displaced persons from Ukraine within the meaning of Article 5 of Directive 2001/55/EC, and having the effect of introducing temporary protection 2022/C 126 I/01 C/2022/1806, [2022] OJ C126I/1.

[26] eur-lex.europa.eu/legal-content/EN/TXT/?uri=CELEX%3A52022XC0321%2803%29&qid=1647940863274.

Other than bottlenecks and inconsistent procedures at EU–Ukraine crossing points, initial arrivals of Ukrainians have generally been facilitated.[27] But the treatment of stateless persons and third-country nationals who had been living in Ukraine was much criticised for the lack of facilitation provided to these persons also potentially within the scope of the scheme.[28]

8.2. Implementation of the TP Scheme

The opening of the TP scheme had an immediate effect, and the Member States started applying it in accordance with their national laws, adopted two decades earlier, transposing the Directive, the final date for which was 31 December 2002.[29] In this section, we will examine the legal foundations for TP rights through a comparison of:

- the international standards contained in the Refugee Convention, which predate the adoption of the Directive;
- the EU Qualification Directive,[30] which post-dates the adoption of the TP Directive and transposes into EU law the rights contained in the Refugee Convention, international human rights conventions to which the Member States are parties and the European Convention on Human Rights (this second group is called beneficiaries of subsidiary protection);[31] and
- the Reception Conditions Directive,[32] also adopted after the TP Directive, which applies to people who claim to be refugees but whose applications have yet to be determined by the authorities.

One of the key legal issues is the application of the principle of non-discrimination contained in Preamble 16 of the TP Directive. It states that regarding the treatment of TP beneficiaries, states are bound by obligations under instruments of international law (ie, the international conventions), which prohibit discrimination. What is missing here is any indication of what discrimination in comparison with whom is within the scope. The possible options as regards the comparator for determining discrimination are: recognised refugees (the position of the European Council on Refugees and Exiles);

[27] D De Coninck, 'The refugee paradox during wartime in Europe: How Ukrainian and Afghan refugees are (not) alike' (2022) 57 *International Migration Review* 578.

[28] C Costello and M Foster, '(Some) refugees welcome: When is differentiating between refugees unlawful discrimination?' (2022) 22 *International Journal of Discrimination and the Law* 244, available at doi.org/10.1177/13582291221116476.

[29] See here for information on national implementing measures: eur-lex.europa.eu/legal-content/en/NIM/?uri=celex:32001L0055.

[30] Directive 2011/95/EU of the European Parliament and of the Council of 13 December 2011 on standards for the qualification of third-country nationals or stateless persons as beneficiaries of international protection, for a uniform status for refugees or for persons eligible for subsidiary protection, and for the content of the protection granted (recast), [2011] OJ L337/9.

[31] Art 15 of the Qualification Directive arguably extends international protection in EU beyond these conventions. See H Storey, 'EU Refugee Qualification Directive: A Brave New World?' (2008) 20 *International Journal of Refugee Law* 1.

[32] Directive 2011/95/EU (n 30).

asylum-seekers; third-country nationals lawfully residing in the territory; and citizens of another Member State exercising treaty rights of residence in the host state or citizens of the state itself. The Refugee Convention, which is the most relevant international standard for the purposes of Preamble 16, sets different standards for different rights, notwithstanding its general non-discrimination provision in Article 3, which requires states the provisions of the Convention to be applied to refugees without discrimination as to race, religion or country of origin. This means that the fallback position, where no specific non-discrimination comparator is provided, is the Article 3 prohibition of discrimination among refugees where the ground is race, religion or country of origin.[33] A very compelling argument is made by Clark and Crepeau 1999[34] that the intersection of the Refugee Convention with international human rights law means that the non-discrimination rights in the latter are also applicable, a position to which we adhere but which, for our purposes here, we will not repeat.

Below we will examine the relevant standards regarding seven rights: free movement; housing; welfare; healthcare; education; access to employment; and family reunification.

8.2.1. Free Movement

The Refugee Convention requires states to accord all refugees lawfully on their territory the right to choose their place of residence and to move freely within its territory (with specific exceptions) (Article 26). There is no specific non-discrimination provision here, so the general rule applies.

The Qualification Directive requires Member States to provide free movement to beneficiaries of international protection within their territory under the same conditions and restrictions as are applicable to other third-country nationals legally resident there (Article 33).

The Reception Conditions Directive, however, provides for the detention of asylum-seekers, although it states that applicants may be detained only under very clearly defined exceptional circumstances laid down in the Directive and subject to the principle of necessity and proportionality with regard to both the manner and the purpose of such detention (Preamble 15 and Article 8).[35] There is no non-discrimination comparator.

[33] A Zimmermann, J Dörschner and F Machts (eds), *The 1951 Convention relating to the status of refugees and its 1967 protocol: A commentary* (Oxford, Oxford University Press, 2011).

[34] T Clark and F Crépeau, 'Mainstreaming Refugee Rights. The 1951 Refugee Convention and International Human Rights Law' (1999) 17 *Netherlands Quarterly of Human Rights* 389; and C Costello and M Foster, (Some) refugees welcome: When is differentiating between refugees unlawful discrimination? (2022) 22 *International Journal of Discrimination and the Law* 244, available at doi.org/10.1177/13582291221116476.

[35] Art 8(3) Reception Conditions Directive: 'An applicant may be detained only: (a) in order to determine or verify his or her identity or nationality; (b) in order to determine those elements on which the application for international protection is based which could not be obtained in the absence of detention, in particular when there is a risk of absconding of the applicant; (c) in order to decide, in the context of a procedure, on the applicant's right to enter the territory; (d) when he or she is detained subject to a return procedure under Directive 2008/115/EC of the European Parliament and of the Council of 16 December 2008 on common standards and procedures in Member States for returning illegally staying third-country nationals, in order to prepare the return and/or carry out the removal process, and the Member State concerned can substantiate on the basis of objective criteria, including that he or she already had the opportunity to access the asylum procedure, that there are reasonable grounds to believe that he or she is making the application for

The TP Directive does not cover free movement, and the Commission's guidelines on free movement only cover movement into the EU and across EU internal borders. Article 11 of the Directive, had it been applied, would have limited free movement for beneficiaries to a single Member State as determined by EU rules.

8.2.2. Housing

The Refugee Convention states that, in relation to housing, refugees lawfully within the territory shall be accorded treatment as favourable as possible and, in any event, not less favourable than that accorded to aliens generally in the same circumstances (Article 21).

The Qualification Directive requires states to ensure that all beneficiaries of international protection have access to accommodation under equivalent conditions as other third-country nationals legally resident in the state (Article 32). These two provisions are close in that, in both cases, the comparator is legally resident non-nationals (aliens for the Refugee Convention, third-country nationals for the Qualification Directive).

The Reception Conditions Directive, in addition to providing for detention which will include housing, allows the housing to be made available in premises at the border or in transit zones, accommodation centres (which guarantee an adequate standard of living) or private houses, flats, hotels or other premises adapted for housing applicants (Article 18(1)). There is no non-discrimination right and thus no comparator here. Further, if asylum-seekers misbehave, the Directive allows states to reduce their reception conditions including access to housing (Article 20, though this has been limited by the case law of the Court of Justice). The standard of housing is obviously inferior to that applicable to aliens or third-country nationals legally resident, other than those who are indigent.

The TP Directive simply provides that states shall ensure that beneficiaries have access to suitable accommodation or, if necessary, the means to obtain it (Article 13(1)), leaving the possibility of arguments regarding standards under which regime.[36]

8.2.3. Welfare

Welfare is covered in all the measures. Starting with the Refugee Convention, Article 23 on public relief requires states to accord refugees the same treatment with respect to public relief and assistance as is accorded to their own nationals. This is the first time

international protection merely in order to delay or frustrate the enforcement of the return decision; (e) when protection of national security or public order so requires; (f) in accordance with Article 28 of Regulation (EU) No 604/2013 of the European Parliament and of the Council of 26 June 2013 establishing the criteria and mechanisms for determining the Member State responsible for examining an application for international protection lodged in one of the Member States by a third-country national or a stateless person. The grounds for detention shall be laid down in national law.' Art 8(4): 'Member States shall ensure that the rules concerning alternatives to detention, such as regular reporting to the authorities, the deposit of a financial guarantee, or an obligation to stay at an assigned place, are laid down in national law.'

[36] J Moritz, 'Non-discrimination and the challenge of integration' in E Tsoudi and P de Bruycker, *Research Handbook on EU Migration and Asylum Law* (Cheltenham, Edward Elgar Publishing, 2022) 342–64.

the non-discrimination comparator has been own nationals, which is the highest level of equal treatment.

The Qualification Directive follows the Refugee Convention requiring the provision of social assistance as provided to nationals of the state (Article 29(1)). However, for beneficiaries of subsidiary protection, social assistance can be limited to core benefits, which are defined as (at least) minimum income support, assistance in the case of illness or pregnancy and parental assistance – but these core benefits must be provided on the basis of non-discrimination with own nationals (Article 29(2)).

The Reception Conditions Directive makes no reference to social assistance or welfare, but states that states shall ensure that material reception conditions are provided which fulfil an adequate standard of living for the applicants and guarantees their subsistence, protecting their physical and mental health (Article 17). There is no non-discrimination requirement.

The TP Directive requires states to make available to beneficiaries necessary assistance in terms of social welfare and means of subsistence (Article 13(2)). There is no non-discrimination provision.[37]

8.3.4. Healthcare

This is not covered in the Refugee Convention (though Clark and Crepeau 1999 argue that this can be inferred from other international human rights conventions).

The Qualification Directive requires states to provide access to healthcare to all beneficiaries of international protection under the same eligibility conditions as their own nationals (Article 30).

The Reception Conditions Directive requires the provision of healthcare, which covers emergency care and essential treatment of illness and serious mental disorders (Article 19).

TP beneficiaries are entitled to medical care, which includes at least emergency care and essential treatment of illness (Article 13(2)), a standard which copies the Reception Conditions Directive rather than its qualification counterpart. There is no non-discrimination requirement. Nonetheless, access to healthcare has been a substantial issue for Ukrainian TP beneficiaries.[38]

8.3.5. Education

Education is covered by all the measures compared here. The Refugee Convention requires equal treatment with own nationals in access to elementary education for refugees (Article 22(1)). As regards other education, states must provide treatment as favourable as possible and, in any event, not less favourable than that accorded to aliens

[37] E Ociepa-Kicińska and M Gorzałczyńska-Koczkodaj. 'Forms of Aid Provided to Refugees of the 2022 Russia–Ukraine War: The Case of Poland' (2022) 19 *International journal of environmental research and public health* 7085.

[38] PB Spiegel, 'Responding to the Ukraine refugee health crisis in the EU' (2022) 399 *The Lancet* 2084.

in respect to education other than elementary, including access to studies, recognition of certificates, diplomas and degrees, and remission of fees/scholarships (Article 22(2)).

The Qualification Directive requires equal treatment with own nationals regarding access to all education for minors and equal treatment with third-country nationals for access of adults to the general education system, training and retraining (Article 27(2)). It also requires the state to provide access for adult beneficiaries of international protection to vocational training, upgrading of skills etc (Article 26(2)). As regards recognition of qualifications, states must ensure equal treatment with own nationals for beneficiaries of international protection (both refugees and beneficiaries of subsidiary protection) in the context of recognition procedures for foreign diplomas, certificates and other evidence of formal qualifications, and to endeavour to facilitate those who cannot provide documentary evidence of qualifications to appropriate schemes of assessment, validation and accreditation (Article 28).

Under the Reception Conditions Directive, minor children, both of applicants and applicants themselves, are entitled to access to education under the same conditions as their own nationals, with the addition that preparatory classes, including language classes must be provided to minors to facilitate their access to and participation in the education system. This education may be provided in accommodation centres (Article 14(1)). Access to secondary education must be continued even after a minor reaches majority. However, there is a let-out where access to the education system is not possible due to the specific situation of the minor, in which case the minor must have access to other educational arrangements (Article 14(3)).

The TP Directive requires for minors under 18 access to the educational system under the same conditions as their own nationals. However, this may be confined to the state education system (Article 14) as well as educational opportunities for adults, vocational training and practical workplace experience without a non-discrimination provision (Article 12). Here again, the TP Directive is closer to the Refugee Convention than the reception conditions alternative.

8.3.6. Employment

The Refugee Convention requires access for refugees to wage-earning employment under the most favourable treatment accorded to resident aliens in the same circumstances (Article 17). However, restrictive measures imposed on aliens to protect that national labour market cannot be applied to a refugee who has completed two (or possibly three) years of residence in the state,[39] has a spouse national of the state of residence or one or more children nationals of the state of residence (Article 17(2). Additionally, states must give sympathetic consideration to assimilating the rights of refugees regarding wage-earning employment to those of nationals (Article 17(3)). As regards labour rights, the Convention requires states to accord refugees the same treatment as nationals in respect of remuneration, family allowances, hours of work, overtime, paid holidays, restrictions on work, minimum age, apprenticeships and training, women and young

[39] Requiring three years of residence would greatly limit the applicability of this solution.

people's work and collective bargaining. Self-employment in the areas of agriculture, industry, handicrafts and commerce, and to establish commercial and industrial companies, is to be accorded to refugees on the basis of non-discrimination with aliens in similar circumstances (Article 18). Regarding self-employment, the Convention only requires states to accord refugees who hold nationally recognised diplomas treatment as favourable as possible and, in any event, no less favourable than that accorded to aliens to practice a liberal profession (Article 19).

The Qualification Directive requires states to authorise beneficiaries of international protection to engage in employment and self-employment subject to generally applicable rules and to apply the general rules of remuneration and access to social security systems to them (Article 26).

Under the Reception Conditions Directive, applicants have access to the labour market with a maximum permitted delay of nine months after the application has been made, so long as there has been no first-instance decision (Article 15(1)). While that access to the labour market must be effective, it can be subject to national rules, including priority for EU and EEA nationals and legally residing third-country nationals, and there is no non-discrimination requirement (Article 15(2)). States may allow access to vocational training, but if it is related to an employment contract, the rules of Article 15 apply (Article 16).

Under the TP Directive, states are required to authorise employment or self-employment subject to a priority of EU and EEA nationals and legally resident third-country nationals (Article 12).

8.3.7. Family Reunification

The Refugee Convention is silent on this matter, though the Final Act adopting the convention calls on states to provide for family reunification of refugees where the head of the family fulfils the conditions or the refugee is an unaccompanied minor.

The Qualification Directive provides that family unity should be maintained, which applies to family members living in the same Member State (Article 23 and Article 2(j)) and to some rights for family members. Still, the main provisions on admission and residence of family members of refugees are found in Directive 2003/86 on family reunification (Articles 9–15). The category includes spouses and minor children with a specific optional provision for the admission of other family members dependent on the refugee. Unaccompanied minors are entitled to family reunification with first-degree family members in the ascending line, his or her legal guardian or any other family member where the refugee has no relatives in the direct ascending line or such relatives cannot be traced. The family relationship had to exist before the flight, and various requirements regarding deadlines for submission of applications can be applied.

The Reception Conditions Directive defines family members as spouses and unmarried partners, minor unmarried children and for unaccompanied minors, the father, mother or another adult responsible for the applicant (Article 2(c)). This Directive applies a somewhat complicated take-charge provision to determine where families should be reunited (though the absence of a visa requirement for Ukrainian family members means that they are able to move to join their family members).

The TP Directive provides for the reunification of spouses and unmarried partners, minor unmarried children and other close relatives who lived together as part of the family unit at the time of the events leading to the mass influx, and who were wholly or mainly dependent on the sponsor at the time (Article 15(a) and (b)). The family relationship must already have existed in the country of origin, and the family members were separated due to circumstances surrounding the mass influx.

From this review of seven areas of particular importance to TP beneficiaries, it is evident that the Directive is less clear than might be wished regarding the regime of equal treatment and with whom (own nationals or resident aliens/third country nationals). It is farthest from the Reception Conditions Directive, where there is no equal treatment either with own nationals or resident aliens/third country nationals. But both the Refugee Convention and the qualification Directive are much more specific about the rights and how the non-discrimination requirement applies. The inclusive implementation of the TP Directive, as proposed by the Commission in its guidelines, encourages states to take an inclusive approach and apply the highest standards of the Refugee Convention and qualification Directive.

The argument that the TP Directive is a measure to protect national administrations from being overburdened by a mass influx of refugees favours an interpretation of rights in accordance with the Refugee Convention and qualification Directive rather than the lower rights of the Reception Conditions Directive. Similarly, it must be born in mind that the Reception Conditions Directive was adopted years later than the TP Directive and with the clear intention to have a far lower level of rights at or just above the minimum of the ECHR cannot be a point of reference for the interpretation of TP Directive rights other than in a negative sense, that is to say, that the TP rights intentionally are better.

8.3. How does the Temporary Protection End, and what Happens Next?

TP ends *collectively* for all protected persons from Ukraine at the same time, either automatically when the maximum duration of three years has been reached on 4 March 2025, or at any time earlier by a Decision of the Council on a proposal of the Commission (Article 6(1)(a) and (b). The Council could make such a decision should the war in Ukraine end before 4 March 2025.

Before the general TP scheme has come to an end, TP may end in *individual* cases on four different grounds. Firstly, because the protected person has exercised his or her right to voluntary return to Ukraine before the end of the scheme other than for a short visit. In such a case, the host Member State should give favourable consideration to a request for a return to that Member State (Article 21(2)), especially when the person is still within the personal scope of the scheme. According to data from the Dutch Statistical Agency, almost 20 per cent of the 100,000+ persons from Ukraine registered since March 2022 had left the Netherlands by November 2022. They either returned to Ukraine or moved elsewhere inside or outside the EU. If they have returned to Ukraine, the provision applies; should they have moved elsewhere in the EU, this would be an exercise of their right to secondary movement, thus remaining within the scope of the scheme. Had they left for a third country outside the EU, they moved outside the scope of the scheme.

Member States may exclude a person from TP for having committed one of the very serious crimes listed in Article 28. Thirdly, an exclusion decision could be based on the ground that the person is not (or no longer) covered by Article 2(2) or (3) of the Council Implementing Decision due to being able to return in safe and durable conditions to his or her country or region of origin (this is relevant for non-Ukrainian TP beneficiaries). Finally, a Member State may exclude a person on the basis that false information was provided at the registration since Union law does not protect rights obtained by fraudulent behaviour.[40] In all such cases, the person excluded from protection is entitled to a reasoned written decision (Article 41 EU Charter), an effective judicial remedy under Article 29 of the Directive and Article 47 EU Charter. In the rest of this section, we will focus on what happens to the overwhelming majority of persons for which the protection will end collectively.

8.3.1. Voluntary or Forced Return?

Chapter V of the Directive deals with return and measures after TP had ended. It provides for rules on voluntary return (Article 21), forced return (Article 22) and prolonged residence and reception conditions in exceptional cases related to health conditions of formerly protected persons or in order to allow their children to complete the current school period (Article 23). All three alternatives are based on the assumption that the formerly protected persons will leave the host Member State. However, other rules in the Directive foresee that some former TP beneficiaries could remain in the host Member State after the end of the TP.

8.3.2. Other Possibilities to Remain in the Host Member State

The legislator was apparently aware that the aforementioned Directive rules cover only some of the alternatives available to ex-protected persons and to the Member States at the end of a TP scheme. Hence, Chapter V of the Directive starts with the general rule in Article 20 that when the TP ends, 'the general law on protection and on aliens in the Member States shall apply, without prejudice to articles 21, 22, and 23'. Most probably, the European Commission, while drafting the proposal, and the Member States, during the negotiations in the Council, on the term 'general law', had in mind international law and the national law of Member States. This is supported by the fact that the Directive makes reference in several places to the Refugee Convention, non-refoulement and human rights and fundamental freedoms.[41]

[40] There is another ground for individual loss of the TP status, where a family member is moved from one Member State to another (Art 15(6) TPD). But this will only exceptionally happen with Ukraine TPs, since they can move freely in the EU and choose residence with their family.

[41] Art 2(b) and (e), Art 3(1) and (2), Art 6(2) and Recital 10.

At the time of the adoption of the Directive in July 2001, the Council had yet to adopt any instrument on migration or asylum of third-country nationals. Today, a series of EU migration and asylum instruments are in force and are part of the 'general law' in force in the Member States. As a consequence, the relevance of EU law increased, and the room for national law has decreased. This is most evident in the area of asylum, but it also applies to the EU migration Directives.

8.3.3. Asylum-seeker Status and International Protection

According to Article 17(1) of the Directive, persons enjoying TP must be able to lodge an application for asylum at any time. Once such an application is filed, the Dublin III Regulation[42] determines which Member State is responsible for dealing with the application with the additional rule of Article 18 TPD making the Member State which accepted the transfer of the TP beneficiary to its territory responsible. The processing of the asylum application today is governed by the Asylum Procedures Directive. In case a Member State has used the possibility of Article 19(1) TPD to provide that TP rights 'may not be enjoyed concurrently with the status of an asylum-seeker while the applications are under consideration', the status of the applicant during the asylum procedure will be governed by the Reception Conditions Directive. Above, we explained that the rights of asylum-seekers to accommodation, employment, social security, education and family reunification under the latter Directive are considerably lower/limited in comparison with those on the basis of the TPD. In 2001 the Union legislator could not have foreseen these differences since the first Reception Conditions Directive was adopted only in 2003.[43]

If no final decision on that asylum application was made when the TP regime ends, the processing of that application should be resumed and completed (Article 17(2)). This implies that for the remainder of the procedure, the rules of the Asylum Procedure Directive and the Reception Conditions Directive are also applicable, and the ex-TP beneficiaries would be treated as asylum-seekers. In case the asylum application was completed during the TP scheme and refugee status or subsidiary protection was granted, the Qualification Directive will continue to apply to that third-country national automatically at the end of the TP scheme (Article 19(2)). The Directive is part and parcel of the CEAS, including where the formerly protected person applies for asylum after the end of the TP scheme.

8.3.4. A New Role for the Legal Migration Directives?

When the TP scheme comes to an end, many protected persons will probably decide to return to Ukraine to contribute to the rebuilding of the country and to resume their

[42] Regulation (EU) No 604/2013 of the European Parliament and of the Council of 26 June 2013 establishing the criteria and mechanisms for determining the Member State responsible for examining an application for international protection lodged in one of the Member States by a third-country national or a stateless person (recast), [2013] OJ L180/31.

[43] Directive 2003/9.

lives there to the extent possible. Others may prefer to stay in the host Member State or another Member State for a myriad of different reasons generally governing the behaviour of migrants: a good job; better prospects for the children; completion of studies; a new family relationship; the home or the city, or both, being destroyed; or nowhere to go in the country of origin.

The experience in the 1960s and 1970s of labour migration to the original six EEC Member States from neighbouring countries like Spain, Portugal, Greece and more distant countries such as Turkey and Morocco, is that the majority of those immigrants, after a few years in Western Europe, returned to their country of origin. The rate of return further increased after the neighbouring countries of origin became EU Member States, and free movement rules made it possible to return to the host Member State if return to the country of origin was unsuccessful. This also applied to many who fled the civil war in the former Yugoslavia in the 1990s. The possibility of making (long) exploratory visits without losing protection status in the host country also stimulated return. The relevant provision in Article 21(1) reflects that experience: 'The Member State shall ensure that the decision of those persons to return is taken in full knowledge of the facts. The Member States may provide for exploratory visits.'[44] The possibility of Ukraine citizens to enter and travel visa-free to and within the Schengen area will support the return movement. The long-term prospect of accession of Ukraine to the EU may also contribute.

8.3.5. Current Exclusion of TP Beneficiaries from the Legal Migration Directives

Currently, seven migration directives are in force; two of them are recast from early directives adopted after 2003. All seven migration directives explicitly or implicitly exclude TP beneficiaries from their personal scope. Article 3(2)(b) Family Reunification Directive provides that this Directive shall not apply where the sponsor is: 'authorised to reside in a Member State on the basis of TP or applying for authorisation to reside on that basis and awaiting a decision on his status'.[45] Similar wording in Article 3(2)(b) of the Long-term Residents Directive and Article 3(2)(f) of the Single Permit Directive exclude all third-country nationals with TP status from the coverage of those two directives. The more recent recast Students and Researchers Directive 2016/901 and the recast Blue Card Directive 2021/1883 exclude from their personal scope third-country nationals those 'who are beneficiaries of TP in accordance with Council Directive 2001/55/EC … in a Member State' (both in Article 3(2)(a)). Third-country nationals with TP status are

[44] The Commission in COM(2000)303 in its proposal for Art 21 explains: 'The voluntary return of persons benefiting or having benefited from temporary protection is the most preferable solution and is regarded as a priority. Accordingly, the Member States must facilitate such returns. Candidates for voluntary return must be fully informed of the conditions under which they will return. The Member States may use exploratory visits as a way of helping candidates. Exploratory visits enable some candidates to visit their country of origin for a short time to see for themselves the security situation and the circumstances of reintegration, before voluntary return is fully completed.'

[45] The Directive does apply to the reunification of Ukraine family members with a non-Ukraine third-country national sponsor.

implicitly excluded from the scope of the two directives adopted in 2014: the Seasonal Workers Directive 20144/36 does not apply to third-country nationals who, at the time of application, reside in the territory of a Member State,[46] and the Intra-Corporate Transfer Directive 2014/66 only applies to third-country nationals who reside outside the territory of the Member States at the time of application and apply to be admitted as an intra-corporate transfer as managers, specialists or trainee employees.[47]

8.3.6. Pending Recast of the Long-Term Residence Directive and the Single Permit Directive

Two months after the second Russian invasion of Ukraine of 24 February 2022, the Commission presented proposals for the recast of the Single Permit Directive and the Long-Term Residence Directive (LTRD).[48] The position of TP beneficiaries is mentioned in the latter recast at one point only. In both proposals, the Commission made no changes to the existing exclusion from the rights and protection of these two directives. In the Council documents on the proposal for the recast of the Single Permit Directive (SPD), there is not a single mention of the four million TP beneficiaries from Ukraine. In the negotiation mandate adopted by the Council in May 2023, TP beneficiaries remain excluded from the scope of this directive, as are other beneficiaries of protection in accordance with international obligations, national law or the practice of a Member State.[49] The effect of this exclusion is that TP beneficiaries employed in Member States are not entitled to the enhanced rights which are granted in Article 11 of the SPD to legally employed workers from non-EU countries. Instead of this protection tailored to the special needs of migrant workers, employed TP beneficiaries have to rely on one single and rather general sentence in Article 12 TP Directive, reading: 'The general law in force in the Member States applicable to remuneration, access to social security systems relating to employed or self-employed activities and other conditions of employment shall apply.' The European Parliament paid more attention to the position of war refugees from Ukraine. In its report for the negotiations with the Council adopted by the LIBE Committee in April 2023 the clause in Article 3(2)(f) of the proposal excluding TP beneficiaries is explicitly deleted.[50]

In his draft report, the European Parliament's rapporteur on the recast of LTRD, Damian Boeselager, proposed to delete the exclusion of TP beneficiaries from the personal scope of the LTRD proposed by the Commission.[51] This position is confirmed in the final European Parliament report on this recast.[52] In practice, this exclusion has fewer negative consequences than the exclusion of TP beneficiaries from the SPD since the LTRD only applies to third-country nationals who, after several years of legal residence, have acquired LTR status. More relevant is how TP beneficiaries can acquire

[46] Art 2(1) Directive 2014/36.
[47] See Art 2(1) Directive 2014/66.
[48] COM(2022)655 and COM(2022)650.
[49] Art 3(2)(f) and (h) SPD in the General Approach in Council document 9474/35 of 26 May 2023.
[50] EP document A9-0140/2023.
[51] Draft Report of 21 November 2022, PE738.503v02-00, 32.
[52] A9-0145/2023 of 13 April 2023, the new text of Art 3(2)(b) proposed in amendment 45.

LTR status. Here two issues are relevant: to what extent the years of residence as TP beneficiary count as the legal residence for LTR status; and the length of the residence requirement for LTR status.

Currently, five years of continuous lawful residence are required.[53] The Parliament in the past repeatedly adopted resolutions asking for a reduction to three years. In 2020, the Commission proposed to reduce the five years to three years for refugees and beneficiaries of subsidiary protection.[54] That proposal did not cover TP beneficiaries.[55] The Commission did not include this proposal in the 2022 recast of the LTRD. The Parliament, in its report on the recast, maintained its previous position that three years should be the general rule.[56] The Swedish presidency included the limited reduction to three years for beneficiaries of international protection, proposed by the Commission in 2020, in the discussion on the recast. This reportedly resulted in the rejection of even this limited reduction by the Council.[57] This issue is likely to be one of the main points of contention in the forthcoming trialogue. If Parliament is unable to convince the Council to accept the general reduction to three years, TP beneficiaries will, in practice, only benefit from the recast if the limited reduction proposed by the Commission in 2020 is accepted as a compromise and the scope of the clause is extended to also cover TP beneficiaries.

In the current LTRD residence on the basis of the TP status is implicitly not taken into account for the calculation of the required five years.[58] The Commission in its recast proposed to take the full period of residence into account, but only where the third-country national concerned has acquired another residence permit which will enable him or her to be granted EU long-term resident status. The Parliament proposes to delete this condition.[59] According to the Swedish presidency, as a compromise for the negotiating mandate of the Council, only the first two years of residence as a beneficiary of TP would be taken into account. The consequence of that rule (and of the Commission's proposal) would be that a TP beneficiary would only qualify for the LTR status after having acquired a residence permit for employment, study or family reunification and after three more years of residence on the basis of that permit (the two other necessary years being as a beneficiary of TP). However, having the TP status, on the one hand, takes away the need to apply for a permit for employment or study and, on the other hand, due to the exclusion of TP beneficiaries from the scope of all legal migration directives, will be an unsurmountable obstacle for most TP beneficiaries to acquire such residence permits until after the end of the TP scheme. The result of the Council's amendment could be that a TP beneficiary could only could apply for LTR status after six years (three years as a TP beneficiary plus three years on the basis of another residence permit).

[53] Art 4(1) Directive 2003/109.

[54] COM(2020) 610, Art 71.

[55] The Commission at the same time proposed to repeal the TP Directive, thus, abolishing TP status, in Art 14 of its proposal for a Crisis-Regulation, COM(2020)613 of 23 September 2020, 33.

[56] The text for Art 4(1) proposed in Amendment 49 of the report A9-0145/2023.

[57] In the presidency's compromise text in Council document 8549/23 of 26 April 2023 the relevant last sentence of Art 4(1) is between square brackets, indicating that the Commission's proposal is not accepted.

[58] Art 4(2) Directive 2003/109.

[59] The text for Art 4(5) proposed in Amendment 52 of the report A9-0145/2023.

The LTRD can only serve as a viable solution for more permanent residence for beneficiaries of TP from Ukraine if the residence requirement for this group is reduced to three years and the full period of lawful residence is taken into account to fulfil this condition. Requiring former TP beneficiaries to first acquire another (temporary) residence permit would create an additional large administrative case load for immigration authorities. It would be unreasonable considering the obstacles to acquire such permits created for TP beneficiaries by their exclusion from the scope of all legal migration directives during the years the TP scheme was in force. Hopefully, the position of TP beneficiaries will be seriously and systematically discussed by the representatives of the Parliament and the Council during their negotiations on the recast of the LTRD.

8.4. The End of the TP Scheme: What Future for the Beneficiaries?

After more than two and a half years of hostilities in Ukraine, it is apparent that there is unlikely to be a rapid resolution of the war. It is also unclear exactly what the end of the war is going to look like. In the meantime, a joint assessment of the World Bank, the Ukraine Government and the European Commission issued on 9 September 2022, sett the cost of the reconstruction of Ukraine at €349 billion.[60] One year on from the invasion, the World Bank estimated that Ukraine's GDP had contracted by 35 per cent in 2022 and that the proportion of the population with income below the national poverty line would reach nearly 60 per cent in 2022, up from 18 per cent in 2021.[61] Further, the World Bank reported that more than 35 per cent of Ukrainians had fled their homes since the start of the invasion, with eight million people now living in poverty, while, generally, poverty increased five-fold in one year, reversing 15 years of development gains.[62] The human and economic costs of this war are catastrophic for the country.

Such devastation will have consequences for those who have fled and are currently receiving TP in the EU, particularly considering that there may be more damage to come. Already, it has been accepted that many of those TP beneficiaries already in the EU will not be able to go back to their country in the short term; for this reason, the scheme has been extended. Whether the circumstances for beneficiaries to return to Ukraine will be more favourable within the next 24 months, the maximum duration of the scheme, is uncertain but unlikely, at least for many of them. While many Ukrainians are determined to go home, and some already have,[63] it is likely that many will not be able to do so, at least in the short term.[64]

[60] www.worldbank.org/en/news/press-release/2022/09/09/ukraine-recovery-and-reconstruction-needs-estimated-349-billion.

[61] www.worldbank.org/en/country/ukraine/overview#3.

[62] www.worldbank.org/en/country/ukraine/overview.

[63] www.euronews.com/my-europe/2022/09/15/you-feel-trapped-why-some-ukrainian-refugees-are-now-heading-home.

[64] www.bruegel.org/policy-brief/will-ukraines-refugees-go-home.

On this basis, we need to consider what the alternative migration statuses may be for those who are currently protected by the TP scheme. The Commission's assessment of the first year of the TP scheme issued on 8 March 2023 specifically recognised the need for a road map into the future for TP beneficiaries.[65] The Commission reiterated the EU's commitment to TP beneficiaries stating that the 'Union will stand in support of those fleeing the Russian aggression against Ukraine for as long as needed.' Determining how long is needed will be a matter of great importance; acknowledging that at least some TP beneficiaries may need to stay longer or, indeed, indefinitely on account of their personal circumstances in the EU is critical. There are a number of possible options which need to be considered. Our co-author, Dzhuliia Lypalo, examines the possibility of the free movement of persons in section 8.6 below

8.4.1. Options to Avoid Status Insecurity and Administrative Chaos at the End of the TP Scheme

In theory, there are four different options for a common solution on the basis of EU law: (1) prolong the TP scheme; (2) use rules from the 2017 EU–Ukraine Association Agreement to enhance the security of residence of Ukrainians exercising economic activities in EU states; (3) amend current secondary EU law to include former TP beneficiaries; or (4) extend the free movement to Ukrainian nationals through a *sui generis* agreement in pursuit of Ukraine's eventual accession to the EU. In their scope, all four options aim at preventing the fifth option: massive asylum procedures and forced return of Ukrainians at the end of the TP scheme.

All these options have advantages and disadvantages, which we will examine below. The determining factor will be the exercise of political will – how far does the EU wish to go? The first option – extending the scheme – is unattractive because of the inherent temporariness against which the Directive itself is designed. The second option of an enhanced use of the Association Agreement could benefit some former TP beneficiaries but not necessarily all, so it could be used in conjunction with at least one of the other options (other than 2). The third option would require the amendment of several directives, which could be undertaken by one legislative act and would provide possibilities of security of residence to many former TP beneficiaries though, once again, this would likely exclude those who have never exercised an economic activity, or been part of a family where one member qualifies or had sickness insurance (as examples). The fourth option – the free movement of persons equivalent to that of EU nationals – would require the greatest exercise of political will, ie a unanimous decision of the Member States, and would probably affect all Ukrainians, not simply those former TP beneficiaries. Because of the interpretation of the right of free movement in EU law, some TP beneficiaries, such as those who are completely dependent on public assistance and/or without family members who qualify, could still be excluded. Further, some would consider this option to be overinclusive. We set out the issues relevant to each option below.

[65] home-affairs.ec.europa.eu/system/files/2023-03/Temporary%20protection%20for%20those%20fleeing%20Russia%E2%80%99s%20war%20of%20aggression%20against%20Ukraine%20one%20year%20on.pdf.

8.4.2. Prolongation of the TP Scheme after Three Years

First, perhaps a simple solution for the EU from the perspective of staying within the CEAS, would be to amend the TP Directive and permit extension of the status beyond the maximum three-year period. The advantage of this approach would be the maintenance of the status quo for those already enjoying protection in the EU. However, the disadvantages would be substantial, not least in the perpetuation of the uncertainty of residence status for those beneficiaries. Beneficiaries have been reconstructing their lives in Europe, finding work, studying and building their futures. For these people, security of residence is necessary if they are to invest fully in their new host states. This does not preclude in any way a safe return to Ukraine once the conditions have been secured. But in the meantime, their contribution to the EU should be acknowledged, and their residence status made more secure.

This solution continues the precarious legal status of the persons concerned and impedes making decisions and choices for their near and longer future. It postpones solving the issues until the end of the extension. The option does not provide security of residence since the Council may decide to end the TP at any time.

8.4.3. Use the 2017 EU–Ukraine Association Agreement

A third option, which the Commission has already signalled, is using the existing Association Agreement between the EU and Ukraine to its maximum to achieve greater integration of the country with the EU during the accession period.[66] A Partnership and Cooperation Agreement was first signed between the EU and Ukraine in 1994 and entered into force in 1998,[67] remaining so until a new Association Agreement replaced it on 1 September 2017.[68] Articles 24–40 of the original agreement provide for equal treatment of Ukrainian workers in the EU with nationals of the host state, liberalisation of self-employment and the establishment of Ukrainian businesses in the EU, including the transfer of their key personnel, and liberalisation of cross-border supply of services between the parties. The new Association Agreement repeats the provisions on the treatment of workers from the previous agreement. It adds a new provision (Article 18) which calls upon Member States to improve existing facilities of access to employment for Ukrainian workers under bilateral agreements (and to enter into such agreements). An Association Council is charged with examining the possibility of granting other more favourable provisions regarding employment in additional areas.

The provisions on establishment in the 2017 Agreement set out as an objective the progressive reciprocal liberalisation of establishment and trade in services (Article 85) and include not only companies as the object of that liberalisation but also natural persons (Article 86(9)). Both the various categories of personnel of Ukrainian companies and independent professionals (as defined) benefit from a right of entry and stay in

[66] ec.europa.eu/commission/presscorner/detail/en/ip_23_461; www.consilium.europa.eu/en/press/press-releases/2023/02/03/joint-statement-following-the-24th-eu-ukraine-summit.

[67] [1998] OJ L 49/1.

[68] eur-lex.europa.eu/legal-content/EN/TXT/?uri=uriserv%3AOJ.L_.2014.161.01.0003.01.ENG&toc=OJ%3AL%3A2014%3A161%3ATOC.

Member States subject to qualifications, limitations and time limits (Articles 92–102). The 2017 Agreement also includes provisions on the movement of persons (Article 19), which provided an additional basis for the lifting of mandatory short-stay visas for Ukrainian nationals that year. The Agreement also provides for a deep and comprehensive free trade area in Title IV, and support for Ukrainian efforts to complete the transition into a functioning market economy by means of, inter alia, the progressive approximation of its legislation to that of the EU.

These provisions provide a basis for further liberalisation of cross-border movement, employment and self-employment of Ukrainians in host Member States including Ukrainians already exercising economic activities there. If the EU–Ukraine Association Council could adopt a decision similar to Decision 1/80 of the Association Council EEC–Turkey, this could help to solve the problems faced by Ukrainian workers (including the self-employed). However, it is unclear whether the competence of the Association Council in Article 18 of the Agreement extends to the adoption of binding rules on admission and rights of family members, students, researchers and other categories of Ukraine nationals. A decision of the Association Council requires unanimity among Member States and the consent of Ukraine. All decisions discussed in the next sub-section can be adopted by a qualified majority in the EU Council of Ministers.

8.4.4. Amend Secondary EU Law

A fourth option would be to amend EU secondary law in order to create a secure residence status for those former TP beneficiaries who do not return immediately at the end of the TP scheme, and to amend the EU instruments on third-country nationals resident or moving to the EU for family, study or economic purposes to specifically include beneficiaries of TP.

At least three possible amendments to existing EU migration and asylum law should be considered: (a) amending the Qualification Directive to allow for collective granting of international protection to categories of former TP beneficiaries; (b) allowing for the acquisition of the long-term resident (LTR) status by former TP beneficiaries at the end of the TP scheme; and (c) deleting the current exclusion of TP beneficiaries in the legal migration directives. These are discussed in turn below.

8.4.4.1. Amend the Qualification Directive

This would allow for collective granting of international protection to former TP beneficiaries, and could be done by introducing a system of prima facie recognition of refugee status or subsidiary protection. This might require a fundamental change in both the Qualification Directive and other asylum directives, which are based on a system of individual decisions. Moreover, the cessation grounds in the Qualification Directive will be a source of insecurity about the loss of the status in case of longer visits and stays in Ukraine.[69] An advantage of his solution is that it would also cover TP beneficiaries irrespective of income or health conditions.

[69] Arts 11(1)(a), 14(1) and 16 Qualifying Directive.

8.4.4.2. Allow for the Acquisition of the LTR Status by Former TP Beneficiaries at the End of the TP Scheme

The pending recast of the LTRD offers a welcome opportunity to allow for the (semi-) automatic acquisition of LTR status at the end of the TP scheme for all former TP beneficiaries with three years of residence in the EU, the last two years of which were in the Member State where LTR status is acquired. This semi-automatic acquisition would considerably reduce the administrative burden. An alternative, with far less reduction of that burden, would be to reduce the five years of residence required in Article 4 LTRD to three years for former TP beneficiaries, leaving the three other conditions (income, health insurance and Integration) in Article 5 in force.

The advantages would be no direct relationship between the residence status and the development of the war (relevant only to the LTRD), no relation between residence rights and economic or other activity of the former beneficiary, and no loss of status on economic grounds (lack of funds). Similarly, former TP beneficiaries would attain a status equal to or better than the rights in the Refugee Convention and the Qualification Directive, while still able to rely on protection against the refoulement of Article 31 Refugee Convention if needed. Moreover, the LTRD allows for long visits/stays in Ukraine (up to one year) without risking loss of status.

8.4.4.3. Delete the Current Exclusion of TP Beneficiaries in Legal Migration Directives

Following discussions in Parliament on the deletion of the clauses excluding TP beneficiaries from the Family Reunification Directive and the Long-Term Residents Directive, there should be a review of the viability (pros and cons) of similar clauses in the other legal migration directives, possibly by additional amendments in the pending recast proposals. Including TP beneficiaries would allow individuals to move from one migration category to another should this become necessary.

These three solutions are not mutually exclusive, and a combination of two or all three should be seriously considered. If a reasonable solution cannot be achieved by amending existing EU instruments, the adoption of a special instrument for former TP beneficiaries from Ukraine could be a last resort, considering the time required for negotiation and adoption of a whole new instrument, which would add to the complexity of the CEAS.

8.4.5. Overwhelming Asylum Procedures, Forced Return and Various National Laws?

Finally, the worst option from the perspective of TP beneficiaries and/or national administrations is foreseen in the TP Directive itself, ie that at the end of the scheme, TP beneficiaries will either transfer into the asylum determination procedure of the Member State (Articles 17–19) or they will be subject to expulsion procedures if the state authorities consider that the conditions in Ukraine permit (Articles 20–23). Where Ukraine is still in no position to receive back its citizens at the end of the TP scheme, the EU should ensure that measures are in place to provide for their continued residence in the EU as a class, not requiring national administrations to determine asylum applications individually, the avoidance of which was the primary objective of the TP scheme. In the event that Ukraine may be able to accommodate some of its citizens who are beneficiaries of TP in the EU, the choice should be up to individuals whether to return or not, and the residence of those who are not in a position to return should be protected by EU law.

What is particularly important is that the arrangements for Ukraine TP beneficiaries at the end of the TP scheme are determined by EU law, not the national law of each Member State. The avoidance of disorder and uncertainty must be a priority, with a common and consistent set of rules regarding their treatment to be adopted at the EU level. The warm welcome the Ukraine TP beneficiaries have received in the EU must not be ruined by a disorganised and fragmented response determined by national, rather than EU, priorities as regards the end of the Scheme.

8.5. Lessons so Far

Stepping beyond the immediate crisis of protection in the context of the Russian invasion of Ukraine and the subsequent war, the EU has a number of lessons to note as a result of the first use of the TP Directive. First, when there is sufficient political will, carefully built by the EU institutions and the Member States, the EU is fully capable of receiving over four million people fleeing war in good conditions of reception in fewer than 12 months. The outcomes in terms of market and social integration have been greatly enhanced by immediate access to the labour market for TP beneficiaries and access to education. Lack of language skills, while posing a barrier, has by no means been the enormous problem to labour and educational integration which some policymakers had feared. The argument that the EU or some of its Member States are 'saturated' by migrant arrivals[70] has proven groundless in this case. It has turned out that the EU has sufficient resources to receive millions of refugees in a single year and to maintain open access to the EU territory for as many people fleeing this war as wish to come. As mentioned above, it is politically unimaginable to reintroduce mandatory visas for Ukrainian nationals to 'slow' the rate of arrivals or diminish the possibilities for TP beneficiaries to return to Ukraine for short stays and return to their EU place of safety.

One of the cornerstones of the CEAS has been the absolute necessity to prevent the secondary movement of asylum-seekers from the first EU country of arrival to another other EU country.[71] This policy of no secondary movement has been an enormous political and practical problem for the EU and refugees – an area without internal borders

[70] V Moreno-Lax, D Ghezelbash and N Klein, 'Between life, security and rights: Framing the interdiction of 'boat migrants' in the Central Mediterranean and Australia' (2019) 32 *Leiden Journal of International Law* 715.

[71] SH Legomsky, 'Secondary refugee movements and the return of asylum seekers to third countries: the meaning of effective protection' (2003) 15 *International Journal of Refugee Law* 567; L Marin, 'Waiting (and Paying) for Godot: Analyzing the Systemic Consequences of the Solidarity Crisis in EU Asylum Law' (2020) 22 *European Journal of Migration and Law* 60.

among (most of) the Member States.[72] In the case of TP beneficiaries, this policy has been reversed. For the largest single group arriving in the EU since the design of the CEAS, secondary movement is touted as a benefit both for states and beneficiaries. The opportunity to move from the first Member State of arrival (usually Poland or Romania) to another Member State, where the beneficiaries may have links, is promoted as an advantage. The surprise for officials across the EU has been the slow uptake of this right to move, especially bearing in mind the difference in the standard of living between some of the first arrival states like Romania and other EU states like Germany.[73] The big test before the EU now is how to provide those TP beneficiaries in need of long-term protection with the security of residence they deserve.

8.6. Addendums

8.6.1. The Option of Free Movement of Persons[74]

Three options discussed in the previous section would greatly contribute to the status of Ukrainian citizens fleeing the war. Nevertheless, there is still scope for another long-term solution to address the most significant migration influx into the EU. It is argued that some form of free movement could be another sustainable solution, duly taking into account the Ukrainian aspiration of European integration. The example of Syrian refugees in Turkey demonstrates the limitations of any temporary arrangements, as they fail to provide certainty and predictability for individuals. As explained above, a more permanent regime would also allow Ukrainians to consider returning to their home country if conditions were conducive while still retaining the option to return to the EU should their return proves unsuccessful.

While the possibility of granting rights stemming from EU citizenship is not discussed for Ukrainians, a limited form of free movement, akin to the example of EFTA states, could offer a viable pathway. Four EFTA Member States (Iceland, Liechtenstein, Norway and Switzerland) already benefit from the free movement of persons while having no intention of seeking membership in the EU. It is not unimaginable that Ukraine could enjoy a similar type of arrangement, especially in light of its candidate status granted by the Council on 23 June 2022.[75] This would ensure that Ukrainian citizens have a secure residence status within the EU, providing them with stability and peace of mind. Furthermore, they would continue to enjoy mobility rights across all 27 Member States, allowing them to travel and explore opportunities within the EU. Lastly, implementing such a measure would serve as a solid political indication by the EU, demonstrating its

[72] M De Somer, 'Schengen and internal border controls' in P De Bruycker, M De Somer and J-L De Brouwer (eds), 'From Tampere 20 to Tampere 2.0: Towards a new European consensus on migration' (European Policy Centre, 2020) 119–31; E Guild, 'Schengen Borders and Multiple National States of Emergency: From Refugees to Terrorism to COVID-19' (2021) 23 *European Journal of Migration and Law* 385.

[73] M Simionescu, 'European economic integration and migration in Romania.' (2019) 32 *Economic research-Ekonomska istraživanja* 3607.

[74] This section is written by Dzhuliia Lypalo.

[75] www.consilium.europa.eu/en/policies/enlargement/ukraine.

support for Ukraine and its unwavering commitment to safeguarding the well-being of Ukrainians under the best possible conditions.

Naturally, granting free movement to Ukrainian citizens poses significant political challenges. Even during the 2004 enlargement, nationals of most of the newly admitted Member States had to wait seven years before enjoying the unrestricted free movement of workers due to transitional arrangements.[76] However, there are crucial differences between these two situations. The previous apprehension towards the free movement of workers was based on the assumption that the combination of a significant migration potential from new Member States and income disparities between old and new EU Member States would result in a mass migration of workers, thus disrupting the labour market. In fact, five million citizens from the new Member States moved to the so-called 'old' Member States in the 10 years following the 2004 enlargement, even with restricted mobility rights for workers. In comparison, the EU has already seen a much more significant movement of four million Ukrainian citizens within one year. The reality is that most individuals who wished to move into the EU (for any reasons, including economic) have already done so under TP, and the influx of migrants feared by national governments has already happened on a much more significant scale than during the previous enlargements.

Nevertheless, even if immediate free movement is not envisaged, a more staged approach could be foreseen. The EU could follow the example of the past enlargements in immediately granting rights to self-employed persons and service providers. This alone would ease the situation for many Ukrainians.

Lastly, while recent new arrivals from Ukraine have stabilised over the past year, significant arrivals after the end of the war would likely include mostly men rejoining their families in the EU following the suspension of martial law. This again emphasises the importance of addressing family reunification for Ukrainian citizens in the EU, which could follow the example of Directive 2004/38 and provide greater protection to those family members in case the free movement approach is followed.

The free movement option raises natural concerns related to the overly inclusive nature of such an approach as it goes beyond the TP holders and could include all 40 million Ukrainian citizens. Moreover, arriving at this solution would necessitate unanimity among 27 EU Member States. Nevertheless, while free movement is not an imminent option, engaging in comprehensive discussions seeking long-term sustainable solutions is crucial considering the growing prospect of Ukrainian membership in the EU.

8.6.2. Addendum: September 2024

At the time of this book going to press, two further important developments have occurred.

On 19 September 2023, the Commission proposed a Council Implementing Decision extending TP for a further year from 4 March 2024 to 3 March 2025.[77] As the

[76] Only nationals of Cyprus and Malta were excluded from these transitional arrangements.
[77] COM(2023) 546 final.

original Decision was adopted on 4 March 2022, by 3 March 2024 the scheme would already have been in place for two years, the maximum permitted under Article 4(1) of the Directive. Article 4(2) allows a further extension of the TP 'by up to one year'. It appears fairly clear that Article 4 of the Directive only permits one extension of one year after the initial two years, and the maximum duration of the scheme is three years. The Commission's proposal on 11 June 2024 to extend the scheme with a fourth year was therefore something of a surprise to the legal community.[78]

The Commission's proposal states that the legal basis for this further extension was Article 4(2) of the Directive itself. The sole argument regarding the additional year set out by the Commission in the proposal was 'This allows for measures that promote a balance of efforts between Member States in receiving such persons and bearing the consequences thereof.' There is no mention of the issue of the maximum length of a TP scheme. The Council duly adopted the decision for the extension of the scheme with a fourth year on 25 June 2024.[79]

The new reading of Article 4(2), isolated from its context, is clearly incompatible with title, text and legislative history of the Directive. The protection status is no longer 'temporary' as clearly intended by the legislator in 2001. It becomes semi-permanent, as it can be extended indefinitely. Article 6 explicitly provides that the protection status has a 'maximum duration'. In the new interpretation of Article 4(2) this maximum has silently been removed. The Commission in 2000 proposed a two-year maximum. From the negotiation documents it appears that Germany wanted three years and France and the Netherlands 12–18 months maximum.

With this new reading of Article 4(2) the Commission's proposal and the Council Decision amount to a de facto amendment of a central element of the Directive with the apparent consent of the Ukrainian Government (but not the co-legislator). This may be politically understandable, but it seems unlawful and unconstitutional notwithstanding the Commission's Legal Service, which gave its blessing to this new interpretation in Autumn 2023. The Commission postponed the introduction of its proposal until two days after the European Parliament elections (6–9 June 2024). The Council then decided favorably two weeks later. During those two weeks the European Parliament was in statis as confirmation of the newly elected MEPs had not yet occurred.

In March 2024, a Dutch court (the Amsterdam Aliens Chamber) asked the CJEU to give a preliminary ruling on the question of the scope of the extension of the scheme (C-244/24, *Kaduna*). A month after the first reference, the Dutch State Council made an additional reference on the same issue on slightly different facts (C-290/24, *Abkez*). Both cases concern several third-country nationals who at the time of the Russian invasion were living in Ukraine on the basis of temporary residence permits. In the first few months after the invasion, they were voluntarily granted TP in the Netherlands on the basis of Article 7(1) of the Directive. The Dutch Government decided to end this non-mandatory TP after a change of the relevant Dutch law during the summer of 2022. Several rulings by Dutch courts forced the Government to repeatedly extend the protection until the State Council held in January 2024 that the non-mandatory protection

[78] COM(2024) 253 final.

[79] Council Implementing Decision (EU) 2024/1836 of 25 June 2024 extending temporary protection as introduced by Implementing Decision (EU) 2022/382 ST/11031/2024/INIT, [2024] OJ L 1836.

would automatically end on 4 March 2024, since the Council Decision of October 2023, extending the protection with a third year, applies only to Ukrainian citizens and third-country nationals mandatorily covered by the 2022 Decision activating the Directive. In February 2024, the Dutch authorities started to issue return decisions to persons outside this scope who, at that time, were still lawfully in the Netherlands in accordance with the State Council's ruling.

Both Dutch courts in their references explicitly held that the maximum duration of the TP, according to Article 4, is three years (District Court The Hague, Amsterdam Chamber at point 2.2 and the State Council in point 5.2.1). Their questions focus on two issues. Firstly, where a Member State has made use of the possibility offered by Article 7(1) of the Directive to grant TP under that Directive to additional categories of displaced persons, does the TP given to that optional group continues both in the case of an automatic extension as referred to in Article 4(1) for the period specified in that provision, but also in the case of a decision to extend the period as referred to in Article 4(2)? The second question boils down to whether Article 6 of the Return Directive precludes a return decision being issued on a date on which the temporarily protected person is still lawfully residing in the territory of a Member State.

The Court joined the two cases and granted the State Council's request for an accelerated procedure (ECLI:EU:C:2024:491). The pleadings before the Grand Chamber took place on 3 September 2024 and the Advocate General presented his conclusions on 22 October 2024. During the hearing neither the judges nor the Advocate General raised the June 2024 Council Decision on the extension of the TP by an additional year beyond that permitted by Article 4(2).

9

EU Defence Capabilities after the War in Ukraine: The Act in Support of Ammunition Production and the Development of an EU Defence Industrial Policy

FEDERICO FABBRINI

9.1. Introduction

In early summer 2023 the European Parliament and the Council of the European Union (EU) approved the Act on supporting ammunition production (ASAP), which was published in the EU official journal on 20 July 2023.[1] The ASAP is an important component of a wide-ranging EU response to the war in Ukraine, which began when Russia illegally invaded its sovereign neighbour in February 2022. The core purpose of the ASAP is to promote through ad hoc EU funding the ramping up of production capabilities of the EU defence industry, thus supporting Ukraine on the battlefield, by providing it with a significant amount of ground-to-ground and artillery ammunitions, as well as missiles. Given the amount of shells which are shot daily by Ukraine and its opponent, in the most high-intensity military conflict in the European continent since the end of WWII,[2] a particular urgency surrounded this new EU defence production effort. Hence the acronym of the new regulation, which reveals the EU's ambition to replenish the Ukrainian stockpiles – as soon as possible.

The purpose of this chapter is to examine the ASAP, as adopted by the EU co-legislator, but also to reflect more broadly at its implications for the EU defence capabilities. The ASAP is, in fact, the latest piece of the puzzle of an ever more comprehensive EU

[1] Regulation (EU) 2023/1525 of the European Parliament and of the Council of 20 July 2023 on supporting ammunition production (ASAP), [2023] OJ L185/7 (ASAP Regulation).

[2] See S Erlanger, 'Ukraine Needs Shells, and Arms Makers Want Money. Enter the E.U.' *The New York Times* (8 March 2023), available at www.nytimes.com/2023/03/08/world/europe/ukraine-eu-shells-ammunition.html.

response to the return of war on the European continent.[3] As a growing body of literature has pointed out, the war in Ukraine has profoundly transformed the EU, leading to unprecedented advances in the field of Common Foreign and Security Policy (CFSP), and Common Security and Defence Policy (CSDP)[4] – but also energy, with the phasing out of Russian fossil fuels, and asylum and migration, with the first ever deployment of the Temporary Protection Directive.[5] Moreover, in response to the war the EU has rolled out several new financial instruments to provide support to the Ukrainian Government and military, which largely tracked the use of common debt experimented in response to COVID-19.[6] At the same time, the war in Ukraine has also led the EU to revive its enlargement process, by granting candidate status to, and starting accession negotiation with, Ukraine (and Moldova);[7] and by setting up a new forum – the European Political Community – to deepen relations with the wider Europe.[8]

Yet, the war in Ukraine has also impacted the EU industrial policy strategy, leading to a rethink of the role of public intervention in the economy in pursuance of geostrategic priorities.[9] In fact, the ASAP is closely connected to a European Defence Industry Reinforcement through common Procurement Act (EDIRPA), which has also been approved by the European Parliament and the Council of the EU in early summer 2023.[10] Moreover, the ASAP relates to other recent legislative priorities of the European Commission, including the Chips Act, and the Critical Raw Materials Act, which have been designed to increase the resilience of EU supply chains, to reduce foreign dependences, and to adjust to the reality of the new, selective, globalisation.[11] Along the lines of this new European economic security strategy,[12] the ASAP Regulation endeavours to support the capacity of the EU defence industry to live up to the challenges posed by the war in Ukraine, while also positioning the EU to address in a supranational way a more threatening geostrategic environment.

[3] This chapter builds on F Fabbrini, 'European Defense Union ASAP' (2024) 29 *European Foreign Affairs Review* 67. The chapter reflects the state of the law and policy up to 30 May 2024. On the topic addressed in this chapter and for a comprehensive analysis of the EU response to Russia's aggression against Ukraine, in the 1,000 days from February 2022 until October 2024, see also, more extensively F Fabbrini, *The EU Constitution in Time of War: Legal Responses to Russia's Aggression against Ukraine* (Oxford, Oxford University Press, 2025).

[4] See S Blockmans, 'The Birth of a Geopolitical EU' (2022) 27 *European Foreign Affairs Review* 155.

[5] See F Fabbrini, '"To Establish Justice": The EU Response to the War in Ukraine in the Field of Justice and Home Affairs' (2024) 49 *European Law Review* 359.

[6] See F Fabbrini, 'Funding the War in Ukraine: the European Peace Facility, the Macro-Financial Assistance Instrument and the Slow Rise of an EU Fiscal Capacity' (2023) 10 *Politics & Governance* 52.

[7] See R Petrov and C Hillion, '"Accession through War" – Ukraine's road to the EU' (2022) 59 *Common Market Law Review* 1289.

[8] See also L Lonardo, 'The European Political Community: A Nebulous Answer to the Strategic Question of How to Unite Europe' (2023) 8 *European Papers* 755.

[9] See Editorial Comments, 'Paying for the EU's Industry Policy' (2023) 60 *Common Market Law Review* 617.

[10] Regulation (EU) 2023/2418 of the European Parliament and of the Council of 18 October 2023 on establishing an instrument for the reinforcement of the European defence industry through common procurement (EDIRPA), [2023] OJ L1.

[11] See H James, 'The new globalization and the economic consequences of Brexit' in F Fabbrini (ed), *The Law & Politics of Brexit. Volume V. The Trade & Cooperation Agreement* (Oxford, Oxford University Press, 2024) 29.

[12] See European Commission & High Representative, 'European economic security strategy' (20 June 2023), JOIN(2023) 20 final.

From this point of view, therefore, the ASAP is a step in the direction of establishing a European defence union, seen both as a combination of military capability and industrial capacity.

Nevertheless, as this chapter maintains, the ASAP cannot be equated to the EU equivalent of the United States (US) Defense Production Act.[13] To begin with, the funding for ASAP charged on the EU budget is remarkably limited – only €500 million for two years. Moreover, the final ASAP Regulation has dropped some of the ambitions of the original Commission proposal, including the power to compel private companies to produce by priority specific defence equipment – a hallmark of the US Defense Production Act. Otherwise, the ASAP is affected by some broader structural limitations of the EU's power in CFSP, CSDP, industry policy and fiscal resources. While the EU itself is a peace project – created to prevent war in the European continent[14] – the war in Ukraine has arguably reinvigorated the leading role of the North Atlantic Treaty Organization (NATO) as the primary security architecture for the European continent. In this framework therefore ASAP constitutes a step towards strengthening the EU defence union. However, if the EU wants to be serious about its defence, given the ongoing conflict and the uncertainties about future US commitment, new EU law and policy initiatives would be much needed.

As such, this chapter is structured as follows. Section 9.2 lays out the context of the ASAP Regulation, explaining the political and military background to its adoption. Section 9.3 examines the content of Regulation (EU) 2023/1525, detailing its main features. Section 9.4 discusses the consequences of ASAP, assessing the choice of legal basis and its significance for the role of the EU in defence industrial policy. Section 9.5, however, critically considers a number of weaknesses of the ASAP, particularly compared to the original Commission proposal, and highlights the unsettled status of the EU defence union. Section 9.6, finally, concludes.

9.2. The Context

The outburst of the war in Ukraine on 24 February 2022 was a shock for the EU and its Member States. The return of land warfare on the European continent for the first time since the end of WWII shattered expectations of a perpetual peace, and forced the EU to face the reality of hard power.[15] Since the Russian illegal military aggression of Ukraine, however, the EU has responded in unprecedented ways – with European integration in security, defence and beyond advancing more in the months since the beginning of the war than it had during the prior three decades. As leaders of the EU institutions and heads of state and government of the 27 Member States acknowledged in a special summit organised by the French Presidency of the Council of the EU in Versailles on 11 March 2022, 'Russia's war of aggression constitutes a tectonic shift in European

[13] Defense Production Act of 1950 (Pub L 81–774).

[14] See M Eilstrup-Sangiovanni and D Verdier, 'European Integration as a Solution to War' (2005) 11 *European Journal of International Relations* 99.

[15] Statement by the HR/VP Josep Borrell, EEAS (27 February 2022).

history.'[16] To face this changing geopolitical scenario, therefore, the EU 'decided to take more responsibility for our security and take further more decisive steps towards building our European sovereignty'[17] – along three key dimensions, namely: 'a) bolstering our defence capabilities; b) reducing our energy dependencies; and c) building a more robust economic base.'[18]

In the field of CFSP/CSDP, in particular, the EU rolled out a series of groundbreaking measures. To begin with, the EU approved a strategic compass designed to outline a united foreign policy and security strategy,[19] and deepened its partnership with NATO.[20] Moreover, between February 2022 and June 2024 the EU approved 14 rounds of sanctions designed to financially target President Vladimir Putin and his inner circle of oligarchs, politically deter Russia, and economically weaken its ability to continue the illegal war of aggression. At the same time, the EU decided for the first time ever to mobilise the European Peace Facility (EPF)[21] – a novel financial instrument established in connection with the new EU multiannual budget – to provide financial support to the Ukrainian military, including funding for the purchase of lethal weapons. Furthermore, the EU also activated a Military Assistance Mission, with the aim to train Ukrainian army officers to the use of advanced weapons.[22]

In particular, as the conflict in Ukraine continued, the EPF emerged as a leading tool in the EU defence strategy. In February 2022, the Council quickly approved a Decision on assistance measure for the supply to the Ukrainian armed forces of military equipment.[23] The Decision empowered the High Representative of the EU for Foreign Affairs and Security to implement the measure,[24] making arrangements with the beneficiary, including ensuring compliance with international human rights law and humanitarian law,[25] and foresaw a disbursement of €450 million.[26] This amount was subsequently doubled in March 2022,[27] and tripled in April 2022 to a total of

[16] Informal meeting of the Heads of State or Government, Versailles Declaration (10–11 March 2022) para 6.

[17] ibid, para 7.

[18] ibid.

[19] See Council of the EU, 'A strategic compass for security and defense – For a European Union that protects its citizens, values and interests and contributes to international peace and security' (21 March 2022) Doc 7371/22.

[20] See also Joint Declaration on EU-NATO Cooperation (10 January 2023).

[21] Council Decision (CFSP) 2021/509 of 22 March 2021 establishing a European Peace Facility and repealing Decision (CFSP) 2015/528, [2021] OJ L102/14.

[22] Council Decision (CFSP) 2022/2245 of 14 November 2022 on an assistance measure under the European Peace Facility to support the Ukrainian Armed Forces trained by the European Union Military Assistance Mission in support of Ukraine with military equipment, and platforms, designed to deliver lethal force, [2022] OJ L 294/25.

[23] See Council Decision (CFSP) 2022/338 of 28 February 2022 on an assistance measure under the European Peace Facility for the supply to the Ukrainian Armed Forces of military equipment and platforms designed to deliver lethal force, [2022] OJ L 60/1.

[24] ibid, Art 4.

[25] ibid, Art 3.

[26] ibid, Art 2.

[27] See Council Decision (CFSP) 2022/471 of 23 March 2022 amending Decision (CFSP) 2022/338 of an assistance measure under the European Peace Facility for the supply to the Ukrainian Armed Forces of military equipment and platforms designed to deliver lethal force, [2022] OJ L96/43.

€1.5 billion.[28] Subsequently, EPF funding to support the Ukrainian military was further tapped in May 2022[29] and July 2022,[30] bringing the total size of the support to €3.1 billion. This, combined with other EPF expenditures towards other third countries carried out in 2022, largely depleted in a single year a budget that had been designed for a seven-year timeframe. As a result, the Council decided in December 2022 upon a €2 billion increase in the EPF for 2023,[31] and in June 2023, the Council agreed to a further €3.5 billion top-up of the EPF, increasing its size to €12 billon.[32]

Yet, the continuation of the war and the need to fund the Ukrainian army in its defence against the Russian aggression forced a further reorganisation of the EPF. Following a request by the European Council in December 2023,[33] the Council agreed in March 2024 to increase the envelope of the EPF by a further €5 billion, ringfencing this new amount for Ukraine only, via a so-called Ukraine Assistance Fund (UAF).[34] Moreover, the Council decided to improve the governance arrangements for the implementation of the UAF, tasking the Facility Committee to decide on the disbursement of this amount within a month.[35] At the same time, the Council agreed to limit after a transition period the ability of Member States to obtain reimbursement from the EPF for the national deliveries of ammunition from stocks to Ukraine,[36] thus promoting joint procurement of new weapons. The latest increase of the EPF – which brings it to a total of over €17 billion, more than three times the original EPF funding of €5.6 billion – constitutes a significant increase. However, the Council acknowledged that 'further comparable annual increases could be envisaged until 2027, based on Ukrainian needs'.[37]

Nevertheless, the war also quickly exposed the limited military capabilities and dwindling arsenals of the EU Member States – a process caused by two interrelated factors. On the one hand, under the post-Cold War peace dividend, Member States had consistently reduced their defence spending. In fact, this had long been a matter of complaint by the US: while in 2014, following Russia's illegal invasion and annexation of Crimea, NATO had set a target of two per cent of GDP national defence spending

[28] See Council Decision (CFSP) 2022/636 of 13 April 2022 amending Decision (CFSP) 2022/338 on an assistance measure under the European Peace Facility for the supply to the Ukrainian Armed Forces of military equipment, and platforms, designed to deliver lethal force, [2022] OJ L117/34.

[29] See Council Decision (CFSP) 2022/809 of 23 May 2022 amending Decision (CFSP) 2022/338 on an assistance measure under the European Peace Facility for the supply to the Ukrainian Armed Forces of military equipment, and platforms, designed to deliver lethal force, [2022] OJ L145/40.

[30] See Council Decision (CFSP) 2022/1285 of 21 July 2022 amending Decision (CFSP) 2022/338 on an assistance measure under the European Peace Facility for the supply to the Ukrainian Armed Forces of military equipment, and platforms, designed to deliver lethal force, [2022] OJ L195/93.

[31] Council Decision (CFSP) 2023/577 of 13 March 2023 amending Decision (CFSP) 2021/509 establishing a European Peace Facility, [2023] OJ L75/23.

[32] Council of the EU, 'European Peace Facility: Council agrees on second top-up of the overall financial ceiling by 3.5 billion' press release (26 June 2023).

[33] European Council conclusions 14–15 December 2023, EUCO 20/23, para 3.

[34] Council of the EU, 'Ukraine Assistance Fund: Council allocates €5 billion under the European Peace Facility to support Ukraine militarily' press release (18 March 2024).

[35] Council Decision (CFSP) 2024/890 of 18 March 2024 amending Decision (CFSP) 2021/509 establishing a European Peace Facility, [2024] OJ L1/4, Art 1.

[36] ibid, Recital 10.

[37] ibid, Recital 15.

on the military,[38] European countries had largely failed to abide by this rule.[39] On the other hand, uncoordinated national military expenditures had led to duplication and waste – a dynamic often called the costs of non-Europe in defence.[40] To address this state of affairs, as requested by the Versailles Declaration,[41] on 18 May 2022 the European Commission and High Representative published a joint White Paper on the defence investment gap and the way forward, in which they outlined options to incentivise joint procurement of military equipment.[42] Building on this policy document, on 19 July 2022 the Commission put forward a legislative proposal for an EDIRPA.[43] This short-term instrument, which had its legal basis in Article 173 TFEU, on industrial policy, was specifically designed to incentivise the EU Member States to procure defence products jointly, addressing the EU's most urgent and critical defence capability gaps and developing the EU Defence Technological & Industrial Base (EDTIB). To this end, the Commission proposed for EDIRPA a dedicated financial envelope of €500 million, to be drawn down from the EU budget. The EDIRPA Regulation was ultimately approved by the European Parliament and the Council in October 2023, but with a smaller budget of €300 million for the period until 31 December 2025.

As the war increasingly turned into a high-intensity conflict of attrition, however, a specific need emerged to supply the Ukrainian army on the battlefield with ammunitions. On 20 March 2023, therefore, the Council of the EU approved a plan in three steps to secure the delivery and joint procurement of ammunition for Ukraine.[44] First, 'The Council call[ed] on Member States to urgently deliver ground-to-ground and artillery ammunition to Ukraine and, if requested, missiles.'[45] Second, 'The Council further call[ed] on Member States to jointly procure 155mm ammunition and, if requested, missiles for Ukraine in the fastest way possible before 30 September 2023.'[46] Third, and finally,

> The Council invite[d] the Commission to present concrete proposals to urgently support the ramp-up of manufacturing capacities of the European defence industry, secure supply chains, facilitate efficient procurement procedures, address shortfalls in production capacities and promote investments, including, where appropriate, mobilising the Union budget.[47]

[38] See Summit Declaration Issued by the Heads of State and Government Participating in the Meeting of the North Atlantic Council in Wales (5 September 2014) para 14.

[39] See F Fabbrini, 'Do NATO Obligations Trump European Budgetary Constraints?' (2018) 9 *Harvard National Security Journal* 121.

[40] See B Ballester, 'The Cost of Non-Europe in Common Security and Defense Policy' (2013) *European Parliament Research Service*, available at www.europarl.europa.eu/RegData/etudes/etudes/join/2013/494466/IPOL-JOIN_ET%282013%29494466_EN.pdf.

[41] Versailles Declaration (n 16) para 11.

[42] See European Commission and High Representative Joint Communication on Defense Investment Gap Analysis and Way Forward, 18 May 2022, JOIN(2022)24 final, 9–10.

[43] See European Commission proposal for a Regulation of the European Parliament and of the Council on establishing the European defense industry Reinforcement through common procurement Act, 19 July 2022, COM(2022) 349 final.

[44] Council of the EU, Doc 7632/23, Annex: Speeding up the delivery and joint procurement of ammunition for Ukraine (20 March 2023).

[45] ibid, para 2.

[46] ibid, para 3.

[47] ibid, para 4.

On this basis, on 3 May 2023, the Commission put forward a proposal for an ASAP Regulation,[48] as a complement to the EDIRPA. The ASAP – which has as its legal bases Article 173 TFEU on industrial policy, and Article 114 TFEU on internal market – was approved by the co-legislators at record speed, indeed much faster than the EDIRPA, and entered into force in July 2023, with a envelope of €500 million, funded from the EU budget, for the period from 25 July 2023 until 30 June 2025.

9.3. The Content

The ASAP Regulation is a relatively lean piece of EU legislation, comprising 24 Articles, structured in five Chapters. The Preamble recalls the historical setting in which ASAP was put forward, including the outburst of the war in Ukraine and the consequential decision taken by heads of state and government in the Versailles summit of 11 March 2022 to 'take further decisive steps towards building European sovereignty'.[49] The Preamble also explains the rationale for the adoption of the ASAP, namely Ukraine's pressing defence need of ground-to-ground and artillery ammunitions and missiles, and the urgent need to increase the production to replenish depleting national stocks.[50] The Preamble furthermore highlights 'the specificities of the defence industry, where demand comes almost exclusively from Member States',[51] clarifying that 'the functioning of the defence industry sector does not follow the conventional rules and business models that govern more traditional markets'.[52] As such, the ASAP emphasises how 'additional [EU] industrial policy measures are necessary to ensure a rapid ramp-up of manufacturing capacities'[53] and stresses that EU 'defence industry is a crucial contribution to the resilience and the security of the [EU]'.[54]

Article 1 of the Regulation states that the purpose of the ASAP is to 'establish[] a set of measures and lay[] down a budget aimed at urgently strengthening the responsiveness and ability of the [EDTIB] to ensure the timely availability and supply of [...] relevant defence products'. This overall purpose if further teased out in Article 4, which clarifies that: 'The objective of the Instrument is to foster the efficiency and competitiveness of the [EDTIB] to support the ramp-up of the production capacity and timely delivery of relevant defence products through industrial reinforcement.' To this end, Article 5 sets aside a budget of €500 million in current prices, 'for the period 25 July 2023 to 30 June 2025'. Indeed, as indicated in Article 24(2), 'This Regulation shall apply until 30 June 2025' – hence with a sunset. Nevertheless, pursuant to Articles 1(2) and 23, 'By 30 June 2024, the Commission shall draw up a report evaluating the implementation of the measures set out in this Regulation and their results, as well as the opportunity to

[48] European Commission proposal for a Regulation of the European Parliament and of the Council on establishing the Act in Support of Ammunition Production, 3 May 2023, COM(2023) 237 final.

[49] ASAP Regulation, Recital 2.

[50] ibid, Recital 4.

[51] ibid, Recital 20.

[52] ibid.

[53] ibid, Recital 6.

[54] ibid, Recital 34.

extend their applicability and provide for their funding'[55] – hence leaving open the door to extend and expand the instrument's funding. Moreover, as stated in Article 6, ASAP funding 'shall be implemented in synergy with other [EU] programmes', with the consequence that an action receiving funding under this Regulation may also gain support from other EU funding schemes, provided alternative contributions do not cover the same costs.

The substantive core of ASAP is enshrined in Article 8. This provision clarifies the eligible actions to be funded, and states that:

> The Instrument shall provide financial support for actions addressing identified bottlenecks in production capacities and supply chains with a view to securing and accelerating the production of relevant defence products in order to ensure their effective supply and timely availability.[56]

The provision, in particular, lists a number of defence production activities, including the optimisation, expansion, modernisation, upgrading or repurposing of existing, or the establishment of new, production capacities, in relation to relevant defence products; the establishment of cross-border industrial partnerships; the testing and reconditioning of defence products; and the training, reskilling or upskilling of personnel. At the same time, Article 8(4) prohibits using ASAP to fund 'actions related to the production of goods or delivery of services which are prohibited by applicable international law; [and] actions related to the production of lethal autonomous weapons'. From this point of view, for example, the ASAP could not be used to produce cluster munitions, which the US controversially decided to provide to Ukraine at its request,[57] but which are banned by an international convention.[58]

From a management viewpoint, the regulation empowers the Commission to lay out a work programme,[59] and directly award ASAP funding to relevant defence industries, based on their applications. According to Article 11(2), the 'Commission shall, by means of implementing acts, award the funding under this Regulation'. Pursuant to Article 10(1) eligible entities include 'public or privately owned [companies], which are established and have their executive management structures in the [EU] or in an associated country'. In fact, as stated in Article 3, ASAP is open also to members of the European Economic Area – basically Norway.

As clarified in Article 11 the award of funding depends on several criteria, including: increase in production capacity in the EU; reduction of lead production time; elimination of sourcing and production bottlenecks; and resilience through cross-border cooperation. As stated in Article 9, the financing rate offered by the EU can fund

> up to 35% of the eligible costs of an eligible action related to the production capacities of relevant defence products, and up to 40% of the eligible costs of an eligible action related to

[55] ibid, Art 23(1).
[56] ibid, Art 8(2).
[57] 'Pourquoi la livraison d'armes à sous-munitions à l'Ukraine annoncée par Washington est controversée' *Le Monde* (7 July 2023).
[58] Convention on Cluster Munitions (CCM).
[59] ASAP Regulation, Art 12.

the production capacities of components and raw materials insofar as they are intended or used wholly for the production of relevant defence products.

However, this percentage can increase further 'where applicants demonstrate a contribution to the creation of new cross-border cooperation' or 'where applicants commit to prioritising, for the duration of the action, orders stemming from … the common procurement of relevant defence products by at least three Member States; [or] the procurement of relevant defence products [… for] Ukraine'.[60]

Moreover, the Regulation introduces further special provision to secure the security of supply. To ensure the timely availability of relevant defence products, Article 13 encourages Member States to accelerate the permit granting process related to the planning, construction and operation of production facilities, transfer of inputs within the EU as well as qualification and certification of end products. To facilitate common procurement during the ammunition supply crisis, Article 14 of the Regulation introduces a derogation to Directive 2009/81/EC on defence procurement,[61] allowing at least two EU Member States to modify existing framework agreements to increase production. At the same time, 'to leverage, de-risk and speed-up investments needed to increase manufacturing capacities' Article 15 authorises the establishment of a ramping-up fund, which the Commission will manage.[62] The Regulation then introduces final provisions on security of information,[63] confidentiality,[64] data protection[65] and publicity,[66] while also foreseeing standard audits mechanisms to protect the financial interests of the EU.[67]

9.4. The Consequences

From an EU legal perspective, ASAP constitutes a significant development for CFSP/CSDP – both in formal and substantive terms. As Panos Koutrakos had explained in detail, the EU institutions, and especially the Commission, had long emphasised the structural and economic problems of the EU defence industries and endeavored to enhance the capacity of the European defence technological and industrial base – but 'for a long time, defence industries were considered to be entirely beyond the reach of EU law'.[68] In fact, a provision of the Treaties dating back to the early stages of European integration, now Article 346(1)(b) TFEU, seemed to exclude a role for the EU in this domain, by stating that 'any Member State may take such measures as it considers necessary for the protection of the essential interests of its security which are connected with

[60] ibid, Art 9(2).

[61] Directive 2009/81/EC of the European Parliament and of the Council of 13 July 2009 on the coordination of procedures for the award of certain works contracts, supply contracts and service contracts by contracting authorities or entities in the fields of defence and security, and amending Directives 2004/17/EC and 2004/18/EC, [2009] OJ L216/76.

[62] ASAP Rgulation, (n 1) Art 7(1).

[63] ibid, Art 17.

[64] ibid, Art 18.

[65] ibid, Art 19.

[66] ibid, Art 22.

[67] ibid, Arts 20 and 21.

[68] P Koutrakos, *The EU Common Security and Defense Policy* (Oxford, Oxford University Press 2013) 252.

the production of or trade in arms, munitions and war material'. However, through several important rulings, the Court of Justice of the EU (ECJ) eventually interpreted this provision strictly.[69] This opened the door for greater EU involvement in the field of defence procurement, although legal commitments in the area of industrial integration proved difficult.[70]

At the time of the Constitutional Treaty, EU Member States agreed to set up an EU forum for coordinating their defence industrial policy and military procurement – the European Defence Agency (EDA) – going beyond purely international mechanisms such as the Organisation for Joint Armament Co-operation (OCCAR), established by a specific convention.[71] Nevertheless, the Member States did so in an intergovernmental fashion.[72] EDA was initially set up through a Council joint action,[73] and then retained by the Lisbon Treaty. According to Article 45 TEU, the EDA shall have as its task among others to 'contribute to identifying the Member States military capability objectives [... to] support defence technology research [... and to] strengthening the industrial and technological base of the defence sector'. The EDA in particular, launched in 2017 a process known as the Coordinated Annual Review on Defence (CARD), which allows Member States to gain a better view of national investment in defence, to coordinate defence procurement and develop opportunities for cooperation.

With the explosion of the war in Ukraine, however, the EU seems to be taking a much more influential role in the area of defence industry – also through a more expansive use of the 'supranational' legal bases available in the Treaties. The legal bases of ASAP in fact are Articles 114 and 173(3) TFEU. While the former is the well-known EU internal market legal basis, the latter is a provision dedicated to industrial policy. Specifically, Article 173(1) states that: 'The Union and the Member States shall ensure that the conditions necessary for the competitiveness of the Union's industry exist' and clarifies that 'in accordance with a system of open and competitive markets' they shall inter alia 'speed[] up the adjustment of industry to structural changes; encourag[e] an environment favourable to initiative and to the development of undertakings [... and] foster[] better exploitation of the industrial potential of policies of innovation, research and technological development'. According to Article 173(3) TFEU, then: 'The Union shall contribute to the achievement of the objectives set out in paragraph 1 through the policies and activities it pursues under other provisions of the Treaties.' Nevertheless, pursuant to the same provision, the European Parliament and the Council, acting in accordance with the ordinary legislative procedure, 'may decide on specific measures in support of action taken in the Member States to achieve the objectives set out in paragraph 1'.

[69] Case C-414/97 *Commission v Spain* (1999) ECR I-5585; Case C-337/05 *Commission v Italy* (2008) ECR I-2173; Case C-157/06 *Commission v Italy* (2008) ECR I-7313.

[70] S Blockmans, 'The EU's Modular Approach to Defense Integration: An Inclusive, Ambitious and Legally Binding PESCO?' (2018) 55 *Common Market Law Review* 1785.

[71] Convention on the Establishment of the Organisation for Joint Armament Cooperation.

[72] M Trybus, 'The new European Defense Agency: A contribution to a common European security and defense policy or a challenge to the Community acquis?'(2006) 43 *Common Market Law Review* 667.

[73] Council Joint Action 2004/551/CFSP of 12 July 2004 on the establishment of the European Defence Agency, [2004] OJ L245/17.

Traditionally, Article 173 TFEU – which is the sole provision of Title XVII of Part III of the TFEU on 'Industry' – had been regarded as a marginal legal basis for EU action. In fact, while the clause – which was originally introduced by the Treaty of Maastricht – brought industrial policy under EU competences, it clearly left the dominant role in this field to the Member States. According to Article 173(2) TFEU: 'The Member States shall consult each other in liaison with the Commission and, where necessary, shall coordinate their action.' The Commission can establish guidelines, and organise the exchange of best practices, in line with the open method of coordination. However, Article 6(b) TFEU explicitly indicates 'industry' as a policy area where the EU 'shall have competence to carry out actions to support, coordinate or supplement the action of the Member States'. This means, pursuant to Article 2(5) TFEU, that the EU shall thereby not 'supersed[e]' the Member States' competence in this area. Moreover, Article 173(3) TFEU specifically 'exclude[s] any harmonisation of the laws and regulations of the Member States'. Finally, pursuant to Article 173(3), final paragraph, TFEU 'This Title shall not provide a basis for the introduction by the Union of any measure which could lead to a distortion of competition or contains tax provisions or provisions relating to the rights and interests of employed persons.'

Article 173(3) TFEU had been used by the EU, together with Article 175 TFEU on cohesion policy, as the legal basis for the adoption of several economic stimulus programmes, such as the 2015 European Fund for Strategic Investment,[74] and the 2021 InvestEU programme.[75] In the field of defence industrial development, Article 173 TFEU had also been used before the war in Ukraine for some early common initiatives – but these were essentially designed to fund defence-related research and development (R&D). In particular, Article 173(3) TFEU was the sole legal basis for the approval in 2018 of a Regulation establishing the European Defence Industrial Development Programme (EDIDP) aiming at supporting the competitiveness and innovation capacity of the Union's defence industry with a two-year R&D budget of €500 million.[76] Moreover, Article 173(3) TFEU was, jointly with other legal bases on research and technological development, the foundation to adopt in 2021 a Regulation establishing the European Defence Fund (EDF),[77] as part of the EU Multi-Annual Financial Framework (MFF) 2021–27. The EDF repealed the EDIDP and set aside a seven-year budget of €7.9 billion to 'support collaborative research that could significantly boost the performance of future capabilities throughout the Union'.[78]

Nevertheless, since the beginning of the war in Ukraine, Article 173(3) TFEU has arguably been used more frequently, and more aggressively. This provision is a legal

[74] Regulation (EU) 2015/1017 of the European Parliament and of the Council of 25 June 2015 on the European Fund for Strategic Investments, the European Investment Advisory Hub and the European Investment Project Portal and amending Regulations (EU) No 1291/2013 and (EU) No 1316/2013 – the European Fund for Strategic Investments, [2015] OJ L169/1.

[75] Regulation (EU) 2021/523 of the European Parliament and of the Council of 24 March 2021 establishing the InvestEU Programme and amending Regulation (EU) 2015/1017, [2021] OJ L107/30.

[76] Regulation (EU) 2018/1092 of the European Parliament and of the Council of 18 July 2018 establishing the European Defence Industrial Development Programme aiming at supporting the competitiveness and innovation capacity of the Union's defence industry, [2020] OJ L200/30.

[77] Regulation (EU) 2021/697 of the European Parliament and of the Council of 29 April 2021 establishing the European Defence Fund and repealing Regulation (EU) 2018/1092, [2021] OJ L170/149.

[78] ibid, Art 3(2)(a).

basis for ASAP, as well as for EDIRPA, and the Chips Act. And ASAP goes beyond simple R&D by specifically funding with EU money the production and procurement of ammunition. This development mirrors to some extent what happened in the response to the pandemic: as Bruno de Witte pointed out, legal bases that 'had originally (after their inclusion in the Treaty text) been dormant [... were] rediscovered' to tackle the socio-economic consequences of COVID-19 and legally engineer an economic policy shift like the establishment of the Next Generation EU (NGEU).[79] Moreover, this confirms that the system of competences in the TFEU is less clear-cut than what may prima facie emerge from reading Article 2 TFEU, which categorises EU competences as either exclusive, shared, coordinating, supporting or supplementing.[80] In fact, the TFEU system of allocation of competences is very complex, particularly in the economic domain.[81] While Article 114 TFEU, the EU internal market competence has conventionally been constructed as a flexible legal basis,[82] if one considers the entirety of the Treaties' provisions one can find support for the view that the EU has significant powers to take legislative action in the field of economic policy *lato sensu*.[83] As a result, the EU law-making institutions have the ability – subject to the principles of subsidiarity and proportionality[84] – to adjust to changing circumstances and act when necessary.

From a substantive point of view, therefore, the adoption of ASAP aligns with the EU effort to enhance its strategic autonomy – a process which began before the war in Ukraine but was accelerated by it.[85] As Frank Hoffmeister has recently pointed out, strategic autonomy has driven the development of a number of new EU policy tools in the field of external trade relations, and CFSP[86] – and arguably ASAP further advances the trend in CSDP. Needless to say, there is much academic and policy debate about the significance and success of the push towards EU strategic autonomy. As political scientists have pointed out, the goal to increase the EU strategic autonomy is in tension with the EU's attempt to deepen transatlantic relations in a more threatening geostrategic environment, and ultimately 'the war underline[d] the dependence on US security guarantees'.[87] Yet, the action taken in response to the war in Ukraine, and ASAP, reveal the effort by the EU to enhance its autonomous capabilities *to act*.

In fact, the adoption of ASAP is all the more significant because, as is well known, Article 41(2) TEU states that 'expenditure arising from operations having military or defence implications' cannot be charged to the EU budget. To be clear, ASAP does

[79] B De Witte, 'The European Union's Covid-19 Recovery Plan: The Legal Engineering of an Economic Policy Shift' (2021) 58 *Common Market Law Review* 635.

[80] See T Tridimas, 'Competence After Lisbon: The Elusive Search for Bright Lines' in D Ashiagbor et al (eds), *The European Union after the Lisbon Treaty* (Cambridge, Cambridge University Press, 2012) 47.

[81] See M Claes and B De Witte, 'Competences' in S Blockmans and A Lazowski (eds), *Research Handbook of EU Institutional Law* (Cheltenham, Elgar, 2016) 9.

[82] See N Nic Shuibhne, *Regulating the Internal Market* (Cheltenham, Elgar, 2006).

[83] See R Bieber, 'The Allocation of Economic Policy Competences in the European Union' in L Azoulai (ed), *The Question of Competence in the European Union* (Oxford, Oxford University Press 2015) 86.

[84] See Art 5 TFEU.

[85] T Verellen and A Hofer, 'The Unilateral Turn in EU Trade and Investment Policy' (2023) 28 *European Foreign Affairs Review* 1.

[86] F Hoffmeister, 'Strategic Autonomy in the European Union's External Relations Law' (2023) 60 *Common Market Law Review*. 667.

[87] N Helwig, 'EU Strategic Autonomy after the Russian Invasion of Ukraine: Europe's Capacity to Act in Times of War' (2023) 61 *Journal of Common Market Studies* 1.

not conflict with Article 41(2) TEU, since Regulation (EU) 2023/1525 is focused on defence production, not defence operations. However, through its internal market and industrial policy competences the EU has taken an inroad into the domain of military capabilities – which until then remained essentially a purview of the Member States, either separately or jointly. In fact, ASAP goes beyond the purely intergovernmental mechanisms experimented within the framework of the EDA by providing a truly supranational solution to the defence industrial challenges posed by the war in Ukraine. Moreover, while Regulation (EU) 2023/1525, in line with Article 42(2) TEU, proclaims that ASAP 'should apply without prejudice to the specific character of the security and defence policy of certain Member States',[88] by leveraging the EU budget to procure weapons it effectively positions the whole EU in the conflict. As such, ASAP contributes to strengthen the EU's role in building common defence capabilities, and can be seen as a positive step towards developing a real EU defence union, as envisaged by Article 42(2) TEU.

9.5. The Critical Aspects

Despite the positive features of the ASAP discussed above, however, the Regulation presents a number of weaknesses, which are worth eviscerating. To begin with, and most obviously, the ASAP budget is fairly negligible – only €500 million for two years, which amounts to 0.04 per cent of the €1074 billion MFF 2021–27 – or even less, 0.02 per cent if one considers also the separate €750 billion of the NGEU, which is on top of the MFF. Needless to say, this figure is very small – even when accounting also for additional EU expenditures on defence industrial production, including the €500 million EDIRPA, and the €7.9 billion EDF. Admittedly, the EU has spent a larger amount of resources to support Ukraine, including the EPF, whose budget now is over €17 billion, a €18 billion Macro-Financial Assistance+ Facility for Ukraine 2023,[89] and a €50 billion Ukraine Facility for 2024–27.[90] However, these figures pale when compared to the defence spending of the main European security provider, ie the US, which for 2023 alone approved a military bill worth a stunning $858 billion.[91] Even without looking across the Atlantic, moreover, the ASAP budget looks very small when compared to the defence spending of individual EU Member States, including France,[92] or Germany – which has recently set up an €100 billion special fund to invest in rearmament.[93]

[88] ASAP Regulation, (n 1) Recital 44.

[89] Regulation (EU) 2022/2463 of the European Parliament and the Council of 14 December 2022 establishing an instrument for providing support to Ukraine for 2023 (macro-financial assistance +), [2022] OJ L322/1.

[90] Regulation (EU) 2024/792 of the European Parliament and the Council of 29 February 2024 establishing the Ukraine Facility, [2024] OJ L1.

[91] See C Edmonson, 'Congress Passed an $858 Billion Military Bill. Here is what's in it' *The New York Times* (16 December 2022).

[92] Loi no 2023-703 du 1er août 2023 relative à la programmation militaire pour les années 2024 à 2030 et portant diverses dispositions intéressant la défense, JORF no 0177 du 2 août 2023.

[93] Gesetz zur Finanzierung der Bundeswehr und zur Errichtung eines „Sondervermögens Bundeswehr", vom 1. Juli 2022 (BGBl. I S. 1030).

Yet, beyond the matter of sheer size, the ASAP also suffers another relevant shortcoming, which becomes apparent when the final Regulation is compared with the original Commission proposal of May 2023. The latter included a proposed Article 14, named 'Priority Rated Orders', that allowed the Commission to compel a private company to produce military materiél needed for European security. Specifically, according to the proposed Article 14(2), the Commission could, 'after the consultation of the Member State of establishment of the concerned undertaking and with its agreement, notify the latter of its intent to impose a priority rated order'. Moreover, under the proposed Article 14(3):

> Where the notified undertaking declines the request … the Commission may, in agreement with the Member State of establishment of that undertaking … adopt an Implementing Act obliging the concerned undertakings to accept or perform the priority rated order, at a fair and reasonable price.

At the same time, the proposed Article 14(5) clarified that a priority-rated order shall 'take precedence over any performance obligation under private or public law'. Furthermore, to increase the coerciveness of the orders, the proposed Article 15 introduced penalties, stating that 'Where an undertaking, intentionally or through gross negligence, does not comply with an obligation to prioritise priority rated orders pursuant to Article 14, the Commission may, by decision, where deemed necessary and proportionate, impose periodic penalty payments.'

The possibility for the Commission to compel a specific economic undertaking to produce on demand defence-related goods needed for national security, trumping any other pre-existing obligation of contract, constituted a severe interference with private property and the right to freedom of enterprise, not to mention the right to due process and defence. As such, consistently with the legal principles enshrined in the EU Charter of Fundamental Rights,[94] the Commission proposal introduced several guarantees. *Ex ante*, the proposed Article 14 set up an administrative procedure that entitled the undertaking to a due process, with the possibility to make its views heard, and provide explanations to object to the Commission request. Moreover, the proposed Article 16 enshrined a right to be heard for the imposition of fines and periodic penalty payments. At the same time, ex post, the Commission proposal introduced an unlimited right of judicial review. Specifically, the proposed Article 15(5) stated that the ECJ 'shall have unlimited jurisdiction to review decisions whereby the Commission has fixed a fine or a periodic penalty payment. It may cancel, reduce or increase the fine or periodic penalty payment imposed'. Finally, to further assuage worries, the Commission proposal explicitly limited in Article 15(7) the above-mentioned powers to a period of three years.

Yet, with the guarantees of judicial review, the Commission proposal to introduce priority-rated orders would have rendered ASAP far more impactful. In fact, from a comparative law perspective, the executive authority to compel production by private companies to ensure the supply of materials and services necessary for national defence constitutes the hallmark of the US Defense Production Act. As is well known, this statute, which the US Congress approved at the dawn of the Korean War, empowers the

[94] See also F Fabbrini, *Fundamental Rights in Europe* (Oxford, Oxford University Press, 2014).

US president to inter alia prioritise contracts and orders which are necessary for the national defence, designate scarce materials whose hoarding is prohibited, and ration energy resources. In the landmark 1952 Steel Seizure Case, *Youngstown Sheet & Tube Co v Sawyer*,[95] the US Supreme Court developed a tripartite scheme to evaluate executive powers and held that 'When the President acts pursuant to an express or implied authorisation of Congress, his authority is at its maximum, for it includes all that he possesses in his own right plus all that Congress can delegate.'[96] As a result, the Defense Production Act has remained a powerful instrument in the US presidency toolbox to deal with issues of industrial capacity, and has been used as recently as during the COVID-19 pandemic, and now the war in Ukraine.

As pointed out in section 9.3, however, the final text of the ASAP Regulation does not include any provision on 'priority rate orders'. The co-legislator, therefore, entirely killed this part of the Commission's original proposal. Unsurprisingly, opposition to this coercive feature of the ASAP emerged from the Member States in the intergovernmental Council. Most likely, the above-mentioned measure smacked too much of a sovereign empowerment of the EU institutions in an area which is still regarded as being at the core of national sovereignty. But would this not be precisely the end goal, if we take seriously the woe of the Versailles Declaration to 'building our European sovereignty'?[97] And is the objective of bolstering the EU defence capabilities realistic if the Commission's power to steer the defence industry is deprived of any teeth, exclusively relying on market operators' goodwill and cooperation, without any authority to direct them?

In fact, the choice to deprive the Commission of any teeth in its power to steer the defence industry, and to exclusively rely on market operators' goodwill and cooperation, ultimately undermined the goals of ASAP. The Council of the EU's ambition enshrined in the March 2023 three steps plan to deliver one million rounds of ammunition to Ukraine within a year fell utterly short. As the High Representative had to acknowledge in January 2024, the EU reached only 'one third of the objective, mainly taken from our stockpiles'.[98] Hence, despite the best intentions, national jealousies and governance obstacles in the EU decision-making system removed from the ASAP Regulation an empowerment in favour of the Commission, which would have been necessary to effectively prioritise defence production.

In sum, the ASAP reflects how the EU foreign affairs and security policy remains a work in progress, and the challenges of developing a fully fledged EU defence union.[99] In the aftermath of the Brexit referendum, the EU had taken a number of important steps to deepen defence cooperation, including the launch of the Permanent Structured Cooperation on Defence (PESCO),[100] as allowed by Article 42(6) TEU; the authorisation

[95] 343 US 579 (1952).
[96] ibid, at 635 (Jackson J concurring).
[97] Versailles Declaration (n 16) para 7.
[98] High Representative/Vice-President Josep Borrell, press remarks (31 January 2024).
[99] See also R Wessel, 'Common Foreign, Security and Defense Policy' in R Wessel and J Larik (eds), *EU External Relations Law* (Oxford, Hart Publishing, 2020).
[100] Council Decision (CFSP) 2017/2315 of 11 December 2017 Establishing Permanent Structured Cooperation (PESCO) and Determining the List of Participating Member States, [2017] OJ L331/57.

of the first PESCO operational projects;[101] and the establishment of an operational planning and conduct capability infrastructure designed to oversee common security and defence policy missions and operations.[102] Nevertheless, the European Parliament had more ambitiously called for the creation of a real EU Defence Union, underpinned by strong and modern military capabilities.[103] In fact, in the aftermath of the Russian invasion of Ukraine, the European Parliament has called for a reinforcement of the EU capacity to act in a more challenging geopolitical context,[104] and underlined 'the urgent need to establish a truly European defence equipment market', with increased financial support from the EU budget.[105] To get there, however, further steps are needed.

Indeed, while the pandemic pushed the EU to develop a centralised fiscal capacity,[106] in the form of NGEU, the war in Ukraine has arguably not yet led the EU to develop unified military capabilities. Rather, NATO has been strengthened as the preeminent organisation for the security of Europe – a dynamic made evident by its enlargement to Finland and Sweden.[107] From an international relations perspective, the decision by these two Member States to abandon their military neutrality dwarfed in importance, eg the decision by Denmark to renounce its output on CSDP.[108] As a matter of fact, NATO is backed by the US military commitment – which makes the mutual defence clause of Article V NATO Treaty credible. At the moment, instead, no similar credibility underpins the EU's mutual defence clause, Article 42(7) TEU – and this is precisely because of the lack of common EU military capabilities and deterrence. Yet, with the war in Ukraine showing no sign of abating, and with future uncertainties about the US commitment to European security,[109] especially in view of the elections of 2024, the EU should move in the direction of a real defence union – asap.[110]

9.6. Conclusion

This chapter has examined ASAP – a new regulation adopted by the European Parliament and the Council to boost the production and procurement of ammunitions

[101] Council Decision (CFSP) 2018/340 of 6 March 2018 establishing the list of projects to be developed under PESCO, [2018] OJ L65/24.

[102] Council of the EU Conclusions, On Progress in Implementing the EU Global Strategy in the Area of Security and Defence, Annex – Concept Note: Operational Planning and Conduct Capabilities for CSDP Missions and Operations (6 March 2017) Doc 110/17.

[103] European Parliament Resolution of 22 November 2016 on the European Defense Union, P8_TA(2016)0435.

[104] See European Parliament resolution of 19 May 2022 on the social and economic consequences for the EU of the Russian war in Ukraine – reinforcing the EU's capacity to act, P9_TA(2022)0219.

[105] European Parliament resolution of 18 January 2023 on the implementation of the common security and defence policy – annual report 2022, P9_TA(2023)0010, para 34.

[106] F Fabbrini, *EU Fiscal Capacity: Legal Integration after Covid-19 and the War in Ukraine* (Oxford, Oxford University Press 2022).

[107] See C Bildt, 'NATO's Nordic Expansion' *Foreign Affairs* (26 April 2022).

[108] See also High Representative/Vice-President Josep Borrell, statement on the outcome of the referendum on the opt-out in defence matters (1 June 2022).

[109] K Engelbrekt, 'Beyond Burdensharing and European Strategic Autonomy: Rebuilding Transatlantic Security after the Ukraine War' (2022) 27 *European Foreign Affairs Review* 383.

[110] See further F Fabbrini, 'European Defense Integration after Trump's Re-election: A Proposal to Revive the European Defense Community Treaty and its Legal Feasibility' (2024) *European Law Journal*, 1, proposing to revive the European Defence Community Treaty of 1952 as a legally feasible way to achieve defense integration in Europe.

and missiles with the aim of supporting Ukraine in the war against Russia. ASAP is the latest piece in a wide-ranging EU response to the war in Ukraine, and pushes the EU into a new terrain; that of industrial defence policy. In particular, through a constructive use of supranational legal bases in the Treaties, ASAP has attributed to the Commission the authority to use resources from the EU budget to fund the industrial production of ammunitions and missiles urgently needed by Ukraine, thus helping to strengthen the EU's role in developing common defence capabilities. Yet, the EU's involvement in the military industrial complex remains limited, as ASAP suffers from a number of weaknesses, including a very tiny €500 million bi-annual budget.

Moreover, contrary to the original Commission proposal, the co-legislator have ditched the power for the Commission to issue priority-rated orders, compelling defence industries to produce specific defence goods on demand. From this point of view, therefore, ASAP cannot be regarded as the EU's equivalent of the US Defense Production Act, a landmark piece of legislation which gives wide authority to the US executive to command the production of materiél needed for the national defence. This state of affairs is hardly surprising, considering the constraints on the EU defence policy. Nevertheless, this state of affairs is at odds with the declared EU aspirations to establish a form of European sovereignty, and may be unsustainable in light of the ongoing war in Ukraine, and uncertainties about future US commitment. Beyond ASAP, the EU therefore needs a defence union – asap.

10

The Administration and Enforcement of EU Sanctions Revisited

ANTIGONI MATTHAIOU AND ISABELLE VAN DAMME*

10.1. Introduction

The EU sanctions against Russia[1] are unparalleled in terms of scope and impact,[2] marking a 'sanctions revolution'.[3] Their objectives are clear and remain strongly supported, including at the multilateral level. They are imposed against a (previously) close trading partner of the EU, which is not the case for many other EU sanctions. Moreover, their effects on the geopolitical framework within which trade and other commercial relations take place are expected to be lasting and transformative.

The EU sanctions against Russia affect most economic sectors, meaning that many economic operators in the EU need to verify and invest in due diligence in respect of their compliance. The EU regulations impose a series of sectoral sanctions affecting trade in goods and technology, trade in services, intellectual property rights and trade secrets, the transport of goods, banking operations, investments, securities transactions, public procurement, etc. Moreover, those sanctions notably target various Russian oligarchs with majority stakes in companies active in key economic sectors, as well as major Russian banks with activities around the world (resulting in an unprecedented interaction between EU targeted and trade/financial sanctions). Although EU sanctions against Russia have existed since Russia's 2014 annexation of Crimea, until early 2022 they were more limited in scope. As a result, starting from 2022, EU operators (as well as

* The authors would like to thank Alexandre Lejeune and Roisin O'Donovan for their research assistance.

[1] Council Regulation (EU) 269/2014 of 17 March 2014 concerning restrictive measures in respect of actions undermining or threatening the territorial integrity, sovereignty and independence of Ukraine [2014] OJ L78/6 (Current consolidated version: 29 October 2024) and Council Regulation (EU) 833/2014 of 31 July 2014 concerning restrictive measures in view of Russia's actions destabilising the situation in Ukraine [2014] OJ L229/1 (Current consolidated version: 14 September 2024). Sanctions against Russia have first been implemented through both Regulations in reaction to the 2014 illegal annexation of Crimea. Following the February 2022 full-scale invasion of Ukraine, these regulations have been substantially expanded by 15 sanctions packages. These latest developments are the main subject of our analysis.

[2] A Carpile and A Delivorias, 'EU sanctions on Russia: Overview, impact, challenges' (2023) *European Parliamentary Research Service*, PE 739.366.

[3] Council of the European Union, Infographic – EU sanctions in response to Russia's invasion of Ukraine, available at www.consilium.europa.eu/en/infographics/eu-sanctions-russia-ukraine-invasion.

non-EU operators) have been confronted with a broad set of sanctions affecting global supply chains and corresponding due diligence obligations.

Against that background, this chapter assesses the administration and enforcement of the EU sanctions against Russia and their implications for the EU's sanctions regimes in respect of other countries. In particular, the assessment focuses on two features of the operation of EU sanctions legislation which, due to the EU sanctions against Russia, are becoming more visible and, also prompting reforms that are bound to affect all EU sanctions regimes: (i) the decentralised administration and enforcement of EU sanctions and how that model might undermine those sanctions' effectiveness; and (ii) the extended reach of EU sanctions affecting businesses well beyond the borders of the EU, despite the EU's principled objection against the extraterritorial effects of EU sanctions legislation.

10.2. The Administration and Enforcement of EU Sanctions

10.2.1. Introduction

This section focuses on the decentralised and fragmented model of administering and enforcing EU sanctions. This model entails that, whilst EU sanctions legislation is negotiated and decided (and interpreted) at EU level, it is administered and enforced at Member State level. Apart from this decentralisation, the model also results in a significant degree of fragmentation in how individual Member States regulate and/or organise their implementation of EU sanctions. In turn, this affects the effectiveness of EU sanctions.[4]

A useful illustration of these differences and the implications of the decentralised and fragmented model is the process for obtaining an authorisation (that is, a licence) based on a derogation ground set out in EU sanctions legislation. In remedying the defects and inefficiencies resulting from that model, the EU and the Member States could resort to informal solutions (not requiring any legislation) and/or EU legislative interventions (in addition to legislative changes and other reforms at Member State level). Both types of solution, at (especially) EU level, are already scheduled or initiated. At the same time, other informal reforms could also help to improve the model of administration and enforcement of EU sanctions legislation on the short term.

[4] The Council has recognised that '[the] uniform and consistent interpretation and effective implementation of the restrictive measures is essential to ensure their effectiveness in achieving the desired political objective'. Council of the European Union, Sanctions Guidelines – update (5664/18, 4 May 2018) 46. One study noted that 'the effective implementation and enforcement of sanctions is a prerequisite for their geostrategic success, credibility and political sustainability'. C Portela and KB Olsen, Implementation and monitoring of the EU sanctions' regimes, including recommendations to reinforce the EU's capacities to implement and monitor sanctions, AFET committee of the European Parliament (PE 702.603, October 2023) viii. These authors observe that the decentralised model has 'resulted in a mosaic of implementation and enforcement practices across the EU, with more than 160 designated competent authorities in Member States'.

10.2.2. The Decentralised and Fragmented Model of Administration and Enforcement of EU Sanctions

EU sanctions are negotiated and adopted by the Council of the EU (Council) in the form of Council decisions.[5] Where the decisions involve measures having economic or financial implications, they are implemented in the form of Council regulations, on the basis of joint proposals from the High Representative and the European Commission (Commission), with the Directorate-General on Financial Stability, Financial Services and Capital Markets Union taking the lead.[6]

The Member States are responsible for implementing and enforcing EU sanctions legislation within their respective jurisdiction.[7] This includes identifying breaches of EU sanctions legislation occurring within their jurisdiction, imposing penalties and granting authorisations for activities falling within their jurisdiction, where so permitted by the Council regulations. Depending on the Member State, various authorities are involved in the implementation and enforcement of EU sanctions legislation.[8] A study by the European Parliament (Parliament) identified more than 160 designated national competent authorities (NCAs) in the Member States.[9] In fact, in several Member States, different national authorities are responsible for granting authorisations for activities that would otherwise violate trade, financial or targeted sanctions.[10]

In addition to preparing joint proposals for Council regulations, the Commission is responsible, subject to the control of the Court of Justice of the European Union (CJEU), for monitoring the uniform application of EU sanctions legislation and coordinating the Member States' actions.[11] To fulfil its coordination role, the Commission issues guidance on the interpretation of EU sanctions legislation. It has clarified that 'National authorities and economic operators may make use of [the Commission's] guidance based on the text, context and purpose of [EU sanctions legislation], to achieve the uniform application of sanctions across the EU'.[12]

The CJEU recently clarified that the Commission's guidance is 'of no consequence', namely that it 'cannot determine, in any manner, the outcome of [the] analysis as to the

[5] Consolidated version of the Treaty on European Union (2012) OJ C 326/01, Art 29.

[6] Consolidated version of the Treaty on the Functioning of the European Union [2012] OJ C 326/01, Art 215.

[7] See Portela and Olsen (n 4), 15–29.

[8] For example, in some Member States, the Ministry of the Economy is involved in the enforcement of economic sanctions (eg in France, the *Ministère de l'Economie et des Finances*). In others, this task is assumed by specialised agencies (eg in Germany, the *Bundesamt für Wirtschaft und Ausfuhrkontrolle* (BAFA)). Sometimes, sanctions are also implemented by the Ministry of Foreign Affairs (eg, in Finland, the *Ulkoministeriö*).

[9] Portela and Olsen (n 4).

[10] For example, in Ireland, the Department of Enterprise, Trade and Employment is in charge of trade sanctions, while the Central Bank of Ireland manages financial sanctions, and the Department of Foreign Affairs enforces travel restrictions. In Belgium, financial sanctions and sanctions on dual-use and advanced goods are implemented at the federal level, while other trade sanctions are enforced by both the Walloon and the Flemish regions.

[11] Treaty on European Union (n 6), Art 17(1).

[12] See, eg European Commission, Consolidated FAQs on the implementation of Council Regulation No 833/2014 (n 1) and Council Regulation No 269/2014 (n 1) (last update: 11 December 2024) 1, available at www.finance.ec.europa.eu/system/files/2023-10/faqs-sanctions-russia-consolidated_en_3.pdf.

proper interpretation to be given' to EU sanctions legislation.[13] Despite this clarification, in practice, the Commission's guidance continues to exercise significant influence on the Member States' implementation of EU sanctions against Russia[14] and operators' strategies aimed at ensuring compliance with their due diligence obligations.

This decentralised and fragmented model is increasingly put under pressure and criticised, because, in the context of the EU sanctions against Russia, the inefficiencies, inconsistencies and gaps resulting from the model's use have become more visible. In practice, the decentralised model governing the administration and enforcement of EU sanctions often leads to the fragmented application of EU sanctions at the expense of EU nationals/operators seeking to ensure their compliance, and to the benefit of those seeking to circumvent or otherwise undermine those sanctions.[15] The EU sanctions against Russia, which are unprecedented in terms of scope and effects, have in essence resulted in a stress test for the administration and enforcement of EU sanctions regimes and already prompted the EU to propose certain reforms that will eventually affect all EU sanctions legislation. In mapping those reforms (either already initiated or available), a distinction can be made between those requiring legislation and others that can be implemented without a legislative initiative.

10.2.3. The Effects of the Decentralised and Fragmented Model of Administering and Enforcing EU Sanctions Legislation: The Granting of Authorisations as a Case Study

The processes and rules for applying and obtaining authorisations illustrate well (the effects of) this decentralised and fragmented model. Activities that fall within the scope of EU sanctions are prohibited except if a derogation ground or a carve-out applies.

[13] Case C-109/23, *Jemerak* [2024] EU:C: 2024:307, [69]. See also C Challet 'Op-Ed: "Request for a preliminary ruling in *Jeremak* (C–109/23): to what extent are notaries prohibited to provide legal services to Russian legal persons?" by Celia Challet' EU Law Live (31 May 2023), available at www.eulawlive.com/op-ed-request-for-a-preliminary-ruling-in-jemerak-c-109-23-to-what-extent-are-notaries-prohibited-to-provide-legal-services-to-russian-legal-persons-by-celia-challet.

[14] For example, in *Islentyeva v Council*, it became evident that the Luxembourg NCA's implementation of the restrictive measures on air transport set out in EU sanctions against Russia was influenced by the guidance published by the Commission and the European Aviation Safety Agency. See Case T-233/22, *Islentyeva v Council* [2023] EU:T:2023:828, [9]–[11]. See also A Matthaiou 'Op-Ed: "The objectives of EU sanctions against Russia as a driver for the interpretation and application of EU sectoral and targeted sanctions (T-233/22 and T-313/22)" by Antigoni Matthaiou' EU Law Live (6 February 2024), available at www.eulawlive.com/op-ed-the-objectives-of-eu-sanctions-against-russia-as-a-driver-for-the-interpretation-and-application-of-eu-sectoral-and-targeted-sanctions-t-233-22-and-t-313-22-by-antigoni-matt. In addition, certain Member States request operators applying for authorisations to identify in their applications any relevant EU guidance published by the Commission. See, eg Central Bank of Ireland, Sanctions Derogation Application Form, Derogation applications pursuant to EU Council Regulations relating to financial sanctions (restrictive measures), available at www.centralbank.ie/regulation/how-we-regulate/international-financial-sanctions/derogations.

[15] See, eg Portela and Olsen (n 4), 27, noting that 'If [authorisations] are hard to obtain due to bureaucratic inconsistencies and a lack of responsibility-division, individuals from one Member State can be seen as experiencing less comprehensive treatment from their own NCAs than they would in another Member State' and highlighting that 'The non-harmonised system for granting exemptions further affords third-country actors ample opportunities for selective shopping between Member States.'

Derogation grounds and carve-outs are provisions negotiated by the Council and expressly set out in the various Council regulations (but specific to the various sanctions regimes). Where an otherwise sanctioned activity falls within the scope of a carve-out, that activity is not covered by the relevant prohibition, meaning that it may be undertaken without obtaining a prior authorisation. However, if a derogation ground applies, the NCAs may grant authorisations to permit an activity otherwise prohibited under EU sanctions legislation, provided that a request for an authorisation is filed. In determining whether to grant authorisations on the basis of derogation grounds, the NCAs enjoy considerable discretion, but nevertheless they cannot grant authorisations where the specific conditions of a derogation ground are not satisfied.[16] In practice, if an authorisation is granted by the NCA, the authorised activity may take place provided that the conditions attached to the authorisation are strictly observed.

The operation of the decentralised and fragmented model, in the context of granting authorisations, leads to a difference in the treatment of persons and economic operators in the various Member States, which gives rise to an uneven playing field between economic operators across the EU. Moreover, it creates uncertainty as to whether EU sanctions are effectively implemented by the Member States and whether the NCAs can support economic operators in ensuring compliance with EU sanctions legislation. It also affords especially non-EU companies that are subject to EU sanctions legislation (because of business done in whole or in part in the EU) the opportunity to engage in forum shopping between the Member States when seeking authorisations under derogation grounds.

These inefficiencies are well illustrated by: (i) the various authorisation processes followed by NCAs; (ii) the differences in the interpretation of the derogation grounds; and (iii) the challenges in identifying the competent NCA to grant an authorisation, especially in the case of multijurisdictional transactions.

First, there is no unified process for applying for an authorisation in the Member States. For example, some Member States have only designated one NCA that is responsible for granting authorisations in relation to all types of EU sanction.[17] Other Member States have designated multiple NCAs that are responsible for the granting of authorisations in relation to different types of sanction.[18] In effect, this means that, on the one hand, even before filing an authorisation request, operators might be required to engage in a complex analysis in order to identify which NCA(s) is/are responsible for granting the authorisation. On the other hand, where operators seek to obtain an authorisation

[16] For example, on the one hand, Art 2(a)(1) of Regulation 269/2014 (n 1) is a carve-out provision to the prohibition to make funds or economic resources available to listed persons that applies in respect of funds or economic resources made available by organisations and agencies which are pilar-assessed by the EU and used for humanitarian purposes ('Article 2(2) shall not apply to …'). On the other hand, Art 4(2)(1)(a) authorises the Member States to grant authorisations for the release of certain frozen funds in specific cases and under such conditions as they deem appropriate ('By way of derogation from Article 2, the competent authorities of the Member States may authorise the release of certain frozen funds or economic resources, or the making available of certain funds or economic resources, under such conditions as they deem appropriate, after having determined that the funds or economic resources concerned are: (a) necessary to satisfy the basic needs of natural or legal persons, entities or bodies listed in Annex I, and dependent family members of such natural persons, including payments for foodstuffs, rent or mortgage, medicines and medical treatment, taxes, insurance premiums, and public utility charges').

[17] For example, in Finland, the only NCA is the Ministry of Foreign Affairs.

[18] This is the case, for example, in Belgium and Ireland (n 10).

in a Member State where only one NCA is designated, they might be confronted with (even more) significant delays. Likewise, some Member States proactively make available guidance in relation to the granting of authorisations, including by making available dedicated templates for specific types of authorisation requests that can be used by operators to streamline the authorisation process,[19] or online systems where operators may automatically file for authorisations.[20] Other Member States only accept authorisation requests by email, and sometimes offer little to no guidance on the authorisation process and the documentation and information to provide as part of an application.[21] Certain Member States make general authorisations available for specific derogation grounds (which the Commission endorses[22]) whereas others only issue individual authorisations for the same derogation ground.[23] Moreover, the time needed to process authorisations is typically not defined. In practice, certain NCAs might take more than a year to process authorisation applications.

Second, derogation grounds are not uniformly interpreted by the NCAs. Measuring the extent of that divergence is difficult because hardly any information about authorisations granted/denied is published (also in respect of transparency about the authorisations granted, the practice is not uniform[24]), and the coordination and information exchange process between NCAs is not clearly defined. A notable illustration of this divergence is the difference in how the Belgian and Luxembourg NCAs have interpreted Article 6b(5) of Regulation 269/2014 in order to take the necessary actions to transfer certain securities from the (Russian) National Settlement Depository (NSD) to Euroclear and Clearstream (based in, respectively, Belgium and Luxembourg). Article 6b(5) sets out the following derogation ground:

> By way of derogation from Article 2, the competent authorities of a Member State may authorise the release of certain frozen funds or economic resources belonging to the entity listed

[19] For example, the Central Bank of Ireland has made available a sanctions derogation application form to be used for requesting authorisations under EU targeted sanctions (n 14).

[20] For example, in France, the 'Service des biens à double usage' of the 'Direction générale des Entreprises' of the 'Ministère l'Économie, des Finances et de la Souveraineté Industrielle et Numérique' which is the NCA competent for granting authorisations under EU sectoral sanctions only receives authorisations through an online portal. See Ministère l'Économie, des Finances et de la Souveraineté Industrielle et Numérique, Le portail de la Direction générale des Entreprises, Obtenir Une Autorisation, available at www.entreprises.gouv.fr/fr/echanges-commerciaux-et-reglementation/service-des-biens-double-usage/obtenir-autorisation.

[21] Until recently, the General Administration of Treasury, the Belgian NCA responsible for EU financial sanctions, only accepted authorisation requests by email. Federal Public Service Finance, General Administration of Treasury, Derogations, available at www.finance.belgium.be/en/treasury/financial-sanctions/derogations.

[22] See, eg European Commission, Consolidated FAQs (n 12) s B sub-s 1, q 12 on interest payments and s G sub-s 6, q 39 on public procurement.

[23] For example, in respect of the derogation grounds under Art 5(c)(1)(f) of Regulation 833/2014 (n 1) and Art 6(5) of Regulation 269/2014 (n 1), the Luxembourg NCA responsible for the implementation of EU financial sanctions issued general authorisations. However, in respect of Art 6(5) of Regulation 833/2014 (n 1), the Belgium NCA only accepted individual licence applications. Moreover, the German NCA has issued a general authorisation (valid until 31 December 2025) covering the supply of enterprise software and services in respect of the derogation ground under Art 5n(10)(h) of Regulation 833/2014 (n 1), available at www.bafa.de/SharedDocs/Kurzmeldungen/DE/Aussenwirtschaft/Ausfuhrkontrolle/20240717_neubekanntgabe_agg42.html.

[24] For example, the Money Laundering Bureau of the Financial Intelligence Unit of Estonia that is responsible for the implementation of EU targeted sanctions publishes information on authorisations granted. See Republic of Estonia, Financial Intelligence Unit, Russian military aggression in Ukraine, available at www.fiu.ee/rahvusvahelised-sanktsioonid/venemaa-sojaline-agressioon-ukrainas#erandid.

> under entry number 101 in Annex I, or the making available of certain funds or economic resources to that entity, *under such conditions as the competent authorities deem appropriate and after having determined that such funds or economic resources are necessary for the termination by 7 January 2023 of operations, contracts or other agreements concluded with, or otherwise involving, that entity before 3 June 2022.*[25]

On 16 December 2022, the Luxembourg NCA issued a general authorisation based on this derogation ground.[26] By resorting to a general authorisation, the authority managed the challenge of having to process a large volume of authorisation applications within a short timeframe, taking into account that: (i) the derogation ground set, as a condition, that operations, contracts and other agreements with NSD needed to be terminated by 7 January 2023 (implying that, for example, any release or transfer of securities needed to occur before that termination, and thus prior to 7 January 2023); and (ii) as a result, individual authorisations would need to be issued well before 7 January 2023. The general authorisation notably required users of the general authorisation to maintain 'records of sufficient detail of any activity purporting to have been permitted under this general authorization in order to enable the verification of the conditions'.

By contrast, the Belgian NCA published a few days later, on 22 December 2022, the 'General conditions for the application of Article 6b(5) of Council Regulation (EU) No 269/2014 of 17 March 2014 concerning restrictive measures with regard to actions endangering or threatening the territorial integrity, sovereignty and independence of Ukraine'.[27] Despite initial confusion about whether this was intended to operate as a general authorisation (similar to what the Luxembourg NCA had issued), these general conditions reflected that authority's understanding of this derogation ground, including the requirement that the authorisation applications be filed, via email, no later than 7 January 2023. However, the derogation ground in Article 6b(5) presupposes that the otherwise prohibited conduct pre-dates (and thus any authorisation covering that conduct be issued before) the termination of relations with NSD by 7 January 2023.

So far, this divergence in approach and interpretation has not yet been resolved, or addressed in Commission FAQs. For example, although Regulation 269/2014 has been amended to expressly refer to the option available to NCAs to grant general authorisations in respect of the release of frozen assets necessary for humanitarian purposes in Ukraine, the NCAs may still opt to only grant individual authorisations.[28] At the same time, the above example in respect of Article 6b(5) of Regulation 269/2014 illustrates that general authorisations might need to be more actively used, to: (i) offer clarity to

[25] Emphasis added.

[26] Ministry of Finance of the Grand Duchy of Luxembourg, General authorization pursuant to article 6b paragraph 5 of Council Regulation (EU) No 269/2014 of 17 March 2014 concerning restrictive measures in respect of actions undermining or threatening the territorial integrity, sovereignty and independence of Ukraine, as amended.

[27] Federale Overheidsdienst Financen, Algemene voorwaarden artikel 6 ter, lid 5, van Verordening (Eu) nr. (269/2014), available at www.financien.belgium.be/nl/over_de_fod/structuur_en_diensten/algemene_administraties/thesaurie/controle-financiële-2-4/algemene.

[28] Regulation 269/2014 (n 1), Art 2a(2): 'In cases not covered by paragraph 1 of this Article, and by way of derogation from Article 2, the competent authorities may grant specific or general authorisations, under such general or specific conditions as they deem appropriate, to release certain frozen funds or economic resources or to make available certain funds or economic resources, provided that the provision of such funds or economic resources is necessary for exclusively humanitarian purposes in Ukraine'.

operators seeking to comply but faced with strict timeframes, under sanctions legislation, to apply for and obtain an authorisation and incomplete guidance, at Member State level, on what information and documentation are needed for that purpose; and (ii) manage the workload of the NCAs, which are, depending on the Member State, incurring considerable delays in processing authorisation applications.[29]

Third, there is no conflict rule in EU sanctions legislation assigning which NCA is competent to issue an authorisation in circumstances where the activity requiring an authorisation has touchpoints with multiple Member States. In general, it is understood that the NCA of the Member State where the applicant is established is competent.[30] This corresponds with the guidance of the Commission.[31] However, in complex transactions, where EU nationals and EU companies of various Member States are involved, or where the activity otherwise takes place within the jurisdiction of various Member States, multiple authorisations need to be requested from different NCAs covering the same facts.

This is aptly illustrated in the case of the derogation ground added with the twelfth package of EU sanctions against Russia to the horizontal services prohibition set out in Article 5n of Regulation 833/2014. Article 5n prohibits the provision of covered services to Russian companies and the Russian Government (regardless of targeted sanctions and any connection of the covered service with a restricted good listed in the various trade sanctions). Article 5n(10)(h) provides that by way of derogation from the horizontal services prohibition:

> [T]he competent authorities may authorise the sale, supply, transfer, export, or provision of the services referred to therein, under such conditions as they deem appropriate, after having determined that this is necessary for … the exclusive use of legal persons, entities or bodies established in Russia that are owned by, or solely or jointly controlled by, a legal person, entity or body which is incorporated or constituted under the law of a Member State, a country member of the European Economic Area, Switzerland or a partner country as listed in Annex VIII.

This derogation ground allows notably EU parent companies providing covered services for the exclusive use of their Russian subsidiaries to request and obtain an authorisation that will enable them to continue engaging in the provision of covered services (previously, they benefited from a carve-out). In the case of multinational groups, covered services might be provided by the EU parent company, as well as by other EU companies of the group to the Russian subsidiary. Moreover, EU (or dual-EU and non-EU) nationals who are employed by the various group companies (including, when working

[29] To address both concerns, the EU legislator could contemplate using transitional periods instead of derogations based on time-barred exceptions. Revisiting the use of limited derogations grounds (which do not anticipate all of the possible effects and applications of prohibitions and other restrictions) instead of promoting broader discretionary derogations grounds is more difficult to implement in the decentralised mechanism because it might further contribute to the lack of coherence and uniformity in how EU sanctions legislation is interpreted and applied at Member State level (and without further institutional reform focusing on creating centralised agencies).

[30] This rule also applies in respect of EU export control legislation. See Regulation (EU) 2021/821 of the European Parliament and of the Council of 20 May 2021 setting up a Union regime for the control of exports, brokering, technical assistance, transit and transfer of dual-use items (recast), [2021] OJ L206/1, 1, Art 12(2).

[31] See, eg European Commission, Consolidated FAQs (n 12) s D sub-s 2, q 7, 16, 18, 19, 27, 28, 29 on export-related restrictions for dual-use goods and advanced technologies.

and/or residing in various Member States) might participate in the provision of covered services to the Russian subsidiary.

In this situation, the provision of covered services will fall within the jurisdiction of the Member States where the various EU companies are incorporated, as well as within the jurisdiction of the Member States of nationality/residence of the EU (or dual-EU and even non-EU) nationals who are employees of the various involved group companies. As a result, an authorisation request should be filled with the NCA of every Member State that has jurisdiction.

The Commission has confirmed that 'Operators must request authorisations in each Member State they are planning to provide services from'. This is because 'An authorisation issued by the national competent authority of a Member State is valid only within that Member State', meaning that 'authorisations are not automatically valid in other Member States e.g. in the case of a parent company and a subsidiary located in different Member States'.[32] This scattered approach risks creating an undue burden for the various EU operators involved, due to the different authorisations processes employed by the NCAs in different Members States, the potential delays resulting from numerous ongoing authorisation procedures in different Member States, as well as the risk that different Member States might adopt a different interpretation of the relevant derogation ground.

In practice, NCAs can coordinate with the NCAs of other Member States that also have jurisdiction over an activity seeking authorisation. This might result in only the Member State with the closest jurisdictional link to the relevant activity issuing an authorisation. For example, in the case of the application of Article 5n(1)(h) to the provision of intra-group services to a Russian subsidiary, this might be the NCA of the Member State where the EU parent company of the Russian subsidiary is established. However, despite this practical coordination among the Member States, there is no guarantee that this coordination shields economic operators from being exposed to the risk of enforcement action in the Member States with (a less predominant) jurisdictional link.

10.2.4. Making the Implementation and Enforcement of EU Sanctions More Effective and Coherent – Legislative and Other Initiatives

As a result of the EU sanctions against Russia, the inefficiencies and incoherence in how EU sanctions are implemented and enforced are becoming more visible, as outlined above. They also lead to an assessment that, historically, there has been under-compliance with EU sanctions legislation.[33] This increased awareness of the need for reform[34] is translating into many types of proposal that broadly can be divided in two categories, depending on whether they require a legislative change.

[32] See, eg European Commission, Consolidated FAQs (n 12) s G sub-s 8, q 35 on provision of services.

[33] European Parliament, Resolution of 9 November 2023 on the effectiveness of the EU sanctions on Russia (2023/2905(RSP), P9_TA(2023)0397) para 6.

[34] ibid.

On the one hand, the EU is already moving forward with legislation that seeks to strengthen enforcement efforts and avoid so-called forum shopping, such as the addition of the violation of restrictive measures to the list of EU crimes, a directive on criminal sanctions and a directive on asset recovery and confiscation.

In November 2022, the Council added the violation of Union restrictive measures to the list of crimes liable to be subject to minimal harmonisation under Article 83(1) TFEU.[35] Consequently, the Parliament and the Council adopted in April 2024 a Directive harmonising the definition of criminal offences and the penalties incurred for violating EU sanctions.[36] This Directive also takes a step forward in the EU-wide coordination of the enforcement of EU sanctions. In particular, it requires the Member States, Europol, Eurojust, the European Public Prosecutor's Office and the Commission to cooperate in circumstances where criminal offences for the violation of EU restrictive measures are suspected to be of a cross-border nature. Finally, the Parliament and the Council also adopted in April 2024 a Directive on asset recovery and confiscation,[37] which requires the Member States to take measures to enable the confiscation of the assets of entities convicted of violating EU restrictive measures.

Many of these legislative developments inevitably raise the question of whether a new EU agency or authority is needed to monitor and coordinate compliance with EU sanctions legislation and possibly assume responsibility in respect of authorisations relating to transactions affecting more than one Member State. In part, the recent creation of the new EU authority for Anti-Money Laundering and Countering the Financing of Terrorism (AMLA) could be a prelude for such an initiative.[38] In fact, AMLA already has some responsibility for monitoring compliance with targeted sanctions. For example, among its tasks, AMLA is required, in respect of certain selected obliged entities, to ensure their compliance with targeted sanctions.[39] As noted by the Council, AMLA is expected to oversee a selection of large credit and financial institutions that represent a high risk of money laundering and financing terrorism, by among others monitoring that they have internal policies and procedures in place to ensure the proper implementation of targeted financial sanctions, asset freezes and confiscations.[40] The Netherlands, in particular, has been promoting, apart from more coordination between the EU and the Member States, the expansion of the toolbox for implementing and enforcing EU sanctions legislation, including through institutionalised cooperation.[41]

[35] Council Decision (EU) 2022/2332 of 28 November 2022 on identifying the violation of Union restrictive measures as an area of crime that meets the criteria specified in Article 83(1) of the Treaty on the Functioning of the European Union [2022] OJ L308/18.

[36] Directive (EU) 2024/1226 of the European Parliament and of the Council of 24 April 2024 on the definition of criminal offences and penalties for the violation of Union restrictive measures and amending Directive (EU) 2018/1673 [2024] OJ L2024/1216.

[37] Directive (EU) 2024/1260 of the European Parliament and of the Council of 24 April 2024 on asset recovery and confiscation [2024] OJ L2024/1260.

[38] Regulation (EU) 2024/1620 of the European Parliament and of the Council of 31 May 2024 establishing the Authority for Anti-Money Laundering and Countering the Financing of Terrorism and amending Regulations (EU) No 1093/2010, (EU) No 1094/2010 and (EU) No 1095/2010 [2024] OJ L2024/1620.

[39] Regulation 2024/1620 (n 38), Art 5(2)(a).

[40] European Council, 'Anti-money laundering: Council and Parliament agree to create new authority' (13 December 2023), available at www.consilium.europa.eu/en/press/press-releases/2023/12/13/anti-money-laundering-council-and-parliament-agree-to-create-new-authority.

[41] Rijksoverheid, 'Non-paper on strengthening EU sanctions capacity and countering sanctions circumvention', available at www.open.overheid.nl/documenten/ronl-9af192a9dbdd615b48854e341be0c3e5b88c2594/pdf.

In this first category fall also amendments of existing sanctions legislation, and in particular the EU sanctions against Russia, seeking to strengthen coordination and information exchange between the NCAs as well as between those authorities and the Commission. For example, Article 2d of Regulation 833/2014 (which imposes trade and financial sanctions against Russia, of which Article 2 prohibits trade in dual use goods and technology to Russia) requires the NCAs to exchange information (also with the Commission) on, notably, authorisation applications that have been denied or granted and applications received that raise concerns about forum shopping.[42] Likewise, the same provision envisages the possibility of information exchange between the Commission and partner countries.[43] Article 6 of the same regulation also establishes a more horizontal coordination mechanism between the Member States and the Commission in respect of authorisations granted or denied, information gathering, violation and enforcement problems, penalties applied for infringements, judgments of Member States courts, infringements, cases (or attempts) of circumvention. A similar mechanism is now provided in Article 12 of Regulation 269/2014 (imposing targeted sanctions against Russia). That Regulation also establishes information exchange mechanisms in function of specific provisions.[44]

Moreover, Regulation 883/2014 provides a framework for managing the possibility of divergent assessments of authorisation applications in respect of identical transactions. In particular, it addresses the situation where a competent authority of a Member State has received an authorisation application and intends to grant the authorisation, but it finds that, in respect of a transaction that is in essence identical to another transaction, another authority has denied granting an authorisation. In those circumstances, that authority must consult with the latter and, if it nevertheless grants the authorisation, it must inform the other Member States and the Commission of that decision and state the information in support of its authorisation.[45]

On the other hand, progress has also been made through initiatives not requiring legislation. For example, the EU has appointed a special sanctions envoy.[46] It has also established a sanctions whistleblower tool[47] and various taskforces to improve coordination at EU level to implement the sanctions against listed persons and entities, such as the 'Freeze and Seize' Task Force, and participates in international task forces such as the Russian Elites, Proxies, and Oligarchs (REPO) taskforce.[48]

[42] Regulation 833/2014 (n 1), Art 2d(1). See also Council Regulation (EU) 2022/328 of 25 February 2022 amending Regulation (EU) No 833/2014 concerning restrictive measures in view of Russia's actions destabilising the situation in Ukraine [2022] OJ L49/1, Art 1(4).

[43] ibid, Art 2(d)(4).

[44] See, eg Regulation 269/2014 (n 1), Arts 2a, 4, 4(2), 5(2), 6(2), 6a(2), 6b(6), 6d(2).

[45] Regulation 833/2014 (n 1), Art 6a.

[46] European Commission, 'EU appoints David O'Sullivan as International Special Envoy for the Implementation of EU Sanctions' (13 December 2022), available at www.ireland.representation.ec.europa.eu/news-and-events/news/eu-appoints-david-osullivan-international-special-envoy-implementation-eu-sanctions-2022-12-13_en.

[47] Although this is a tool applicable to all sanctions regimes, it was launched in March 2022, only a few days after the Russian invasion of Ukraine. Online portal available at www.eusanctions.integrityline.com/frontpage.

[48] European Commission, 'Enforcing sanctions against listed Russian and Belarussian oligarchs: Commission's "Freeze and Seize" Task Force steps up work with international partners' (17 March 2022), available at www.eurojust.europa.eu/eu-freeze-and-seize-task-force; European Commission, 'Russian Elites, Proxies, and Oligarchs Task Force Joint Statement' (29 June 2022), available at www.ec.europa.eu/commission/presscorner/detail/e%20n/statement_22_4232.

In addition, informal methods of coordination are increasingly used and demanded.[49] Notably, the Commission is in regular contact with the Member States and the industry to explain the measures, discuss their impact, ensure compliance with EU sanctions and prevent their misapplication from indirectly supporting the Russian war. It is also understood that various dedicated IT tools have been put in place to facilitate exchanges between the Member States and the Commission. The Member States also participate in the Commission's Expert Group on Sanctions Implementation, where challenges in the implementation of sanctions are discussed with the Commission and other Member States. Moreover, the Commission holds ad hoc stakeholder meetings to provide guidance and to discuss implementation aspects of Russia sanctions with operators.[50] In addition, it appears that the Commission is increasingly focusing on engagement with private stakeholders involved in sanctions investigations in an effort to benefit from lessons learned by the private sector in the development of future sanctions implementation tools.[51]

At the Member State level, it is also understood that the Member States (are encouraged[52] to) coordinate with each other in respect of authorisation applications, especially in cases where companies apply to multiple NCAs (due to touchpoints in different Member States). Although the details and results of that coordination remain to a large extent unclear, Estonia, Latvia and Lithuania published in December 2023 a joint declaration recognising that 'closing loopholes and ensuring the effective implementation of sanctions is of critical importance in strengthening the impact of sanctions and disrupting Russia's ability to continue its war of aggression against Ukraine' and pledging to adopt a uniform approach to regional sanctions implementation within 2024.[53] Almost a year later, in November 2024, Estonia, Latvia and Lithuania agreed to establish a common regional list of controlled battlefield items subject to export restrictions to Russia and Belarus.[54]

Apart from those initiatives, there are various types of informal change that can be introduced to promote and enhance compliance with EU sanctions legislation. For the purpose of this chapter, we focus on identifying a few changes that specifically pertain to authorisations, building on experience in advising on sanctions compliance.[55]

[49] See, eg European Parliament, Effectiveness of the EU sanctions on Russia (n 33), para 14.

[50] European Parliament, answer given by Ms McGuinness on behalf of the European Commission (E-003306/2023, 20 December 2023), available at www.europarl.europa.eu/doceo/document/E-9-2023-003306-ASW_EN.pdf.

[51] See, eg the invitation extended by the Directorate-General for Financial Stability, Financial Services and Capital Markets Union to stakeholders to give feedback on Article 12g of Regulation 833/2014 (n 1), available at www.finance.ec.europa.eu/eu-and-world/sanctions-restrictive-measures/sanctions-adopted-following-russias-military-aggression-against-ukraine_en.

[52] See also Sanctions Guidelines – update (n 4), para 29, inviting the Member States to 'communicate to the EEAS and to the Commission data collected in applying these exemptions in order to improve the quality of the identifiers referred to above'.

[53] Republic of Estonia, Government, The Baltic states adopt a common approach to the implementation of EU sanctions (22 December 2023), available at www.valitsus.ee/en/news/baltic-states-adopt-common-approach-implementation-eu-sanctions.

[54] Government of the Republic of Lithuania, As Lithuania Concludes its Presidency of the Baltic Council of Ministers, Prime Ministers Discuss Defence and Security, Support for Ukraine and Infrastructure Projects (22 November 2024, available at www.lrv.lt/en/news/as-lithuania-concludes-its-presidency-of-the-baltic-council-of-ministers-prime-ministers-discuss-defence-and-security-support-for-ukraine-and-infrastructure-projects.

[55] For a broader set of suggestions, see Portela and Olsen (n 4).

First, a central and publicly available database could be developed where redacted versions of authorisations granted (and denied) in the various Member States can be consulted, and where statistics on authorisations granted or denied (in respect of specific derogation grounds) are published. Amendments made to Regulations 269/2014 and 883/2014 (in respect of the EU sanctions against Russia) indicate that, in any event, this information is becoming available and is exchanged between the Member States and with the Commission. Provided that confidentiality concerns are properly addressed, persons and entities seeking to comply with EU sanctions legislation could greatly benefit from better understanding whether, for example, the Member States are actively granting (or denying) particular types of authorisation, the intensity of their process for granting authorisations, and possibly the NCAs' interpretation of particular derogation grounds and their application to frequently occurring similar transactions. As things stand, some Member States publish information about authorisations (granted or denied);[56] others do not offer any transparency in this respect.

Second, based on closer coordination between the Member States and with appropriate facilitation of the Commission, uniform templates for requesting authorisations could be used. The authorisation application procedures are uncertain and diverse, ranging from detailed and instructive templates provided by certain NCAs to the simple recommendation to send an authorisation application to a specified NCA email address. Eventually, it could be proposed to develop a central register, administered by the Commission, through which authorisation applications may be filed and distributed to the competent authorities (in a way that would also facilitate the process among the Member States for establishing who takes the lead for the full assessment of the relevant transaction). The latter would be particularly welcome to deal with the fact that there are no conflict rules for establishing the competent NCA in respect of a transaction having multiple touchpoints in different Member States, and there is no regulated mechanism of mutual recognition of authorisations granted.

Third, as already mentioned, a broader use of general authorisations (and coordination at Member State level on the use of those authorisations and the conditions – including reporting obligations – attached to them) could promote (uniform) compliance with EU sanctions legislation, offer more legal certainty for companies, and ensure that the derogation grounds are more effective and used by individuals and operators needing to comply with EU sanctions legislation. Although EU sanctions against Russia only refer to general authorisations for humanitarian purposes in Ukraine, the Commission has confirmed that NCAs may issue general authorisations (or 'block authorisations') in respect of other derogation grounds, and even recognised the benefit of that type of authorisation.[57]

[56] For example, the Money Laundering Bureau of the Financial Intelligence Unit of Estonia that is responsible for the implementation of EU targeted sanctions publishes information on authorisations granted. See Republic of Estonia, Financial Intelligence Unit, Russian military aggression in Ukraine, available at www.fiu.ee/rahvusvahelised-sanktsioonid/venemaa-sojaline-agressioon-ukrainas#erandid.

[57] See, eg European Commission, Consolidated FAQs (n 12) s G sub-s 6, q 39 on public procurement and s B sub-s 1, q 12 on asset freeze and prohibition to make funds and economic resources available.

10.3. Compliance with EU Sanctions Legislation Affects Businesses Well Beyond EU Borders

10.3.1. Introduction

The EU opposes extraterritoriality and has contended that EU sanctions have no extra-territorial effects.[58] In particular, the EU considers that secondary sanctions, namely restrictive measures imposed on persons and entities that are not nationals of the relevant state and are outside that state's jurisdiction, violate international law.[59] For example, the Parliament has noted that

> some states, particularly the US, seek to apply their laws outside their territory in a manner which may precipitate conflicts with other states or international organizations. These measures are referred to as 'secondary sanctions', as opposed to 'primary sanctions' which are aimed at targets within the sending state's jurisdiction.[60]

Likewise, the Commission has stressed that 'EU restrictive measures should only apply in situations where links exist with the EU, as the EU refrain from adopting legislative instruments having extra-territorial application in breach of international law'.[61]

Despite the EU's strong opposition to the extraterritorial application of sanctions, the reality of EU sanctions compliance is that EU targeted and sectoral sanctions (and especially EU sanctions against Russia) have effects well beyond the border of the EU. Although these effects do not necessarily result in extra-territoriality, they significantly extend the reach of EU sanctions. Following Russia's invasion of Ukraine and the extension of the substantive scope of EU sanctions against Russia, it has become apparent that the wide reach of EU sanctions results from, notably: (i) the interpretation and application of the jurisdictional clause found in the

[58] See also J Borrell, 'Some clarifications on the circumvention of EU sanctions against Russia' (19 May 2023), available at www.eeas.europa.eu/eeas/some-clarifications-circumvention-eu-sanctions-against-russia_en; T Ruys and C Ryngaert, 'Secondary Sanctions: A Weapon out of Control? The International Legality of, and European Responses to, US Secondary Sanctions' BYIL (20 September 2020), available at www.academic.oup.com/bybil/advance-article/doi/10.1093/bybil/braa007/5909823; T Ruys and FP Silvestre, 'Secondary Sanctions After Russia's Invasion of Ukraine – A Whole New World?" (September 2023), available at www.law.ugent.be/grili/sites/default/files/working-paper/grili_working_paper_ruys-rodriguez_silvestre_chapter_handbook_secondary_sanctions_sept_2023.pdf; J Dunin-Wasowivz, 'Op-Ed: "The Long Arm of EU Sanctions" by Jan Dunin-Wasowicz' EU Law Live (25 October 2022), available at www.eulawlive.com/op-ed-the-long-arm-of-eu-sanctions-by-jan-dunin-wasowicz.

[59] Sanctions Guidelines – update (n 4), paras 51–52. The EU is opposed to the extraterritorial application of third-country sanctions, which led to the adoption of a Blocking Statute nullifying their effects in the EU. Its recitals state: 'Whereas a third country has enacted certain laws, regulations, and other legislative instruments which purport to regulate activities of natural and legal persons under the jurisdiction of the Member State … Whereas by their extra-territorial application such laws, regulations and other legislative instruments violate international law'. Council Regulation (EC) No 2271/96 of 22 November 1996 protecting against the effects of the extra-territorial application of legislation adopted by a third country, and actions based thereon or resulting therefrom [1996] OJ L309/1 (current consolidated version 7 August 2018) 1.

[60] Policy Department for External Relations, Extraterritorial sanctions on trade and investments and European responses (PE 653.618, November 2020) 18, available at www.europarl.europa.eu/RegData/etudes/STUD/2020/653618/EXPO_STU(2020)653618_EN.pdf.

[61] European Parliament, Answer given by High Representative/Vice-President Borrell i Fontelles on behalf of the European Commission (P-003090/2022, 12 October 2022), available at www.europarl.europa.eu/doceo/document/P-9-2022–003090-ASW_EN.pdf.

Council regulations setting out the various EU sanctions regimes; (ii) the widespread use of sanctions due diligence clauses in contracts with counterparties located outside the EU; and (iii) the new listing grounds included in EU sanctions against Russia.

This section explores how compliance with EU sanctions affects global transactions taking place outside the EU territory and highlights how the extended reach of EU sanctions raises the level of difficulty for EU and non-EU operators seeking to comply with EU sanctions, potentially leading to overcompliance.

In particular, three key mechanisms allow the effects of EU sanctions to extend well beyond the borders of the EU and stress-test the EU's long-established position against the extraterritorial application of EU sanctions. First, the broad scope of the long under-appreciated jurisdictional clause found in EU sanctions covers any business done in whole or in part within the EU, as well as the involvement of EU parent companies and EU (and dual-EU) nationals in the activities of non-EU companies (which, as we analyse below, has now also been codified under the fourteenth package of EU sanctions against Russia). The practice of sanctions compliance that has emerged after Russia's invasion of Ukraine shows that, as long as the scope of this jurisdictional clause is not interpreted by the CJEU, the jurisdictional net of EU sanctions is being cast widely, often capturing transactions taking place well outside the EU. Second, the due diligence obligations imposed on EU operators lead to the adoption of contractual arrangements that impose on non-EU counterparties otherwise not subject to EU sanctions the obligation to comply with EU law. Notably, in a novel turn marked by the twelfth package of EU sanctions against Russia, the Council introduced for the first time an obligation on EU operators to contractually require their foreign counterparts to respect EU sanctions prohibiting exports to Russia. Third, the new listing grounds adopted by the Council allow the imposition of targeted sanctions not only to operators that facilitate EU actors to circumvent EU sanctions, but also to operators that undertake activities that significantly frustrate EU sanctions. The broad and still untested concept of 'significant frustration' challenges the EU's opposition to extraterritoriality as it appears to allow the Council to list persons and entities on the basis of conduct that has no link with the EU.

10.3.2. The Jurisdictional Clause in EU Sanctions Legislation

As mentioned above, the rules governing the application of EU sanctions legislation are set at EU level. The Council regulations setting out the various EU sanctions regimes contain, since 2001,[62] an almost identical jurisdictional clause stipulating that EU sanctions apply:

(a) within the territory of the Union;
(b) on board any aircraft or any vessel under the jurisdiction of a Member State;

[62] See, eg Council Regulation (EC) No 2580/2001 of 27 December 2001 on specific restrictive measures directed against certain persons and entities with a view to combating terrorism [2001] OJ L344/70, Art 10; Council Regulation (EU) No 753/2011 of 1 August 2011 concerning restrictive measures directed against certain individuals, groups, undertakings and entities in view of the situation in Afghanistan [2011] OJ L199/1, Art 14; Council Regulation (EU) 2017/1509 of 30 August 2017 concerning restrictive measures against the Democratic People's Republic of Korea [2017] OJ L224/1, Art 1; Council Regulation (EU) 2023/1529 of

(c) to any person inside or outside the territory of the Union who is a national of a Member State;
(d) to any legal person, entity or body, inside or outside of the territory of the Union, which is incorporated or constituted under the law of a Member State; and
(e) to any legal person, entity or body in respect of any business done in whole or in part within the Union.[63]

As the jurisdictional clause indicates, EU sanctions legislation applies to EU (and dual-EU) nationals and companies at all times. Moreover, it applies in respect of non-EU nationals, when they are present within the territory of the EU, including on board any aircraft or vessel under the jurisdiction of a Member State. When it comes to non-EU companies, according to jurisdictional rule (e), EU sanctions legislation applies in respect of 'any business', namely any form of commercial activity, done in whole or in part within the EU territory.[64]

10.3.2.1. Any Business Done in Whole or in Part in the EU Territory

Jurisdictional rule (e) has been a standard feature of EU sanctions legislation. Nevertheless, its effects have started to become tangible following Russia's 2022 invasion of Ukraine. Up until 2022, when EU sanctions legislation generally affected a more limited number of economic sectors, there was an underappreciation of what jurisdictional rule (e) meant and what its effects on global supply chains were. However, ever since the 2022 EU sanctions against Russia introduced an unprecedented set of restrictions covering activities taking place across entire supply chains, economic operators started to look more closely into this jurisdictional rule.[65] The renewed focus on

20 July 2023 concerning restrictive measures in view of Iran's military support of Russia's war of aggression against Ukraine [2023] OJ L186/1, Art 16.

[63] Jurisdictional rule (e) was first included in the sanctions regulations adopted in the wake of the 9/11 terror attacks. The original version of this jurisdictional ground, included in Council Regulation (EC) No 2580/2001, was worded more narrowly ('to any legal person, group or entity doing business within the Community', Council Regulation (EC) No 2580/2001 of 27 December 2001 on specific restrictive measures directed against certain persons and entities with a view to combating terrorism [2001] OJ L344/70, Art 10), as compared to the wording of the jurisdictional clause included in more recent sanctions regulations ('to any legal person, group or entity doing in respect of any business done in whole or in part within the Community' Council Regulation (EC) No 765/2006 of 18 May 2006 concerning restrictive measures against President Lukashenko and certain officials of Belarus [2006] OJ L, Art 10).

[64] The term 'any business' indicates that all forms of commercial activities performed by non-EU companies are potentially covered This understanding is supported by certain other language versions of EU sanctions legislation, which indicate that the term 'business' can also be understood as commercial 'transactions'. For example, the German language versions of the relevant legislative acts translate 'business' as 'Geschäfte', whereas the Dutch language versions refer to 'transacties'.

[65] For example, the jurisdictional clause set out in Art 9 of the original version of Regulation 2465/96 (Council Regulation (EC) No 2465/96 of 17 December 1996 concerning the interruption of economic and financial relations between the European Community and Iraq [1996] OJ L337) stipulated that 'This Regulation shall apply within the territory of the European Community including its air space and on any aircraft or any vessel under the jurisdiction of a Member State and to any person elsewhere who is a national of a Member State and any body which is incorporated or constituted under the law of a Member State.' Despite the fact that these jurisdictional rules have been featured in EU sanctions legislation for almost three decades, their effects have become particularly apparent with the expansion of EU sanctions against Russia in and after 2022 following Russia's invasion in Ukraine (see Regulation 833/2014 (n 1) and Regulation 269/2014 (n 1)).

jurisdictional ground (e) is illustrated by the twelfth package of EU sanctions against Russia. In December 2022, the Council prohibited the sale of tankers for the transport of crude oil intended to monitor more closely how tankers might be used to circumvent the oil price cap.[66] According to the text of the new Article 3q of Regulation 833/2014, this prohibition applies to 'any national of a Member State, natural person residing in a Member State, and legal person, entity or body which is established in the Union'. For the first time, the Council expressly limited the jurisdictional scope of the sanctions to EU nationals/residents and EU companies in the text of a single provision, thus signalling that at least with respect to certain types of sanction the broad reach of jurisdictional ground (e) may *not* be justified.[67]

Despite the urgent need for clarification of its scope, the CJEU has not (yet) interpreted jurisdictional rule (e).[68] However, it is highly likely that the CJEU (probably in a preliminary ruling procedure), will soon be asked to interpret this jurisdictional rule. In the meantime, the far-reaching effects of this jurisdictional ground, as they are particularly apparent in the context of the application of EU sanctions against Russia (and the FAQs of the Commission on those sanctions), are resulting in a new understanding of the scope of application of all EU sanctions regimes.

The key question that arises under jurisdictional rule (e) is when a commercial activity is 'done in whole or in part' within the EU territory. The practice adopted by several operators is that from the moment the EU territory is crossed, or an EU company or EU (or dual-EU) national/resident is in any way involved in a transaction, eg, as an insurer or payment intermediary, the transaction falls under the jurisdictional scope of EU sanctions legislation. As long as the scope of jurisdictional rule (e) remains unaddressed by the CJEU, under a broad interpretation, this approach does not appear to be overly cautious.

The plain meaning of the phrase 'any business done in whole or in part within the Union' signals that the commercial activities of a non-EU company must be conducted in accordance with EU sanctions when those activities take place within the EU territory. However, jurisdictional rule (e) cannot be understood to require the non-EU company itself to be physically present (ie, via its representatives, branches, etc) in the EU for that entity to do business 'within' the EU territory.[69] To conclude differently

[66] See Regulation 833/2014 (n 1), Art 3(q). See also Council Regulation (EU) 2023/2878 of 18 December 2023 amending Regulation (EU) No 833/2014 concerning restrictive measures in view of Russia's actions destabilising the situation in Ukraine [2023] OJ L2878, Art 1(15).

[67] A similar limitation on the jurisdictional scope of certain restrictive measures introduced with the 14th sanctions package was adopted in respect of Articles 3l and 5ac of Regulation 833/2014 (n 1). See also Council Regulation (EU) 2024/1745 of 24 June 2024 amending Regulation (EU) No 833/2014 concerning restrictive measures in view of Russia's actions destabilising the situation in Ukraine.

[68] The General Court of the European Union (GCEU) has referred to this phrase in passing. In Cases T-496/10 *Bank Mellat v Council* [2013] EU:T:2013:470 and T-8/11 *Bank Kargoshaei and Other v Council* [2013] EU:T:2013:470, the GCEU considered that, because EU sanctions apply to a legal person, entity or body incorporated or constituted outside the European Union only with respect to 'business done in whole or in part within the European Union', those measures are 'not capable of imposing legal obligations on a financial institution established in a non-Member country *and* constituted under the law of that country', with respect to 'transactions carried out outside the European Union' (emphasis added). See *Bank Mellat* [122]–[123].

[69] Joined Cases C-89/85, C-104/85, C-114/85, C-115/85, C-116/85, C-117/85, and C-125/85 to C-129/85 *A Ahlström Osakeyhtiö and Others v Commission of the European Communities* [1994] EU:C:1988:447, [18].

would render the phrase redundant, given that EU sanctions always apply to persons and entities within the territory of the EU.

In this respect, the Commission has commented on the type of activity which might constitute business done in whole or in part in the EU:

> EU sanctions are never extraterritorial and do not apply to non-EU companies or individuals that do business entirely outside the Union. By way of example, a non-EU company shipping agricultural products from Russia directly to a non-EU country has no obligations vis-à-vis EU sanctions. However, if the same company imports the products via the Union or carries out payments in the Union, then it has to comply with EU sanctions as it is entering the EU internal market.[70]

The Commission seems to consider that whenever a transaction becomes operative within the EU internal market, for example because goods cross the EU territory or the banking channels used involve an EU bank, the transaction at issue is to be considered as 'done' (at least) 'in part' within the EU territory. This approach echoes the effects doctrine of EU competition law, which extends the reach of EU competition rules to conduct that can foreseeably have 'an immediate and substantial effect in the European Union'.[71] The CJEU has considered that the effects doctrine is permissible under EU competition law because 'the applicability of [EU] competition law [was] made to depend on' whether the relevant agreement, decision or concerted practice becomes 'operative on the territory of the internal market' and not 'on the place where [it] was formed'.[72] Although up until now the Commission, in its limited guidance, has always required an EU link to exist for jurisdictional rule (e) to apply, absent concrete guidance from the CJEU, the line between the territoriality principle and the effects doctrine might become harder to draw.

Overall, as things stand, any commercial transaction undertaken by a non-EU company that has a (remote) link with the territory of the EU or EU operators, must comply with EU sanctions. Therefore, when assessing whether business is done in whole or in part within the EU, it is relevant to assess inter alia not only whether a party to the transaction operates within the EU, but also whether, as part of a transaction, any party to that transaction must perform obligations within the territory of the EU, or whether the transaction otherwise, in view of its nature, has a touchpoint in the EU internal market. In effect, transactions where goods cross or are destined for the territory of the EU, where services are supplied, directly or indirectly, to recipients within the territory of the EU, where EU banks are used, where EU transport, logistics, insurance etc. companies are involved, or even where intellectual property rights are licensed by an EU company, run the risk of being captured by jurisdictional rule (e).

[70] European Commission, Consolidated FAQs (n 12), s F sub-s 1, q 7 on trade in agricultural and related products from Russia.

[71] Case C-413/14 P *Intel v Commission* [2017] EU:C:2017:632, [40]–[47].

[72] Case C-413/14 P *Intel v Commission* [2017] EU:C:2017:632, [43]–[44]. See also EM Fox, 'Extraterritorial Jurisdiction, Antitrust, and the EU Intel Case: Implementation, Qualified Effects, and the Third Kind' (2019) 42 *Fordham International Law Journal* 981, 982.

10.3.2.2. EU Operators' Liability for the Actions of Non-EU Companies

The broad scope of the jurisdictional clause in EU sanctions does not only bring non-EU companies within the jurisdictional scope of the sanctions; it can also result in EU operators incurring liability for the activities of non-EU companies. As has become clear in the context of EU sanctions against Russia, the obligation to ensure EU sanctions compliance indirectly extends to the conduct of non-EU companies, either because they are subsidiaries of EU companies or because EU (or dual-EU) nationals are part of their employee structure or governance. Moreover, as a result of the fourteenth package of EU sanctions against Russia, a direct obligation was imposed on EU parent companies to undertake best efforts to ensure that the activities of non-EU companies that they own or control do not undermine EU sectoral sanctions against Russia.

To illustrate, where EU (or dual-EU) nationals/residents act as employees or executives of a non-EU company or exercise their voting rights as part of the board of directors or the shareholders' meeting of a non-EU company, they must comply with EU sanctions legislation.[73] This means that they may not approve or otherwise facilitate or support a transaction of the non-EU company, unless that transaction complies with EU sanctions. In this respect, the Commission has cautioned that:

> EU nationals working for [a non-EU company] are personally bound by EU sanctions and can be held personally liable for participating in transactions which breach EU sanctions. For example, if the [company] itself entered the transaction, EU nationals facilitating the transaction could still be covered by the anti-circumvention clause if they 'participate in activities' the object or effect of which was to circumvent the main prohibition.[74]

In practice, this means that if the CEO of a non-EU company has EU (or dual-EU) nationality/residence, he or she is prohibited from approving or in any way facilitating a transaction of the non-EU company that contradicts EU sanctions, eg, a transaction involving the sale of sanctioned goods to a sanctioned territory, such as Russia.

Likewise, where an EU parent company directs or controls the activities of its non-EU subsidiary, whether directly or indirectly, it must comply with EU sanctions. In this respect, the Commission has stressed that:

> [I]t is prohibited for EU parent companies to use their Russian subsidiaries to circumvent the obligations that apply to the EU parent, for instance by delegating to them decisions which run counter the sanctions, or by approving such decisions by the Russian subsidiary.[75]
>
> …
>
> decisions taken by the foreign subsidiary that need to be cleared/greenlighted by the EU parent company would be relevant, in that the latter is bound in respect of its own actions.[76]

The involvement of an EU parent company in the activities of its non-EU subsidiary might take the form of delegation or approval of decisions in accordance with the articles of association of the non-EU subsidiary, the company group management structures and policies, or otherwise the applicable law or contractual framework.

[73] European Commission, Consolidated FAQs (n 12) s C sub-s 3, q 3 on investment funds.
[74] ibid s D sub-s 2, q 34 on export-related restrictions for dual-use goods and advanced technologies.
[75] ibid.
[76] ibid 12, q 14.

For example, in multinational group of companies, a series of decisions taken by group companies are typically approved at the group level, either by the direct or ultimate parent company or by executives who participate in global or regional management teams. As a result, where an EU company has delegated or is required to approve a commercial activity of its non-EU subsidiary, EU sanctions must be respected.

In addition to formal delegation or approval, an EU parent company's involvement in the activities of a non-EU subsidiary might also take the form of informal participation, by means of direction, clearing or green-lighting a commercial activity.[77] This is the case, for example, where the non-EU subsidiary informally seeks strategic input from the EU parent company in respect of a prospective business activity or where the non-EU subsidiary enters a transaction on the basis of business policy directions issued by its EU parent company. In those instances, the EU parent company must ensure that the relevant action of its non-EU subsidiary complies with EU sanctions. In practice, this might involve the communication of instructions to the non-EU subsidiary requiring EU sanctions compliance, as well as the adoption of measures, whether formal or informal, that are reasonably available to the EU parent company and can guarantee that the non-EU subsidiary complies with the instructions.

The implications of this broad understanding of the jurisdictional scope of EU sanctions are highlighted by a judgment of the Court of Amsterdam. The Dutch Court, in the context of a civil case, considered that the Russian company Boskalis LLC was required to comply with EU sanctions when performing its contractual obligations towards its Dutch counterparty, Saren BV, because its parent company, Boskalis Westminster Dredging BV, was incorporated in the Netherlands, while its sole director was a Dutch national. Focusing on the obligation imposed on EU nationals and EU companies to not participate in the circumvention of EU sanctions, the Court of Amsterdam found that:

> In this light and in view of the purpose and scope … of the Sanctions Regulation and [the prohibition on circumvention] in particular, it is assumed for the time being that the sanctions are not only aimed at the Dutch (grand)mothers of Boskalis LLC and its Dutch director, but also on Boskalis LLC itself.
>
> The second interim conclusion is that it is assumed for the time being that Boskalis LLC falls under the Sanctions Regulation and was therefore obliged to cease work.[78]

Although this approach does not oppose the jurisdictional principles of territoriality and nationality, it extends the effects of EU sanctions well beyond the borders of the EU, to global transactions having no other touchpoint with the EU than the place of incorporation of the corporate UBO or the CEO of one of the counterparties. This is the case, for example, where a joint venture is registered in a Member State and needs to approve an acquisition where the acquiring and acquired entities and all other involved parties are outside the EU.

In practice, EU (and dual-EU) nationals/residents and companies that direct or control the conduct of non-EU companies, incur a series of practical difficulties when seeking to verify compliance of non-EU companies with EU sanctions. On

[77] ibid.

[78] Rechtbank Amsterdam, Case C/13/717154/KG ZA 22-388 *Boskalis LLC et al* [2022] ECLI:NL:RBAMS:2022:3141, [4.22]–[4.23].

the one hand, this might relate to the lack of adequate information flow to assess the non-compliance risks arising from a particular activity. On the other hand, any counter-sanctions imposed by the third country of incorporation of the non-EU company might raise barriers to compliance with EU sanctions. For example, this has been the case with the Russian counter-sanctions. Even where EU parent companies issue concrete instructions to their Russian subsidiaries to comply with EU sanctions, the obligations imposed under Russian law to those subsidiaries often limit their ability to act in accordance with EU law.

Moreover, the liability of an EU parent company under EU sanctions may be engaged where it obtains information, through formal or informal channels, or otherwise has reasonable cause to suspect that its non-EU subsidiary, including through its own subsidiaries or joint ventures, undertakes or plans to engage in activities contradicting EU sanctions. In those circumstances, if the EU parent company fails to issue instructions to its non-EU subsidiary and adopt reasonably available measures to ensure that the non-EU subsidiary refrains from or ceases non-compliant conduct, it risks being found in breach of EU sanctions.

Overall, as the recent practice of EU sanctions compliance shows, transactions of non-EU companies can easily have a touchpoint in the EU. In this respect, the uncertainty about the interpretation and application of the jurisdictional clause set out in EU sanctions might result in overcompliance affecting the interests of both EU and non-EU companies.

What is more, in view of the decentralised and fragmented model of sanctions administration, as long as there is no guidance from the CJEU, the application of the jurisdictional clause in particular instances by NCAs might vary. Even more, where an NCA finds that a non-EU company is subject to compliance with EU sanctions in respect of a particular activity, that same company might not be subject to the enforcement jurisdiction of the relevant Member State. Although efforts are being made to create a common framework governing the enforcement of EU sanctions across the Member States, as discussed in the first section of this chapter, the jurisdictional clause set out in EU sanctions might not necessarily be fully aligned with the rules governing the enforcement jurisdiction of individual Member States.

Following the fourteenth package of EU sanctions against Russia,[79] as of 25 June 2024, EU parent companies are expressly required – at the threat of incurring liability for the violation of EU sanctions – to 'undertake their best efforts to ensure that' any foreign, namely established outside the European Union, company 'that they own or control', eg, any of their foreign subsidiaries, joint-ventures etc, including those that are established in Russia, 'does not participate in activities that undermine the restrictive measures provided for' in Regulation 833/2014 (best-efforts obligation).[80] As things stand, the best-efforts obligation only applies in respect of sectoral sanctions against Russia,[81] without yet covering targeted sanctions against Russia.[82]

[79] Regulation 2024/1745 (n 67).
[80] Regulation 833/2014 (n 1), Art 8a.
[81] Regulation 833/2014 (n 1).
[82] Regulation 269/2014 (n 1).

This new accountability mechanism further extends the reach of EU sanctions. Apart from requiring EU parent companies to ensure that any explicit or implicit involvement in the activities of their foreign subsidiaries complies with EU sanctions, the new mechanism obliges an EU parent company to actively seek to gain awareness of a foreign subsidiary's activities and intervene to prevent any activities which 'undermine'[83] sectoral sanctions against Russia.[84]

In its recent guidance on the best-efforts obligation,[85] the Commission took the position that EU parent companies must perform all necessary and feasible actions to ensure their own awareness of the activities conducted by their foreign subsidiaries and their foreign subsidiaries' understanding of the types of activities that risk undermining sectoral sanctions against Russia. According to the Commission, that necessary and feasible action might involve 'internal compliance programs, systematic sharing of corporate compliance standards, sending newsletters and sanctions advisories, setting up mandatory reporting or organising mandatory sanctions trainings for staff, as well as setting up procedures to rapidly react to sanctions violations'. Although the Commission recognised that no liability arises in circumstances where the EU parent company has no control over its foreign subsidiary, it stressed that no mitigation of liability will be accepted in situations where control is lost due to the actions of the EU parent company. Especially in respect of Russian subsidiaries, taking into account Russian legislation that 'unjustly target[s] assets of companies from 'unfriendly countries', including EU Member States',[86] the Commission cautioned that inadequate risk assessment and management, as well as risk-prone decisions of an EU parent company, might be taken into account – on a case-by-case basis – as circumstances that 'contributed to the loss of control'.

10.3.3. The Use of Sanctions Due Diligence Clauses in Contracts with Non-EU Counterparties

Apart from the jurisdictional clause set out in EU sanctions regulations and the new accountability mechanism for EU parent companies introduced in sectoral sanctions against Russia, contractual clauses can also operate in a way that makes EU sanctions legislation applicable (or, at least, relevant) to non-EU companies or conduct taking place outside the EU.

[83] On the concept of 'undermining', the Commission has considered that a foreign subsidiary would 'undermine the restrictive measures' when it engaged in activities 'resulting in an effect that [the] restrictive measures seek to prevent, for example, that a recipient in Russia obtains goods, technology, financing or services of a type that is subject to prohibitions under Regulation (EU) No 833/2014'. To reach this interpretation, the Commission relied on the CJEU's case-law on the circumvention prohibition set out in EU sanctions legislation, thus signaling the broad reach of the best-efforts clause.

[84] Regulation 2024/1745 (n 67), recital 30.

[85] European Commission, Consolidated FAQs (n 12) s A sub-s 4.

[86] In its guidance, the Commission referred to Presidential Decree No 302 of the Russian Federation of 25 April 2023, which allows the Russian Government to take control of Russian assets owned or managed by investors associated with 'unfriendly' foreign States, such as the European Union, the United States etc. See European Commission, Consolidated FAQs (n 12) s A sub-s 4 q 4.

Following in particular the adoption of the 2022 EU sanctions against Russia, a key tool used by operators to mitigate the risk of non-compliance with EU sanctions is the incorporation of sanctions due diligence clauses in their contracts, including with counterparties established and operating outside the EU. These clauses impose a contractual obligation on counterparties (which might, depending on the circumstances, not otherwise be subject to EU sanctions legislation) to comply with various aspects of EU sanctions in respect of transactions that could potentially engage the liability of their EU counterparts.

Operators subject to EU sanctions legislation are not liable for violating EU sanctions if they did not know, and had no reasonable cause to suspect, that their actions would infringe EU sanctions legislation.[87] This means that operators subject to EU sanctions legislation must, prior to engaging in a business activity, exercise due diligence to ensure that their activities do not violate the applicable EU sanctions.[88] As part of the fourteenth package of EU sanctions against Russia, the Council clarified the liability clause by noting that:

> the protection against liability that is granted to Union operators if they did not know, and had no reasonable cause to suspect, that their actions would infringe Union restrictive measures cannot be invoked where Union operators have failed to carry out appropriate due diligence. It is appropriate for publicly or readily available information to be duly taken into account when carrying out such due diligence. Therefore, for example, a Union operator cannot successfully invoke such protection when it is accused of breaching the relevant restrictive measures because it has failed to carry out simple checks or inspections.[89]

According to the Commission's recommendations, contractual sanctions due diligence clauses, that give rise to liability in case of a breach, are a key due diligence tool for operators seeking to limit the risk of incurring liability for non-compliance with EU sanctions resulting from actions taken by their business partners downstream or upstream their supply chains.[90]

For example, contractual sanctions due diligence clauses are extensively used to mitigate the risk of diversion of sanctioned goods and technology to sanctioned countries. Various EU sanctions regimes prohibit the direct or indirect sale, supply or export of sanctioned goods to or for use in a sanctioned country, as well as the circumvention of this export-related prohibition. As a result, operators subject to EU sanctions are required to exercise due diligence to ensure that, when they sell, supply or export sanctioned goods to counterparties in non-sanctioned countries, those sanctioned goods are diverted to or for use in a sanctioned country. In this respect, in its due diligence

[87] See Regulation 833/2014 (n 1), Art 10; Regulation 269/2014 (n 1), Art 10(2).

[88] European Commission, Consolidated FAQs (n 12) s A sub-s 2, q 1 and 10 on circumvention and due diligence.

[89] Council Regulation (EU) 2024/1739 of 24 June 2024 amending Regulation (EU) No 269/2014 concerning restrictive measures in respect of actions undermining or threatening the territorial integrity, sovereignty and independence of Ukraine [2024] OJ L2024/1739, recital 3. See also, Regulation 2024/1745 (n 67), recital 36. Moreover, the fourteenth sanctions package against Russia expressly codified the due diligence obligation in respect of common high-priority items. See, Regulation 833/2014 (n 1), Art 12gb. See also European Commission, Consolidated FAQs (n 12) s D sub-s 14 on enhanced due diligence for operators manufacturing and/or trading with CHP items.

[90] European Union, Notice to economic operators, importers and exporters [2022] OJ C145 I/01.

and circumvention guidance issued in the context of EU sanctions against Russia, the Commission recommended that:

> [W]hen exporting goods subject to restrictions, [operators subject to EU sanctions] should include, in particular, contractual clauses with their third-country business partners prohibiting further re-exports of the items to Russia and Belarus. For example, such a clause may oblige the importer in third countries not to export the concerned goods to Russia or Belarus, and not to resell the concerned goods to any third party business partner unless that partner commits not to export the concerned goods to Russia or Belarus. It is vital that the contractual clause gives rise to liability and can be enforced under the law applicable to the contract. The clause may also entail ex post verifications, and may be identified an essential element of the contract.[91]

Therefore, to ensure that their own conduct, neither directly nor indirectly, raises the risk of non-compliance with EU sanctions, many EU operators have been incorporating sanctions due diligence clauses in their contracts with non-EU companies.

Building on the Commission's recommendations, in December 2023, the twelfth package of EU sanctions against Russia imposed a novel obligation on EU exporters to contractually prohibit re-exportation to and for use in Russia of certain sensitive and common high-priority items, as well as firearms and ammunition.[92] Article 12g of Regulation 833/2014 will in practice enable the customs authorities of the Member States to block exports of covered items unless the exporters present at the time of export a copy of the contract underlying the relevant sale that includes clauses prohibiting re-export to or for use in Russia. Moreover, the Commission has published a non-mandatory template of those clauses.[93]

Overall, the widespread, and now in certain cases mandatory, use of sanctions due diligence contractual clauses, shows that even where the jurisdictional clause of EU sanctions legislation does not apply, non-EU companies might still be required to comply EU sanctions legislation on the basis of contractual arrangements.

10.3.4. The New Listing Grounds as a Driver for Non-EU Businesses to Comply with EU Sanctions

Whilst the jurisdictional grounds, the new accountability mechanism for EU parent companies and the sanctions' due diligence contractual clauses still rely on a touchpoint (even if remote) in the EU in terms of territory, nationality or residence, the adoption of new listing grounds in the EU sanctions against Russia has resulted in more uncertainty regarding whether the EU maintains its principled opposition to extra-territoriality.

The listing grounds set out in the sanctions legislation differ from the jurisdictional grounds in that they do not, in principle, define who must comply with EU sanctions.

[91] European Commission, Guidance for EU operators: Implementing enhanced due diligence to shield against Russia sanctions circumvention (last update: 19 February 2024), available at www.finance.ec.europa.eu/publications/guidance-due-diligence_en.

[92] Regulation 833/2014 (n 1), Art 12g; see also Regulation 2023/2878 (n 66), Art 1(28).

[93] European Commission, Consolidated FAQs (n 12) s D sub-s 13, q 6 on 'no re-export to Russia' clause.

Instead, they enable the Council to designate and, thus, impose targeted sanctions against individuals and entities that engage in certain conduct, irrespective of whether they are required to comply with EU sanctions.

Aiming to tackle circumvention of sanctions legislation but confronted with the limits of the jurisdictional grounds and the enforcement jurisdiction of the Member States, the Council adopted two new listing grounds allowing it to designate individuals and entities that facilitate the circumvention of or frustrate EU sanctions. Although this development was specific to the EU sanctions against Russia, it has already spread to other EU sanctions regimes.[94] As a result, targeted sanctions are now also being used to attach consequences (often more far-reaching than those resulting from the violation of EU sanctions) to activities that facilitate the circumvention of or frustrate the sanctions, even if undertaken by non-EU operators. In this regard, the new listing grounds broaden the effects of EU sanctions legislation and result in an indirect enforcement of EU sanctions outside the EU territory. Concretely, on 6 October 2022, as part of the eighth package of EU sanctions against Russia, the Council added a new ground for the listing of persons and entities in Annex I to Regulation 269/2014.[95] The new Article 3(1)(h) of Regulation 269/2014 provided that:

> Annex I shall include:
>
> (h) natural or legal persons, entities or bodies *facilitating infringements of the prohibition against circumvention* of the provisions of this Regulation, of Council Regulations (EU) No 692/2014 …, (EU) No 833/2014 … or (EU) 2022/263 … or of Council Decisions 2014/145/CFSP …, 2014/386/CFSP …, 2014/512/CFSP … or (CFSP) 2022/266 …; (emphasis added)

The prohibition against the circumvention of EU sanctions is included (in almost identical terms) in all EU sanctions regimes and provides that: 'It shall be prohibited to participate, knowingly and intentionally, in activities the object or effect of which is to circumvent prohibitions in this Regulation.' This prohibition applies to individuals and entities that are subject to EU sanctions. Thus, it presupposes that the jurisdictional clause of EU sanctions applies in respect of the conduct that amounts to circumvention.

Prior to the introduction of Article 3(1)(h), instances of circumvention of EU sanctions were subject to Member States' penalties, as set out under national law and enforced by national courts. The listing ground introduced with the eighth package enables the Council to list in Annex I – and thereby impose targeted sanctions on – natural or legal persons, entities or bodies, irrespective of their nationality or place of incorporation, that 'facilitat[e]' the circumvention of the EU sanctions by individuals and entities that are subject to EU sanctions.

[94] For example, under EU sanctions against Belarus, the Council may target individuals and entities that 'have been identified … as facilitating infringements of the prohibition against circumvention of the provisions [EU sanctions against Belarus] or as otherwise significantly frustrating those provisions.' See Council Regulation (EU) 2024/1865 of 29 June 2024 amending Regulation (EC) No 765/2006 concerning restrictive measures in view of the situation in Belarus and the involvement of Belarus in the Russian aggression against Ukraine [2024] OJ L2024/1865.

[95] Council Regulation (EU) 2022/1905 of 6 October 2022 amending Regulation (EU) No 269/2014 concerning restrictive measures in respect of actions undermining or threatening the territorial integrity, sovereignty and independence of Ukraine [2022] OJ L259 I/76, Art 1(1) (emphasis added).

Although the concept of circumvention is particularly board, the listing ground only applies to facilitation of circumvention, for example to activities which serve, are instrumental to or make possible the circumvention of EU sanctions legislation.[96] This choice on the part of the Council might have been driven, as already mentioned, by: (i) increased concerns that operators in certain non-EU jurisdictions, such as Türkiye, Kazakhstan or the UAE,[97] participate in the circumvention of EU sanctions, and the need to deter those practices; (ii) the fact that under the national laws of certain Member States, the applicable liability standards might not bring within the scope of the circumvention prohibition, acts which facilitate circumvention, even if perpetrated by EU operators;[98] and (iii) the fact that companies not subject to EU jurisdiction (and therefore, not subject to Member States' penalties for violating EU sanctions) facilitate circumvention, but escape liability on jurisdictional grounds.

In its public communications around the time of the adoption of the eighth package, the Council stressed that the adoption of the new criterion intended 'to prevent any loopholes or circumvention' and 'fores[aw] the possibility to list individuals who help EU actors circumvent sanctions'.[99] Indeed, on a strict reading, this listing ground presupposes a finding of circumvention of EU sanctions. In practice, to face the risk of listing, a non-EU operator must have 'facilitated' an EU operator to engage in circumvention. As a result, until the adoption of the eleventh package of EU sanctions against Russia, activities that had the effect of circumvention but where no EU operators were involved, were not captured.

However, with the eleventh package, another listing ground was added to Article 3(1)(h), that further broadened the consequences attached to activities that result in circumvention. In addition to the listing ground covering facilitation of circumvention, the new listing ground allows the listing of persons or entities that significantly frustrate EU sanctions.[100] In practice, under this listing ground, which covers both EU and non-EU operators, non-EU operators who participate in an

[96] See, eg the Commission's interpretation of the term facilitation found elsewhere in EU sanctions legislation (European Commission, Consolidated FAQs (n 12) s G sub-s 1, q 2 and 7 on media). In the context of individual rights of EU citizens, the CJEU has understood the term 'facilitate' as encompassing acts that 'make possible' a certain outcome (Case C-83/11 *Rahman and* others [2012] EU:C:2012:519, [21]–[22]). The broad scope of acts that could be deemed to facilitate circumvention is further indicated by the types of conduct that the Council has considered to constitute facilitation of certain Russian activities that warranted the listing of Russian persons and entities in Annex I to Regulation 269/201, prior to the adoption of Article 3(1)(h) (Regulation 269/2014 (n 1) Annex I Part A entry no 1195, Reasons, entry no 1243, Reasons).

[97] See, eg European Commission, High risk third countries and the International context of anti-money laundering and countering financing of terrorism, available at www.finance.ec.europa.eu/financial-crime/high-risk-third-countries-and-international-context-content-anti-money-laundering-and-countering_en#200507.

[98] European Commission, Questions and Answers on the eighth package of restrictive measures against Russia (6 October 2022), available at www.ec.europa.eu/commission/presscorner/detail/en/qanda_22_5990.

[99] European Commission, Statement by Commissioner McGuinness on the outcomes of the first meeting of the high-level meeting on sanctions implementation (24 October 2022), available at www.finance.ec.europa.eu/news/statement-commissioner-mcguinness-outcomes-first-meeting-high-level-meeting-sanctions-implementation-2022-10-24_en.

[100] Council Regulation (EU) 2023/1215 amending Regulation (EU) No 269/2014 concerning restrictive measures in respect of actions undermining or threatening the territorial integrity, sovereignty and independence of Ukraine [2023] OJ LI159/330, Art 1(1).

activity that might frustrate EU sanctions and who might otherwise fall outside the jurisdictional scope of sanctions legislation or escape the enforcement jurisdiction of the Member States, may nevertheless bear consequences for their activities.

In particular, following the eleventh package, Article 3(1)(h) provides that:

> Annex I shall include:
>
> (h) natural or legal persons, entities or bodies:
>
> (i) *facilitating infringements of the prohibition against circumvention* of the provisions of this Regulation, of Council Regulations (EU) No 692/2014 …, (EU) No 833/2014 … or (EU) 2022/263 … or of Council Decisions 2014/145/CFSP …, 2014/386/CFSP …, 2014/512/CFSP … or (CFSP) 2022/266 …; or
>
> (ii) otherwise significantly frustrating those provisions; (emphasis added)

The listing ground in Article 3(1)(h)(ii) does not require the involvement of EU operators in the activity leading to the targeting of a non-EU operator by the Council. Without any guidance from the CJEU on the meaning of the new concept of 'significant frustration', it cannot be excluded that the conduct of non-EU companies that has no EU link but due to its specific modalities or magnitude operates in a way that frustrates the purpose or operation of EU sanctions, might serve as a basis for listings.[101] In this respect, the question of whether the listing ground in Article 3(1)(h)(ii) still falls within the limits of the principles of territoriality and nationality under public international law is inescapable.[102] On a strict textual approach, this listing ground appears to allow the Council to adopt a form of secondary sanctions bringing within the purview of EU sanctions operators that fall well outside the jurisdiction of the EU.[103] In fact, as long as the meaning of the new listing ground is not clarified by the CJEU, its broad text might be used to justify listings on the basis of conduct that not only is far removed from the EU, but also exerts no direct or indirect effects on EU operators.

The new listing grounds in Article 3(1)(h)(i) and (ii) have already been put to use. Several (dual-)EU[104] and Russian[105] persons and entities have been listed either exclusively on the basis of one of the two new listing grounds, or on the basis of those new listing grounds combined with a pre-existing one.[106] For example, several Russian individuals and companies have been designated for their involvement in 'parallel imports' to Russia of goods falling under EU sanctions, without the consent of the EU

[101] The only available Commission guidance relates to the oil price cap measures set out in Art 3n of Regulation 833/2014 (n 1). In particular, the Commission has commented that 'The Council can impose asset freezes and travel bans against third country individuals or entities for circumvention or other forms of frustration of EU sanctions. Depending on the specifics of the case, this may also apply to actors withholding pricing information in order to circumvent the price cap provisions.' See European Commission, Consolidated FAQs (n 12) s E sub-s 5, q 48 on the oil price cap.

[102] C Ryngaert, *Jurisdiction in International Law*, 2nd edn (Oxford, Oxford University Press, 2015).

[103] We recall that the European Parliament has expressly called for 'a secondary sanctions mechanism that would close any loopholes' in the EU's sanctions against Russia'. European Parliament, Resolution of 16 February 2023 on one year of Russia's invasion and war of aggression against Ukraine (2023/2558(RSP)), para 22.

[104] Regulation 269/2014 (n 1), Annex I, Part A, Entries No 1637, 1821.

[105] Regulation 269/2014 (n 1), Annex I, Part A, Entries No 1723, 1825; Part B, Entries No 241, 296, 412, 441, 475, 476, 477.

[106] Regulation 269/2014 (n 1), Annex I, Part A, Entries No 1645, 1724, 1789 Part B, Entries No 334, 425, 442.

manufacturer. Although these Russian individuals and companies remain outside the jurisdictional scope of the sanctions legislation, they nonetheless have become subject to targeted sanctions due to the fact that they engaged in trading activities that frustrate EU sanctions.

The Commission has clarified that the Council is 'not asking operators who are outside EU jurisdiction to comply with our sanctions', but

> when foreign operators partake in the circumvention of EU sanctions, for instance by re-exporting sanctioned EU goods to Russia, this can be of such nature as to undermine the objectives of EU sanctions. This can then result in CFSP measures taken against them, such as a listing activating financial sanctions and, for natural persons, also a travel ban.[107]

The use of the listing grounds has already resulted in a challenge of the lawfulness of Article 3(1)(h), which is – at the time of writing – pending before the CJEU.[108] In addition to any considerations of compatibility of the new listing grounds with EU law, the Council's decisions to list individuals or entities also needs to meet an adequate evidentiary standard regardless of what criterion is used. As stressed by the CJEU, although the Council enjoys a broad discretion in respect of the general criteria to be taken into consideration for the purpose of adopting restrictive measures, it is required to engage in a careful assessment of the evidence gathered and the facts allegedly established by that evidence and sufficiently substantiate why the listing a of person or entity is warranted in view of the relevant criteria.[109]

10.4. Conclusions

The practice of sanctions compliance indicates that, in respect of past and other sanctions, there has likely been a considerable degree of undercompliance. That compliance concern has become visible as a result of the unprecedented EU sanctions against Russia. However, despite the common agreement on the importance of EU sanctions against Russia, the practice of sanctions compliance raises significant concerns relating, notably, to the decentralised and fragmented model of administration and enforcement of EU sanctions, and the far-reaching effects of EU sanctions that materialise well beyond the borders of the EU and challenge the EU's strong position against the extraterritorial application of EU sanctions. These concerns have become tangible in any everyday business operations of EU and non-EU operators, thus prompting the need for reforms (at EU and Member State level) with effects across the board of all EU sanctions regimes and an increased investment in sanctions compliance strategies and

[107] European Commission, Questions and answers on the eleventh package of restrictive measures against Russia (23 June 2023), available at www.ec.europa.eu/commission/presscorner/detail/en/qanda_23_3449 (emphasis original).

[108] Case T-492/24 Action brought on 20 September 2024 – *Beloglazov v Council*, C/2024/6663.

[109] See Case C-280/12 P *Council v Fulmen and Mahmoudian* [2013] EU:C:2013:775, [64], and the case law cited.

programmes (especially at the business level), due to the EU sanctions against Russia. These initiatives are moving forward, even if many of the underlying legal questions have yet to be addressed by the CJEU.

At the same time, these developments (as well as the case law of the CJEU on, especially, interpretive questions but also the extensive FAQs produced by the Commission) will affect all EU sanctions regimes, and not solely EU sanctions against Russia.

11

The EU's Response to War Crimes

CHLOÉ BRIÈRE

11.1. Introduction

War crimes are usually understood as crimes committed in the context of an armed conflict leading to extremely severe violations of human rights, as civilians are targeted by armed forces in the context of their military operations, violating the applicable international humanitarian law rules. Their legal definition can be notably found in the Nuremberg Principles,[1] later integrated into the Statute of Rome establishing the International Criminal Court.[2]

The EU has repeatedly marked its intention to ensure accountability and avoid the impunity of perpetrators. The European Council has stressed the EU's firm commitment 'to holding to account all commanders, perpetrators and accomplices of war crimes and the other most serious crimes committed in connection with Russia's war of aggression against Ukraine',[3] and the EU's support to investigations by the Prosecutor of the International Criminal Court (OTP-ICC).[4] Its position finds echoes among the other EU institutions, such as the European Commission,[5] the High Representative of the Union,[6] or the European Parliament,[7] that have also insisted the necessity to fight against impunity and support the investigations undertaken on the ground.

The EU is not alone in supporting accountability and ensuring that all perpetrators of war crimes committed in Ukraine are brought to justice. The support of EU

[1] International Law Commission, 'Report of the International Law Commission to the General Assembly' 5 UN Gar Supp No 12, Principle Vi, UN Doc a/1316 (1950).

[2] Rome Statute of the International Criminal Court, United Nations Treaty Series, vol 2187, 3, and in particular its Art 8.

[3] European Council, Conclusions of 9 February 2023, EUCO 1/23, §4.

[4] See also European Council, Conclusions of 15 December 2022, §8.

[5] Statement by President von der Leyen on the establishment of the International Centre for the Prosecution of Crimes of Aggression against Ukraine, 4 March 2023, STATEMENT/23/1363; or Opening remarks by Commissioner Reynders at the Justice Ministers Conference on Support to the International Criminal Court and its Investigations into the Situation in Ukraine, 20 March 2023, SPEECH/23/1786.

[6] Statement on the deadly attack in Kupiansk, 5 October 2023.

[7] European Parliament resolution of 19 May 2022 on the fight against impunity for war crimes in Ukraine, [2022] OJ C479/68, or European Parliament resolution of 19 January 2023 on the establishment of a tribunal on the crime of aggression against Ukraine, [2023] OJ C214/109.

institutions integrates itself among other national, regional and international initiatives and actions led by the EU Member States, third states, specialised intergovernmental organisations or the International Criminal Court (ICC).

This chapter investigates the impact of the war in Ukraine on EU law through an assessment of the EU's role in combating impunity for war crimes to determine whether, since February 2022, it has seen a 'paradigm shift', leading to the development of exceptional measures.

The chapter will demonstrate that the EU has always been involved in supporting international criminal justice, with variations in time in its support mirroring the salience of the issue at the international level. Such support relies on its external competences and activities promoting the respect for international law, and cooperation with specialised international courts and tribunals. It also mobilises internal competences in criminal matters, mostly to accompany the Member States' exercise of their (universal) jurisdiction, but also to support their cooperation with third countries. Since 2022, the intensification of the war in Ukraine returned the issue to the front stage and prompted the adoption of diverse measures. Yet, the main shift relates to the scale of the measures taken, rather than to their nature, with one notable exception: the role of Eurojust, which saw a clear evolution in its mandate and competences.

Section 11.2 addresses the EU's consistent support of international criminal justice, tracing it back to the mid-1990s, and appraising its evolution notably in the mid-2010s. Section 11.3 focuses on the EU's measures adopted in relation to Ukraine since 2014, and those adopted up to 30 November 2023, to ascertain whether they constitute a paradigm shift.

11.2. Tracing the EU's Support to International Criminal Justice

The EU, and its Member States, have supported international criminal justice, notably through the establishment of specialised international jurisdictions, and the adoption and implementation of measures aimed at fighting impunity. Such support is not a surprise, as all EU Member States are parties to the international treaties criminalising international core crimes, including war crimes, such as the Geneva Conventions and their two additional protocols, or the Convention of the Prevention and Punishment of the Crime of Genocide. Furthermore, the issue is 'located at the crossroads of human rights, the rule of law and compliance with international law',[8] and presents inextricable links with the EU's objectives enshrined in Articles 3 and 21 TEU.

Subsection 11.2.1 below retraces how the EU and its Member States promoted in the late 1990s and early 2000s the establishment of ad hoc and permanent international jurisdictions, and the adoption of instruments facilitating their own cooperation, notably to prosecute the criminals who attempted to flee justice in Europe. Subsection 11.2.2

[8] E Aoun, The European Union and International Criminal Justice: Living Up to Its Normative Preferences? (2012) 50 *Journal of Common Market Studies* 21.

then addresses how they reactivated some of these mechanisms since the mid-2010s, notably in relation to the civil war in Syria.

11.2.1. The EU's Support of International and European Accountability Mechanisms

The first initiatives undertaken by the EU to support the fight against the impunity of war criminals can be traced back to the early 1990s. At the time, international criminal justice resurfaced in the discussions of the international community due to the genocide in Rwanda and the mass killings committed during the wars in ex-Yugoslavia. The United Nations Security Council encouraged and supported the creation of ad hoc international criminal tribunals,[9] and the idea of creating a permanent international criminal court was raised by the United Nations General Assembly in several resolutions, leading to the organisation of the UN Diplomatic Conference of Plenipotentiaries on the Establishment of an International Criminal Court in 1997.[10] The EU and its Member States supported these initiatives, and engaged in a multifaceted series of actions aiming to combat impunity for international core crimes, supporting the activities of specific ad hoc tribunals, the establishment of a permanent criminal court, as well as through the adoption of internal instruments supporting cross-border cooperation between EU Member States.

11.2.1.1. Support to the ICTY Through Enlargement Conditionality

The creation of the International Criminal Tribunal for ex-Yugoslavia (ICTY) had special importance for the EU, as it had failed to prevent the eruption of the war and elaborate a common position about the war in the Balkans. In the Stability Pact for Southeast Europe, proclaimed by the international community, the EU was granted a leading role in promoting stability and growth in the region. The EU institutions adopted a new framework for cooperation with the countries of the region: the Stabilisation and Association Process,[11] launched at the Thessaloniki Summit of 2003. This process represented a shift in the EU's approach 'from post-conflict stabilisation and reconstruction (security) to democratic consolidation and European integration (enlargement)'.[12]

References to the cooperation with the ICTY were frequent and consistent, with the EU making use of its leverage to incite countries to cooperate with the ICTY.

[9] UN Security Council, Resolution 827 (1993) [Establishment of the International Tribunal for Prosecution of Persons Responsible for Serious Violations of International Humanitarian Law Committed in the Territory of the Former Yugoslavia since 1991], 25 May 1993, S/RES/827(1993), and UN Security Council, *Resolution 955 (1994)* [Establishment of the International Criminal Tribunal for Rwanda], 8 November 1994, S/RES/955(1994).

[10] United Nations, Codification Division, Office of Legal Affairs, United Nations Diplomatic Conference of Plenipotentiaries on the Establishment of an International Criminal Court, available at legal.un.org/diplomaticconferences/1998_icc.

[11] Commission, Communication on the Stabilisation and Association Process for countries of South-East Europe, COM(1999) 235; and European Council, Cologne, 3–4 June 1999, Conclusions, §§ 72–77.

[12] E Prifti, 'Introduction: from stabilisation to integration' in E Prifti (ed), *The European future of the Western Balkans: Thessaloniki @10* (Paris, EU Institute for Security Studies, 2013) 15.

The Thessaloniki Declaration, adopted in June 2003, stressed the importance of 'full and unequivocal cooperation with the ICTY', including the transfer of all remaining indictees.[13] This echoed the Thessaloniki Agenda for the Western Balkans, in which the Council clearly expressed the conditionality attached to such cooperation 'in particular with regard to the transfer to The Hague of all indictees and full access to documents and witnesses' for further movement towards the EU.[14] The importance of such cooperation, presented as inextricably linked to respect for the states' international obligations, was additionally stressed in the European Partnerships as a key priority and figured among the essential elements underlying the application of the Stabilisation and Association Agreements.

Such 'ICTY-conditionality' was particularly noticeable in the documents and texts concerning Serbia and Croatia. Non-cooperation with the ICTY became a point of tension in the relations between Serbia, the EU and other international partners due to the non-extradition of indictees.[15] In this situation, the EU did not hesitate to stall the accession process as long as cooperation was insufficient,[16] even though it eventually lowered its threshold and granted progress in the country's relations with the EU.[17] The same pressure was applied to Croatia, leading to similar consequences for the country, namely a pause in the accession negotiations between December 2004 and October 2005,[18] as long as indictees were not transferred to the Hague.

Additionally, the Council adopted restrictive measures in direct support of the effective implementation of the ICTY's mandate. It pronounced the freezing of the funds and economic resources of natural persons remaining at large despite their indictment by the ICTY.[19] Such restrictive measures were later extended to restrictions on admission of persons engaged in activities helping them or obstructing the ICTY's effective implementation of this mandate.[20] These measures were amended and renewed as long as ICTY indictees were at large, and the Council ended them only in October 2011 when Goran Hadzic, the last indictee at large, was transferred into the custody of the ICTY.[21]

[13] EU-Western Balkans Summit Thessaloniki, Declaration, 21 June 2003, doc 10229/03 (Presse 163).

[14] ibid, Conclusions.

[15] M Pawelec, and S Grimm, 'Does national identity matter? Political Conditionality and the Crucial Case of Serbia's (Non-)Co-operation with the ICTY' (2014) 52 *Journal of Common Market Studies* 1296.

[16] MA Vachudova, 'EU leverage and national interests in the Balkans: The Puzzles of Enlargement Ten Years On' (2014) 52 *Journal of Common Market Studies* 122. See also Commission, Serbia 2006 Progress Report, SEC (2006)1389, 4.

[17] KH Brodersen, 'The ICTY's Conditionality Dilemma – On the Interaction of Influences of the European Union's Conditionality Policy and the ICTY on the Development of Rule of Law in Serbia' (2014) 22 *European Journal of Crime, Criminal Law and Criminal Justice* 229.

[18] Commission, 2005 Progress Report for Croatia, SEC(2005) 1424, 3; and 2006 Progress Report for Croatia, SEC(2006) 1385, 13.

[19] Council Common Position 2004/293/CFSP of 30 March 2004 renewing measures in support of the effective implementation of the mandate of the ICTY, [2004] OJ L94/65. See also Council Regulation (EC) 1763/2004 of 11 October 2004 imposing certain restrictive measures in support of effective implementation of the mandate of the ICTY, [2004] OJ L315/14.

[20] J Wouters and S Basu, 'The creation of a global criminal justice system: the European Union and the International Criminal Court' in C Ryngaert (ed), *The Effectiveness of International Criminal Justice* (Cambridge, Intersentia, 2009) 124.

[21] Council Decision 2011/705/CFSP of 27 October 2011 repealing Decision 2010/145/CFSP renewing measures in support of the effective implementation of the mandate of the ICTY, [2011] OJ L281/27.

The EU's support was not restricted to the ICTY, even though the latter benefited from the mobilisation of the EU pre-accession leverage to ensure full cooperation from the concerned national authorities. Still within the enlargement policy, the principle of complementarity between international and national proceedings was implemented as the EU insisted and provided support to domestic investigations and prosecutions of international core crimes. It did so through the monitoring of the establishment and work of specialised chambers and tribunals,[22] or the inclusion in the mandate of the EU Rule of Law Mission in Kosovo the assistance to the prosecution of war crimes.[23]

The EU's commitment to international criminal justice was also demonstrated through its financial support to the International Criminal Tribunal for Rwanda,[24] and its coordination with international efforts of EU Member States and other countries in supporting the arrest and transfer of a suspect.[25]

11.2.1.2. Support of the Creation and Work of the ICC

The period was also marked by diplomatic negotiations aiming to create a permanent international criminal court. All the EU Member States (EU-15) participated in the negotiations of the Rome Conference that prepared the Statute of the ICC. However, no common position was initially formulated due to the divergent positions of the UK and France on matters relating to the Court's jurisdiction, the role of the UN Security Council or the independence of the Prosecutor.[26] Their divergences later resolved as they negotiated clauses addressing their concerns.[27] EU unity was restored upon the completion of the negotiations in 1998 with all Member States voting in favour of the Statute of the ICC and ratifying it shortly after, counting among the first 60 required state parties for its entry into force.

Their position and support for the ICC contrasted with the positions adopted by other countries. China, Israel, India, Russia and the US clearly marked their opposition. The Bush Administration notably withdrew the US signature of the Rome Statute and negotiated bilateral immunity agreements (BIAs) aiming at excluding the jurisdiction of the ICC in cases in which US nationals would be suspected of having committed international core crimes and arrested in a foreign state.[28] The EU Member States reacted to these developments by promoting further the role of the ICC, supporting its universal ratification. The Council adopted several Common Positions on the ICC,[29] as well as

[22] See eg Commission, Bosnia and Herzegovina 2011 Progress Report, SEC(2011) 1206, 20.

[23] Council Joint Action 2008/124/CFSP of 4 February 2008 on the European Union Rule of Law Mission in Kosovo (EULEX KOSOVO), [2008] OJ L42/92, Art 3.

[24] unictr.irmct.org/en/news/european-commission-fund-tribunal-projects.

[25] Council's reply to the written question E-4831/2006(ASW), [2006] OJ C329/159.

[26] MLP Groenleer and LG Van Schaik, 'United We Stand? The European Union's International Actorness in the Cases of the International Criminal Court and the Kyoto Protocol' (2007) 45 *Journal of Common Market Studies*, 977.

[27] ibid.

[28] M Groenleer, 'The United States, the European Union, and the International Criminal Court: Similar values, different interests?' (2015) 13 *International Journal of Constitutional Law* 924.

[29] Council Common Position of 11 June 2001 on the International Criminal Court, [2001] OJ L155/19, amended by Council Common Position of 20 June 2002, [2002] OJ L164/1 and Council Common Position of 16 June 2003, [2003] OJ L150/67.

Council Conclusions defining the EU Guiding Principles on BIAs that would restrict their scope.[30] An Action Plan, adopted in 2002, and revised in 2004, defined a series of actions to attain universal ratification and assist third countries in the implementation of the Statute.

The EU's actions[31] included but were not limited to diplomatic statements in multilateral forums,[32] references to the ICC Statute and its ratification in political dialogues with third countries, support to technical assistance measures,[33] or even conditioning cooperation with the EU to the ratification of the ICC Statute.[34] The EU and its Member States also provided financial support to the ICC,[35] and the EU was the first regional organisation signing a cooperation agreement with the ICC in 2006.[36] The agreement focuses on technical aspects regarding the exchange of information and documents, immunity waiver for EU staff, or the EU's assistance in training legal professionals,[37] and it was complemented by security arrangements for the protection of classified information and bilateral cooperation agreements between EU Member States and the ICC.[38] The EU's commitment lasted beyond the 'inception phase' of the ICC, as evidenced by a 2011 Council Decision on the ICC, repeating the EU's support of the widest possible ratification, acceptance, approval and accession to the Rome Statute and its implementation.[39]

11.2.1.3. Adoption of Internal Instruments Supporting International Criminal Justice

The late 1990s and early 2000s were also key for the establishment and the development of the EU area of criminal justice. Favoured by the modernisation of the Treaty provisions defining the objectives and competences of the EU in the field of police and judicial cooperation in criminal matters, the Council, sole legislator at the time, adopted a series of EU secondary law instruments that participate in the creation of an ecosystem favourable to the effective prosecution of international core crimes within the EU Member States and/or before the ICC.

[30] Council, Conclusions on the International Criminal Court, 30 September 2002, doc 12488/1/02.

[31] S Huiriki, *The Institutionalization of the International Criminal Court* (London, Palgrave Macmillan, 2019) 149–50.

[32] EU Presidency Statement at the Assembly of States Parties of the Rome Statute of the International Criminal Court (New York), PRES02-238EN, 2002.

[33] Groenleer and Van Schaik (n 26) 978.

[34] Agreement amending the Partnership Agreement between the members of the African, Caribbean and Pacific Group of States, of the one part, and the European Community and its Member States, of the other part, signed in Cotonou on 23 June 2000 – Final act -Declarations, [2005] OJ L287/4, Article 11(6).

[35] L Davis, 'Discreet effectiveness: The EU and the ICC' in E Drieskens and LG van Schaik (eds), *The EU and Effective Multilateralism* (Abingdon, Routledge, 2014) 89.

[36] Council Decision 2006/313/CFSP of 10 April 2006 concerning the conclusion of the Agreement between the International Criminal Court and the European Union on cooperation and assistance, [2006] OJ L115/49.

[37] O Bekou and A Antoniadis, 'The European Union and the International Criminal Court: An Awkward Symbiosis in Interesting Times' (2007) 7 *International Criminal Law Review* 633.

[38] C Behrmann, 'Strengthening the International Criminal Court Cooperation Regime from the European Union's Perspective' in O Bekou and D Birkett (eds), *Cooperation and the International Criminal Court, Perspectives from Theory and Practice* (Leiden, Brill, 2016) 300–01.

[39] Council Decision 2011/168/CFSP of 21 March 2011 on the International Criminal Court and repealing Common Position 2003/444/CFSP, [2011] *OJ* L76/56.

These internal instruments present a particular relevance in relation to the decision of some EU Member States to revise their national criminal legislation to establish the universal jurisdiction of their courts for international core crimes committed abroad and allowing for instance domestic courts to judge suspected perpetrators of crimes in Rwanda or in the Balkans who attempted to flee justice by taking up residence abroad. This echoes their support to the ICC, and in particular the complementary nature of its jurisdiction.[40]

The Framework Decision on the European Arrest Warrant,[41] adopted in 2002, provides that the mechanism for surrender may be used for persons suspected or convicted for 'crimes falling within the jurisdiction of the ICC'.[42] The latter were subsequently listed in the Annexes defining the scope of application of the EU instruments based on the principle of mutual recognition, facilitating cross-border cooperation between national authorities,[43] including in the execution of judgments.[44] The Framework Decision defining the conditions to establish a joint investigation team[45] (JIT) could also be mobilised for the investigation of such crimes.

In addition, the Council enacted two instruments favouring the implementation by EU Member States of their international obligations under the ICC statute. A Framework Decision adopted in 2003 calls on the Member States to increase cooperation between their respective specialised units.[46] It also provides for measures inciting them to inform law enforcement authorities of the presence of alleged perpetrators and ensure exchange of information between national law enforcement and migration authorities. It was preceded by a Decision creating the EU network for investigation and prosecution of genocide, crimes against humanity and war crimes, later known as the EU Genocide Network.[47] The network has been tasked to support cooperation in these investigations among EU Member States, but also with the EU's external partners. National authorities are represented through national contact points (prosecutors, investigators and authorities specialised in mutual legal assistance) and the Network may further include representatives of ad hoc international tribunals and the ICC.

Lastly, the EU agencies specialised in supporting cross-border cooperation in criminal matters may also support the investigation and prosecution of core international crimes. Eurojust, whose task is to support judicial cooperation, hosts the secretariat of the EU Genocide Network since 2011. It signed in 2007 a Letter of Understanding with the OTP-ICC, in order to enhance contacts between the two organisations and explore areas of cooperation.

[40] Groenleer (n 28) 929.

[41] Council Framework Decision 2002/584/JHA of 13 June 2002 on the European arrest warrant and the surrender procedures between Member States, [2002] OJ L190/1.

[42] ibid, Art 2(2).

[43] See eg Directive 2014/41/EU of the European Parliament and of the Council of 3 April 2014 regarding the European Investigation Order in criminal matters, [2014] OJ L130/1, Annex D.

[44] Council Framework Decision 2008/909/JHA of 27 November 2008 on the application of the principle of mutual recognition to judgments in criminal matters imposing custodial sentences or measures involving deprivation of liberty for the purpose of their enforcement in the European Union, [2008] OJ L327/27.

[45] Council Framework Decision of 13 June 2002 on joint investigation teams, [2002] OJ L162/1.

[46] Council Decision 2003/335/JHA of 8 May 2003 on the investigation and prosecution of genocide, crimes against humanity and war crimes, [2003] OJ L118/12.

[47] Decision 2002/494/JHA setting up a European network of contact points in respect of persons responsible for genocide, crimes against humanity and war crimes, [2002] OJ L167/1.

All these mechanisms, either relying on the EU's external competences, or on its internal competences in criminal matters, demonstrate that the EU institutions and Member States have been neither silent nor absent from international efforts aiming at ensuring the accountability of individuals suspected or accused of having committed international core crimes. They translate their commitment to support international courts and tribunals, and the implementation of the international obligations binding upon the EU Member States. Yet the question remains whether they would be mobilised in response to war crimes committed in other conflicts than those that took place in the 1990s.

11.2.2. Appraisal of EU Mobilisation Pre-2022

The EU's support for international criminal justice was for a time mostly envisaged as an external issue, and the EU's role in combating impunity focused on financial support to international criminal tribunals and courts. Since the creation of the ICC, EU Member States have been its main contributors. Until July 2007, the assessed contribution of the EU Member States had amounted to roughly 75 per cent of the total assessed contributions to the Court, and this percentage decreased to 60 per cent following the accession of Japan in July 2007, which became the biggest contributor.[48] From 2008 onwards, five (and later four) EU Member States, namely Germany, the UK, France, Italy and Spain, have been among the top 10 largest contributors.[49] In addition to these national fundings, the European Commission also directly supported various ICC activities of the (internships and visiting programmes, training, etc),[50] and provided indirect support to its activities,[51] for example by funding of specialised NGOs carrying out ratification campaigns.

However, the EU's approach started to evolve in the mid-2010s 'in part because of the violence of the conflicts (in Belarus, Iraq, Libya and Syria to name a few), and in part owing to their geographical proximity to the EU and direct impact on refugee flows'.[52] The Genocide Network adopted in 2014 a Strategy,[53] endorsed a year later by the Council,[54] which led to various initiatives, such as the instauration of an EU Day against Impunity every 26 May, or the development of the network up to 150 contact points representing EU Member States; observer states, such as Canada, Norway, Switzerland and the USA; EU institutions and agencies; specialised actors (ICC, Interpol, etc) and civil society organisations.[55] As a consequence, the number of cases opened for the

[48] Council, General Secretariat, The European Union and the International Criminal Court, May 2010, 17.

[49] E Wiebelhaus-Brahm and K Ainley, 'The evolution of funding for the International Criminal Court: Budgets, donors and gender justice' (2023) 22 *Journal of Human Rights* 31, and the data set they constituted.

[50] Council, General Secretariat (n 48) 16.

[51] Davis (n 35) 89.

[52] Genocide Network and Eurojust, '20 Years On: Main Developments in the Fight against Impunity for Core International Crimes in the EU' (2022).

[53] Genocide Network Secretariat, 'Conclusions of the 17th meeting of the European Network of Contact Points for investigation and prosecution of genocide, crimes against humanity and war crimes' (2014).

[54] Council, Conclusions on strengthening the fight against impunity for the crime of genocide, crimes against humanity and war crimes within the EU and its Member States, 2015, Doc 15584/2/14.

[55] EU Genocide Network, Strategy to combat impunity for the crime of genocide, crimes against humanity and war crimes within the European Union and its Member States, 2014, 25.

investigation and prosecution of international core crimes within EU Member States increased, even though gaps and loopholes remain.

This can be illustrated through the investigation of crimes committed in the context to the civil war in Syria.[56] Two permanent members of the UN Security Council vetoed the referral of the situation in Syria to the ICC, and the international response was limited to the establishment of an Independent International Commission of Inquiry on the Syrian Arab Republic (IIIM).[57] Its mission is to consolidate, preserve and analyse evidence of violations and prepare files that may facilitate criminal proceedings.[58] Backed with the consensus expressed in the EU strategy for Syria, the EU actors fully supported the IIIM, and decided for instance to include a contact point of the IIIM within the EU Genocide Network. However, they also mobilised the various instruments and mechanisms available in the EU Toolbox.

The EU and the Member States continue to rely on the EU's external competences and its diplomatic role. For instance, the EU organises an annual international Brussels Conference on 'Supporting the future of Syria and the region' gathering EU institutions, states' representatives and international organisations, including the United Nations. On these occasions, accountability for international crimes may be addressed,[59] and the conference also raises funds for humanitarian and resilience assistance projects, including projects to support the collection and analysis of evidence material related to potential crimes under international criminal and humanitarian law.

The EU actors also supported the identification of persons who have left Syria and reside within the EU, either victims or witnesses of international core crimes, or perpetrators.[60] Several EU Member States launched investigations against former members of Syrian authorities suspected of war crimes and other international core crimes, relying on their national legislations granting universal or extraterritorial jurisdiction to their courts.[61] In that regard, the EU internal instruments proved their added value, as Member States were able to coordinate their actions through the EU Genocide Network, or the establishment of a joint investigation team between France and Germany in the 'Caesar case',[62] building upon the 'Caesar files', a document containing over 26,000 pictures of the torture of victims in mass detention centres of the Syrian regime. While the investigations have already led to the convictions of two persons by the Higher Regional Court of Koblenz,[63] they also reveal limits in national

[56] For an account of the crimes, see Report of the Fact-finding Mission on Syria, 2011, available at www.ohchr.org/en/press-releases/2011/08/syria-un-human-rights-office-publishes-fact-finding-mission-report; or the work of the Independent International Commission of Inquiry on the Syrian Arab Republic, available at www.ohchr.org/en/hr-bodies/hrc/iici-syria/independent-international-commission.

[57] 'International, Impartial and Independent Mechanism to assist in the investigation and prosecution of persons responsible for the most serious crimes under International Law committed in the Syrian Arab Republic since March 2011.'

[58] UN General Assembly, Resolution 71/248, 11 January 2017, A/RES/71/248.

[59] See eg, the programme for the 2023 edition with a panel on 'Furthering justice and accountability for the Syrian people – state of play of ongoing efforts by civil society, international organisations and national jurisdictions and the way forward'.

[60] O Bekou, 'State of play of the existing instruments for combating impunity for international crimes' (2020) European Parliament, PE 603. 499, 62.

[61] W Kaleck and P Kroker, 'Syrian Torture Investigations in Germany and Beyond' (2018) 16 *Journal of International Criminal Justice* 173, including an account of convictions in Germany, Sweden, Austria or Spain.

[62] For an overview, see Bekou (n 60) 60.

[63] Eurojust, 'Syrian official sentenced to life for crimes against humanity with support of joint investigation team assisted by Eurojust' Press release (13 January 2022).

legislations regulating the exercise of universal or extraterritorial jurisdiction in relation to core crimes committed abroad.[64] For example, French law the requirement of 'double criminality'[65] must be met to prosecute foreign perpetrators residing on French territory. In 2021, the French Court of Cassation found that the condition was not met for a case in which a Syrian national was prosecuted for acts of torture and barbary, crimes against humanity and complicity for such crimes. The Court pointed out that Syrian law does not provide for an offence comparable to the crimes against humanity as defined under French law, subsequently quashing the judgment and declaring all French jurisdictions incompetent to judge the case.[66] The judgment could have potentially jeopardised other ongoing proceedings but was thankfully overruled in two posterior judgments rendered in 2023.[67]

In parallel to such developments, the mandates of Eurojust and Europol, the two EU actors competent in criminal matters, were extended, as both received a clear competence and additional means to support cross-border cooperation in combating genocide, crimes against humanity and war crimes.[68] This reform induced an increased attention to international crimes in their work. Europol established an Analysis Project Core International Crimes (AP CIC), an operational analysis platform and database to collect, cross-check and analyse various types of information and intelligence related to core international crimes, notably used to support the ICC's work.[69] Besides its work to support the JITs eventually created to investigate such crimes, Eurojust identified the ICC as one of the international organisations with whom operational cooperation could be developed.[70]

These examples demonstrate how the EU and its Member States have supported the development of international criminal justice and the combatting of the impunity of perpetrators of international core crimes with the adoption and implementation of a dense array of instruments, networks, measures and practices. They constitute classical forms of EU actions, relying on the competences granted to the EU in criminal matters and/or in external relations. The most striking element is potentially the dynamism of the EU itself on a subject traditionally perceived as closer to Member States' sovereignty, and the support of national intra-EU actors for such a role being played by the EU. The mechanisms put in place in the late 1990s and early 2000s were relied upon to assist the investigation and prosecution in the EU of those involved in the commission of international crimes in Syria. New competences were granted to Europol and Eurojust, demonstrating the shift that occurred, putting an end to the perception that international criminal justice concerned only external competences and actions.

[64] Genocide Network and Eurojust (n 56) 8.

[65] ibid. This means that: '(i) the suspect must be a national of a State Party to the Rome Statute; (ii) the crime must have been committed on the territory of a State party; or (iii) the offences must be punishable under the law of the State where they were committed.'

[66] Cour de cassation, Pourvoi no 21-81.344, 24 November 2021.

[67] Cour de Cassation, Assemblée Plénière, 12 May 2023, Pourvoi no 22-82.468 and Pourvoi no 22-80.057.

[68] Regulation (EU) 2018/1727 of 14 November 2018 on the European Union Agency for Criminal Justice Cooperation (Eurojust), [2018] OJ L295/138, Annex I, and Regulation (EU) 2016/794 of 11 May 2016 on the European Union Agency for Law Enforcement Cooperation (Europol), [2016] OJ L135/53, Annex I.

[69] See Europol's web pages on genocide, crimes against humanity and war crimes: www.europol.europa.eu/crime-areas-and-trends/crime-areas/genocide-crimes-against-humanity-and-war-crimes.

[70] Eurojust's website: www.eurojust.europa.eu/states-and-partners/third-countries/international-agreements.

The EU's response to the war crimes committed in Ukraine thus does not intervene in a legal vacuum, and the EU has clearly perceived the importance of these questions. Yet, the scale of the violations committed in Ukraine, as well as the international context favourable to the mobilisation of international, regional and national accountability mechanisms, may influence the EU's role in such matters.

11.3. Assessing the EU's Response to the Situation in Ukraine: Is there a Qualitative Shift?

The situation in Ukraine and the tensions surrounding the country's aspirations towards closer cooperation with the EU precede the Russian invasion in February 2022. In 2014 and 2015, Russia's annexation of the Crimean Peninsula and the start of the conflict in the Donbas region triggered the application of mechanisms for accountability for core international crimes. Russia is not party to the Rome Statute, but, after twice accepting the ICC's jurisdiction as provided in Article 12(3) of the Rome Statute, Ukraine became a State party from 1 January 2025. The first declaration was made concerning the 'Maidan crimes', and the second one for the alleged crimes in Crimea and eastern Ukraine from 20 February 2014 onwards.[71] In December 2020, the ICC Prosecutor Fatou Bensouda closed its preliminary examination, concluding 'that a reasonable basis exists to believe that a broad range of crimes falling within its jurisdiction have been committed in Ukraine',[72] by different sides to the conflict.[73] However, she left the decision to request the opening of an investigation to her successor due to capacity constraints of her office, and the situation appeared stalled from the perspective of the ICC.

Within the EU, the response was at the time mostly focused on foreign policy actions, with the signature of the Association Agreement with Ukraine in 2014; diplomatic measures, such as the cancellation of an EU–Russia Summit, or the suspension of bilateral discussion on visa matters; and the adoption of autonomous EU sanctions relying on its competences in the field of CFSP.[74] The latter also included the deployment of the Advisory Mission for Civilian Security Sector Reform Ukraine, tasked to assist Ukraine in the field of civilian security sector reform, including police and rule of law,[75] whose aim was to improve accountability of security services and restore public confidence in them following their use of violence during the Euromaidan protests.[76]

The EU's instruments in the field of criminal justice were also mobilised, especially after Malaysian Airlines flight MH17 was shot on 17 July 2014 while overflying the airspace above Donetsk, a territory held by pro-Russian separatists. The resulting

[71] I Marchuk and A Wanigasuriya, 'The ICC concludes its preliminary examination in Crimea and Donbas: What's next for the situation in Ukraine?' EJIL:Talk! (16 December 2020).

[72] Statement of the Prosecutor, Fatou Bensouda, on the conclusion of the preliminary examination in the situation in Ukraine.

[73] Marchuk and Wanigasuriya (n 71).

[74] European Council, Statement of the Heads of State or Government on Ukraine Brussels, 6 March 2014.

[75] Council Decision 2014/486/CFSP of 22 July 2014 on the European Union Advisory Mission for Civilian Security Sector Reform Ukraine (EUAM Ukraine), [2014] OJ L217/42.

[76] NIM Nováky, 'Why so Soft? The European Union in Ukraine' (2015) 36 *Contemporary Security Policy* 244.

crash caused the death of all 298 passengers and crew, coming from 16 different countries. The Dutch authorities addressed an urgent request for assistance to Eurojust, which organised a series of coordination meetings and assisted in the setting up in a Joint Investigation Team between the Netherlands, Australia, Malaysia, Belgium and Ukraine. The possible qualification and prosecution of this event as a war crime was initially envisaged,[77] but was later discarded due to insufficient evidence.[78] Nevertheless, three of the four defendants were convicted for causing the flight's crash and the murder of those occupants.[79]

The EU's mobilisation significantly increased after the Russian invasion of Ukraine in February 2022, due to the gravity of the situation, with repeated reports of civilian buildings being targeted, or the discovery of the atrocities committed in Bucha. While the EU is not the only actor engaging in diverse activities to report and assist the investigation of the war crimes committed in Ukraine, the following sections will cover the mechanisms it supports, with a view to ascertaining to what extent they may constitute a qualitative shift in the EU's role in combating impunity for war crimes.

11.3.1. The EU's Reliance on Foreign Policy Measures: A Change in Scale, not in Nature

In contrast with the investigation and prosecution of war crimes committed in Ukraine before 2022, the OTP-ICC decided very quickly to open an investigation into the situation in Ukraine on 2 March 2022, after receiving a State Party referral from Lithuania, followed by a joint referral from 38 state parties the next day (including the remaining 26 EU Member States, the EEA countries, the UK, Switzerland, etc).[80] Although it is difficult to isolate strictly the EU's role, this section analyses the EU's measures adopted in the framework of its external competences. Such measures demonstrate not only how the issue remains partially envisaged as a foreign policy matter, but also offer us the opportunity to assess whether they constitute innovations in the EU's role in combating impunity.

The EU and its Member States intensified their financial support to the ICC's investigations, notably through the adoption of an exceptional assistance measure regarding Ukraine and the need to strengthen the investigation and prosecution capacities of the ICC.[81] The attribution of exceptional resources was called for by the OTP-ICC in February 2022, when he announced seeking 'partnerships and contributions of all States in order to address our needs for additional recourse across all situations addressed for my office'.[82] The EU and its Member States responded and announced the

[77] Council, Conclusions on strengthening the fight against impunity (n 54).

[78] Dutch Public Prosecution Service, Report 'Findings of the JIT MH17 investigation into the crew members of the buk TEAR and those responsible in the chain of command' (February 2023) 64.

[79] The Hague District Court, Judgments of 17 November 2022, ECLI:NL:RBDHA:2022:12216/12217/12218.

[80] ICC, 'Situation in Ukraine', ICC-01/22, available at www.icc-cpi.int/situations/ukraine.

[81] Commission Implementing Decision of 8 June 2022 on an exceptional assistance measure regarding Ukraine, C(2022) 3734 final.

[82] ICC-OTP, Statement of ICC Prosecutor, Karim A.A. Khan QC, on the Situation in Ukraine: Receipt of Referrals from 39 States Parties and the Opening of an Investigation, 2 March 2022.

allocation of extra resources.[83] The EU relied on its main fund for its external activities known as the Global Europe Fund,[84] and the funds allocated therein for exceptional and unforeseen situations, including the support for international criminal tribunals.[85] As described in the Commission Implementing Decision, the EU provided €7.25 million to support the investigation and prosecution capacities of the ICC, notably to upscale the data storage and processing infrastructure of the Office of the Prosecutor, and increase analytical and forensic capacity for new types of evidence, including digital.[86] To measure the scale of the EU's response, it is worth highlighting that the EU's support to the ICC had traditionally involved a much lower sum. For example, the direct EU financial support to the ICC was €2.5 million in 2000–06; €2 million in 2007–09[87] and €7 million in 2021–27.[88] This means that the amount attributed in 2022, to be spent in a period of maximum 18 months, corresponds to the same amount granted to support the ICC over a period of six years. Such increased financial support in times of crisis is symptomatic of the instability of the funding granted to the ICC and its sensitivity to the geopolitical context, which may continue to nourish the 'widespread perception of the ICC as an expensive slow and unbalanced court in which some donors have disproportionate influence'.[89] It does not however constitute an exceptional measure for the EU to implement, as the possibility to provide additional support had already been envisaged in the fund Global Europe.

Beyond their support to the ICC, the EU and its Member States are supporting the investigation and prosecution of war crimes, crimes against humanity and other war-related offences by the Ukrainian authorities. The number of cases opened in the country reached more than 80,000 cases in 2023, placing an additional burden on the national criminal justice system.[90] Building on the principle of complementarity between international and domestic criminal proceedings, the EU's support led to the revision of the mandate of the EU Advisory Mission (EUAM) Ukraine on 13 April 2022 to provide for its 'support to Ukrainian authorities to facilitate the investigation and prosecution of international crimes'.[91] This includes notably the provision of strategic advice on the investigation and prosecution of core international crimes, the necessary amendments of the national legislation or the related communication strategy; as well as the donation of funds and equipment to national authorities. Such changes in the national legislation were necessary to, for instance, foresee the possibility for the OTP-ICC to perform its investigations on Ukrainian territory and allow the transfer to the ICC of materials and

[83] A Singh, 'International Criminal Court: How is the Court Funded?' (London Politica, June 2023).

[84] Regulation (EU) 2021/947 of the European Parliament and of the Council of 9 June 2021 establishing the Neighbourhood, Development and International Cooperation Instrument – Global Europe, [2021] OJ L209/1.

[85] ibid, Annex IV, 1(e).

[86] Commission Implementing Decision of 8 June 2022 on an exceptional assistance measure regarding Ukraine, Annex 3.

[87] Davis (n 35) 89.

[88] international-partnerships.ec.europa.eu/system/files/2022-01/mip-2021-c2021-9620-human-rights-democracy-annex_en.pdf.

[89] Wiebelhaus-Brahm and Ainley (n 49) 43.

[90] European Commission, Ukraine 2023 Report, SWD(2023) 699 final, 20.

[91] Council Decision (CFSP) 2022/638 of 13 April 2022 amending Decision 2014/486/CFSP on the European Union Advisory Mission for Civilian Security Sector Reform Ukraine (EUAM Ukraine), [2022] OJ L117/38.

evidence gathered by national authorities,[92] to legalise the use of foreign forensic expert opinions, or improve the activities of a joint investigation team.[93] These reforms did not block domestic criminal proceedings. As of November 2023, 66 perpetrators had been convicted according to the Ukrainian Prosecutor General[94] and trials, whose legality is doubtful, also took place in the Russian-occupied territories.[95]

The change in the EUAM's mandate does not represent a novelty, as the mandates of previous EU missions had included activities linked to the fight against impunity,[96] and impunity for core international crimes.[97] It is not even the most ambitious as the EUAM is not directly involved in the conduct of investigations and prosecutions. It differs from the mandate granted to the EU mission in Kosovo, which is currently under scrutiny before the CJEU due to the actions for damages brought by individuals who lost family members due to the commission of war crimes and claim that the EU mission did not properly investigate these crimes.[98] Other EU activities to support domestic proceedings include specialised forensic training organised jointly by CEPOL, the EUAM Ukraine and the Council of Europe,[99] and training organised by the EU European Judicial Training Network (EJTN)[100] and the EU Genocide Network.[101]

These actions are coordinated with the efforts of other international actors (OSCE Moscow Mechanism, UN Commission of Inquiry), through the Atrocity Crimes Advisory Group, set up in May 2022 by the USA, the EU and the UK.[102] They are furthermore complemented by the judicial decisions taken in several Member States to open investigations on international crimes committed in Ukraine relying on their universal jurisdiction,[103] or the detachment of national experts to Ukraine. All these activities, either implemented by the EU, or the Member States, correspond to rather classic forms of cooperation and assistance. The war in Ukraine nevertheless had an important impact on the conclusion of an international agreement, today known as the Ljubljana–The Hague Convention, to facilitate extradition and mutual legal assistance

[92] O Kaluzhna and K Shunevych, 'Liability Mechanisms for War Crimes Committed as a Result of Russia's Invasion of Ukraine in February 2022: Types, Chronicle of the First Steps and Problems' (2022) 5 *Access to Justice in Eastern Europe* 185.

[93] ibid, 191.

[94] 'Ukraine says it has evidence of 109,000 Russian war crimes', Politico (US edition) (18 November 2023).

[95] Amnesty International, 'Ukraine: Prisoners of war "sentenced" to prison following sham trials in Russian-occupied territories' (10 March 2023).

[96] Council Decision 2014/219/CFSP of 15 April 2014 on the European Union CSDP mission in Mali (EUCAP Sahel Mali), Art 2(2)(c).

[97] Council Joint Action on EULEX KOSOVO (n 25).

[98] Advocate General Ćapeta, Opinion delivered on 23 November 2023, Joined cases C-29/22P and C-44/22P, ECLI:EU:C:2023:901.

[99] EU Agencies Network, EU Agencies repository on actions concerning Ukraine, 9.

[100] EJTN, 6 December 2022, available at ejtn.eu/news/ejtn-is-addressing-the-challenges-of-the-war-in-ukraine-through-training-for-ukrainian-judiciary.

[101] Council, Options paper on ensuring full accountability of individuals responsible for international crimes in Ukraine, doc 15321/22, 9.

[102] www.eeas.europa.eu/eeas/helping-ukraine-bring-war-criminals-account_en.

[103] Kaluzhna and Shunevych (n 92), 187–88. See also Council, Judicial responses and the fight against impunity regarding crimes committed in connection with Russia's war of aggression against Ukraine – State of play, doc 12838/22, 2.

in the prosecution of international core crimes, an initiative in which several Member States, notably Belgium, the Netherlands and Slovenia, prominently participated.[104]

Lastly, the EU mobilised the regime of sanctions it put in place in 2014 to pressure Russia into ending its actions in Ukraine.[105] Since February 2022, the EU has expanded significantly the scope of this regime through no less than 22 amendments (as of December 2023). The Council added to the list of targeted persons, ie individuals who are suspected to have been involved in the commission of war crimes. The list notably includes, since June 2022, 65 individuals belonging to the Russian Armed Forces, ranging from colonels (nos 1,111–1,116), lieutenant colonels (nos 1,116–1,130) to majors (nos 1,131–1,155), who were leading the actions of military units which killed, raped and tortured civilians in Bucha.[106] Although their actions are referred to as constituting 'crimes against humanity and war crimes', the statements of reasons relies on the general listing criteria, namely their responsibility for undermining or threatening the territorial integrity, sovereignty and independence of Ukraine, or stability or security in Ukraine.

The same criteria was mobilised to add to the list persons who denied the responsibility of the Russian Armed Forces for the war crimes committed in Bucha (no 1,391 and no 14,878), as well as participants in other atrocities, such as Mikhail Mizintsev, identified as the commander overseeing the siege of Mariupol (no 1,157), or 36 persons involved in the illegal transportation of Ukrainian children to Russia, among whom Maria Alekseyevna Lvova-Belova (no 1,210, listed as of 21 July 2022), subject of an arrest warrant issued by the ICC on 17 March 2023.[107] Their inclusion in the list of the persons covered by the sanction regime against Russia differs from the restrictive measures taken to support the investigation of the ICTY, which targeted persons who had been indicted, or persons assisting them to escape justice. In contrast, the persons now listed are included on the list before criminal investigations and trials took place.

These sanctions serve to signal the EU's commitment to international norms,[108] and rely on the assumption that EU restrictive measures are administrative in nature, even when they are increasingly used in response to international crimes.[109] It is for instance foreseen under the EU sanction regime against serious human rights violations and abuses,[110] under which restrictive measures may apply against natural and legal

[104] B de Oliveira Biasatti and E Amani, 'The Ljubljana–The Hague Convention on Mutual Legal Assistance: Was the Gap Closed?' EJIL:Talk! (12 June 2023).

[105] Council Decision 2014/145/CFSP of 17 March 2014 concerning restrictive measures in respect of actions undermining or threatening the territorial integrity, sovereignty and independence of Ukraine, [2014] OJ L78/16.

[106] Council Decision (CFSP) 2022/883 of 3 June 2022 amending Decision 2014/145/CFSP, [2022] OJ L153/92. A reference to their accountability for violations of international humanitarian law can be found in the Preamble (§3).

[107] ICC, 'Situation in Ukraine: ICC judges issue arrest warrants against Vladimir Vladimirovich Putin and Maria Alekseyevna Lvova-Belova' Press release (17 March 2023).

[108] A Hofer, 'The Punitive Effect of the EU's Restrictive Measures against Russia' in F Bossuyt and EP van Elsuwege (eds), *Principled pragmatism in practice: The EU's policy towards Russia after Crimea* (Leiden, Brill, 2021) 87.

[109] A Moiseienko, 'Crime and Sanctions: Beyond Sanctions as a Foreign Policy Tool' (2023) ANU College of Law Research Paper No 23.4.

[110] Council Decision (CFSP) 2020/1999 of 7 December 2020 concerning restrictive measures against serious human rights violations and abuses, [2020] OJ L410I/13.

persons who are responsible or providing support for acts of genocide, crimes against humanity, and behaviours that may correspond to war crimes (torture, extrajudicial, summary or arbitrary executions, etc). On that basis, sanctions were enacted against Gabriel Moses Lokujo, Major General of the South Sudan People's Defence Forces, as his forces remained in an area in which civilians were displaced and the safety and security of the civilian communities continue to be in jeopardy. This instrument is also used to target the Wagner Group and associated individuals suspected of having been involved in torture, extrajudicial, summary or arbitrary executions and killings in Syria, Libya, Sudan or Central African Republic.[111]

The paragraphs above highlight that in reaction to the war in Ukraine, the EU has mobilised the instruments it traditionally relies on for the pursuit of foreign policy objectives. These measures do not constitute a fundamental change, even though the scale of the EU's response is different. The financial resources made available are higher than before, and the restrictive measures have targeted a higher number of persons on a relatively short timeframe and prior to the issuance of arrest warrants against them. This new trend in EU sanctions regimes may mostly be explained by the ambition to counteract the impunity the alleged perpetrators may enjoy in their home country.[112]

11.3.2. The EU's Competences in Criminal Matters and the New Role Granted to Eurojust

The EU's response to the war crimes committed in Ukraine also mobilised the legal basis available in the TFEU for the EU's actions in criminal matters. Some actions complement foreign policy measures, such as the amendment of the list of euro-crimes foreseen in Article 83(1) TFEU to include as a crime the violation of EU restrictive measures,[113] and the negotiation of a Directive providing minimum rules on the definition of the offences and sanctions applicable.[114] However, the EU and its Member States also mobilised tools and actors specialised in supporting cross-border cooperation in criminal matters, among EU Member States but also with third countries.

The setting up of a Joint Investigation Team (JIT) with the support of Eurojust constitutes a clear example of that trend. The JIT was set up on 25 March 2022 initially among the Polish, Lithuanian and Ukrainian judicial authorities, which were later joined by judicial authorities from Estonia, Latvia, Slovakia (May 2022) and Romania (October 2022), as well as Europol (October 2023). The purpose of the JIT is to facilitate the exchange of information and evidence, and support the criminal investigations into the crimes committed in Ukraine. It is not the first JIT supported by Eurojust involving Ukrainian authorities, as they previously participated in the one set up to investigate the

[111] Listing nos 16–26 (for natural persons) and nos 6– 12 (for legal persons).

[112] Moiseienko (n 109) 31.

[113] Council Decision (EU) 2022/2332 of 28 November 2022 on identifying the violation of Union restrictive measures as an area of crime that meets the criteria specified in Article 83(1) TFEU, [2022] OJ L308/18.

[114] Commission, Proposal for a Directive on the definition of criminal offences and penalties for the violation of Union restrictive measures, COM(2022) 684.

crash of the MH17 airplane. While its participation has been facilitated by the posting of a Ukrainian Liaison Prosecutor at Eurojust since 2018,[115] the support of Eurojust remains similar to the support provided to other JITs (operational, legal and financial support). Other JITs have been set up for the prosecution of war crimes, such as the one to investigate crimes committed by foreign terrorist fighters against the Yezidi population in Syria and Iraq.[116]

A few elements nevertheless demonstrate the unprecedented international attention focused on the prosecution of war crimes committed in Ukraine. For the first time the OTP-ICC is participating in a JIT,[117] and the US Department of Justice and the seven participating national authorities signed a Memorandum of Understanding to enhance the coordination in their respective investigations.[118] More generally, the 2022 annual meeting of the Network of National JIT Experts focused on supporting JITs in times of conflict, addressing directly some of the issues faced in the prosecution of core international crimes and the implication of the ICC in a JIT.[119] Additionally, Eurojust prepared with the EU Genocide Network and the OTP-ICC guidelines for civil society organisations on 'Documenting international crimes and human rights violations for criminal accountability purposes', providing information on how to collect and preserve information related to international crimes and human rights violations, which may become admissible evidence in court.[120] These developments nourish the EU's efforts in combating impunity, reflect the evolutions in the field of criminal justice, notably regarding the role of private actors, and are relevant beyond the prosecution of those committed in Ukraine.

The main change in the EU's response to the war crimes committed in Ukraine might be found in the new tasks granted to Eurojust, whose role evolved substantially after February 2022, giving a new impetus to its operational activities and capacities. Eurojust has long been compared with its sister agency, Europol, pinpointing notably their different capacities in the processing and analysis of information. The gap between the two agencies has started to close in recent years, for instance through the development by Eurojust of a Judicial Counter-Terrorism Register, allowing the agency to identify links between investigations, signal coordination needs and analyse the casework to pinpoint ways to improve the judicial response to terrorism, including the protection of its victims. The Regulation, proposed in 2021 to improve its functioning and integrate it better into Eurojust's Case Management System, was adopted in October 2023.[121]

[115] Eurojust's website, page on Ukraine: www.eurojust.europa.eu/states-and-partners/third-countries/liaison-prosecutors/ukraine.

[116] Eurojust, 'Belgium and Netherlands sign up to joint investigation team targeting crimes against Yezidi victims in Syria and Iraq' Press release (26 June 2023).

[117] Eurojust, Highlights of the Annual Meeting of the Network of National Experts on Joint Investigation Teams (The Hague, 5 and 6 October 2022), Doc 16201/22.

[118] Eurojust, 'Joint investigation team into alleged core international crimes in Ukraine: one year of international collaboration' Press release (24 March 2023).

[119] Eurojust (n 117).

[120] Eurojust, Documenting International Crimes and Human Rights Violations for Criminal Accountability Purposes: Guidelines for Civil Society Organisations (21 September 2022).

[121] Regulation (EU) 2023/2131 of the European Parliament and of the Council of 4 October 2023 as regards digital information exchange in terrorism cases, [2023] OJ L2023/2131.

However, the war in Ukraine prompted another change in the mandate of the agency, negotiated and adopted in little more than a month.[122] Eurojust is entrusted with the new task of creating a data management and storage facility enabling the preservation, analysis and storage of digital judicial evidence of 'genocide, crimes against humanity and war crimes and related offences, including those that may be committed in Ukraine in the context of the current hostilities.'[123] The agency shall enable the exchange of such evidence, or otherwise make it directly available to the competent national and international judicial authorities, in particular the ICC.[124] The measure is justified by the risk that evidence related to core international crimes and related criminal offences cannot be safely stored on the territory where the hostilities take place,[125] and Eurojust's expertise can serve to support the preservation, analysis and storage of evidence as far as its admissibility before courts and its reliability are concerned, thus assisting in building cases in national and international investigations.[126] The Core International Crimes Evidence Database (CICED) became operational in February 2023, and is 'fed' only by competent national authorities from EU Member States and countries with Liaison Prosecutors at Eurojust, filtering the information coming from individuals and non-governmental or civil society organisations.

This qualitative step forward is multifaceted. Firstly, the CICED is not solely envisaged as a tool destined to support intra-EU cooperation, but foresees close cooperation with non-EU and international judicial actors. It is the first time an EU database foresees equal access for EU Member States and external partners, the latter being usually left out of such databases (eg no access to Eurojust's case management system or Europol's databases) and relying on more classic mechanisms of information exchange.[127] Secondly, Eurojust is competent to analyse the evidence centrally stored in the CICED, both for operational and strategic purposes. Eurojust has long developed such capacities to identify potential links between cases (operational analysis) or recurring issues in judicial cooperation (strategic analysis) on the basis of the information stored in Eurojust's Case Management System, or the Judicial Counter-Terrorism Register. Yet, the agency's analytical tasks within the CICED are more extensive. They should serve to identify evidentiary gaps, parallel investigations and *advise on prosecution strategies* (operational analysis), and to prepare thematic reports on specific aspects, such as sexual and gender-based violence (strategic analysis).[128] They also serve the *protection of victims*, as Eurojust maintains a complete overview of all evidence collected, including through

[122] Regulation (EU) 2022/838 of the European Parliament and of the Council of 30 May 2022 as regards the preservation, analysis and storage at Eurojust of evidence relating to genocide, crimes against humanity, war crimes and related criminal offences, [2022] OJ L148/1. The proposal was published on 25 April 2022.

[123] Regulation (EU) 2022/838, Preamble, §7 and amendment to Art 4(1).

[124] ibid.

[125] ibid. Preamble, §9.

[126] ibid. §§10–11.

[127] C Brière, 'Cooperation of Europol and Eurojust with external partners in the fight against crime: a legal appraisal' in M Chamon, E Vos and H Hofmann (eds), *The External Dimension of EU Agencies and Bodies* (Cheltenham, UK, Edward Elgar, 2019).

[128] Eurojust, CICED leaflet (2023), available at www.eurojust.europa.eu/sites/default/files/assets/ciced-leaflet.pdf.

interviews with victims, with a view to avoiding revictimisation through repeated interviews.[129]

This evolution makes Eurojust as a central player in the prosecution of the war crimes committed in Ukraine, and its position is further emphasised by its other task of supporting the International Centre for the Prosecution of the Crime of Aggression against Ukraine. This Centre is mandated to prepare and contribute to any future prosecutions of the crime of aggression, irrespective of the jurisdiction before which these will be brought. It is, like the additional financial support to the ICC, funded by the European Commission's Service for Foreign Policy Instruments (starting at €8.3 million).[130]

The role of the EU in supporting accountability for international core crimes has thus evolved, albeit in a limited manner. Its position remains centred around supporting international and national competent authorities responsible for bringing perpetrators to justice. Nevertheless, while it continues to play such a role, the EU's role has acquired a new dimension since 2022, notably due to the new competences granted to Eurojust, which also reflects how internal integration within the EU area of criminal justice has progressed. The creation of the CICED opened to competent authorities from third countries or the participation of the OTP-ICC and the USA to the JIT investigating international core crimes in Ukraine illustrates how the EU, and especially Eurojust, have acquired the trust of national and international actors, as well as better visibility on the international scene.

11.4. Conclusions

The purpose of this chapter was to assess the role of the EU in combating impunity for war crimes, to determine the impact of the war in Ukraine on EU law. The EU's commitment to international criminal justice has been constant and repeatedly expressed since the mid-1990s. The war in Ukraine is unfortunately not an exceptional circumstance in which the tools and mechanisms established internationally and within the EU are mobilised to investigate, prosecute and convict perpetrators of war crimes within and outside Europe. From a legal perspective, the main impact of the war on EU law has been identified in relation to Eurojust, whose mandate has been revised and expanded.

However, the war in Ukraine reflects the influence of the international context on the EU's response to war crimes. The openness and willingness of the Ukrainian authorities to collaborate with international partners, including the ICC, in the prosecution of these crimes, as well as the consensus within the international community on the need to ensure accountability, have allowed the EU to fully mobilise the instruments at its disposal. This demonstrates its clear responsiveness to the expectation that, as an actor dedicated to the respect for international law and human rights,

[129] ibid.

[130] eu4ukraine.eu/en/whats-happening-en/news-en/history-in-the-making-en.html.

it plays a key role in combating impunity, especially when the commission of war crimes takes place within its close neighbourhood. This contrasts with the EU's struggles in agreeing on and maintaining a common position on the conflict between Israel and Hamas,[131] even though attacks on civilians are reported almost daily since 7 October 2023, illustrating further the sensitivity of the EU's response to the international context.

[131] 'Israel-Hamas war: Tensions flare across EU ahead of leaders' summit' Euronews (6 December 2023).

12

The Impact of the Russian War against Ukraine on EU Environmental Law: Environmental Deregulation in Times of Energy Crisis?

ERRIKETI TLA DA SILVA*

12.1. Introduction

The EU is facing the dual challenge of ensuring energy security and compliance with environmental commitments in the wake of geopolitical turmoil. Russia's aggression in Ukraine prompted a reassessment of the EU's energy situation, with the need to focus on reducing reliance on Russian fossil fuels, and revealed the intricate web of connections between energy and environmental policies.

Russia's invasion of Ukraine disrupted energy supplies and initially sent Europe into a state of panic. The EU, heavily dependent on Russian fossil fuels, faced an unprecedented energy crisis. This situation led to demands from the industry, agriculture and fisheries sectors to delay the implementation of environmental regulations and to ask for greater financial support. The immediate impact on energy supply and prices, as well as the urgent need to reduce dependency on Russian fossil fuels, demanded a fast response. However, tackling this crisis had to be reconciled with the ultimate goal of achieving climate neutrality by 2050 as part of the European Green Deal.[1]

In order to address this unprecedented crisis, the EU launched the REPowerEU plan,[2] representing a big step towards energy transition and reducing dependency on Russian fossil fuels. A series of targeted amendments to existing energy and environment legislation and to the Recovery and Resilience Facility were introduced in order

* I would like to express my sincere gratitude to Professor Dr N Notaro for his invaluable guidance and expertise during the process of writing this chapter.

[1] Commission, Communication from the Commission, 'The European Green Deal' [2019] COM(2019) 640 final.

[2] Commission, Communication from the Commission to the European Parliament, the European Council, the Council, the European Economic and Social Committee and The Committee of the Regions, REPowerEU Plan [2022] COM(2022) 230 final.

to increase renewable energy production and to ensure the financing of the plan, while demonstrating a commitment to accelerate the green transition. It has been claimed that this rapid shift could advance the green transition by five to 10 years, signalling a significant commitment to the acceleration of the deployment of renewable energy.[3]

While the EU's swift response through the REPowerEU plan and its related legislative amendments reflects a commitment to accelerate the green transition, this complex set of legislative changes needs careful analysis and implementation to avoid environmental degradation. Amidst the urgency of addressing energy security, crucial environmental considerations come to the forefront as the Union is facing a twofold challenge. Firstly, the direct consequences of the war, including pollution and destruction of nature and infrastructure in Ukraine,[4] raised the imperative to align post-war reconstruction efforts with EU environmental standards. This monumental task necessitates comprehensive coordination and funding to rebuild infrastructure and restore natural ecosystems, and is essential in order to ensure Ukraine's path towards membership. Secondly, while addressing energy security is paramount, the EU faces the challenge of avoiding environmental deregulation. The response to the energy crisis, if not carefully managed, could undermine environmental protection, so the EU has to find the right balance to ensure that energy security measures align with its commitment to environmental sustainability.

This chapter analyses the impact of the REPowerEU plan and its related legislative initiatives, triggered by the Russian war of aggression against Ukraine, on EU environmental law. More specifically, the analysis will focus on Regulation (EU) 2023/435 regarding the addition of REPowerEU to the Recovery and Resilience Plans,[5] Directive 2018/2001 on the promotion of energy from renewable sources[6] and Council Regulation 2022/2577 laying down a framework to accelerate the deployment of renewable energy.[7] The chapter will explore whether the introduced amendments of EU environmental legislation amount to an impermissible reversal of environmental standards.

12.2. The REPowerEU Plan

In May 2022, only three months after the Russian invasion of Ukraine, the European Commission presented the REPowerEU Plan in response to the disruption of the global energy market because of the war, which highlighted the vulnerability of Europe's energy

[3] 'War and subsidies have turbocharged the green transition' *The Economist* (13 February 2023), available at www.economist.com/finance-and-economics/2023/02/13/war-and-subsidies-have-turbocharged-the-green-transition.

[4] OECD, 'Environmental impacts of the war in Ukraine and prospects for a green reconstruction' [2022] 4.

[5] Regulation (EU) 2023/435 of the European Parliament and of the Council of 27 February 2023 amending Regulation (EU) 2021/241 as regards REPowerEU chapters in recovery and resilience plans and amending Regulations (EU) No 1303/2013, (EU) 2021/1060 and (EU) 2021/1755, [2023] OJ L63/1.

[6] Directive (EU) 2023/2413 of the European Parliament and of the Council of 18 October 2023 amending Directive (EU) 2018/2001, Regulation (EU) 2018/1999 and Directive 98/70/EC as regards the promotion of energy from renewable sources, and repealing Council Directive (EU) 2015/652, [2023] OJ L2023/2413.

[7] Council Regulation (EU) 2022/2577 of 22 December 2022 laying down a framework to accelerate the deployment of renewable energy, [2022] OJ L335/36.

supply. In summary, the plan represents a comprehensive strategy to enhance Europe's energy security and to end its reliance on Russian fossil fuels, while accelerating the green transition in light of the Union's commitments under the European Green Deal.[8]

The plan emphasises the importance of energy-efficiency measures as the quickest and most cost-effective way to address the energy crisis. It proposed increasing the binding energy efficiency target and implementing short-term measures to reduce gas and oil demand.[9]

The REPowerEU aims to swiftly diminish Europe's reliance on Russian fossil fuels, hastening the transition to cleaner energy and fostering a more resilient Energy Union. The plan, building upon the Fit for 55 proposals[10] and addressing energy security and storage, outlines actions to significantly increase the production of energy from renewable sources. The overarching objective is to ensure the long-term sustainability, cost-effectiveness and security of the EU's energy supply by gradually reducing dependency from the Russian Federation.[11] To achieve these goals, the plan incorporates short-, mid- and long-term targets across four pillars: demand reduction; diversification of fossil fuel suppliers with infrastructure futureproofing; acceleration of the shift to renewable energy sources; and smart investments in order to fund the transition.[12]

The REPowerEU plan represents a pivotal moment in EU energy policy. It aims to accelerate the transition to renewable energy sources, reduce fossil fuel dependency, and achieve carbon neutrality by 2050. The plan encompasses several components, including substantial investments in renewable energy infrastructure and the promotion of clean technologies. Thus, it strives to balance immediate energy security needs with long-term environmental sustainability goals.

The implementation of this very ambitious plan required the introduction of multiple legislative measures. The following sections analyse Regulation 2023/435 regarding the REPowerEU chapters in Recovery and Resilience Plans, Directive 2023/2413 regarding the promotion of energy from renewable sources, and Council Regulation (EU) 2022/2577 laying down a framework to accelerate the deployment of renewable energy.

12.3. Regulation 2023/435 Regarding the REPowerEU Chapters in Recovery and Resilience Plans

In order to finance the REPowerEU plan, Regulation 2023/435 was adopted to amend the Regulation establishing the Recovery and Resilience Facility[13] (RRF Regulation).

[8] REPowerEU Plan (n 3) 1–2.

[9] The revised Energy Efficiency Directive (Directive (EU) 2023/1791 of the European Parliament and of the Council of 13 September 2023 on energy efficiency and amending Regulation (EU) 2023/955 (recast), [2023] OJ L 231) increased the energy-efficiency target-setting goal of reducing energy consumption by 11.7% by 2030, compared to projected energy use for 2030.

[10] Communication from the Commission to the European Parliament, the Council, the European Economic and Social Committee -and the Committee Of The Regions, 'Fit for 55': delivering the EU's 2030 Climate Target on the way to climate neutrality [2021] COM(2021)550 final.

[11] REPowerEU Plan (n 3) 1–2.

[12] ibid.

[13] Regulation (EU) 2021/241 of the European Parliament and of the Council of 12 February 2021 establishing the Recovery and Resilience Facility, [2021] OJ L57/17.

Regulation 2023/435 requires Member States to seek financing for reforms and investments that promote the REPowerEU by adding a new chapter to their Recovery and Resilience Plans.

Regulation 2023/435 has generated considerable debate due to its exemption for oil and gas from the Do Not Significantly Harm (DNSH) principle. More specifically Article 21c(6) provides for an exemption for reforms and investments aiming to improve energy infrastructure and facilities to meet 'immediate security of supply needs' for gas, including liquified natural gas and in some exceptional cases oil from the DNSH principle.[14] In order for the exemption to be granted the measure should be necessary and proportionate to meet 'immediate security of supply needs', it should not jeopardise the attainment of climate targets, it should be operational by 31 December 2026, and the Member State concerned should take appropriate mitigation measures.

This preferential exemption for only some specific projects which, by their very nature, are likely to harm the environment, seems to prioritise immediate energy security concerns over environmental protection. The current privileged treatment of oil and gas seems at odds with the obligation to aim at a high level of environmental protection and to integrate environmental protection requirements into all EU sectoral policies, as stipulated, respectively, in Articles 191(2) and 11 TFEU as well as in Article 37 of the Charter of Fundamental Rights. It is also questionable how a dedicated exemption to the benefit of fossil fuels could be considered as not jeopardising the climate targets.

The exemption discriminates against environmentally friendly projects, such as renewables or energy-efficiency projects that need to abide by the DNSH principle, in favour of environmentally harmful new fossil fuel infrastructure that is not required to respect the DNSH standard. This discriminatory clause establishes a negative precedent and runs counter to the fundamental goals of the RRF, including the pursuit of 'smart, sustainable, and inclusive growth'.[15] The preference for oil and gas, as opposed to renewable alternatives with inherently lower environmental impacts, lacks a clear and transparent justification. While it may serve as a short-term, pragmatic response to energy security threats, it should have been framed by much more stringent and clearer criteria.

Ambiguities in the Regulation, in particular concerning essential definitions, have generated legal uncertainty especially in Article 21c(6) of the Regulation.[16] The vagueness of terms like 'significant harm' or 'emergency situation' leaves room for

[14] Art 21c(6) Regulation 2023/435 (n 6).

[15] Regulation (EU) 2021/241 of the European Parliament and of the Council of 12 February 2021 establishing the Recovery and Resilience Facility, [2021] OJ L57/17, Recitals 10 and 13, Art 3(c).

[16] Article 21c(6) of Regulation 2023/345 (n 6) provides that: 'By derogation from Article 5(2), Article 17(4), Article 18(4), point (d), and Article 19(3), point (d), the principle of "do no significant harm" shall not apply to the reforms and investments under paragraph 3, point (a), of this Article, subject to a positive assessment by the Commission that the following requirements are met: (a) the measure is necessary and proportionate to meet immediate security of supply needs in accordance with paragraph 3, point (a), of this Article taking into account cleaner feasible alternatives and the risk of lock-in effects; (b) the Member State concerned has undertaken satisfactory efforts to limit the potential harm to environmental objectives within the meaning of Article 17 of Regulation (EU) 2020/852, where feasible, and to mitigate harm through other measures, including the measures in the REPowerEU chapter; (c) the measure does not jeopardise the achievement of the Union's 2030 climate targets and the objective of EU climate neutrality by 2050, based on qualitative considerations; (d) the measure is planned to be in operation by 31 December 2026.'

interpretation that can result in litigation and potential project implementation delays. The notion of 'immediate security of supply needs' seems to contradict the requirement of the measures to be operational by the end of 2026. Furthermore, using the expression 'planned to be in operation' means the actual operationalisation of the measures could occur many years later than 2026, undermining their urgent nature.

Regulation 2023/435 was initially framed as a response to immediate security of supply needs. However, the energy landscape has evolved, and the gas prices have considerably decreased.[17] This changed context raises strong doubts about the continuation of the 2022 emergency situation and many concerns on the potential fossil fuels lock-in effect which could hinder the transition to sustainable energy sources. Thus, a reassessment of the Regulation's relevance and alignment with current energy realities is crucial.

In conclusion, Regulation 2023/435 causes concerns, related especially to the exemption of oil and gas from the DNSH principle, which introduced legal uncertainties and inconsistencies with EU climate and environmental goals and legal requirements while not being based – at least no longer – on an energy security emergency.

12.4. The Revised Renewable Energy Directive (Directive 2023/2413)

Directive 2023/2413 seeks to simplify and accelerate the permit procedure for renewable energy projects, aiming to expedite their deployment. To this end, Article 1(2) raises the EU's binding renewables target for 2030 to a minimum of 42.5 per cent, from the previous 32 per cent target, aiming to reach 45 per cent. However, while this primary goal is laudable, the implications of the simplification of permitting procedures require careful consideration.

The explanatory memorandum of the Directive's proposal underlines the need to accelerate the permitting process, since the heavy administrative requirements hinder significantly the effective deployment of renewable energy.[18] Pursuant to the Interim Report of the RES Simplify Study, administrative burdens are nearly half of the identified obstacles to the deployment of renewable energy.[19]

The following sub-sections will analyse the main amendments introduced by Directive 2023/2413.

[17] 'Eurostat, Electricity and gas prices stabilise in 2023' Eurostat (26 October 2023), available at ec.europa.eu/eurostat/web/products-eurostat-news/w/ddn-20231026-1#:~:text=After%20a%20significant%20increase%20in,and%20gas%20prices%20are%20stabilising.

[18] Commission, 'Proposal for a Directive of the European Parliament and of the Council amending Directive (EU) 2018/2001 on the promotion of the use of energy from renewable sources, Directive 2010/31/EU on the energy performance of buildings and Directive 2012/27/EU on energy efficiency' [2022] COM(2022) 222 final, 1.

[19] Commission, Directorate-General for Energy, 'Technical support for RES policy development and implementation Simplification of permission and administrative procedures for RES installations' (RES simplify: interim report)' [2022] 36.

12.4.1. Designation of Renewable Acceleration Areas

The increase of areas dedicated to energy production sought by the REPowerEU Plan adds pressure on natural habitats and wildlife, creating a dilemma involving competing societal priorities. Spatial planning, accompanied by strategic environmental assessments, plays a crucial role in reconciling these interests by identifying areas on land and at sea where the environmental impacts would be lower and which could therefore be prioritised for renewable energy projects.

Directive 2023/2413 focuses on the importance of strategic planning in order to secure adequate land and sea areas for the deployment of renewable sources. More specifically, pursuant to Article 15b of the Directive, by 21 May 2025 Member States shall carry out a coordinated evaluation in order to identify areas in their territories that will be used for the deployment of renewable energy in order to meet the 2030 target, ensuring that there is sufficient land, inland water and sea space for renewable energy installations. The size of these areas should be determined based on the specific needs and characteristics of the technologies to be deployed. Article 15b provides concrete criteria that should be considered when identifying the areas to be used for renewable energy production in order to meet the 2030 target. These criteria encompass renewable resource availability, production potential, projected demand, and grid infrastructure and storage.

According to Article 15c of Directive 2023/2413, by 21 February 2026, Member States shall designate within the areas mapped pursuant to Article 15b, renewable acceleration areas ('go-to' areas) for one or more types of renewable energy sources. Article 15c provides guidance to Member States, emphasising the promotion of renewable energy integration with existing infrastructure while minimising the use of environmentally sensitive areas. This approach prioritises artificial and built surfaces and excludes areas designated as Natura 2000 sites, areas designated under national protection schemes for nature and biodiversity conservation, and 'major bird and marine mammal migratory routes'.[20] However, the language used in this provision is non-committal and does not create a clear prohibition for Member States to exclude environmentally sensitive areas from areas of accelerated renewable energy deployment. It also creates legal uncertainty by introducing undefined notions such as 'major birds and mammal migratory routes'. This expression seems to imply a quantitative element, but how many specimens should one count before a migratory route is considered 'major'?

Prior to their approval, plans that designate go-to areas must go through a strategic environmental assessment (SEA) in line with Directive 2001/42/EC (SEA Directive).[21] If these plans are likely to have a significant impact on Natura 2000 sites, they must also undergo an appropriate assessment as specified in Article 6(3) of Directive 92/43/EEC (Habitats Directive).[22] Essentially, Article 15c of Directive 2023/2413 aims to ensure compliance with Articles 11 and 191 of the TFEU by incorporating environmental

[20] Article 15c(1)(a)(ii) of Directive 2023/2413 (n 7).

[21] Directive 2001/42/EC of the European Parliament and of the Council of 27 June 2001 on the assessment of the effects of certain plans and programmes on the environment (SEA Directive), [2021] OJ L197.

[22] Council Directive 92/43/EEC of 21 May 1992 on the conservation of natural habitats and of wild fauna and flora [1992], OJ L206.

concerns into strategic planning, thereby facilitating the attainment of a 'high level of protection' for the environment'.[23] These plans need to be made public and be re-evaluated at least every two years, coinciding with the updates to the national energy and climate plans.

Additionally, pursuant to Article 15c(4), Member States have the option to start more rapidly the deployment of renewable sources by designating, by 21 May 2024, as 'renewable acceleration areas' those areas that have been already identified as suitable for the expedited deployment of renewable energy technologies if they are not within the Natura 2000 network or other protected zones, have undergone a SEA and, if applicable, an appropriate assessment under the Habitats Directive, and provided that suitable rules are implemented to mitigate any potential adverse environmental impacts.

12.4.2. Exemption from Environmental Assessments

Article 16a(3) introduces a very important exemption. In renewable acceleration areas, projects are exempted from the requirement for an environmental impact assessment (EIA),[24] provided that the relevant authority determines during the screening process that significant unforeseen adverse effects are unlikely, after considering the environmental sensitivity of the location. Moreover, in the same areas, renewable energy projects must not be subject to an assessment of their implications for Natura 2000 sites provided that appropriate mitigation measures have been taken.

This exemption is based on the rationale that the plans designating the renewable acceleration areas have already undergone a strategic environmental assessment (SEA). Additionally, if these plans were expected to significantly affect Natura 2000 sites, they would have undergone an appropriate assessment in line with Article 6(3) of the Habitats Directive. However, it is important to note that conducting a SEA at the plan level cannot replace the need for assessments at the project level, since SEA and EIA operate at different and complementary levels. While the SEA looks at plans which identify broadly the areas where future projects may be developed, the EIA concerns individual projects in specific locations, also looking into cumulative impacts from different individual projects in the same area. Therefore, the EIAs provide a more specific evaluation of the potential consequences of individual projects that can, by no means, be replaced by a SEA alone.[25]

The new exemption does not make EIAs completely irrelevant for renewable energy projects. Following a screening process according to Article 16a(4), the EIA and appropriate assessment can still apply to projects that are deemed 'highly likely to give rise to significant adverse effects' that were not anticipated in the plan. However, the

[23] Art 191(2) TFEU provides that 'Union policy on the environment shall aim at a high level of protection taking into account the diversity of situations in the various regions of the Union'.

[24] Directive 2014/52/EU of the European Parliament and of the Council of 16 April 2014 amending Directive 2011/92/EU on the assessment of the effects of certain public and private projects on the environment Text with EEA relevance (EIA Directive), [2014] OJ L124, Arts 2–4.

[25] B Dalal-Clayton and B Sadler, 'Strategic environmental assessment: A rapidly evolving approach. A Directory of Impact Assessment Guidelines'(1999) *Environmental Planning Issues* 2.

terminology used, ie 'highly likely' and 'significant unforeseen adverse effects', departs from the Habitats and EIA Directives, thereby limiting the possibility for the authorities to require an assessment only to exceptional cases.[26]

Thus, Directive 2023/2413 introduced implicit amendments to key provisions of the Habitats and EIA Directives, which are an essential part of EU environmental legislation. This becomes even clearer when one looks at the legal bases for Directive 2023/2413, which include Article 192(1) TFEU, the environmental legal basis, in addition to Article 194(2), the energy legal base. The exemptions from the EIA and the appropriate assessment under the Habitats Directive put at risk the attainment of their respective goals. While streamlining permits could accelerate renewable energy projects, it remains to be demonstrated that environmental requirements are a key factor slowing down the approval process rather than the lack of administrative capacity of national authorities, the poor quality of the projects that are submitted for authorisation, or the opposition of local populations that do not wish to see wind and solar farms in their backyard.

Safeguards must be put in place to prevent hasty approvals that compromise environmental protection. Assessing the environmental impact of a project before its authorisation is vital to respect the principles of prevention and precaution enshrined Article 191(2) TFEU. In addition to the climate crisis, the world is facing a biodiversity crisis which is topical also in the EU. Most protected habitats and species in the EU are in poor conservation status[27] and habitat fragmentation is one of the key causes for this. Therefore, considering projects' adverse environmental effects on nature during the authorisation phase is crucial. In addition, these amendments are a significant departure from the stringent approach followed by the Court of Justice, which favours case-by-case evaluations and does not allow pre-emptive exemption of entire categories of projects.[28]

Moreover, excluding projects within acceleration areas from environmental assessments is likely to result in less predictability for project developers and investors. The Habitats and EIA Directives have a long history of application based on established case law, providing a reliable and well-understood legal framework. The above amendments are likely to disrupt this system, creating legal uncertainties because of the vague notions they introduce and increasing litigation during the project permitting process which would, in turn, lead to unnecessary delays.

While it is true that the environmental assessments can be time-consuming, the above almost complete exemption from an EIA and from an appropriate assessment is disproportionate and was not included as a proposal to reduce the administrative complexities of permitting in the RES Simplify Study[29] nor in the Fitness Check of the Birds and Habitats Directives.[30]

[26] Art 6(3) of the Habitats Directive (n 23) and Art 2(1) of the EIA Directive (n 25) use the terms 'likely' and 'significant effects'.

[27] European Environmental Agency Report No 10/2020 (2020) 'State of nature in the EU' (Luxembourg, Publications Office of the European Union).

[28] Case C-66/06 *Commission v Ireland* [2008] ECR I-00158, [65].

[29] RES simplify: interim report' (n 20) 36.

[30] Commission Staff Working Document Fitness Check of the EU Nature Legislation (Birds and Habitats Directives) Directive 2009/147/EC of the European Parliament and of the Council of 30 November 2009 on the conservation of wild birds and Council Directive 92/43/EEC of 21 May 1992 on the conservation of natural habitats and of wild fauna and flora [2016] SWD(2016) 472 final, ch 6.2.7.

These concerns are further increased by the introduction of Article 16a(6) which allows, for renewable projects in acceleration areas, permitting applications to be authorised without an explicit decision from the competent authority, unless the project would be subject to an EIA or where the principle of positive administrative silence does not exist in the national legal system of the Member State concerned. This automatic granting of permits without the express approval of a competent authority raises legal and environmental concerns since, potentially, the projects at stake could have significant impacts. Considering the 45-day timeframe in Article 16a, there is a significant risk for competent authorities to be unable to come to a decision within that timeline and for major projects to – tacitly – get very close to final approval. This concern is partly mitigated by the clause in Article 16a(6) stating that tacit approval 'shall not apply to final decisions on the outcome of the permit-granting procedure, which shall be explicit'. Alternatively and less likely, competent authorities might choose to require an environmental assessment provided they can argue that the project is 'highly likely to give rise to significant adverse effects'.

Thus, Directive 2023/2413 effectively leads to the almost automatic authorisation of renewable projects in acceleration areas, marginalising the significance of environmental assessments, which are considered by the Court of Justice one of the 'fundamental environmental protection mechanisms'.[31]

12.4.3. Short Screening Deadlines

Article 16a(4) outlines a requirement for Member States to conduct a screening of permit applications for renewable projects in designated acceleration areas. As mentioned above, this screening aims to identify if the project is 'highly likely' to lead to unforeseen significant adverse environmental effects that were not previously considered during the designation of these renewable areas. Furthermore, this Article suggests that such screening should be completed within a very short timeframe of 30 or 45 days, depending on the project type.

From a practical standpoint, these short deadlines may pose challenges for public authorities, which are often under-resourced.[32] These tight timelines could create an incentive to expedite the process, potentially leading to the oversight of significant environmental impacts of a project. Therefore, this provision is likely to generate complexities and uncertainties, which could be avoided if the screening process were integrated into the standard EIA procedure. It is essential to ensure that these assessments are conducted thoroughly so that the potential environmental impacts can be identified.

Article 16a(4) specifies that the project developer is obliged to provide, inter alia, details regarding the project's characteristics and its adherence to the rules and measures outlined in Article 15c(1b) and (1c). Supplying the competent authority with

[31] Case C-261/18, *Commission v Ireland (Derrybrien Wind Farm)* [2019] ECLI:EU:C:2019:955, [116].

[32] It should be noted that the proposal provided even tighter deadlines of 15 and 30 days depending on the project type (see Proposal for a Directive of the European Parliament and of the Council amending Directive (EU) 2018/2001 (n 18), Art 16a(4).

sufficient information to effectively screen the project is crucial, primarily because the request for additional information is limited to what already exists. This approach does not consider the potential gaps, lack of biodiversity or other environmental data in the information provided by the developer. It also deviates from the interpretation offered by the Court of Justice concerning the Habitats Directive, which calls for the use of 'the best scientific knowledge in the field'.[33]

12.4.4. Presumption of Compliance of Mitigation Measures with the Birds and Habitats Directives and the Water Framework Directive

Article 15c(1b) creates a presumption that mitigation measures against the potential detrimental effects of renewable energy projects to the environment would automatically ensure projects' compliance with key environmental obligations related to the preservation of species, habitats and surface water bodies. More specifically, it provides that if appropriate and timely mitigation measures are taken and applied in a proportionate manner to ensure compliance with the Habitats and Birds Directives (Nature Directives) and the Water Framework Directive and to avoid deterioration of the environment, these measures are sufficient to presume that the projects to which they apply are compliant with the environmental law obligations stemming from these legislative instruments.

Mitigation measures refer to actions taken to reduce the potential adverse environmental impact of a project. These measures operationalise the principle of prevention, which calls for actions to minimise environmental harm from the outset, rather than addressing it after it has occurred. Integrating mitigation measures into plans and projects ensures that the development of renewable energy sources is carried out in a way that minimises environmental harm.

However, the presumption bypasses requirements set by the Nature Directives and the Water Framework Directive and risks to be used as means to circumvent important protective provisions outlined in these legislative instruments.

12.4.5. Compensation or 'Pay to Kill' Provisions

Article 16a(5) provides that wind and solar photovoltaic installations, which are expected to provide most of the renewable electricity by 2030[34] can, in the event of justified circumstances (including to accelerate the deployment of renewable energy to achieve the climate and renewable energy targets), be put in place without assessments under the EIA and the Habitats Directives, even if potential adverse environmental consequences were identified during the screening process, provided that the developer adopts proportionate mitigation measures. If such measures are deemed unavailable,

[33] Case C-254/19, *Friends of the Irish Environment* [2020] ECLI:EU:C:2020:680, [50] and [51].
[34] See Recital 35 of Directive 2023/2413 (n 6).

the developer should adopt compensatory measures which, if other compensatory measures are unavailable, can take the form of monetary compensation to be paid, in case of impacts on species protection, into species protection programmes during the whole plant's operation, in order to ensure or improve the conservation status of the species affected.

Regarding plans to designate dedicated areas for grid and storage projects, pursuant to Article 15e, they should as a rule exclude Natura 2000 sites since there are fewer limitations on their placement. In such areas, Member States should be able to exempt projects from assessments under the EIA and the Habitats and Birds Directives under justified circumstances, including where needed to accelerate the grid expansion to support the deployment of renewable energy to achieve the climate and renewable energy targets. Should Member States choose to rely on such exemptions, the designated projects should undergo an efficient screening process, akin to the process outlined for areas dedicated to accelerating renewable energy projects, and this process should rely on existing data. If the screening reveals projects with a high likelihood of causing significant unforeseen adverse effects, the competent authority must ensure the adoption of appropriate and proportionate mitigation measures. When it is not possible to adopt such measures, the mitigation might take form of a 'monetary compensation for species protection programmes' in order to ensure or improve the conservation status of the species affected.

In relation to the above-described special regime for both wind/solar photovoltaic installations and grid/storage projects, it is to be recalled that monetary compensation is an ex-post measure and does not align with the principle of prevention which underscores EU environmental law. Moreover, monetary compensation does not qualify as compensatory measure under the Habitats Directive.[35] Thereunder, compensatory measures must be measures of an ecological nature that address the specific habitats and species affected by the project in order to ensure the overall coherence of the Natura 2000 network of protected areas.

In both projects related to grid and storage infrastructure under Article 15e as well as for exceptional cases regarding wind and photovoltaic projects under Article 16a, it is emphasised that mitigation measures have to be proportionate. However, the Directive does not provide guidance on what would constitute a proportionate mitigation measure in these cases. This lack of clarity in the terminology could lead to legal disputes if mitigation measures are rejected on the grounds of being disproportionate. Moreover, further uncertainties are likely to arise regarding the definitions of 'monetary compensation' and 'species protection programmes' and what constitutes an amount consistent with the goal of ensuring or improving the conservation status of the species. Lastly, regarding the timeframe of these measures for wind and solar photovoltaic projects, Article 16a(5) limits compensation to 'the duration of the operation of the renewable power plant', which could be problematic as projects may have long-lasting effects even after the plant ceases operation, and nature might need more time and support to restore after the end of the projects' activities.

[35] See European Commission, Directorate-General for Environment, Managing Natura 2000 sites – The provisions of Article 6 of the 'Habitats' Directive 92/43/EEC, Publications Office [2019] 62.

12.4.6. 'Deliberate Killing or Disturbance' and 'Novel Mitigation Measures'

Pursuant to Article 16b, outside renewable acceleration areas, if 'appropriate mitigation measure' has been 'adopted' for a specific project, the killing or disturbance of species protected under the Nature Directives would not be considered 'deliberate'. It is worth noting that the term 'adopted' may suggest that mere adoption is enough and effective implementation is not required. Moreover, this approach seems to depart from the case law of the Court of Justice, which underlines that the mere acceptance of the possibility of capture, disturbance or killing is enough to qualify the action as 'deliberate' and stands at odds with the precautionary and prevention principles which underscore the Habitats Directive.[36] This is particularly so if the authorities and/or project developer have no obligation to implement and monitor the effectiveness of the mitigation measures in question and to impose/take additional measures in case they prove ineffective.

Both in renewable acceleration areas (Article 15c) and outside of them (Article 16b), the Directive allows the temporary use of 'novel mitigation measures' in pilot projects if they have not been 'widely tested' and their effectiveness is 'closely monitored' before implementation, with appropriate steps taken immediately if they are proven ineffective. It remains to be seen how these mitigation measures will be considered when determining if the project adversely affects the integrity of the site or the species. The case law of the Court of Justice suggests that the precautionary principle should be applied in a strict manner and has underlined that only measures whose effectiveness has been confirmed through 'definitive data' can guarantee the integrity of the protected site or species.[37]

12.4.7. Presumption that Renewables Projects Constitute an Overriding Public Interest

Article 16f introduces a presumption that the development of renewable energy projects is considered an 'overriding public interest' and 'serving public health and safety' for the purpose of the Nature Directives and the Water Framework Directive. However, these Directives already include an 'overriding public interest' test, which allows certain activities, plans or projects to proceed for reasons of public interest when their harmful impacts have been extensively assessed.[38] Any application of such test should be done through a case-by-case evaluation, to ensure that projects that cause significant adverse environmental effects that cannot be avoided or mitigated are only authorised when, balancing environmental protection with another public interest, the latter prevails.

[36] Case C-221/04 *Commission v Spain* [2006] ECLI:EU:C:2006:329, [71].

[37] Case C-142/16 *Commission v Germany* [2017] ECLI:EU:C:2017:301, [37]–[45].

[38] See, eg, Art 6(4) Habitats Directive (n 22), which provides for an 'overriding public interest' test and requires the Member State to prove that there are no 'alternative solutions' to the proposed development.

The rationale for proposing this presumption is to simplify the assessment process for renewable projects by facilitating their approval. Yet, there is a concern that this provision may not actually simplify the assessment but could instead lead to confusion in the application and interpretation of existing EU legislation. The concept of 'overriding public interest' within the context of the Nature Directives is already subject to a substantial body of case law and Commission guidance.[39] Most importantly, given the current case law, according to which the security of energy supply has been accepted as an 'overriding public interest',[40] renewable projects that aim at generating a substantive amount of energy are already likely to be considered as in the overriding public interest. On the other hand, small projects with a big impact on nature should not benefit from such a generous presumption which is, therefore, either unnecessary or potentially damaging to the environment for no good reason, depending on the project to which it will apply.

12.4.8. The Lack of an Impact Assessment

Impact assessments are required for all legislative instruments and their amendments which are expected to have significant economic, environmental and social impacts and are part of the legislators' obligation to state reasons. This obligation derives from the Aarhus Convention,[41] Regulation 1367/2006,[42] Article 41 of the EU Charter of Fundamental Rights and Article 296 TFEU, and is stipulated in Paragraph 13 (Chapter III) of the Inter-institutional Agreement between the European Parliament, the Council of the European Union and the European Commission on Better Law-Making.[43]

Reasons of political sensitivity and urgency were invoked to justify the lack of an impact assessment for the proposal for the revision of Directive 2018/2001.[44] However, it is precisely due to the political sensitivity of the amendments introduced and of their potentially significant environmental impact that an impact assessment was essential.

The invoked urgency reasons are not persuasive since conducting an impact assessment should not result in undue delays in the legislative process[45] and resources can be shifted to face the urgency and develop the assessment more quickly. Furthermore,

[39] Commission Notice, Assessment of plans and projects in relation to Natura 2000 sites – Methodological guidance on the provisions of Article 6(3) and (4) of the Habitats Directive 92/43/EEC [2021] OJ C437/01, ch 3.3.2.

[40] See, eg, Case C-411/17 *Inter-Environnement Wallonie et Bond Beter Leefmilieu Vlaanderen* [2019] ECLI:EU:C:2019:622, [159].

[41] UNECE Convention on Access to Information, Public Participation in Decision-Making And Access to Justice in Environmental Matters done at Aarhus, Denmark, on 25 June 1998 (Aarhus Convention), Art 5.

[42] Regulation (EC) No 1367/2006 of the European Parliament and of the Council of 6 September 2006 on the application of the provisions of the Aarhus Convention on Access to Information, Public Participation in Decision-making and Access to Justice in Environmental Matters to Community institutions and bodies (Aarhus Regulation), [2006] OJ L264, Art 4.

[43] Interinstitutional Agreement between the European Parliament, the Council of the European Union and the European Commission on Better Law-Making, [2016] OJ L123, paras 12–18.

[44] See Proposal for a Directive of the European Parliament and of the Council amending Directive (EU) 2018/2001 (n 18).

[45] Case C-128/17 *Poland v Parliament and Council* [2019] ECLI:EU:C:2019:194, [83]; Interinstitutional Agreement on Better Law-Making (n 43), para 12.

when considering the overall duration of the ordinary legislative procedure and the proposal's long-term goals, the additional time required for completing an impact assessment seems insignificant,[46] especially as the effects of the proposal had been largely anticipated through the 'emergency regulation' discussed in section 12.5 below. Bypassing the impact assessment is hardly justifiable, especially since the Directive is intended for long-term application.

12.4.9. Scarce Public Participation

The limited consultation process for the adoption of the legislative framework to implement the REPowerEU plan has raised concerns regarding the lack of inclusivity, the potential hindering of well-informed decision-making on environmental legislation and the need to uphold the principles of the Aarhus Convention.

More specifically, Articles 6–8 of the Aarhus Convention apply to the preparation of 'generally applicable legally binding normative instruments' that may significantly affect the environment.[47] Moreover, Article 9 of Regulation 1367/2006[48] and paragraph 19 of the Inter-institutional Agreement outline a public consultation process intended to ensure the broadest possible participation.[49]

Concerning the REPowerEU plan, various activities, including a call for evidence and a public consultation,[50] were conducted to gather input from competent authorities and the public on potential modifications to permit-granting procedures. While these actions align with the Interinstitutional Agreement on Better Law-Making, non-governmental organisations (NGOs) have expressed reservations about their comprehensiveness.[51] They argued that, due to the urgency of the situation, the public consultation was notably limited. Environmental NGOs and civil society organisations were not considered part of the 'target audience' and were not consulted during the creation of the RES Simplify Study.[52] The primary stakeholder group that had significant opportunities for involvement consisted mainly of the energy sector, including renewable energy companies, energy communities and industry associations. Consequently, the feedback gathered from the consultation lacks comprehensiveness, and the process failed to capture diverse input from stakeholders with varying interests.[53]

Regarding the substance of the Directive, it addresses public participation in Article 15d, providing that Member States shall comply with the public participation requirement outlined in Article 6 of the SEA Directive by granting 'early and effective

[46] Directive 2023/2413 (n 6) entered into force on 20 November 2023 and the proposal (n 18) was published on 18 May 2022.

[47] Aarhus Convention (n 41), Arts 6–8.

[48] Aarhus Regulation (n 42), Art 9.

[49] Interinstitutional Agreement between the European Parliament on Better Law-Making (n 43), para 19.

[50] Factual Summary Report of the Stakeholder Consultation on 'Renewable energy projects – permit-granting processes & power-purchase agreements', Ref. Ares(2022)8484514 –7 December 2022, available at eur-lex.europa.eu/legal-content/EN/TXT/?uri=pi_com%3AAres%282022%298484514.

[51] Client Earth, Briefing: RePower EU Proposal for a REDII amendment Expediting renewable technologies' permitting procedures (June 2022), available at www.clientearth.org/media/itejqaby/clientearth_repowereu-permitting-amendments-briefing_july-2022.pdf.

[52] Factual Summary Report (n 50).

[53] Client Earth, Briefing (n 51).

opportunities' for public participation. While public consultation is an obligation pursuant to the SEA Directive, the lack of public participation at a project level due to the exemption from the obligation to conduct an EIA in renewable acceleration areas coupled with the short assessment deadlines may negatively affect the possibility for meaningful public participation.

In conclusion, and given the fundamental role of effective public participation in projects with potentially significant environmental effects, these gaps constitute a major flaw in the adoption of the proposal and raise serious doubts about its compatibility with the Aarhus Convention principles and the duty to ensure transparent and inclusive environmental decision-making processes.

12.5. Council Regulation (EU) 2022/2577: Accelerating Renewable Energy Deployment

Council Regulation (EU) 2022/2577[54] aims to urgently tackle the need to end dependency on Russian fuels by expediting renewable energy deployment and was adopted under Article 122(1) TFEU, which provides for an emergency legislative procedure when there are severe difficulties regarding energy supply. The Regulation entered into force originally for 18 months (ie, until July 2024), but its duration was extended to 30 June 2025 by virtue of Council Regulation (EU) 2024/223.[55]

Regulation 2022/2577, similarly to the Directive analysed in the previous section, introduces the overriding public interest presumption (Article 3), provisions for accelerating the permitting process for solar energy equipment (Article 4), fast-track procedures for the repowering of renewable energy projects (Article 5), exemptions from environmental assessments for renewable energy projects and related grid infrastructure, essential for integrating renewables (Article 6), and provisions regarding the acceleration of the deployment of heat pumps (Article 7). In essence, it introduced the main amendments of Directive 2023/2413 before the enactment of the Directive, in view of the urgent need to accelerate the deployment of renewable energy and the lengthy negotiations between the co-legislators that the ordinary legislative procedure entails. The substantive concerns regarding these amendments are analysed in the previous section of this chapter.

While the objective of the Regulation is to deal with the situation in an urgent manner, concerns emerge about its scope of application, as the Regulation covers renewable projects whose impacts will only materialise many years beyond its expiry, prompting questions about whether an emergency situation will still exist at that time.

In addition, environmental NGOs have raised concerns regarding the respect of the prerogatives of the European Parliament in light of the use of Article 122(1) TFEU as the legal base.[56] Pursuant to this Article, an act can be adopted by the Council upon

[54] Council Regulation (EU) 2022/2577 (n 7).

[55] Council Regulation (EU) 2024/223 of 22 December 2023 amending Regulation (EU) 2022/2577 laying down a framework to accelerate the deployment of renewable energy, [2023] OJ L2024/223, Art 8.

[56] *CEE Bankwatch Network z.s., Ökobüro – Allianz der Umweltbewegung v Council of the European Union* (Case T-535/23) (C/2023/221).

a proposal by the Commission without the participation of the European Parliament when there are severe difficulties regarding the supply of energy products. Since the emergency Regulation significantly alters legislative acts of paramount importance in EU environmental law, ie, the EIA, the Nature and the Water Framework Directives, all adopted through the ordinary legislative procedure, the exclusion of the European Parliament and the reliance on Article 122(1) should be truly exceptional. Instead, and as we have seen, there are strong doubts about the correspondence between the need to ensure immediate security of energy supply and the effect of the measures included in the Regulation. Therefore, compliance with democratic principles is questionable due to the limited public participation and the disrespect of the European Parliament's prerogatives. Striking the right balance between expeditious energy measures and environmental integrity is a difficult exercise that requires mechanisms for parliamentary scrutiny and robust public participation.

The emergency Council Regulation 2022/2577 was challenged by two environmental organisations[57] under the internal review procedure provided in Article 10 of the Aarhus Regulation.[58] The environmental organisations argued that the contested Regulation would result in environmental degradation which is not permitted pursuant to a combined reading of Articles 191 and 194 since these provisions suggest that existing environmental protection levels should not be decreased. In this context, Article 191 of the TFEU outlines the objectives of EU policy on the environment, which include preserving and protecting, but also improving, environmental quality. Additionally, Article 194 of the TFEU highlights the importance of 'preserving and improving' the environment in the context of the energy sector. The NGOs argue that the EU's policy is designed to achieve a high level of protection and automatically prohibits the reversal of environmental standards. To this end, the exemptions of certain renewable projects from EIAs under Article 5 of the contested Regulation contradicts the objective of 'improving the quality of the environment'.

In addition, the NGOs argued that Article 3 of the contested Regulation effectively presumes that all renewable energy projects requiring derogations from the EIA and the Nature Directives are automatically in the overriding public interest, regardless of the extent of harm they may cause to protected habitats, species or water quality. They contend that this provision primarily benefits the most environmentally damaging renewable energy projects. In addition, since even before the Regulation renewable energy projects could be recognised on case-by-case basis as being of overriding public interest and approved in spite of their significant impacts,[59] the NGOs maintain that the introduction of this presumption was not necessary.

They also argue that the Regulation breaches the Aarhus Convention by excluding the affected public from participating in the procedure due to the exemption of certain

[57] ibid.

[58] Aarhus Regulation (n 42), Art 10.

[59] CEE Bankwatch Network zs, Ökobüro – Allianz der Umweltbewegung v Council of the European Union Request for Internal Review under Title IV of the Aarhus Regulation ch 5.1.1. The NGOs referred the Schwarze Sulm and Gratkorn hydropower plants in Austria as examples of projects that received derogations under these Directives, available at bankwatch.org/wp-content/uploads/2023/03/Request-for-an-Internal-Review-of-Council-Regulation-EU-2022_2577-of-22-December-2022_consolidated.pdf.

projects from EIAs, and by failing to grant access to courts for challenging the procedure's outcomes.[60]

The NGOs also consider that legal basis of the Regulation is inappropriate since, as mentioned above, the Regulation was adopted via a procedure that excludes the European Parliament, instead of relying on Article 192 TFEU, which constitutes the legal basis to adopt environmental legislation and provides for the ordinary legislative procedure, except in some instances that are not relevant in the case at hand. The NGOs also claim that the Regulation is a non-legislative act and is hierarchically inferior to legislative acts; and, therefore, it cannot introduce amendments to other legislative acts such as the EIA and the Nature Directives.[61]

On 13 June 2023, the Council dismissed the complaint. The environmental organisations proceeded to two actions for annulment before the General Court arguing that their main arguments for the legal challenge were not refuted in a meaningful way by the Council. The actions would challenge the Council's response rather than the Regulation itself but would likely have a significant impact on the discussion of fast track permitting. At the time of writing the cases are still pending.

12.6. Is Environmental Deregulation Permitted?

Notwithstanding the urgent need to accelerate the energy transition towards the use of renewable sources in order to end the dependency on Russian fossil fuels, the introduced amendments present a backward step regarding their environmental ambition. Undoubtedly legitimate goals should not come at the expenses of environmental protection through environmental deregulation.[62] The amendments to EU environmental legislation, to the detriment of nature and broader environmental protection, may be characterised as a reversal of environmental protection standards and it is worth examining whether such regression is permitted under EU law.

According to one international definition of the non-regression principle, public authorities should 'refrain from allowing activities or adopting norms that have the effect of reducing the global level of environmental protection guaranteed by current law'.[63] The principle is gaining recognition in international environmental law and a non-regression or progression obligation is included in the Paris Agreement.[64] Moreover, non-regression has been recognised as a general principle by the Court of Justice regarding the protection of the rule of law.[65]

Various terms are employed to describe the concept of non-regression, creating a diversity of potential definitions for the same principle. Some refer to it as

[60] ibid, chs 5.1.2.1 and 5.2.2.

[61] ibid, ch 5.1.2.

[62] CJ Durá-Alemañ et al, 'Climate change and energy crisis drive an unprecedented EU environmental law regression' (2023) 16 *Conservation Letters*.

[63] Definition of the International Group of Experts for the Pact (IGEP), 'Draft Global Pact for Environment' (2017), Art 17.

[64] Paris Agreement to the United Nations Framework Convention on Climate Change, 12 December 2015, TIAS No 16-1104, Art 3s and 4(3).

[65] Case C-896/19 *Repubblika* [2021], ECLI:EU:C:2021:311, [64].

'non-regression', while others call it 'standstill principle'[66] or even the 'principle of progression'.[67] This array of terminology underpins a variety of definitions, leading to a central question: should the principle be interpreted in a factual sense, encompassing any tangible environmental degradation, or solely in a legal sense, addressing rollbacks in the level of protection?

It needs to be noted that non-regression is not an explicit principle of EU environmental law and is not enshrined in the Treaties. Some argue that introducing a non-regression principle is necessary to maintain the high level of protection the EU aims to achieve.[68]

Despite progress on the global stage in the recognition of 'non-regression', the only new environmental principle incorporated into Article 191 TFEU through the years has been the precautionary principle, introduced by the Maastricht Treaty.[69] This prompts the question of whether one can draw additional environmental principles from EU environmental law beyond the explicit provisions outlined in the Treaties.

The notion of non-regression is not entirely new in EU environmental law since non-regression clauses appear in various pieces of sectoral legislation with environmental significance. Factual non-regression clauses are incorporated in Article 4(1) Water Framework Directive, Article 4(4) Birds Directive and Article 6(2) Habitats Directive. The Court of Justice refers to these clauses as 'prohibition of deterioration'.[70] The Strategic Plans Regulation for the Common Agricultural Policy introduced a legal non-regression obligation in Article 105(1), obliging Member States to increase ambition regarding environmental and climate-related objectives.[71]

It can be argued that a combined reading of Articles 11 (principle of integration) and 191(2) TFEU, Article 37 and Recital 6 of the Charter of Fundamental Rights referring to 'responsibilities and duties with regard to … future generations' suggests that the reversal of environmental protection standards is prohibited, since the concept of progressivity is inherent in environmental protection.[72]

More specifically, Article 11 TFEU provides for the obligation of the EU to take into account environmental considerations in its policies and activities with a view to promoting sustainable development. The choice of the word 'must' – the most imperative wording possible for an obligation by the Treaty drafters – demonstrates

[66] I Hachez, 'Le principe de standstill dans le droit des droits fondamentaux : une irréversibilité relative' in M Prieur and G Sozzo (eds), *La non régression en droit de l'environnement* (Brusells, Bruylant, 2012) 484–88.

[67] N de Sadeleer, *Environmental Principles: From Political Slogans to Legal Rules*, 2nd edn (Oxford, Oxford University Press, 2020) 69.

[68] M Prieur, 'Plaidoyer pour un principe de non régression environnementale' in C Cournil and AS Tabau (eds), *Politiques climatiques de l'Union européenne et droits de l'homme* (Brusells, Bruylant, 2013) 303–09.

[69] L Krämer, 'The Genesis of EC Environmental Principles' in R Macrory, I Havercroft and R Purdy (eds), *Principles of European Environmental Law* (Groningen, Europa Law Publishing, 2004) 38.

[70] Case C-346/14 *Commission v Austria* [2016] ECLI:EU:C:2016:322, [45]; Case C-504/14 *Commission v Greece* [2016] ECLI:EU:C:2016:847, [100].

[71] Regulation (EU) 2021/2115 of the European Parliament and of the Council of 2 December 2021 establishing rules on support for strategic plans to be drawn up by Member States under the common agricultural policy (CAP Strategic Plans) and financed by the European Agricultural Guarantee Fund (EAGF) and by the European Agricultural Fund for Rural Development (EAFRD) and repealing Regulations (EU) No 1305/2013 and (EU) No 1307/2013, [2021] OJ L435.

[72] M Prieur, 'Plaidoyer pour un principe de non régression environnementale' in Cournil and Tabau (n 68) 304.

that there is, undoubtedly, a clear obligation to ensure the integration of environmental objectives in sectoral policies. Nevertheless, the presence of this provision alone is evidently inadequate in ensuring environmental integration across all EU policies and activities. For environmental integration to play a substantial role in achieving policy coherence, it needs to possess a well-defined objective. To this end, an interpretation of Article 11 TFEU, considering natural science and more specifically using the planetary boundaries[73] as non-negotiable ecological limits which must be respected, is crucial in rendering Article 11 TFEU truly effective.[74]

In principle, environmental considerations should be integrated in energy policy, including the REPowerEU plan. However, while it is generally accepted that Article 11 is legally binding, the wording of the Article does not give the full picture regarding its legal effects and, most importantly, its potential limits. This is why the principle of proportionality plays a crucial role in the balancing exercise between ensuring energy security and safeguarding environmental standards. Within this context, the conceptual framework for planetary boundaries calls for a precautionary approach by setting the boundary value at the lower end of the uncertainty range.[75] In the case at hand, an interpretation using the limits set by the planetary boundaries as a starting point would suggest that legislative amendments that undermine the role of the EIA and introduce unjustified presumptions is in breach of the obligation to integrate environmental considerations in other sectoral policies.

The principle of coherence, as enshrined in Article 13(1) TEU and Article 7 TFEU, should be applied in this context, ensuring that energy and environmental policies are implemented in a coherent manner. Consistency in policy goals can help the EU reconcile energy security and environmental protection, and the effective integration of environmental considerations into energy policy can ensure a harmonious approach in tackling emergency situations.

Regarding Article 37 of the EU Charter, although it can be seen as a repetition of Article 3(3) TEU, which is part of the general provisions setting forth core objectives of the Union, and of the environmental integration clause of Article 11 TFEU, it can also be seen as an additional 'persuasive authority'[76] for the obligation to effectively integrate environmental considerations in other sectoral policies. It should be noted, however, that Article 37 falls within the 'principles' category of the Charter and thus it does not confer any independently justiciable entitlement to environmental protection.[77]

[73] The concept of planetary boundaries refers to a set of nine Earth system processes or 'boundaries' that, if exceeded, could lead to abrupt and irreversible environmental changes, negatively impacting the stability and resilience of the Earth's systems. These boundaries were proposed by a group of scientists led by Johan Rockström and Will Steffen in 2009. See: M Leach, K Raworth and J Rockström, 'Between social and planetary boundaries: Navigating pathways in the safe and just pathway for humanity' World Social Science Report 2013: Changing Global Environments (OECD, 2013) 84–90.

[74] B Sjåfjell, 'The Environmental Integration Principle: A Necessary Step Towards Policy Coherence for Sustainability' in F Ippolito, ME Bartolino and M Condinanzi (eds), *The EU and the Proliferation of Integration Principles under the Lisbon Treaty* (Abingdon, Routledge, 2019) 105–08.

[75] ibid.

[76] G Marin-Duran and E Morgera 'Commentary on Article 37 of the EU Charter of Fundamental Rights – Environmental Protection' (2013) *Europa Working Paper* No 2013/2, 26.

[77] Art 52(5) Charter of Fundamental Rights, See also: Explanations relating to the Charter of Fundamental Rights [2007] OJ C 303, which explicitly mention Art 37 as a Charter principle and not a right.

This Article provides for an absolute obligation to integrate a high level of environmental protection and the improvement of the quality of the environment in the sectoral policies of the EU. The concept of a 'high level' of environmental protection holds significant importance as a fundamental principle in EU environment policy which is enshrined in Article 191(2) TFEU.

The Court of Justice has clarified that the level of protection does not have to be the utmost technically achievable,[78] but this does not imply adopting the lowest common denominator in environmental standards.

This perspective aligns with the possibility granted to Member States under Article 193 TFEU to implement more stringent environmental protection measures than those at the EU level. Consequently, the EU legislator is not obligated to adopt the highest environmental protection standard found within a specific Member State. Overall, the 'high level' principle embodies a dynamic objective, constantly advancing environmental protection within the EU. The notion of 'improvement of the quality of the environment', which is also present in Article 191(1) TFEU, is comparatively more straightforward as it suggests that any action leading to environmental deterioration contradicts the spirit of Article 37 of the Charter.

In the case at hand, given that the level of environmental protection does not need to be the highest possible, one could argue that a short and temporary lowering of environmental standards is not in breach of the Treaties and the Charter. However, one should recall that the amendments to the Renewable Energy Directive are not temporary and that even the changes introduced by the 'emergency' Regulation (EU) 2022/2577 amount to a partial deregulation of renewable energy projects, with long-lasting effects that extend beyond the duration of the adopted provisions. Arguably, the presumptions and the exemptions introduced by these legislative changes can be characterised as a reversal of environmental standards that would be prohibited under the principle of non-regression underscoring the EU Treaties.

12.7. Conclusion

The Russian invasion of Ukraine brought to the fore the intrinsic links between energy security and environmental sustainability. The EU's swift response through the REPowerEU plan and legislative amendments has been presented as a commitment to accelerating the green transition. However, striking the right balance between energy security and environmental protection is essential for a resilient and sustainable European future. Instead, the REPowerEU plan accentuates the silos between biodiversity protection and climate change mitigation.

The REPowerEU plan brings many opportunities but also challenges in the context of energy security and environmental sustainability. While short-term deviations may be necessary in times of crisis, they must be approached with caution. Continuous review, adaptation and monitoring of emergency measures are essential to avoid prolonged deregulation, reaching a level of impermissible environmental regression.

[78] Case C-284/95 *Safety High-Tech v S & T Srl* (Safety High-Tech) [1998] ECR I-4301, [49].

Thus, measures should focus on the very difficult exercise of balancing immediate security needs with long-term environmental objectives, ensuring a harmonious coexistence. The rigorous application of the principle of proportionality in compliance with the TFEU and the Charter to integrate environmental protection in other sectoral policies is key in this regard.

To this end, the DNSH principle should be fortified with clear criteria to guide decision-making. The funding of new fossil fuel infrastructure risk creating long-term carbon dependencies and hindering the energy transition in the long term. Therefore, exemptions, when granted, should be well justified and should not compromise environmental standards. Moreover, EIAs should remain a key element of permitting processes, as they provide transparency and accountability, even in fast-track permitting procedures. Expedited permitting demands clear definitions and guidance, public participation and justification of decisions, in order to be truly efficient. Finally, emergency measures introduced during crises should be monitored and revised continuously to assess their relevance and alignment with constantly evolving situations, since adaptation and recalibration are essential to avoid lock-in effects. In this regard, parliamentary oversight is paramount in order to enhance democratic accountability. The amendments introduced by the REPowerEU plan result in a deregulation of the energy sector, creating risks for environmental backsliding if not monitored cautiously.

The complex relationship between the fight against climate change and the halting of biodiversity loss is evident in the REPowerEU plan, which could have been an opportunity to break the silos and bridge the gap between energy and the environment, combining renewable energy sources with robust environmental conservation frameworks. Biodiversity conservation and climate change mitigation should be seen as goals that support each other. In this direction, the new EU Strategy on Adaptation to Climate Change recognises the need to increase synergies with areas like biodiversity for creating a climate resilient Europe.[79] Policy coherence is crucial, even within various environmental realms and it is essential to recognise that biodiversity and climate change mitigation are inextricably linked. Climate change is a significant driver of biodiversity loss, jeopardising protected species by destroying their habitats and threatening their extinction. At the same time, preserved nature plays a fundamental role in climate change mitigation, through carbon sequestration, and adaptation, eg through the prevention/reduction of floods' damage exacerbated by climate change.[80]

While it can be argued that the introduced amendments serve the goal of ensuring a 'high level of environmental protection' since they accelerate the deployment of renewable energy contributing to climate change mitigation, the very purpose of environmental assessments is to identify the basis to deliberate on trade-offs between various public interests, including opposing environmental goals. Thus, curtailing those assessments can only lead to ill-based decisions.

Renewable energy installations are essential in fighting climate change, but they can also lead to biodiversity loss in the areas where they are implemented. This creates a

[79] Communication from the Commission to the European Parliament, the Council, the European Economic and Social Committee and the Committee of the Regions, Forging a climate-resilient Europe – the new EU Strategy on Adaptation to Climate Change [2021] COM(2021) 82 final, 2.

[80] M Fitzmaurice, 'Biodiversity and Climate Change' (2021) 23 *International Community Law Review* 230.

contrast between the benefits of such projects for climate change mitigation and the potential harm they may cause to biodiversity. The best way to maximise such benefits and reduce harm is to conduct solid environmental impact assessments for these projects. The REPowerEU plan has chosen the opposite direction, potentially leading to more policy and social conflict in the local communities that will host the projects, which is turn may lead to projects' delays.

The EU should move away from compartmentalised thinking acknowledging climate change and biodiversity as 'two sides of the same coin'. In this regard, the Nature Restoration Law[81] should be implemented alongside REPowerEU to restore and rehabilitate degraded ecosystems, enhancing their resilience to climate change and bolstering their ability to sequester carbon.

In conclusion, the application of EU environmental law during emergencies should not be seen as an obstacle but as an opportunity to address immediate challenges and end silos between different environmental policies without compromising long-term sustainability. By addressing immediate energy security concerns while upholding long-term environmental commitments, the EU can emerge as a global leader in both energy resilience and environmental sustainability.

[81] Proposal for a Regulation of the European Parliament and of the Council on nature restoration [2022] COM(2022)304 final.

13

The Impact of War on EU Food Security

CHRISTIAN MESTRE

13.1. Introduction

As a legal issue, food security rose up the agenda after the Mad Cow Disease scandal,[1] but the purpose was first to give consumers back confidence, and the content of the food security policy was mainly in relation with the sanitary conditions for the food commodities.[2] With the Russian aggression against Ukraine, the vision and the goal are changed; today the main concern is the supply of foodstuffs and the security of food supply chains.[3]

As we know, Russia and Ukraine are recognised as significant exporters of certain produce. A large proportion of the grains or seeds used by the European population and European farmers comes from Russia and Ukraine,[4] and this dependency extends to other countries beyond the Ukrainian borders, in Africa (eg, Benin and Somalia) and the Middle East (eg, Syria or Yemen).[5] In this very particular context, the outbreak of the war has created a huge and global upheaval and jeopardised the food trade.[6]

The war's impact on food supplies has taken many forms: the fear of possible food shortages; sharp increases in prices; and the continuance of food assistance for vulnerable populations. Moreover, the occupation by the Russian forces of a part of Ukraine,

[1] PM Lledo, *Histoire de la vache folle* (Paris, PUF, 2001); J Butault, *Les causes juridiques de la crise de la vache folle* (Paris, Dalloz, 2010); *United Kingdom v Commission*, ECLI:EU:C:1998:192; M Blanquet and N de Grove-Valdeyron, 'Les relations entre la PAC, la politique de santé et la politique de sécurité alimentaire' (2011) 4 *Revue des Affaires Européennes* 707.

[2] A Mahiou and F Snyder (eds), *La sécurité alimentaire/ Food security and food safety* (Leiden, Martinus Nijhoff, 2006).

[3] Y Petit, 'L'invasion russe en Ukraine: l'Union européenne face au défi de la sécurité alimentaire' (2022) *Revue de Droit Rural*, no 504, étude 24.

[4] Commission Implementing Decision (EU) 2022/500, 25/03/2022 establishing the military aggression of Russia against Ukraine as the occurrence of an exceptional event causing a significant disruption of markets: 'The crisis is likely to have serious consequences as the supply of grain, vegetable oils and white fish from Ukraine and Russia to the Union'; [2022] OJ L101/45.

[5] P Weil and G Zachmann, 'The impact of the war in Ukraine on food security' Bruegel Blog (21 March 2022); Y Petit, 'L'Union européenne et la sécurité alimentaire suite à l'agression russe en Ukraine' (2022) *Revue des Affaires Européennes*, no 507, alerte 256.

[6] E Ducros, 'Crise alimentaire mondiale : entre repli et responsabilité, l'Europe doit choisir' Fondation Robert Schuman (4 April 2022).

the destruction of infrastructure and agricultural land and the blockage of the Black Sea Ukrainian ports have reduced significantly Ukraine's export capacities. In 2022 and 2023, the land on which to grow cereal crops has reduced and, subsequently, the grain harvest has been impacted.

There are two important points to make. Firstly, politicians and journalists tend to prefer the term 'food sovereignty' over 'food security'.[7] In 2022, during the first semester of the French presidency of the Council, the French Head of State Emmanuel Macron referred only to 'food sovereignty', and likewise, to 'energetic sovereignty'.[8] Secondly, at the same time, the French Government decided to change the name of the Ministry of Agriculture to the Department of Agricultural and Food Sovereignty.[9] To my mind, this demonstrates a gap between political weight and political will: to speak about food sovereignty recalls the introduction of the Common Agricultural Policy (CAP), when the goal of the European Community was food independency, but it is impossible to make a real distinction between sovereignty and independency.

However, whatever the term used, the substance is the same, and in relation to food security, there are four pillars:[10] availability; access; utilisation; and stability. The first one is concerned with having enough supplies of suitable food; the second with having sufficient resources to obtain food; the third with having a healthy diet; and the fourth with understanding the stability of food supplies, and protecting the European population against unexpected events, weather conditions and cyclical events.[11]

The issue of access was the most important in relation to the international food system at the time Russian invaded Ukraine. A number of events were affecting access at that time: the COVID pandemic;[12] climate change-induced drought;[13] and rising food prices. Of course, the war has deepened these food vulnerabilities, but they were present before. For example at the end of November 2021, the European Commission adopted both a contingency plan for ensuring food supply and food security in times of crisis[14] and measures against market disturbance in compliance with the general Common Market Organisation Regulation.[15] To quote, 'Increasing uncertainty as well as price and supply volatility are affecting production capacity and distribution through the food

[7] S Alahyane, 'La souveraineté alimentaire ou le droit des peuples à se nourrir eux-mêmes' (2017) 3 *Politique Etrangère* 167.

[8] M Pariset et M Hocque, 'Discours d'Emmanuel MACRON à la Sorbonne, 26/09/2017, Pour une Europe de la sécurité et de la souveraineté parlementaire' *Le Monde* (13 July 2002).

[9] Décret no 2022/840, 1 June 2022 relatif aux attributions du ministre de l'agriculture et de la souveraineté alimentaire, JORF no 127, 2 June 2022.

[10] FAO, 'Food Security' Policy Brief (June 2006, Issue 2).

[11] S Mahieu and K Merten-Lentz (eds), *Sécurité alimentaire, Nouveaux enjeux et perspectives* (Brussells, Bruylant, 2013); D Bianchi, 'Souveraineté alimentaire: les outils juridiques au niveau européen à la lumière de la récente réforme de la PAC et du Green Deal' (2022) 2 *Revue du droit d 175 e l'Union européenne* 175.

[12] UN Policy Brief, 'The Impact of COVID-19 on Food Security and Nutrition' (June 2020); Y Petit, 'L'Union européenne face à la déstabilisation de l'agriculture par la pandémie de COVID-19' (2020) *Revue de Droit Rural* étude 20; H Basquin Fané, Impact of COVID-19 on food security, ALIMENTERRE 2020, available at www.alimenterre.org/impact-of-the-covid-19-crisis-on-food-security.

[13] UN Office for Disaster Risk Reduction, Special Report on Drought 2021.

[14] COM(2021) 689 final, 12 November2021; creation of the European Food Security Crisis preparedness and response Mechanism (EFSCM).

[15] Regulation (EU) no 1308/2013 of the European Parliament and of the Council of 17/12/2013 establishing a common organization of the market in agricultural products, [2013] OJ L347/671.

supply chain.'[16] This statement dates to exactly three months before the outbreak of the Russian invasion.

This chapter consists of two main sections; section 13.2 provides a general overview of the impact of the Russian aggression on food supplies, then section 13.3 concerning the European response to the situation.

13.2. The Impact of the Russian Aggression on Food Security

The war caused a deep disruption to the agricultural and food markets in the EU and beyond mainly because of the weight of both Russia and Ukraine in the grain supply chain.

13.2.1. The State of Dependency

Russia and Ukraine are major providers of cereals, sunflower and fertilisers. According to the European Parliament, Ukraine represents around 15 per cent of cereals in the world market[17] and Russia over 20 per cent (wheat, barley, corn). Including sunflower (seeds, cake and oil), Ukrainian exports can feed around 400 million people.[18] Both Russia and Ukraine are key players for basic agricultural and food commodities, and their grain exports are crucial for many countries, in European as well as Africa. This dependency creates a demand for a large number of other imports, such as animal feed, additive feed, and a wide range of agricultural fertilisers (eg ammonia, nitrogen, phosphate and potassium).[19]

Russian forces in Ukraine have destroyed some storage (silos storage) and transport infrastructures, harbour facilities, and the blocking of Black Sea Ukrainian ports have reduced Ukraine's export capacities by 90 per cent. Before the war, the volume of goods, mainly cereals, shipped by sea per month was five–six million tonnes. In 2022 alone, the fall-off in agricultural production was one-third to one-half.[20] Therefore, crops could not be planted as the agricultural lands are concentrated in the conflict areas.

In this crisis, food commodity prices reached record highs and, most importantly for consumers, inflation rose dramatically. Of course, high prices also mean rising costs

[16] COM(2021) 689 final, pt 4; D Gadbin, 'La sécurité alimentaire dans tous ses états: le besoin de politique commune agricole' (2022) *Revue de Droit Rural*, no 507, repère 9.

[17] European Council, Council of the EU, 'Food for the world. What EU countries are doing to mitigate the impact of Russia's war', pt 2: 'Ukraine: the world's bread basket', available at www.consilium.europa.eu/en/food-for-the-world-eu-countries-mitigate-impact-russia-war; Ukraine, Agriculture et alimentation (January 2021); available at www.tresor.economie.gouv.fr.

[18] P9_TA (2022)099 (24 March 2022),'Need for an urgent E.U. action plan to ensure food security inside and outside the E.U. in fight of the Russian invasion of Ukraine', pts K and L.

[19] COM(2022) 590 final, 9 November 2022, Ensuring availability and affordability of fertilizers, Annex 2, 8.

[20] Europe Daily Bulletin, 9 April 2022, no 12929.

of seeds, livestock feed for producers and farmers. According to the FAO Food Price Index, the price of cereals rose nearly 17 per cent from February to March 2022, while for wheat, the increase was 70per cent.[21] The price of sunflower oiluring the period rose from €550 euros to more than €1000 per tonne.[22] The same trend can be seen over a range of goods, such as meat and vegetable oil.

The price of fertilisers rose even more significantly due to higher gas prices, following Russia's decision in March 2022 to stop the export of nitrogen fertilisers. Facing this new financial and economic environment, some farmers and companies have opted to cease farming or switch to different crops.

13.2.2. The Threat of Food Insecurity

The European Economic Treaty set out five objectives for the CAP, among them the requirement to ensure the availability of supplies, to guarantee affordable prices for consumers and to ensure a fair standard of living for farmers.[23] Of course, the crisis has jeopardised the achievement of these latter objectives. However, the reports of the Commission and the European Parliament suggest that each institution assesses this situation quite differently. Thus for the Commissioner in charge of agricultural area (M Janucz Wojciechowski) and more largely for the whole European Commission, consumers have absolutely nothing to fear: in all key agricultural products (cereals, animal and dairy product), the Union is largely self-sufficient.[24] The Commission nonetheless recognises that the price level can impede low-income households (already affected by the COVID pandemic) in obtaining food essentials. Furthermore, in 2022, according the official Eurostat figures, the Union recorded a drop in food consumption of eight per cent, and in 2023 of almost of three per cent – which is unprecedented.

The European Parliament does not share the Commission' position. While the Union is not immune to food shortages, it recalls, in several resolutions,[25] the interdependencies of the agricultural and food markets, and refers to Russia and Ukraine as 'grain giants'. In response this situation, the European Parliament made recommendations to improve food independency, and to reduce food waste. The light-touch response is surprising and raises the question whether they understand the measure of the challenges for the Union brought about by the war. Moreover, we note the contrast with the Versailles declaration of EU heads of state or government at the beginning

[21] S Favier, 'Pourquoi les prix du blé flambent-ils?' *Le Monde* (20 May 2022); FAO, Food Price Index, 3 March 2023.

[22] L Girard, 'Le tournesol a perdu la boussole' *Le Monde* (27/28 March 2022); La France Agricole 29/04/2022, available at infodoc.agroparistech.fr/index.php?lvl=bulletin_display&id=170636.

[23] Art 39 TFEU; D Bianchi, *La politique agricole commune (PAC), Précis de droit agricole européen*, 2nd edn (Brussells, Bruylant, 2012).

[24] COM(2022) 133 final, 23 March 2022, Safeguarding food security and reinforcing the resilience of food systems, 1: 'Food supply is not at stake in the EU today. The EU is largely self-sufficient for key agricultural products, being a main wheat and barley exporter and largely able to covers its consumption for other staple crops such as maize or sugar. The EU is also largely self-sufficient for animal products, including dairy and meat, with the notable exception of seafood.'

[25] P9_TA (2022)0099, 24 March 2022, pt W; P9_TA (2022)0219, 18 May 2022, pt H.

of March 2022, which was an alarmist statement pointing out the risks to global food security.[26]

Beyond the EU, the first victims of food insecurity are the Ukrainian people; mainly those living in areas controlled or bombed by Russian forces. At least half of the Ukrainian people have been affected by diet restrictions and shortages,[27] and access to food communities in many areas is challenging. In addition, many countries with dependence on Russian and Ukrainian supplies (eg from North Africa, Middle East or Central Asia) lost a significant proportion of their imports (mainly grain), market disruptions and rising prices weakening the economic situation of the people of these countries. In May 2022, according to the UN, the number of severely food insecure people worldwide reached nearly 300 million.[28] From March to July of the same year, there was a total halt in grain export, and in the same time, over 14 million tonnes of wheat could not leave the Black Sea ports.

13.3. EU Responses

In early March 2022, the EU leaders invited the Commission[29] to present proposals and actions in order to safeguard food security and to support mainly the EU producers.

13.3.1. Strengthening Food Security

Food security was the main topic during the informal European Council session at Versailles in 2022 during the French presidency. Quickly the Commission adopted a communication on 'Safeguarding food security and reinforcing the resilience of food systems'[30] alongside a package of measures: some intended for Union agriculture and others based on solidarity with Ukraine and a multilateral approach. In the resolution following the Commission communication, the European Parliament gave its support to the planned actions, and called for an 'urgent EU action plan to ensure food security inside and outside the EU in light of the Russian invasion of Ukraine'.[31]

For Ukraine, the EU adopted an emergency support programme of €330 million mainly to secure access to basic goods and to protect them:[32] this involved humanitarian assistance, monitoring food insecurity and rebuilding infrastructure. In addition,

[26] Informal meeting of the Heads of State or Government 11–12 March 2022, The Versailles Declaration, pt 21: 'We will impose our food security by reducing our dependencies on key imported agricultural products and inputs, in particular by increasing the E.U. production of plant-based proteins' available at www.consilium.europa.eu.

[27] World Food Programme, Ukraine Food Security Report (May 2022); NS George, 'Beyond the Holodomor: current hunger in Ukraine and global food insecurity' (2024) 3 *Public Health Challenges* 1.

[28] Security Council Resolution 24 May 2022, S/RES/2417 Conflict and Food Security.

[29] The Versailles Declaration (n 26) pt 21.

[30] COM(2022) 133 final, 23 March 2022.

[31] P9_TA (2022)0099, 24 March 2022.

[32] QANDA/22/1964, 23 March 2022, Questions and Answers: Commission acts to safeguard global food security and support EU farmers and consumers.

the EU worked with other western countries and in relation to international organisations and bodies, such as G7 and G20. In March 2022, alongside G7 members and the African Union, on the proposal of President Macron,[33] the EU adopted a mechanism to address the food crisis and to ensure food security in the most vulnerable countries, named 'international Food and Agriculture Resilience Mission (FARM)".[34]

Three months later, G7 members and the World Bank Group established a Global Alliance for Food Security (GAFS) as a concerted response to the unfolding global hunger crisis.[35] A few days later, the European Council conclusions invited the Commission, in a section about food security, to propose actions to help developing countries and to support Africa's sustainable agri-food production capacities.[36]

During the last G20 meeting in November 2022, the heads of state made some commitments to enhance the mechanism of information exchange about agricultural storage and flow, named G20 AMIS.[37] They have requested the renewal of the international Black Sea Grain Initiative concluded under the care of UN. This international meeting carried on the substance of the declaration of leader's summit on global food security held on September 2022 in the margins of the United Nations General Assembly (UNGA).[38]

Among the others actions or programmes, two are particularly significant: Solidarity Lanes; and, as mentioned above, the Black Sea Grain Initiative. Solidarity Lanes is an action plan established by the Commission in May 2022[39] 'for the establishment of alternatives routes using all transport modes, linking the E.U. to Ukraine, while Ukraine's access to black Sea routes is restored'. As a result, 33 million tonnes of grain, oil, seeds and other agricultural products were exported this way between the launch and July 2023.[40]

Moreover, on 19 July 2022, the UN, Ukraine, Russia and Turkyie brokered an agreement to open a safe corridor in the Black Sea, known as the Black Sea Grain Initiative.[41] For its implementation, the states involved and UN held a center of joined coordination in Istanbul. Concluded after 60 days, it was extended for 120 days in November and subsequently to 120 days after Russia accepted new terms. Thanks to this agreement

[33] Communiqué conjoint du ministère de l'Europe et des Affaires étrangères et du ministère de l'Agriculture et de l'Alimentation, 5 April 2022, Sécurité alimentaire: mise en œuvre de l'initiative FARM.

[34] UN World Food Programme, 26 July 2022, France and World Food Programme launch FARM Solidarity Initiative; Europe Daily Bulletin no 12928, 7 April 2022.

[35] The World Bank, Joint Statement 19 May 2022, 'G7 and World Bank Group establish Global alliance for food security to catalyze response to food crisis'; European Parliamentary Research Service, 'Russia's war on Ukraine: impact on global food security and EU response,' PE 733.667 (September 2022) 11.

[36] European Council Conclusions, 23–24 June 2022, pt 9.

[37] G20 Bali Leader's Declaration, Bali, Indonesia, 15/16 November 2022, pt 7: 'We support the international efforts to keep food supply chains functioning under challenging circumstances. We are committed to addressing food security by ensuring accessibility, affordability, and sustainability of food end food products for those in needs, particularly in developing countries and least developed countries.'

[38] UN General Assembly (77) 21–22 September 2022, Declaration of Leaders' Summit on Global Food Security, available at www.consilium.europa.eu.

[39] COM(2022) 217 final, 12 May 2022, An action plan for E.U.-Ukraine Solidarity Lanes to facilitate Ukraine's export and bilateral trade with the EU.

[40] www.consilium.europa.eu/en/infographics/ukrainian-grain-exports-explained.

[41] M Jego, 'A Istanbul, un accord sur l'exportation des céréales ukrainiennes et russes soumis à la bonne foi de Vladimir Poutine' *Le Monde* 23 July 2022; A Belkaid, 'Un fragile corridor contre la faim' *Le Monde Diplomatique* (March 2003).

(Istanbul Agreement), from July 2022 to March 2023, nearly 25 million tonnes of food were shipped.[42] However, in mid-July 2023, Russia refused to extend the agreement.

Finally, for the 90th anniversary of the outbreak of the Holodomor (Ukrainian famine)[43] at the end on November 2023 – this tragedy being quite symbolic of the relations with Russia – the Ukrainian President Vladimir Zelenskyy launched a food initiative named Grain from Ukraine at the food security summit held in Kyiv.[44] At a second international summit at the end of that month he decided to extend this humanitarian initiative.[45] The entities participating in the project buy agricultural products from Ukrainian producers and transfer them mainly to African countries, where populations are on the brink of starvation. Over 30 countries, plus the EU, participate in this programme, and it has provided food to over five million people; for example, 170,000 tonnes of Ukrainian grain were delivered to Somalia, Ethiopia, Kenya and Yemen, and their donations totalled €200 million.

13.3.2. Support for EU Farmers and Consumers

From the start of the invasion, the Commission adopted a range of measures to contain the impact of rising prices and input costs in favour of European farmers,[46] and the European Parliament[47] and the European Council approved them[48] while inviting the Commission to propose new actions.

The first measure concerns half a billion euros in support[49] from two separate budget lines: the reserve for crisis of €350 million planned by the CAP,[50] which was used for the first time in 2013; and special provisions within the CAP budget specifically for farmers. By relating to this main action, the Commission decided to authorise more advance direct payments to farmers from 16 October 2022. The second, more targeted, measure aims to help pork production sector, which needed particular support.[51]

The third measure – and perhaps the most debated – is an exceptional derogation of the fallow land policy. To increase the production capacity of food and feeds

[42] www.consilium.europa.eu.

[43] P9_TA (2022)0449, European resolution of 15 December 2022 on 90 years after the Holodomor: recognising the mass killing through starvation as genocide 1932/1933, VINGTIEME SIECLE. REVUE D'HISTOIRE, 2014, no 121, 121; A Applebaum, *Red Famine: Stalin's War on Ukraine* (London, Allen Lane, 2017).

[44] 'President Zelenskyy opens first international summit to implement grain from Ukraine program initiated by Ukraine, designed to help countries suffering from hunger' (26 November 2022), available at www.president.gov.ua.

[45] mfa.gov.ua grain.ukraine.

[46] COM(2022) 133 final, Safeguarding food security and reinforcing the resilience of food systems.

[47] P9_TA (2022)099 (n 18).

[48] European Council meeting, 24–25 March 2022, EUCO 1/22, CO EUR 1 CONCL 1, pt 23.

[49] Commission Delegated Regulation (EU) 2022/467, 23 March 2022 providing for exceptional adjustment aid to producers in the agricultural sectors, [2022] OJ L96/4, Art 1.

[50] Regulation (UE) no 1306/2013 of the European Parliament and of the Council of 17/12/2013 on the financing, management and monitoring of the CAP, [2013] OJ L347/549, Arts 4 and 106; Regulation (UE) 2021/2116 of the European Parliament and of the Council of 02/12/2021 on the financing, management and monitoring of the CAP and repealing regulation (EU) no 1306/2013, [2021] OJ L435/187.

[51] Commission Implementing Regulation (EU) 2022/470, 23/03/2022 granting aid private storage for pigmeat and fixing the amount of aid in advance, [2022] OJ L96/39.

commodities, the Commission agreed to temporarily renounce a key environmental measure, while maintaining the full level of the greening payment.[52] Concerning this question, a large gap appeared between the Commission and the European Parliament: some the Commission's members defended the farmers' trade unions' position in order to suppress or reduce the fallow land obligation. However, the best yields rarely came from the former fallow land. Therefore, the Commission did not want to waive an emblematic measure of its 'Green deal',[53] or to change its priorities in the environmental area.[54] Nevertheless, in a conciliatory spirit, the Commission announced the postponement of two Green Deal legislative proposals: the revision of the Sustainable Use of Pesticides Directive; and the nature restoration targets.[55] However, in June 2022, the Commission decided to submit a proposal of regulation on pesticides.[56]

At the same time, the Commission established a self-standing Temporary Crisis Framework that enables farmers and fertiliser producers[57] to receive national aid to offset the rising prices for inputs in compliance with the competition law. This mechanism is in force after renewal on 28 October 2022 by the Commission.[58] As during the first semester of 2023 the Member States had to send to the Commission their CAP strategic plans, which could include investments measures and actions to recover independency on fertilisers and pesticides, and all inputs.[59]

For consumers, the EU allows the Member States to apply reduced rates of value added tax and encourages economic operators to contain retail prices.[60] For their low-income and deprived citizens, the Member States can have recourse to the Fund for European Aid to the Most Deprived[61] (FEAD), founded in 2020.[62] In response to the COVID-19 pandemic, European institutions amended this Fund several times,[63] and of course, it was appropriate to address this new challenge.

[52] Commission Implementing Decision (EU) 2022/484, 23/03/2022, providing for derogations from regulation (EU) no 1307/2013 of the European Parliament and of the Council and from Commission Delegated Regulation (EU) no 239/2014 as regards the implementation of certain conditions relating to the greening payment for claim year 2022 (notified under document C (2022)1875), [2022] OJ L 98/105.

[53] COM(2019) 640 final, 11 December 2019.

[54] COM(2020) 380 final, 20 May 2020, European Union Biodiversity Strategy for 2030. Bringing nature back into our lives; COM(2020) 381 final, 20 May 2020, A Farm to Fork Strategy for a fair, healthy and environmentally friendly food system.

[55] European Commission, 'Green deal: pioneering proposals to restore Europe's nature by 2050 and halve pesticide use by 2030' Press release, 22 June 2022.

[56] COM(2022) 305 final, 22 June 2022, Proposal for a regulation on the sustainable use of plant production products and amending regulation (EU) 2021/2115.

[57] Communication from the Commission, Temporary Crisis Framework for State Aid measures to support the economy following the aggression against Ukraine by Russia, [2022] OJ CI131/1; see Amendment to the Temporary Crisis Framework, [2022] OJ C280/1.

[58] [2022] OJ C426/1; see also [2023] OJ C/2023/1188 amendment by the Commission.

[59] Europe Daily Bulletin no 12925, 5 April 2022, Agriculture: European Commission publishes overview of its observations on 19 CAP strategic plans.

[60] COM(2022) 133 final, 23 March 2022, pt 3-1.

[61] ibid: 'Member States can draw from EU funds such as the Fund for European Aid to the Most Deprived (FEAD) which supports EU countries' actions to provide food and/or basic material assistance to the most deprived, reaching over 15 million people with food aid.'

[62] Regulation (EU) no 223/2014 of the European Parliament and of the Council, 11 March 2014 on the Fund for European Aid to the most Deprived, [2014] OJ L72/1.

[63] Regulation (EU) 2020/559, 23 April 2020, [2020] OJ L130/7; Regulation (EU) 2021/177, 10/02/2021, [2021] OJ L53/1.

13.4. Conclusion

Born out of the Mad Cow Disease crisis, food security was one of the main issues underlined by the outbreak of the war. This was the first time that heads of states and governments (and politicians generally) recognised both the importance of food security and the weight of dependency. All the measures and actions taken since the beginning of the conflict aimed to ensure food security in a European and international framework and restore the EU's food independency. These challenges should fundamentally change the philosophy and purposes of the CAP, and restore the balance between the production of food commodities and the respect for environmental protection.

14

(Almost) All Roads Lead to Kyiv: How Russia's War against Ukraine Changed EU Transport Policy for Good

PIERPAOLO SETTEMBRI* AND MARGHERITA CORSARO

14.1. Introduction

This chapter sheds light on how an external event – the 2022 Russia's war against Ukraine – impacted and changed profoundly one of the oldest and most successful policies of the European Union (EU), notably its transport policy. The criteria that guided the selection of the evidence presented here are whether the war altered directly the EU transport policy and whether it did so in an irreversible way. The examples are those for which both questions are answered in the affirmative. They concern in particular the opening of new transport and trade routes, the EU infrastructure policy and maps, a significantly altered geopolitical (transport) landscape, military mobility and the implementation of the Association Agreement's transport provisions towards Ukraine's accession to the EU. The chapter does not cover the measures taken against Russia – such as sanctions – nor does it take into account the new landscape of EU energy suppliers, although their impact on EU transport policy is also substantial.

14.2. New Transport Routes: The 'Solidarity Lanes'

When, on 24 February 2022, Russia invaded Ukraine – a country sharing a 2,235km border with the EU – the bloc was unequivocal in its solidarity with the attacked nation. As many other policy instruments, transport was also mobilised to deliver on the promised assistance. As a response to Russia's blockade of Black Sea ports, which hampered primarily agricultural exports from Ukraine, the European Commission and bordering EU Member States established in May 2022 the so-called 'Solidarity Lanes'[1] to enable

* The author is employed at the European Commission. He writes in a personal capacity and his views cannot be construed as representing the position of the European Commission.

[1] Communication from the European Commission: 'An action plan for EU-Ukraine Solidarity Lanes to facilitate Ukraine's agricultural export and bilateral trade with the EU', COM(2022)217, 12 May 2022.

such exports through alternative routes using all other available transport modes (rail, road and inland waterways). Today these Solidarity Lanes are not just a nice addition to the pre-existing options: they are the lifeline for the Ukrainian economy overall and – sadly since Russia halted its participation in the Black Sea deal in July 2023 – the only remaining available option.

While they were created primarily to solve the specific problem of the grain exports (and to do so quickly before the 2022 harvest), today they are used to export much more than just grains and, most importantly, to enable Ukraine import the goods it needs. Between May 2022 and July 2024, the Solidarity Lanes allowed Ukraine to export around 150 million tonnes of goods (including around 81 million tonnes of agricultural products), and to import around 58 million tonnes of goods. The total value of trade via the Solidarity Lanes since May 2022 is estimated at around €170 billion, with around €52.5 billion for Ukraine's exports and around €117.5 billion for imports.

The measures taken by the EU to guarantee Ukraine's exports and imports draw upon a solid legal framework and a jointly defined path towards the approximation of Ukraine to the EU. This represents a radical fast-forward in the bilateral relations between the EU and Ukraine – a path whose ultimate destination is the accession.

14.3. EU Infrastructure Policy

Partly as a consequence of the Solidarity Lanes, the war changed the EU's infrastructure policy, and not only towards Ukraine. In July 2022 the Commission put forward a proposal[2] to extend into Ukraine (and Moldova) four corridors of the Trans-European Transport Network (TEN-T), notably the North-Sea Baltic Corridor via Lviv and Kyiv to Mariupol; the Baltic–Black–Aegean Sea Corridor to Odesa via Lviv and via Chişinău as well as the Baltic Sea–Adriatic Sea and the Rhine-Danube Corridors to Lviv.

Given the political momentum, the process of extending the TEN-T core network to Ukraine (and Moldova) was remarkably short, taking only a few months for the high-level understanding between the Commission and Ukraine to be signed (29 June 2022). Following the finalisation of the maps, with the agreement of Ukraine and Moldova, a high-level understanding on the adaptation of the indicative TEN-T was signed in December 2023. As a term of comparison, the integration process of the Western Balkans in TEN-T, from the establishment of the Transport Community until the signature of the High-Level Agreement between the Commission and the six concerned states (Bosnia and Herzegovina, Montenegro, North Macedonia and Serbia) took around six years. The corridors under the amended TEN-T, which follow a gradual development and whose fully fledged completion is expected by end 2050, add up to, and in certain cases are aligned with, the Solidarity Lanes. While the latter are meant to provide highly needed, targeted support to Ukrainian agricultural exports and thus to the Ukrainian economy, the former are expected to provide the needed infrastructure

[2] Amended proposal of the European Commission for a Regulation on Union guidelines for the development of the trans-European transport network, amending Regulation (EU) 2021/1153 and Regulation (EU) No 913/2010 and repealing Regulation (EU) 1315/2013, COM(2022)384, 27 July 2022.

connections in the framework of the reconstruction of Ukraine, while drawing lessons learnt from the operation of these commercial routes.

Far from being just a few lines on a map, this development represents a fundamental policy change, with significant implications, some of which are even immediate. For one, the Connecting Europe Facility (CEF) – the EU funding instrument that provides financing for projects under TEN-T – already received in the September 2020 call applications for more than €230 million of support for nine joint projects on border crossing points between frontline Member States (Poland, Slovakia, Hungary and Romania) and Ukraine or Moldova. Even more requests for support are expected to come in the 2023 CEF call, which for the first time allows Ukraine and Moldova to request funding for infrastructure investments along the Solidarity Lanes, following an agreement signed earlier this year by the European Commission for transport Adina Vălean and Deputy Prime Minister of Ukraine Oleksandr Kubrakov.

The international political resonance of the association of Ukraine to CEF transport and its integration in the TEN-T network was highlighted once again by the decision of the Commission and the international financial institutions – the European Investment Bank (EIB), the European Bank for Reconstruction and Development and the World Bank – to mobilise €1 billion euros to increase the capacity of the Solidarity Lanes and improving overall connectivity with Ukraine (and Moldova). Indeed, these funds are expected to complement the allocations under CEF 2022 call, thus financing projects on the TEN-T network. As TEN-T grows to a continental transport network, its indicative maps and related projects have provided orientation to international financial institutions, among other investors, on where to focus their funding and activities in the concerned regions.

Another significant example is rail gauge. Despite its technical nature, the issue is highly political. The fact that the network in the Eastern Partnership countries is equipped with the 1,520mm rail track gauge, whereas the Union standard gauge is narrower (1,435mm), represents a notable obstacle to the integration of the rail network of Ukraine with that of the EU. For instance, Ukrainian goods following the North Sea Baltic Corridor and reaching the port of Klaipeda on Ukrainian trains have to be transhipped at the border between Poland and Ukraine (on trains with the European standard nominal track gauge of 1,435 mm), and then transhipped again at the border between Poland and Lithuania (on 1,520 track gauge trains).

There are other cases of EU Member States having a different gauge from the the European standard, most notably Spain and Portugal, but the Commission never proposed to harmonise it. In fact, two months before the beginning of the war the Commission had put forward a proposal to revise the EU infrastructure policy – the TEN-T network – and did not include anything on this specific issue. A few months later, because of the war and the specific updates made necessary by the situation in Ukraine, the Commission proposed to oblige all Member States with a land rail connection with other Member States to include a requirement to develop all new TEN-T railway lines with a European standard track gauge of 1,435 mm and also to develop a migration plan towards this European standard nominal track gauge for all existing lines of the European Transport Corridors.

To prepare for the integration of Ukrainian (and Moldovan) rail system in the EU, the Commission together with the European Investment Bank conducted a pre-feasibility study[3] for a new EU standard-gauge railway corridor connecting Poland, Ukraine, Romania and Moldova, possibly up to Odesa. The report, which delivers on Action 18 of the Action plan for the EU–Ukraine Solidarity Lanes, goes beyond the initial objective to assess the workability of the extension of the EU logistical paths into Ukraine, and provides a good overview of the general rail network and operations of the two third countries. In so doing, it not only serves the purpose of defining a path towards more interconnectivity between the EU and Ukraine, but it considers the transport network linking the bloc to its neighbourhood as a whole and aims to contribute to its resilience by reducing the vulnerability of logistical chains to exceptional events.

From a broader perspective the war has also shown the strategic dimension of railways. All the leaders that visited President Zelensky, including President Biden, reached Kyiv by train. On 27 March 2023 the head of Ukrainian Railways – Alexander Kamyshin – was appointed Minister for Strategic Industries. The notion of critical infrastructure is now much higher on the agenda, including from the angle of cyber security. This highlights the critical role of traffic management systems in rail and aviation, and the future for autonomous cars. This is not limited to Ukraine but extends to the entire EU infrastructure network. As President Eisenhower once said: 'You will not find it difficult to prove that battles, campaigns, and even wars have been won or lost primarily because of logistics.' And logistics is the great protagonist of this war, be it for the transport of grains, refugees or weapons.

Beyond CEF, the war in Ukraine has led to a wide-ranging repurposing of other EU funding programmes, including regional funds and external action instruments for Ukraine, geared at improving connectivity between the EU and the country. This is a strong signal, adding up to the exceptionally quick regulatory activity, that the Union is also increasing its ambitions as regards its enlargement outlooks in the Eastern part of Europe. As a matter of fact, 'Each of the EU enlargements was accompanied by a strong growth of transport activity'.[4]

14.4. A New Geopolitical (Transport) Landscape

Beyond reframing the EU–Ukrainian relationships as regards the transport and infrastructure policy, the July 2022 proposal concerning the extension of the TEN-T network had an extensive impact on the EU transport infrastructure policy with other third countries. First, the text suggested downgrading last-mile connections of the core network road and railway sections to Russia and Belarus under the Norther Dimension Partnership.

Second, the war highlighted the urgent need to identify alternative, reliable, safe and efficient trade routes between Europe and Asia,[5] thus breathing new life into the project to build a Trans-Caspian International Transport Route. The study on

[3] See: transport.ec.europa.eu/system/files/2023-07/Integration_of_the_UAMD_railway_system_into_the_EU_transport_system.pdf.

[4] Commission Staff Working Document accompanying the 2011 White Paper, SEC(2011) 391 final, 7.

[5] See: transport.ec.europa.eu/transport-themes/international-relations/study-sustainable-transport-connections-central-asia_en.

sustainable transport connections with Central Asia,[6] initiated in November 2021 and published in June 2023, aimed, among other things, to identify the most sustainable transport network connecting five Central Asian countries (Kazakhstan, the Kyrgyz Republic, Tajikistan, Turkmenistan and Uzbekistan) with the EU's extended TEN-T network. It concluded that the Central Trans-Caspian International Transport Route (also known as the Middle Corridor) provides the most sustainable transport connections between Europe and Central Asia. Goods on this corridor enter the Caucasus through the port of Baku, Azerbaijan, and continue to Georgia, from where two alternative routes can be taken before entering the EU via Bulgaria or Romania, one of which is the maritime route via the Black Sea. Indeed, the 'bridging role of the Black Sea basin' in terms of interconnectivity had been already acknowledged by the 2018 EU–Asia Connectivity Strategy.[7] Once again, the network effect resulting from a deeper integration of Ukraine in the EU transport policy, together with an EU-backed post-war reconstruction of the country, is powerful and does not only exceed the EU borders, but even Europe's ones.

Finally, the Solidarity Lanes influenced the external transport policy that the EU has been pursuing with the Western Balkans in the framework of the Transport Community, notably with the integration of Ukraine (and Moldova) in the Transport Community Treaty.

14.5. Military Mobility

For reasons that would be even superfluous to explain, the war in Ukraine made military mobility a necessary priority of the EU. The project was put forward jointly by the Commission and the High Representative (and agreed by the Member States) during the mandate of President Junker.[8] It reluctantly made it to the 2021–27 financial framework with a budget of €1.69 billion (reluctantly, because the Commission had proposed €6.5 billion).

The first call was launched before Russia's aggression against Ukraine for an amount of €330 million, attracting applications for 26 projects. Due to the war, the second call for the same amount (€330 million) was frontloaded to May 2022 and attracted almost three times as many (63). The third call, whose results were published in January 2024, attracted 112 project proposals with 4.5 times oversubscription, of which 38 will be supported with a budget of €807 million. This call, which was frontloaded to May 2023, exhausted the entire budget of military mobility foreseen until 2027.

With the extension of four of the nine corridors of the TEN-T network to Ukraine and Moldova proposed in July 2022, the Commission is de facto also reinforcing

[6] See: ransport.ec.europa.eu/system/files/2023-06/Sustainable_transport_connections_between_Europe_and_Central_Asia.pdf.

[7] Commission Staff Working Document (SWD) replacing the 2010 SWD accompanying the Communication from the Commission on the European Union Strategy for the Denube Region, SWD(2020)59, 9.

[8] Joint Communication from the European Commission and the High Representative of the Union for Foreign Affairs and Security Policy on an Action Plan on Military Mobility, JOIN(2018)5, 28 March 2018.

military mobility towards these countries because the infrastructure standards required for these new corridors are compliant with the military needs foreseen under military mobility. Moreover, CEF military mobility can support also additional actions such as upgrading airports and roads, which would not be possible under the traditional CEF.

For the future, the war in Ukraine may provide the necessary political support to look at foreign direct investments more strategically. Investments such as the one planned by a third country in the port of Hamburg, will more than ever before have to be considered also from the perspective of the new geopolitical landscape. Allowing a third country – especially one that is friendly to Russia – to own a strategic European port makes that infrastructure unattractive and unusable also for military purposes, thereby creating a hole in the EU network.

14.6. Accelerated Implementation of the Association Agreement

Pressure to make Solidarity Lanes a success brought back to the European agenda old sensitive issues such as the liberalisation of road transport between the EU and Ukraine. When the Association Agreement was notoriously not signed by President Yanukovych in November 2013 in Vilnius the EU and Ukraine did initial an aviation agreement (Air Services Agreement). To sign and provisionally apply that agreement took until October 2021 due to a dispute with the UK on the airport of Gibraltar – a problem that it was only possible to overcome after Brexit. It shows that back then the focus was primarily (and almost exclusively) on aviation. Other areas, especially road transport, were far more sensitive. According to the Association Agreement, which was then signed in 2014, the liberalisation of transport was to be defined in possible future transport agreements. Yet a road transport agreement was not in sight. In fact, the issue of the road transport permits granted (bilaterally) to Ukrainian road operators remained a constant irritant in the relationship between Ukraine and the EU and in particular with some Member States, especially Poland. This is because Article 136 of the Association Agreement prescribed that, prior to the conclusion of a dedicated transport agreement, the conditions of mutual market access should have not been made more restrictive as compared to the situation existing before the Association Agreement entered into force.

Today, because of the war and especially to make sure that Solidarity Lanes could increase their capacity, the EU adopted temporary road transport agreements with Ukraine, essentially creating a legal basis for Ukrainian and EU hauliers to transit through and operate between each other's territories. These agreements also include clauses on the recognition of Ukrainian driving licences and certificates of professional competence to further support Ukrainian drivers – something that had so far been an exclusive prerogative of Member States. Of course, they are temporary and linked to the war situation, but they have already been extended once until June 2024 and, subsequently, until June 2025. In the first year of operation, the volume of freight transport increased by more than 50 per cent. As the EU and Ukraine jointly put it, the extension is meant to contribute to the reconstruction of Ukraine 'beyond Russia's war of aggression against Ukraine'.[9]

14.7. Conclusion

Russia's war of aggression against Ukraine changed EU transport policy for good. Measures such as the Solidarity Lanes, which were taken as an emergency reaction to address a specific problem, have created new trade and transport routes that are today stable, essential and irreversible (and growing). The corridors of the TEN-T network have been redesigned and extended to reflect this new reality and to accelerate the integration of Ukraine (and Moldova) into the EU. This effort has been matched by corresponding changes in the way EU infrastructure policy is funded, notably by extending CEF to Ukraine and Moldova, repurposing other EU funds and involving international financial institutions to mobilise up to €1 billion just to increase the capacity of the Solidarity Lanes. In turn, partnerships with other third countries have been deprioritised and alternative global routes are being reconsidered, with the consequence that the broader transport landscape is undergoing a major shake-up. The war underscored the importance of military mobility and accelerated the consumption of its limited budget, especially for projects on the Eastern front. Historically sensitive EU issues, such as the difference in rail gauge and the road transport agreements with third countries, have been brutally bumped to the top of the EU agenda, often leading to bold decisions that were unthinkable just months before the war. Overall, the EU reaction the Russia's war of aggression against Ukraine showed the flexibility and adaptability of both the EU transport sector and the EU transport policy, in line with past experience that all enlargements are accompanied by a strong growth of transport activity.

[9] Decision No 2/2023 of the Joint Committee established by the Agreement between the European Union and Ukraine on the carriage of freight by road of 16 March 2023 as regards the continuation of the Agreement, Recital no 8.

PART III

Institutional Views

15

European Integration: From Fatigue to Revival Through Crisis

EUGENIA DUMITRIU SEGNANA*

15.1. European Integration – Beyond Process, the Question of Legitimacy

A lot has been written on the origins of the European project, so I will recall in only a few lines that in its early days, European integration had first and foremost at its heart the development and the fostering of economic ties between the Member States. The objective was, in the words of Robert Schuman, to create '*une solidarité de fait*':[1] economic integration would almost mechanically induce a degree of material codependence between the participating States which would, in turn, necessarily be translated into political cooperation and integration. Furthermore, the material codependence between the Member States would lead to the emergence of a genuine solidarity between European nations. This vision certainly held true for several decades, which saw the gradual increase of the Union's attributed competences as well as several waves of geographic expansion. The project of European integration is, as recalled by Mateij Avbelj in chapter two of this book,[2] shaped by our common commitment to peace and a common fear of war. After WWII and in the early days of the Cold War, peace was not only a key aim of European integration, but was also, as Mateij Avbeij points out, the main normative value and an enduring source of legitimisation of European integration.

In this process, beyond the values and the objectives that continue to bring together the Member States, the efficiency and the legitimacy of the Union's institutional and legal framework condition the degree of mutual trust amongst the citizens, their national governments and the institutions of the Union.

The EU integration puzzle, as set out in Article 10(1) TEU, rests on the notion of representative democracy and is expressed by institutions which bring together different

* The views expressed by the author are strictly personal and do not engage the institution for which she works. The author wishes to thank Mr Théo Verdi for his help related to this contribution.

[1] Robert Schuman, Déclaration du 9 mai 1950.

[2] The Enduring Legitimisation of European Integration by Reference to Peace?

interests and correspond to distinct legitimacies. The European Parliament, which together with the Council of the European Union (hereinafter, the Council) exercises legislative and budgetary functions, derives its legitimacy from the direct representation of European citizens who directly elect its members every five years.[3]

The European Council, which provides the Union with the necessary impetus for its development and defines its general political directions and priorities, is composed of the Heads of State or Government of the Member States[4] who are themselves democratically accountable either to their national parliaments or to the citizens. The Council is composed of representatives of each Member State at ministerial level that can commit the government of their Member State and cast its vote. Governments of the Member States are also, as recalled by Article 10(2) TEU, democratically accountable either to their national parliaments or to their citizens. Both institutions are, as acknowledged by Article 10(2) TEU, the fora where national interests are represented.

The European Commission, in charge of promoting the general interest of the Union, in particular by overseeing the application of Union law under the control of the Court of Justice, is composed of members chosen on the ground of their general competence and European commitment from persons whose independence is beyond doubt (Article 17(3) TEU). The Commission's legitimacy is in particular based on the role that the European Parliament, the European Council and Council play in its appointment and its accountability. For instance, the person nominated to stand as Commission President is taking into account the results of the elections to the European Parliament and, after having held the appropriate consultations, proposed to the European Parliament by the European Council, acting by a qualified majority. He or she is elected by the latter by a majority of its component members (Article 17(7) TEU). As a body, the Commission is subject to a vote of consent by the European Parliament and is responsible to it, while having the European Council and Council involved in the appointment procedure.[5] To fulfil its mission as defined in Article 17(1) TEU, the Commission enjoys an important degree of independence and a very powerful (but not exclusive in all areas) right of initiative, under the terms of Article 17(2) TEU.

The other three institutions – the Court of Justice, the European Central Bank and the Court of Auditors – derive their legitimacy from their own independence.

That complex institutional framework aims to serve the interests of the Union, its citizens and the Member States as explicitly envisaged in Article 13(1) TEU. The role of the institutions in the integration process is complemented by important principles and mechanisms that ensure mutual trust between the institutions and Member States, but also the trust of Union citizens in the process. One of those key principles is conferral,

[3] Art 14(3) TEU.

[4] See Art 15(2) TEU. According to this provision, the President of the European Council and the President of the Commission are also part of the European Council; however, in accordance with Art 6(4), second subparagraph, of the European Council Rules of Procedure (European Council Decision of 1 December 2009 adopting its Rules of Procedure [2009] OJ L315/51), they do not take part in the voting, when the European Council decides by vote.

[5] See in particular Art 17 TEU and Art 246 TFEU.

which is recalled under Article 1, first paragraph, and Article 5(2) TEU: 'the Union shall act only within the limits of the competences conferred upon it by the Member States in the Treaties to attain the objectives set out therein'. In other words, there is no possibility for the Union or its institutions to unilaterally, in circumstances not foreseen by the Treaties themselves, broaden its competences, without such conferral by the Member States.

While the conferral of competences to the Union by the Member States is of paramount importance to ensure that future legal obligations will be accepted and complied with, this should not be interpreted as meaning that the demarcation between the areas of exclusive Union competence and the competences that are shared with the Member States is static. On the contrary, as permitted by Article 3(2) TFEU, this delineation develops and evolves each time common rules are defined in different areas. Union institutions must also act within the limits of the powers that have been conferred to them in the Treaties, and in conformity with the procedures, conditions and objectives set out in them. They have a duty to practice mutual sincere cooperation, in accordance with Article 13(2) TEU. In this regard, the case law of the Court of Justice, which is often called upon to assess the boundaries of the Union's competences, is also an element that dynamically influences the deliniation of competences between the institutions, as well as between the Union and its members.[6]

Fulfilling the objectives of the Union is a task that is exclusive neither to the Union institutions nor to the Member States. Instead, it results from the combination of actions at both levels, as expressed by Article 4(3) TEU, first subparagraph, that 'pursuant to the principle of sincere cooperation, the Union and the Member States shall, in full mutual respect, assist each other in carrying out tasks which flow from the Treaties'. In certain cases, the common response is dictated by the Treaties, for instance in the areas of exclusive competence of the Union (Article 3 TFEU). In those areas, the action and reaction of individual Member States is either clearly framed or even prohibited. It is the Union, through its institutions, and within the remit of their respective competences, that is in charge of the response in the name of the entire Union, including of the Member States that compose it. This is for instance the case for the trade agreements with third countries, which are negotiated by the European Commission pursuant to the Union's common commercial policy and then concluded by the Council on the basis of Article 207 TFEU, following the procedure laid down in Article 218 TFEU.

In other areas – for instance the internal market, environment, energy, or the area of freedom, security and justice – the Union and its Member States share competences (Article 4 TFEU). In these situations, both are able to legislate and adopt legally binding acts. However, Member States may only exercise their competence to the extent that the Union has not exercised, or has decided not to exercise, its competence. By contrast, in certain specific areas, the Treaties provide that the Union can only play a role of coordination and support to the action of the Member States, for instance in relation to culture, tourism or administrative cooperation (Article 6 TFEU).

[6] See in particular the pivotal judgment of the Court of 31 March 1971: *Commission of the European Communities v Council of the European Communities* European Agreement on Road Transport, Case 22-70, ECLI:EU:C:1971:32.

As regards competences that remain in the hands of the Member States, their exercise is not entirely unaffected by Union law. To take the example of national security, the Court of Justice has clarified that

> although it is for Member States to take the appropriate measures to ensure their internal and external security, it does not follow that such measures are entirely outside the scope of European Union law …. It cannot be inferred that the Treaty contains an inherent general exception excluding all measures taken for reasons of public security from the scope of European Union law. The recognition of the existence of such an exception, regardless of the specific requirements laid down by the Treaty, would be liable to impair the binding nature of European Union law and its uniform application.[7]

In yet another very sensitive field of competence – nationality – the Court has developed a similar reasoning in connection with Union citizenship:

> [I]t is for each Member State, having due regard to Community law, to lay down the conditions for the acquisition and loss of nationality … Nevertheless, the fact that a matter falls within the competence of the Member States does not alter the fact that, in situations covered by European Union law, the national rules concerned must have due regard to the latter. It is clear that the situation of a citizen of the Union … in a position capable of causing him to lose the status conferred by Article 17 EC and the rights attaching thereto falls, by reason of its nature and its consequences, within the ambit of European Union law.[8]

Hence, the existence of a specific responsibility recognised as belonging to the Member States does not prevent the exercise of that competence from being subject to compliance with the fundamental provisions of the Treaty, economic freedoms and citizenship rights under the control of the Court.[9] In other words, the 'exercise' of a power, even if retained by the Member States, does not escape the application of Union law. The intertwined nature of the various competences and responsibilities and the far-reaching effects and scope of Union law are all factors that underlie, support and foster European integration.

European integration is therefore a constantly evolving process which relies on different tools, which in turn rely to a large extent on the existence of a degree of mutual trust, built on several forms of legitimacies.

15.2. 'Community Method' vs Intergovernmentalism

The academic literature sometimes has the tendency to oppose different methods of European integration. Quite commonly, authors have considered that the 'Community method', initially envisaged by Jean Monnet and his colleagues, was the only valid way

[7] See judgment of the Court of Justice of 4 March 2010, in Case C-38/06, *European Commission v Portuguese Republic*, ECLI:EU:C:2010:108, [62], but also Judgment of the Court (Grand Chamber) of 6 October 2020, in Joined Cases C-511/18, C-512/18 and C-520/18, *La Quadrature du Net and Others v Premier ministre and Others*, ECLI:EU:C:2020:791, [99].

[8] See judgment of the Court of Justice of 2 March 2010, in Case C-135/08, *Janko Rottmann*, ECLI:EU:C:2010:104, [39], [41] and [42].

[9] L Azoulai, 'Constitution économique et citoyenneté de l'Union européenne' (2011) 4 *Revue internationale de droit économique* 16.

forward to foster it. While the concept of 'Community method' should probably be pluralised since it encompasses different nuances and has evolved since the 1950s, it usually stresses the importance of the European Commission's role in the process of European integration. Indeed, the Community method naturally places the Commission, which promotes, within the meaning of Article 17(1) TEU and under the control of the Court of Justice, the general interest of the Union, and the use of the ordinary legislative procedure in which European Parliament and Council (acting as a rule by qualified majority voting) act as co-legislators, at the very heart of the decision and policy-making architecture.

The intergovernmental method, often described as based on decision-making processes that rely primarily on the action of the Member States and is characterised by decision-making by unanimity or consensus, is viewed by some as less optimal since it seeks to preserve Member States' individual interests to the detriment of harmonisation, without requiring them to consider the repercussion of their decisions on the wider *intérêt general européen.*[10] In this vein, the European Council is sometimes described as 'the main intergovernmental body',[11] while some authors like Uwe Puetter considers that it 'embodies the new intergovernmentalism in post-Maastricht EU integration'.[12] The European Council's growing role in certain policy areas, for instance economic governance, employment and social policy coordination as well as in the area of foreign and security policies, including its role in relation to the Union's restrictive measures,[13] is seen as an illustration of a political ambition to govern certain areas 'through coordinated action rather than autonomous supranational resources'.[14] Similarly, the Council is labelled as an intergovernmental entity par excellence, an image clearly influenced by its membership. As recalled above, the Council is composed of representatives of each Member State at ministerial level 'who may commit the *government* of the Member State in question and cast its vote' (Article 16(2) TEU, emphasis added). Since Council members are representatives of national executives, it seems clear to several observers and commentators of European affairs that the Council is only a *forum* in which self-centred individual national interests compete with one another and where the compromises produced are only the result of an accommodation of diverse national preferences.

In other words, there is a tendency in literature to consider that where the European Council and Council play a predominant part, the Union's action should be considered intergovernmental in nature. Several important qualifications should however be made in this respect.

Firstly, I would argue that in the specific political and institutional context of the Union, the term 'intergovernmental' should be reserved to common action of the

[10] D Dero-Bugny, 'La dilution de la méthode communautaire et la diversification des pratiques intergouvernementales' (2014) 3 *Revue de l'OFCE* 67.

[11] S Smeets and D Beach, 'Intergovernmentalism and its implications, new institutional in major EU reforms'(2020) 27 *Journal of European Public Policy* 1137.

[12] U Puetter, *The European Council and the Council: New intergovernmentalism and Institutional Change* (Oxford, Oxford University Press, 2014) 68.

[13] V Szép, 'New Intergovernmentalism meets EU sanctions policy: the European Council orchestrates the restrictive measures imposed against Russia'(2020) 42 *Journal of European Integration* 855.

[14] U Puetter, *The European Council and the Council: New intergovernmentalism and Institutional Change* (Oxford, Oxford University Press, 2014), see notably 68 and 142.

Member States acting outside the institutional framework provided by the Treaties. The actions of the European Council and the Council fall entirely within the Union's legal framework. The powers bestowed on these institutions by the Treaties are exercised under clear parameters, in particular under the supervision of the Court of Justice; it is recalled in this context that the exception to the jurisdiction of the Court of Justice provided for in the final sentence of the second subparagraph of Article 24(1) TEU and in the first paragraph of Article 275 TFEU is to be interpreted narrowly, and for instance does not apply where institutions or bodies of the Union adopt acts the legality of which is normally reviewed by the Court if adopted in a procedure unrelated to CFSP.[15]

In this sense, it can hardly be argued that said actions are intergovernmental. The opposing view would lead to the contradictory argument that the European Council and the Council are similar to any other international *fora* for cooperation between sovereign tates set out under classic public international law mechanisms. On the contrary, the Union legal order – which includes its institutional framework – does not proceed from the same logic as other public international structures which are solely based on intergovernmentalism. The conclusion to be drawn from the Treaties – to put it in the words of the Court of Justice – is that 'the Community (the Union) constitutes *a new legal order* of international law for the benefit of which the States have limited their sovereign rights' (emphasis added),[16] which also determines the manner in which these two institutions act and take decisions. The European Council and the Council are fully fledged institutional actors of this 'new legal order'. Consequently the nature of their actions should be assessed taking due account of this specific context.

When Member States participate in the adoption of Union acts as members the European Council and/or the Council, they transcend their own national sphere through the collective exercise of the powers vested to them by the Treaties, and they operate within the procedures set out by the Treaties, as well as under the direct or indirect judicial supervision of the Court of Justice. The discussions that take place in a forum that gather the 27 Member States bringing different perspectives to the table, in the presence of the Commission and where appropriate of other institutions or bodies of the Union, the support given by the General Secretariat of the Council in these discussions, the search for compromise in order to reach an agreement that fits the different realties and interests, show that the decisions taken by the European Council or the Council are not the simple sum of individual positions of its component members.

Secondly, both the European Council and the Council are more complex in their functioning than a purely intergovernmental body. They play a pivotal role in advancing the broader European general interest. The Lisbon Treaty brought the European Council within the institutional framework of the Treaties (Article 14(1) TEU). This was a significant change, as it meant that after years of operating outside (or in the margins) of the Union's institutional framework, the European Council is now acting within the Treaties. While its composition may seem to confer on the European Council

[15] See in particular: judgment of the General Court of 25 October 2018, T-286/15: *KF v European Union Satellite Center (SatCen)*, ECLI:EU:T:2018:718, [91]ff, confirmed in appeal by the judgment of the Court of 25 June 2020 in case C-14/19 P, ECLI:EU:C:2020:492.

[16] Judgment of the Court of 5 February 1963, Case 26–62: *NV Algemene Transport- en Expeditie Onderneming van Gend & Loos v Netherlands Inland Revenue Administration*, ECLI:EU:C:1963:1.

the status of an intergovernmental structure *par excellence*, the institution is not an intergovernmental conference and it embodies the complexity of the institutional architecture of the European legal order.[17] Indeed, the European Council's role transcends the mere representation of the addition of the national interests of its members. The institution serves as the Union's strategic guidepost, setting the direction for the Union's policies and priorities and in doing so, is bound to acknowledge the importance of a broader and genuinely European perspective that goes beyond national considerations. The European Council's role is a forum where leaders engage in discussions that aim to foster unity and cohesion. It is inherent in political dialogue to include considerations which go beyond the immediate national context and rely on shared values, objectives and political commitments.

In this regard, the role of the President of the European Council must be underlined. The President is elected by a qualified majority of the Heads of State or Government for a renewable term of two and half years. Article 15(6) TEU provides that the President shall, in particular, 'drive forward' and ensure 'the preparation and continuity' of the European Council's work while facilitating cohesion and consensus between its members. Additionally, the President is tasked with representing externally the Union on issues related to the common foreign and security policy 'at his level and in his capacity', without prejudice to the powers of the High Representative of the Union for Foreign Affairs and Security Policy (Article 15(6) TEU). The question of the Union's external representation is interesting in this regard. Indeed, it must be noted that when the President of the European Council is tasked with representing the Union internationally, he or she does not represent the interests or the agenda of one or of a specific group of Member States, but rather the collectively determined European interest.

Thirdly, one cannot overlook the essential role played by the Member States in the continued process of legitimation of the Union's actions, ensuring in particular that the Union's policy and constitutional choices remain closely aligned with the interests of the Union and of its citizens, as well as in its application. National governments serve as the primary bridge between the Union institutions and the diverse needs and preferences of the Union's citizens. In many respects, national authorities are directly attuned to the aspirations of their citizens – whose satisfaction or dissatisfaction can make or break national governments – and their valuable input is thoroughly enriching to the Union's decision-making process. Conversely, Member States ensure that Union law directly applies (through implementation, for which, according to Article 291(1) TFEU they are the first responsible, or where applicable, transposition) to those same citizens.

Through their representation in the Council of the European Union and their contribution to the decision-making process, Member States act as guardians of national interests while working towards common goals. This dual responsibility ensures that the Union remains responsive to the concerns of its citizens. This contributes to reinforcing the democratic character of the European project, underscoring the vital connection between Member States, the Union's institutions, and the citizens they collectively represent.

[17] H Flavier, *La contribution des relations extérieures à la construction de l'ordre constitutionnel de l'Union européenne*, Collection Droit de l'Union européenne (Brusells, E Bruylant, 2012) 680.

Fourthly, coming now to what in my view is correctly termed 'the intergovernmental method', is where Member States act outside the format or functions of the institutions or the Treaties. I advocate not only its compatibility with the Union legal framework but also its usefulness in certain crucial moments for the European integration.

It is a fact that intergovernmentalism in the strict sense was very popular among certain heads of States, as illustrated by the French President Nicolas Sarkozy's Toulon speech in 2011: 'c'est par l'intergouvernmental que passera l'intégration européenne, parce que l'Europe va devoir faire des choix stratégiques, des choix politiques'.[18] In the words of Sergio Fabbrini:

> Once the financial crisis arrived to Europe in 2009–2010, the EU intergovernmental constitution *enjoyed the support of a powerful constellation of political leaders and public opinions*. After all, once the EU entered the throes of a crisis after the failure of the Constitutional Treaty in the French and Dutch popular referendum of 2005, *the intergovernmental approach emerged as the only feasible strategy for promoting integration*.[19]

Intergovernmentalism allowed the European integration to progress, when the Community method was not within reach, as several examples testify. The development of the Schengen area is a good illustration in this respect. By signing the Schengen Agreement on 14 June 1985, five Member States decided to remove controls at their internal borders and to introduce freedom of movement in particular for all their nationals. The Schengen construction evolved between 1985 and 1995, and the resulting 'Schengen acquis', was in the end integrated into the Union framework in 1999, before making its way into the Treaties themselves through the Lisbon Treaty. Indeed, the Schengen construction is a very eloquent example of a 'parallel path'[20] to the Community method that became 15 years later one of the major achievements of the EU. On 14 June 1985, five Member States decided the gradual abolition of checks at their common border. The Schengen Agreement was originally signed independently of the European Economic Community, as a purely intergovernmental agreement. In 1990 it was supplemented by a convention aimed at strengthening external border checks, harmonising right of asylum procedures, and taking measures against drug trafficking. This implementing convention was aimed at establishing a number of mitigating measures needed to counterbalance the unhindered freedom of movement, which could obviously also be used for purposes other than purely economic ones. All the resulting 'Schengen acquis' was integrated into the Union framework through the Treaty of Amsterdam by means of Protocols, allowing also to provide for the variable geometry inherent to Schengen.

Another example of this parallel path is the Prüm Convention, an intergovernmental treaty in the field of police cooperation that seven EU Member States signed in 2005 and whose core components were incorporated into the Union legal framework by the Lisbon Treaty.

[18] Which can be translated into 'European integration will take place at intergovernmental level, because Europe is going to have to make strategic and political choices.'

[19] S Fabbrini, 'Intergovernmentalism and its limits: assessing the European Union's answer to the euro crisis' (17 June 2013) *Comparative Political Studies* 8, available at ssrn.com/abstract=2411959 (emphasis added).

[20] See Y Pascouau, 'La politique migratoire de l'Union européenne (De Schengen à Lisbonne)' (Paris, LDGJ, 2010) 66–74.

It is also the search for adequate responses to the financial crisis that brought into the picture solutions designed outside the framework of Union Treaties. The Treaty Establishing the European Stability Mechanism (ESM) was signed by the Member States belonging to the eurozone in 2012, under classic international law mechanisms. The main objective of the ESM is summarised in Article 3 of the ESM Treaty:

> "*The purpose of the ESM shall be to mobilise funding and provide stability support under strict conditionality, appropriate to the financial assistance instrument chosen, to the benefit of ESM Members which are experiencing, or are threatened by, severe financing problems, if indispensable to safeguard the financial stability of the euro area as a whole and of its Member States* [...]".[21]

The ESM operates as a permanent crisis resolution mechanism, offering financial support through loans and other financial instruments on the basis of conditionality to ensure that all contracting parties follow responsible and balanced fiscal behaviour. The ESM is an intergovernmental structure which has its own institutional framework (a Board of Governors, a board of directors and managing directors) as well as its own staff;[22] however, it is linked to the Union legal framework, notably through the role of the Court of Justice as the ultimate arbiter:

> Disputes concerning the interpretation and application of this Treaty arising between the Contracting Parties or between the Contracting Parties and the ESM should *be submitted to the jurisdiction of the Court of Justice of the European Union*, in accordance with Article 273 of the Treaty on the Functioning of the European Union ('TFEU').[23]

As underlined by Sacha Garben, in chapter three of this book, the Member States belonging to the euro area decided to engage, via the ESM in particular, in 'wide-scale financial assistance packages, while facing consequences of the economic downturn themselves'.[24] As she puts it, this was a clear act of solidarity between Member States, and in this sense the ESM Treaty – while intergovernmental and outside the Union's legal framework – can reasonably be considered as being a crucial steppingstone in European integration, further demonstrating that this process may take on different forms.

The Treaty on Stability, Coordination and Governance in the Economic and Monetary Union (TSCG),[25] signed on 2 March 2012 by all but two[26] of the then Member States, and which entered into force on 1 January 2013, is another agreement lying outside the framework of the Treaties that contains specific fiscal obligations for the contracting parties. The TSCG covers specific enforcement mechanisms, whereby the failure to duly incorporate into national law the balanced budget rule may lead to an action before the Court of Justice of the EU for breaching the obligations under the Treaty (Article 8 TSCG). On 26 April 2023, the European Commission presented

[21] Art 3 ESM Treaty (emphasis added).

[22] See in particular ESM Treaty Art 4(1) 'Structure and Voting', Art 5 'Board of Governors', Art 6 'Board of Directors', Art 7 'Managing Directors', Art 33 'Staff of the ESM'.

[23] See Recital 16 and Art 37(3) ESM Treaty.

[24] See ch 3, section 3.3.3.

[25] www.consilium.europa.eu/media/20399/st00tscg26_en12.pdf.

[26] UK and Czech Republic.

proposals for a Regulation of the European Parliament and the Council on the effective coordination of economic policies and multilateral budgetary surveillance and repealing Council Regulation (EC) No 1466/97,[27] for a Council Regulation amending Regulation No 1467/97[28] on speeding up and clarifying the implementation of the excessive deficit procedure and for a Council Directive 2011/85/EU on requirements for budgetary frameworks of the Member States[29] (referred together herewith as the 'Economic Governance Review (EGR) package'). These aim, inter alia, to implement the requirement set out in Article 16 TSCG by incorporating the substance of the Fiscal Compact into Union law.[30] At the end of April 2024, the three acts that are part of this package were adopted.[31]

A similar trend and preference for a certain degree of intergovernmentalism is also reflected in certain features of an important pillar of the Banking Union: the Single Resolution Mechanism. The Single Resolution Mechanism is structured around two main components: the Single Resolution Board and the Single Resolution Fund. The former is a typical illustration of the Community method and was established by Article 42(1) of Regulation (EU) No 806/2014,[32] a legal instrument adopted on the basis of Article 114 TFEU. The latter was established via an intergovernmental treaty. This dual approach constituted a necessary step for Member States to accept at that point in time the pulling together of resources for the benefit of the financial stability of all.

Beyond the fact that this mode of integration is not necessarily at odds with the method of integration through Union law, the recourse to such an intergovernmental mechanism was even tolerated if not validated by the Court of Justice, as the famous judgment in *Pringle* shows.[33] In that case, the Court considered that Member States have the power to conclude between themselves an agreement for the establishment of a stability mechanism such as the ESM Treaty provided that the commitments undertaken by the Member States, who are parties to such an agreement, are consistent with Union law. Furthermore, the Court also accepted that the fact that the EU institutions play certain roles for the purposes of the ESM Treaty is also compatible with Union law, as long as the duties conferred on the Commission and the European Central Bank do not alter the essential character of the powers conferred on those institutions by the Union Treaties. The Court, however, framed the intervention of the institutions outside

[27] COM(2023) 240 final.

[28] COM(2023) 241 final.

[29] COM(2023) 242 final.

[30] COM(2023) 240 final, Recital 32; COM(2023) 241 final, Recital 23; and COM(2023) 242 final, Recital 8.

[31] Regulation (EU) 2024/1263 of the European Parliament and of the Council of 29 April 2024 on the effective coordination of economic policies and on multilateral budgetary surveillance and repealing Council Regulation (EC) No 1466/97, [2024] OJ L 1263; Council Regulation (EU) 2024/1264 of 29 April 2024 amending Regulation (EC) No 1467/97 on speeding up and clarifying the implementation of the excessive deficit procedure, [2024] OJ L1264; Council Directive (EU) 2024/1265 of 29 April 2024 amending Directive 2011/85/EU on requirements for budgetary frameworks of the Member States, [2024] OJ L1265.

[32] Regulation (EU) No 806/2014 of the European Parliament and of the Council of 15 July 2014 establishing uniform rules and a uniform procedure for the resolution of credit institutions and certain investment firms in the framework of a Single Resolution Mechanism and a Single Resolution Fund and amending Regulation (EU) No 1093/2010.

[33] Judgment of the Court (Full Court), 27 November 2012, Case C-370/12: *Thomas Pringle v Government of Ireland and Others*, ECLI:EU:C:2012:756.

the Union Treaties a few years later, in its judgment in the *Ledra* case.[34] The Court underlined that when acting within the framework of such intergovernmental mechanism, the Commission continues to be bound by both Article 17(1) TEU, which confers upon it the general task of overseeing the application of EU law, and Article 13(3)–(4) of the ESM Treaty, which requires it to ensure that the memoranda of understanding concluded by the ESM are consistent with Union law and with the fundamental rights guaranteed by the Charter.

It must also be noted that, in specific circumstances, the Treaties themselves contemplate recourse to the intergovernmental method. An illustration of this can be found in the process of appointing judges and Advocates-General to the Court of Justice, as well as judges to the General Court. According to Article 19(2) TEU; 'they shall be appointed *by common accord of the governments of the Member States for six years*' (emphasis added). Another illustration pertains to the determination of the location of the Union's institutions with Article 341 TFEU providing that: 'the seat of the institutions of the Union shall be determined *by common accord of the governments of the Member States*' (emphasis added).

15.3. Crises-solving and European Integration

We have established that the institutional and specific legal framework of the Union are crucial elements of the integration process. However, the political and geopolitical context of the last two decades, characterised by several crises, is also essential. Crises can shape and to a certain degree reinvigorate the European integration process, thus illustrating Jean Monnet's famous words: 'Europe will be forged in crises and will be the sum of the solutions adopted for those crises'. While different methods have been used to address them, a new pattern has emerged since the Brexit referendum, which favours Union-based approaches, with the institutions at the centre of the response. This does not necessarily mean that recourse to the Community method is generalised, but rather that even in absence of clear Union competences, cooperation and coordination through institutions is favoured over a pure 'intergovernmental' reaction.

Over the past two decades, the EU has faced significant challenges that have undeniably left their mark on the intricate process of European integration. These crises cover a broad spectrum of political, economic and social dimensions, each presenting unique obstacles to the Union's cohesion and progress. The financial crisis, for instance, which was followed by the sovereign debt crisis in a number of Member States, shed light on a number of shortcomings of the eurozone and tested the resilience of the Union's economic governance as well as its reaction capabilities in times of difficulties. However, the financial crisis also led to some very concrete realisations. For instance, having witnessed important vulnerabilities within the European banking system, the crisis prompted the development of the Banking Union and the ESM. While the Banking Union is not yet complete, significant progress has been made since 2008, in

[34] Judgment of the Court (Grand Chamber) of 20 September 2016, Joined Cases C-8/15 P to C-10/15 P: *Ledra Advertising Ltd and Others v European Commission and European Central Bank (ECB)*, ECLI:EU:C:2016:701.

particular through the establishment of the Single Supervisory Mechanism[35] and the Single Resolution Mechanism.[36] Such progress has only been possible by a combination of Community and intergovernmental methods.

Crises can weaken or even undo European integration. This is perhaps best exemplified by the UK's decision to leave the EU. If in June 2016, after the British referendum, the question that tortured all pro-European minds was whether the EU would survive, the unity and the solidarity between Member States prevailed very quickly. The coordination that took place, with the European Council's direct involvement and acting as a catalyst to unity, was key to that effect. The method of work of the European Council, based on consensus, alleviated the concerns that certain Member States could be 'left behind'. The result of this unprecedent unity is the Withdrawal Agreement, which marked, in the history of European integration an important moment, not only because it recalled the added value of the Union from an economic perspective but also in relation to fostering peace in particular on the island of Ireland. In addition, the Trade and Cooperation Agreement was signed at the end of 2020, as a Union-only agreement based on Article 217 TFEU. It is unprecedented to have such broad agreement concluded as a Union-only agreement, even though this was undeniably helped by the fact that the legal basis relied upon (Article 217 TFEU) required unanimity within the Council.

Similarly, the COVID-19 pandemic posed significant and novel challenges to the Union and its Member States. While the pandemic impacted severely the fundamentals of the internal market, especially at the outset, it also turned out to be an opportunity to explore novel tools. Indeed, the initial response, which saw unilateral border closures, bans on exports of certain supplies and deep disagreements over the appropriate fiscal responses, betrayed a lack of a genuinely 'European' response. However, the pandemic also acted as a catalyst to strengthen European integration in several respects, be it the creation of Next Generation EU (NGEU), the EU's €800 billion temporary recovery instrument to support the economic recovery from the coronavirus pandemic, which marked a historic step towards European fiscal solidarity,[37] or the joint purchase of vaccines through the European Commission, instead of separate and most likely less efficient actions by each Member State. In the same vein, the unprecedented budgetary construction of the NGEU and its financing[38] have proved to be a very efficient tool for responding to the crisis.

[35] Regulation (EU) No 468/2014 of the European Central Bank of 16 April 2014 establishing the framework for cooperation within the Single Supervisory Mechanism between the European Central Bank and national competent authorities and with national designated authorities (SSM Framework Regulation) (ECB/2014/17), [2014] OJ L141/1.

[36] Regulation (EU) No 806/2014 of the European Parliament and of the Council of 15 July 2014 establishing uniform rules and a uniform procedure for the resolution of credit institutions and certain investment firms in the framework of a Single Resolution Mechanism and a Single Resolution Fund and amending Regulation (EU) No 1093/2010, [2014] OJ L225/1.

[37] See for illustration F Fabbrini, 'Next Generation EU: Legal Structure and Constitutional Consequences' (2022). REBUILD Centre Working Paper No. 3, available at ssrn.com/abstract=4121330 or dx.doi.org/10.2139/ssrn.4121330.

[38] See in particular P Dermine, 'Le plan de relance et les équilibres institutionnels de l'Union' in *Le plan de relance 'Next Generation EU' de l'Union européenne*, 1st edn (Brusells, Bruylant, 2023) ch 6, but also the Opinion of 24 June 2020 of the Council Legal Service on the matter, document ST 9062/20, available at data.consilium.europa.eu/doc/document/ST-9062-2020-INIT/en/pdf.

The European response to the war of aggression waged by the Russian Federation against Ukraine is in line with this recent trend. The negotiation and adoption of a collaborative instrument for the procurement of defence products is a perfect illustration of this collective approach to addressing common challenges. Indeed, to address a wave of orders from Member States for such products, the Commission proposed a regulation on establishing an instrument for the reinforcement of the European defence industry through common procurement (EDIRPA),[39] based on Article 173(3) TFEU. The instrument was to provide grants to Member States who would engage in joint procurement in consortia of minimum three of them, rather than individually, with the view to offset the high burden and costs of such a procurement method and, most importantly, to incentivise cooperation and coordination of needs and specifications for the products. Furthermore, faced with the urgency of Ukraine's ammunition stock rapid depletion, the Council agreed on a 'three track approach with the aim to, in particular, speed up the delivery and *joint procurement* aiming at one million rounds of artillery ammunition for Ukraine in a joint effort within the next twelve months'.[40] Subsequently, the Commission put forward a proposal for a Regulation in Support of Ammunition Production (ASAP),[41] based on Articles 114 and 173(3) TFEU, which was swiftly adopted by the co-legislators. The Regulation aims at ensuring that defence companies established and managed within the Union are able to increase their production capacity and strengthen the responsiveness and capability of the Union's defence industry to ensure the timely supply of relevant defence products (ground-to-ground and artillery ammunition, missiles) through the provision of financing for the development of such production capacity. This Union-based solution, in a policy field which is extremely sensitive for the Member States and where the demarcation between competences is complex, as it relates not only to defence but also to industrial policy, would have been unthinkable a decade ago.

This overview reveals a renewed impetus for European integration after a period of fatigue, illustrated by increased recourse to European solutions, making full use of the Union institutions and the legal framework foreseen in the Treaties. Collective responses to common challenges are discussed within the Union, in line with the aim of the Union of creating 'a process of creating an ever-closer union among the people of Europe' (Article 1 TEU).

15.4. The External Angle: Gradual Integration?

The Union's relations with its neighbours can often be analysed through the prism of the degree of integration with the internal market even if, as it is the case with the EEA

[39] Regulation (EU) 2023/2418 of the European Parliament and of the Council of 18 October 2023 on establishing an instrument for the reinforcement of the European defence industry through common procurement (EDIRPA), [2023] OJ L2418.

[40] See 'outcomes of proceedings' as approved by the Council on 20 March 2023 (Council document no 7632/23).

[41] Regulation (EU) 2023/1525 of the European Parliament and of the Council of 20 July 2023 on supporting ammunition production (ASAP), [2023] OJ L185/7.

members which are not Member States (Lichtenstein, Iceland, Norway), Switzerland or to a certain extent, the UK, the end of the path is not necessarily accession.

The European Economic Area Agreement (EEA Agreement), which was signed in 1992 and entered into force two years later, is an interesting example of deep and thorough integration in the Union of third States which constitutes an alternative to a fully fledged membership to the Union. Indeed, while the Preamble of the EEA Agreement reads that: 'the conclusion of this Agreement shall not prejudge in any way the possibility of any EFTA State to accede to the European Communities', in reality, the prospect of Iceland, Norway or the Principality of Liechtenstein acceding is not today on the agenda. Despite accession playing such a marginal role, the EEA Agreement provides for a significant level of integration. Its aim, which is recalled under the first paragraph of its first article is to 'promote a continuous and balanced strengthening of trade and economic relations between the Contracting Parties with equal conditions of competition, and respect the same rules, with a view to creating a homogenous European Economic Area'.[42] This ambitious objective is implemented through partial integration in the Union, mainly in its internal market. The EEA Agreement includes provisions analogous to the four Fundamental Freedoms of the Internal market, the free movement of goods, persons, services and capital, as well as a system ensuring the non-distortion of competition.[43] In a similar fashion, the relationship between the Union and Switzerland, which is also based on far reaching economic integration, is entirely decoupled from the accession process.

One should also mention the Trade and Cooperation Agreement with the United Kingdom, an association agreement based on Article 217 TFEU including different forms of cooperation that are very deep, for instance participation in certain Union programmes. That Agreement can obviously not be characterised as being premised on, or even envisaging, eventual accession to the EU. This is why, for instance, during the negotiations, it was important to avoid creating the impression of integration.

In the context of the war of aggression against Ukraine, the situation is very different, and the concept of European integration has a different form of attractiveness. This is illustrated by the current debate about whether countries involved in the enlargement process, could enjoy a closer relationship with the Union already now, before becoming full members of the Union/before concluding Accession Treaties with the Union.[44] Of course, we should not lose sight of the fact that the merit of each country in meeting the Copenhagen criteria, as well as the Union capacity to absorb new members, remains a crucial step in the accession process.

However, the concepts of 'accelerated' or 'gradual' integration within the context of the enlargement process have not emerged with the Russian war of aggression against Ukraine. The Commission Communication of 5 February 2020,[45] which aimed at creating a positive conditionality that would serve as a leverage for the reform process,

[42] Art 1(1), Agreement on the European Economic Area (emphasis added).

[43] See in particular Art 1(2) and Parts II–V of the Agreement on the European Economic Area.

[44] See in particular, P Van Elsuwege and G Van der Loo, 'The EU-Ukraine Association Agreement as a Stepping-stone towards EU Membership?' Op-Ed (28 March 2022) EU Law Live Symposium on the Accession of Ukraine to the European Union.

[45] COM(2020) 57 final, 'Enhancing the accession process – A credible EU perspective for the Western Balkans'.

in particular in the field of the so-called 'enlargement fundamentals', used the term 'accelerated integration'. The Commission considered that clear and tangible incentives of direct interest to citizens should be offered to reward results arising from demanding reforms and the process of political, economic and societal change. Through sufficient progress on the reform priorities agreed in the negotiations, according to the Commission, countries could move faster to integration with the EU, creating incentives to work for accelerated integration and 'phasing-in' to individual EU policies, the EU market and EU programmes, while ensuring a level playing field and increased funding and investments – including through performance-based and reform-oriented Instrument for Pre-accession support and closer cooperation with International Financial Institutions to leverage support.

The European Council of 23 and 24 June 2022 resorted to the term 'gradual integration'[46] when, in relation to Western Balkans, it invited 'the Commission, the High Representative and the Council to further advance the gradual integration between the European Union and the region already during the enlargement process itself in a reversible and merit-based manner', building on a revised methodology.[47] This term appears again in December 2022, in the 'Enlargement conclusions' approved by the General Affairs Council:

> Recalling the European Council conclusions of June 2022, the Council encourages the further advancement of gradual integration between the European Union and partners already during the enlargement process in a reversible and merit-based manner. The Council welcomes the sectoral measures already taken in this regard, in line with the revised enlargement methodology. In this context, the Council takes note of the mapping of the existing and potential integration measures and looks forward to examining proposals for further implementation of such measures, in particular in areas of mutual interest.[48]

However, beyond its attractiveness as a concept, it has to be recalled that any advancement of gradual integration should ensure the preservation of the integrity of the Union's Single Market. This was acutely relevant in the context of the negotiations between the UK and the Union on a future relationship post-Brexit. Indeed, among the core principles set out by the European Council in its 'guidelines following the United Kingdom's notification under Article 50 TEU',[49] were the following:

> [P]reserving the integrity of the Single Market excludes participation based on a sector-by-sector approach. A non-member of the Union, that does not live up to the same obligations as a member, cannot have the same rights and enjoy the same benefits as a member. In this

[46] This is a term that already appears in the 2014 Association Agreements concluded between the Union and Ukraine, Republic of Moldova or Georgia, respectively. See for illustration Art 1(2)(d), 'Association Agreement between the European Union and the European Atomic Energy Community and their Member States, of the one part, and Ukraine, of the other part', [2014] OJ L161/3. The Association Agreement with Ukraine is by far the most modern and far-reaching agreement and provides greater opportunities for gradual integration as it is broader in scope and governs the cooperation between the Parties in greater detail. It also contains measures aimed at ensuring level playing field.

[47] See para 16 of the EUCO Conclusions, available at www.consilium.europa.eu/media/57442/2022-06-2324-euco-conclusions-en.pdf.

[48] See General Affairs conclusions of 13 December 2022, para 11, available at www.consilium.europa.eu/media/60797/st15935-en22.pdf.

[49] See Guidelines adopted by the European Council after the special meeting of 29 April 2017, EUCO XT 20004/17, available at www.consilium.europa.eu/media/21763/29-euco-art50-guidelinesen.pdf.

> context, the European Council welcomes the recognition by the British Government that the four freedoms of the Single Market are indivisible and that there can be no 'cherry picking'.

Furthermore, among the guiding principles for the negotiations in the Brexit context, there was an unequivocal focus on ensuring also a balance of rights and obligations, preserve a level playing field, and avoid upsetting existing relations with other third countries. This approach, which stresses the importance of the degree of stability and continuity, has been maintained in the Trade and Cooperation Agreement between the EU and the UK.

15.5. Conclusion

Recent years, marked by an unusually high number of severe and multifaceted crises, have shown that the process of European integration, in both its internal and external dimensions, is alive and well. Internally, new tools have emerged, sometimes at crossroads between different methods of integration, and new areas of common action have been developed. Externally, the integration with the Union is a powerful tool in our relationship with our partners, not necessarily coupled with tangible accession prospects. These developments show that European integration, far from being a mere academic or policy concept, remains a tangible reality. One question that may deserve further scrutiny is whether this renewed relevance was achieved despite of, or thanks to, the complexity of the Union's institutional architecture and decision-making processes ….

16

The Impact of War (in Ukraine) on the EU

MARTA ARPIO*

16.1. The EU Treaties and the Ukraine War

When speaking about the impact of the war (in Ukraine) in the EU Constitutional blueprint, the first thing to note is that the response of the EU to the war has demonstrated the capacity and flexibility of the EU Treaties to cope with new unexpected situations, as the Russian unprovoked and unjustified military aggression against Ukraine was. On the basis of the EU Treaties, the EU has been able to adopt, in a very short timeframe, far-reaching actions and measures to face the situation, some of them previously unthinkable.

First of all, under the general political direction of the European Council, the Council has adopted several packages of restrictive measures. These packages, covering sanctions against individuals and entities (assets freezes and travel bans) as well as economic sanctions, restrictions on media, and diplomatic and visa measures, have been adopted in a record time and concern a very large number of sectors: finance (SWIFT ban for 10 Russian Banks, restrictions on Russia's access to the EU's capital and financial markets, ban on transactions with the Russian Central Bank, etc); transport (closure of EU airspace to all Russian-owned aircraft, ban on Russian road transport operators, closure of EU ports to Russian vessels, etc); energy (ban on imports from Russia of oil and coal, ban on exports to Russia of goods and technologies in the oil refining sector, etc); defence (ban on exports to Russia of dual-use goods and technology for military use, of arms and ammunition, of semiconductor materials, etc); services, etc. Article 29 TEU, which empowers the Council to adopt decisions on Common Foreign and Security Policy (CFSP) matters, has been the main legal basis for the establishment of these sanctions, and Article 215 TFEU has ensured their uniform application across the EU.

Secondly, the EU and its Member States have provided extraordinary military support to Ukraine through joint and coordinated actions, from the purchase of military equipment for Ukraine to the decision to provide Ukraine with artillery

* The opinions expressed in this chapter are strictly personal and in no way engage the Council of the European Union or the European Council.

ammunition, either from existing stocks, or by joint procurement concerning the new production. For the first time in its history, the EU has given a direct military assistance to a third country. In this framework, in October 2022 the Council adopted a decision establishing a Military Mission in support of Ukraine (EUMAM Ukraine),[1] based on Articles 42(4) and 43(2) TEU, which empower the Council to adopt decisions on Common Security and Defence Policy (CSDP). European Union Military Assistance Mission (EUMAM) Ukraine intends to provide individual, collective and specialised training to Ukraine's armed forces through a coordinated action of the participating EU Member States. All these supporting actions have been given with the assistance of the European Peace Facility (EPF) instrument,[2] an important tool for Common Foreign and Security Policy (CFSP)/CSDP established by the Council in order to enhance the EU's ability to prevent conflicts, build peace and strengthen international security. EPF is financed by contributions from Member States, which were substantially increased in order to assist Ukraine.

Thirdly, as an answer to the energy crisis in 2022, a consequence of Russia's aggression against Ukraine, the EU has taken important steps to decrease its energy dependence on Russia and to develop an autonomous energy policy. In March 2022, the European Council asked the Commission to elaborate, in close coordination with the Member States, an action plan aimed at phasing out the EU dependency on Russian gas, oil and coal imports. Several long-term legislative and non-legislative measures, such as the gas and hydrogen package, are currently on the table or have been adopted, eg, the Repower EU Plan.[3] Moreover, the Union has adopted a range of emergency measures concerning inter alia gas storage, coordinated demand-reduction measures for gas, solidarity concerning gas purchases, market correction mechanisms, and measures to address high energy prices. Most of these measures were adopted on the basis of Article 194 TFEU (the energy legal basis) and the emergency measures were adopted on the basis of Article 122 TFEU, which empowers the Council to determine the measures appropriate to the economic situation if severe difficulties arise in the supply of certain products, notably in the area of energy. This provision has already been used to adopt urgent measures in past crises: establishment of the European Stability Financial Mechanism during the eurozone crisis;[4] the Emergency Support Instrument Regulation during the refugee crisis;[5] the SURE Regulation;[6] and the Regulation establishing an EU Recovery Instrument during the COVId-19 crisis.[7]

[1] Council decision 2022/1968 of 17 October 2022 on a European Union Military Assistance in support of Ukraine (EUMAM Ukraine).

[2] Council decision 2021/509 of 22 March 2021 establishing a European Peace Facility.

[3] Regulation (EU) 2023/435 of the European Parliament and of the Council of 27 February 2023 amending Regulation (EU) 2021/241 as regards REPowerEU chapters in recovery and resilience plans and amending Regulations (EU) No 1303/2013, (EU) 2021/1060 and (EU) 2021/1755, and Directive 2003/87/EC of the European Parliament and the Council of the European Union.

[4] Council Regulation (EU) 407/2010 of 11 May 2010 establishing a European financial stabilization mechanism.

[5] Council Regulation (EU) 2016/369 on the provisions of emergency support within the Union.

[6] Council Regulation (EU) 2016/672 0f 19 May 2020 on the establishment of a European instrument for temporary support to mitigate unemployment risks in an emergency (SURE) following the COVID-19 outbreak.

[7] Council Regulation (EU)2020/2094 of 14 December 2020 establishing a European Recovery Instrument to support the recovery in the aftermath of the COVID-19 crisis.

Fourthly, on 4 March 2022, the Council activated unanimously and for first time the 2001 Temporary Protection Directive,[8] based on Article 63(2) of the Treaty establishing the European Community, to allow Ukrainian displaced people fleeing the war to enjoy harmonised rights across the EU, including residence permits, access to the labour market and suitable accommodation and housing, medical care and access to education for children. This temporary protection has been extended until March 2025.

Finally, an exceptional financial assistance through the macro-financial assistance instrument[9] was established by an EU regulation based on Article 212 TFEU related to the EU economic, financial and technical cooperation measures with third countries, and guaranteed by the Member States, not by the EU budget, due the veto of one Member State.

These far-reaching measures have been adopted, making full use of the provisions and flexibilities of the Treaties. This has been possible due to the common will in the EU Institutions and the Member States to face the brutality of the war in Ukraine, by mobilising all the necessary instruments and by taking all the necessary steps in order to allow the Union to respond to this war in the most effective way. The European Council has played a crucial role in creating this necessary consensus through its successive formal and informal meetings held immediately after Russian's military aggression. The European Commission, whose President is member of the European Council, and the High Representative of the Union for Foreign Affairs and Security Policy, who takes part in its work, have also played their full role in the process. On 24 February 2022, the first day of the aggression, a special meeting of the European Council took place and condemned Russia's unprovoked and unjustified military aggression in the strongest terms, confirmed its unwavering support for the independence, sovereignty and territorial integrity of Ukraine, and agreed on further restrictive measures on Russia and work towards providing Ukraine with political, financial, humanitarian and military support. This consensus has been key to reaching the unanimity required for the adoption of an important part of the CFSP measures to respond to this aggression, given that in CFSP unanimity in the Council is the voting rule by default. This has been the case, for example, for the adoption of the different packages of restrictive measures against Russia. This unanimity has facilitated the implementation and enforcement of the restrictive measures, given that, to be efficient, these measures require to be implemented and enforced uniformly within EU.

By mobilising all the instruments at the disposal of the EU Institutions and Member States, the EU's reaction to Russia's aggression has also demonstrated the complementarity of national and supranational actions to face a major crisis such as this one. Translated in terms of competences and governance in the specific field of CFSP/CSDP, it has demonstrated the utility of mixed instruments (national and supranational) in order to combine the national capabilities and powers with the strength of the EU Institutions. This has been, for example, the case of the EUMAM, where the resources

[8] Council Directive 2001/55 on minimum standards for giving temporary protection in the event of a mass influx of displaced persons and on measures promoting a balance of efforts between Member States in receiving such persons and bearing the consequences thereof.

[9] Regulation (EU) 2022/2463 of the European Parliament and of the Council of 14 December 2022 establishing an instrument for providing support to Ukraine for 2023 (macro-financial assistance).

and instructors of the different Member States are coordinated under the command of the EU, which also coordinates the EU efforts with those of third countries (US, UK, Canada, etc).

16.2. The War in Ukraine and the Conference on the Future of Europe

The Conference on the Future of Europe, the first exercise of participatory democracy at the level of the EU, contains in its final report very relevant proposals in the framework of the war in Ukraine. After a year of intensive work and collective citizens deliberations, in particular in the framework of the European and National Citizens' Panels, 49 proposals and 326 related measures reflecting the priorities of the European citizens for the years to come were presented on 9 May 2022 to the presidents of the European Parliament, the Council and the European Commission. Several of those proposals and measures underline the need to reinforce the EU's efficiency and its strategic autonomy, and pledge for a stronger EU in the world scene that promotes peace and security.

Russia's aggression against Ukraine occurred in the middle of the Conference, when the Recommendations of the European and National Citizens' Panels were being finalised. When the war started, the citizens participating in the panels were asked if any of their Recommendations, and in particular those related to the 'Europe in the world' panel, needed to be reviewed following Russia's aggression against Ukraine. The citizens' answer was that the Recommendations were more valid than ever, and that a strong EU on the world scene was needed more than ever. Some of the proposals of the Conference, in particular those related to 'Europe in the world', are highly relevant in the context of the war in Ukraine, particularly the following points:

(a) Proposal 17: Reducing dependency of EU from foreign actors in economically strategic sectors:

> We propose the EU takes measures to strengthen its autonomy in key strategic sectors such as agriculture products, strategic economic goods, semiconductors medical products, innovative digital environmental technologies and energy, through:
>
> [Measures …].

(b) Proposal 18: Reducing dependency of EU from Foreign actors in energy:

> We propose that the EU reach more autonomy in the field of energy production and supply, in the context of the ongoing green transition by:
>
> Measures:
>
> 1. Adopting a strategy to be more autonomous in its energy production … […].

(c) Proposal 21: Decision making and cohesion within the Union

> We propose that the EU improve its capacity to take speedy and effective decisions, notably in Common foreign and security (CFSP), speaking with one voice and acting as a truly global player …. notably through:

Measures:

1. In particular in the area of CFSP, issues that are currently decided by way of unanimity to be changed, normally to be decided by way of a qualified majority.
2. Basing cooperation in security and defence policy on the recently endorsed Strategic Compass and making use of the European Peace facility.
3. [...]
4. Agreeing on a strong vision and a common strategy to consolidate the unity and decision taking capacity of the EU in order to prepare the EU for further enlargement.

[...]

(a) Proposal 23: The EU as a strong actor on the world scene in peace and security

'We propose that the EU continue to act to promote dialogue and guarantee peace and a rules-based international order, strengthening multilateralism and building on long standing EU peace initiatives which contributed to its award of the Nobel Prize in 2012, while strengthening its common security through:

[Measures]

(d) Proposal 24: The EU as a strong actor on the world scene in relationship building:

We propose that the EU should, in its relations with third countries:

Measures:

1. Make greater use of its collective political and economic weight, speaking with one voice and acting in a unified way ....
2. Strengthen its ability to sanction States, governments, entities, groups, or organisations as well as individuals that do not comply with its fundamental principles, agreements and laws and ensuring that sanctions that already exist are quickly implemented and enforced.

[...]

The EU's response to the war in Ukraine is in line with all these proposals, in particular on CFSP/CSDP and on energy. In this sense, the Eurobarometer launched by the Commission some weeks after the start of the war confirmed the positive opinion of the respondent citizens about the various elements of the EU's reaction to the war in Ukraine. 93 per cent approved providing humanitarian support to the people affected by the war and 88 per cent approved welcoming in the EU people fleeing the war. 80 per cent approved the economic sanctions against Russia and about two-thirds approved financing the purchase and supply of military equipment to Ukraine. More than 80 per cent considered that the EU should reduce its dependency on Russian gas and oil, and supported EU measures to secure energy supply and to mitigate rising energy prices. Most agreed that the war in Ukraine shows the need for greater military cooperation within the EU.

The Conference did not propose any specific change concerning the role of Institutions on CFSP/CSDP, except to strengthen the role of the High Representative to ensure that the EU speaks with one voice (see proposal 21.3) and on Council decision-making (see proposal 21 above and proposal 39.1).

Concerning Council decision-making, the follow-up work to this proposal by the Council started immediately after the presentation of the final report of the Conference to the presidents of the three Institutions. This ongoing work has been pushed with the perspective of a possible future enlargement of the Union, in the framework of the examination of the so-called 'EU's absorption capacity', which refers to the EU's capacity to maintain and deepen its own development after the enlargement.[10] In an enlarged EU, the Council decision-making when unanimity is required will be challenging due to the increased number and heterogeneity of Member States and to the possible increased use of vetoes.

In the Granada Declaration on 6 October 2023 the heads of state and government stated:

> Looking ahead to the prospect of a further enlarged Union, both the EU and future Member States need to be ready … We will address key questions related to our priorities and policies as well as our capacity to act. This will make the EU stronger and will enhance European sovereignty.

Therefore, the EU's capacity to act, including the decision-making of the Council, in particular in CFSP, will have an important place in future discussions in the framework of the Council.

16.3. Council Decision-Making in CFSP

As the latest reforms of the EU Treaties have demonstrated, the issue of the Council decision-making, and in particular the voting rule in the Council, is a sensitive and divisive issue, which has been largely discussed in the different intergovernmental conferences (IGC) that have modified the Treaties, including in the IGC that preceded the Lisbon Treaty. Concerning in particular the possible switch from unanimity to qualified majority voting for the adoption of CFSP Council decisions, the EU Treaties offer important flexibilities that the Council has started to explore. These flexibilities are reflected in the so-called 'passerelle clauses', in the possibility of 'constructive abstention' when the Council decides by unanimity, and in the so-called 'emergency brake' when the Council decides by qualified majority.

16.3.1. General Considerations

Before exploring these three 'flexibilities', some general considerations can be made. Firstly, the qualified majority vote is already possible in the area of CFSP in several cases mentioned in Article 31(2) TEU:[11]

(1) When the Council adopts a decision on the basis of a decision of the European Council relating to the EU's strategic interests and objectives.

[10] The integration of new Member States in the EU depends on the fulfilment of the criteria laid down at the June 1993 European Council in Copenhagen, in their different aspects: (i) those that are addressed to the candidate countries; and (ii) the one that is addressed to the EU itself, on its capacity to maintain and deepen its own development, including its capacity to integrate new members ('absorption capacity').

[11] This shall not apply to decisions having miliary or defence implications.

(2) When the Council adopts a decision a proposal of the High Representative following a specific request from the European Council.
(3) When the Council adopts any decision implementing a Council decision, for example to implement a CFSP decision establishing restrictive measures. Therefore, a more extensive conferral of implementing powers by the Council would increase the use of qualified majority.
(4) When the Council appoints a special representative (Article 33 TEU).

Secondly, unanimity has not been an obstacle for the Union to act in CFSP when a strong common political will and unity of objectives exist, as has been the case with the EU's response to Russia's war against Ukraine. In such circumstances, even when the unanimity rule exists in the Council's decision-making, previous situations have generally shown that it is possible to reach compromises and to take decisions beyond the addition of purely national interests. The right balance is necessary between the protection of the 'vital interests' of the Member States and the need to protect the interests of the Union as a whole and to find EU solutions to the problems that so require.

Thirdly, sometimes unanimity contributes to the efficiency and implementation of CFSP Council decisions, as it has been the case with economic sanctions, which are only effective if they are applied uniformly across the whole EU, without putting at risk the integrity of both the internal market and the Schengen area.

Fourthly, veto power as a mechanism to allow the defence of 'vital interests' of EU Member States is sometimes used for reasons not related to the defence of these 'vital interests'. When it is the case, unanimity requirements could weaken the EU's capacity to act and therefore could create mistrust among EU Member States. With a more diverse EU, the differences in views have sometimes been more prominent in the recent years.

16.3.2. The 'Passerelle Clauses'

The change of the rule of vote from unanimity to qualified majority in CFSP is possible in most cases through the flexibilities offered by the current Treaties. The passerelle clauses included in the EU Treaties by the Treaty of Lisbon allow the modification of the rule of vote in the Council from unanimity to qualified majority within the current Treaty framework. Concerning CFSP, the TEU contains two passerelle clauses: a general one (Article 48(7) TEU); and a specific one (Article 31 TEU) that empowers the European Council to decide (by unanimity, with or without the consent of the European Parliament respectively) to move from unanimity to qualified majority. There is only one exception: the decisions with military implications or those in the area of defence given that defence capabilities and assets are in the hands of the Member States. The Council is currently examining to what extent some of the existing passerelle clauses could be triggered.

16.3.3. The Emergency Brake

Decision-making in CFSP allows to protect some 'vital interests' from Member States when qualified majority is the Council voting rule. To this aim, the TEU provides for an 'emergency brake procedure' in order to find a solution acceptable by all Council Members when a member of the Council declares that, for 'vital and stated reasons of national policy', it intends to oppose the adoption of a decision to be taken by qualified majority. In such a case, the vote is not taken, and the High Representative will, in close consultation with the concerned Member State, try to find an acceptable solution. If the High Representative does not succeed, the Council may, acting by reinforced qualified majority (*cf* Article 238(2) TFEU), request that the matter is referred to the European Council for a decision by unanimity.[12]

In addition, the so-called Ioannina mechanism,[13] applicable to all the cases where the Council acts by qualified majority, aims at reinforcing the 'practice of the Council to devote every effort to strengthening the democratic legitimacy of decisions taken by a qualified majority' by requiring the Council to continue discussing a draft legal act in situations where a qualified majority is within reach, but the minority is close to a blocking minority, to try to reach a satisfactory solution to address the concerns raised. However, given the existence in the CFSP area of the emergency brake procedure, the 'Ioannina mechanism' as it stands seems more relevant in EU policies other than CFSP.

16.3.4. Constructive Abstention

When the Council acts by unanimity in CFSP, the Treaty provides for another important element of flexibility, the constructive abstention[14] (*cf* Article 31(1) TEU, second subparagraph). Pursuant to this provision, when abstaining in a vote by unanimity, any member of the Council may qualify its abstention by making a formal declaration. In that case, it shall not be obliged to apply the decision, but shall accept that the decision engages the Union. In a spirit of mutual solidarity, the Member State concerned shall refrain from any action likely to conflict with or impede Union action based on that decision and the other Member States shall respect its position. Moreover, if the members of the Council qualifying their abstention in this way represent at least one-third of the Member States comprising at least one-third of the population of the Union, the Council decision shall not be adopted.

In practice, constructive abstention has been used in the context of the establishment of an EU civilian mission (EULEX) in Kosovo in 2008, where a Member State constructively abstained and therefore enabled the EU to act despite the political differences. And more recently for the adoption of the European Peace Facility Decision to provide Ukraine with lethal and non-lethal military assistance, where some Member States constructively abstained concerning lethal assistance but contributed to the non-lethal support. Nevertheless, constructive abstention may not be used when adopting CFSP restrictive measures, given that those measures require to be implemented and enforced uniformly within the EU and its internal market.

[12] An emergency brake" mechanism also exists outside the CFSP for the coordination of social security systems (Art 48 TFEU), for judicial cooperation in criminal matters (Art 82 TFEU) and for the establishment of common rules for certain criminal matters (Art 83 TFUE).

[13] Council Decision 2009/857/EC of 13 December 2007.

[14] Constructive abstention also has been included in other policies as JAI, social, etc.

Taking into account that constructive abstention allows Member States to keep their national specificities without blocking the others, an increased use of the constructive abstention by the Council members would facilitate decision-making in the Council in CFSP matters when Member States constructively abstain instead of using their veto power.

In addition to all these existing possibilities in the framework of the current Treaties, other possibilities could facilitate the Council decision-making, but may need Treaty change. This would be the case, eg, if modifying the voting rule on Treaty provisions where the passerelle clause does not apply or if introducing in the Treaty a reinforced qualified majority voting outside the cases when such a reinforced majority already exists.

16.4. Conclusion

Russia's aggression against Ukraine has confronted the EU with a new and unexpected geopolitical environment in which the instruments and mechanisms provided for in the Treaties have been used to their fullest. The existence of a common will amongst the EU Member States to find responses to this war has been key to deliver the EU's far-reaching and swift response. The very valuable and complementary work of the EU institutions and the Member States through the different existing mechanisms to respond to the war echoes several of the proposals of the Conference on the Future of Europe. The proposal of the Conference concerning the Council decision-making deserves a particular attention in the perspective of a possible future enlargement of the EU.

17

The Impact of War on EU Law and Policy

DANIEL CALLEJA*

17.1. Introduction

The war in Ukraine has been ongoing since 2014, resulting in a humanitarian crisis, loss of life, and significant political and economic instability in the region. However, its impact has not been limited to Ukraine alone: it has deeply affected our Union.

The list of policy and legal areas that have been affected by the war is very long. The adoption of sanctions against Russia, the provision of significant financial support and humanitarian support to Ukraine, seeking to ensure accountability for war crimes, working towards the use of Russia's frozen and immobilised assets for Ukraine's future reconstruction, tackling migration into the Union, the related energy crisis, challenges to our food security, and the provision of military equipment to Ukraine, illustrate how profound and far-reaching the impact of the war on EU law and policy has been. The conclusions of the European Council of 23 March 2023 show this very well, Ukraine being once again at the top of the agenda. And with this long list of issues, the legal questions we have had to address have been numerous and complex.

Yet, it is my conviction that these unprecedented challenges arising from the war have best demonstrated the ability of the Union to act legally. The solidarity and promptness of the Union response was crucial. And the Union has managed to deliver, using the law as its guiding principle and its most effective tool. Let me illustrate that, by way of example, focusing on three key elements of the EU's legal response: our work on sanctions against Russia; how we have tackled the EU's energy crisis; and the further strengthening of the EU's defence policy.

17.2. Sanctions

In the context of Russia's war of aggression against Ukraine, the EU's sanctions policy was pushed to the fore again. Sanctions became the EU's primary tool for responding to

* The views expressed are personal and cannot bind in any way the Commission. The text reflects the state of play as of 16 January 2025.

Russia's actions, and the different sanctions packages have been the most far-reaching, in terms of content, and the most promptly adopted, in terms of timing, in the EU's history.

17.2.1. Sanctions Revolution

Soon after 24 February 2022, in response to Russia's military aggression against Ukraine, the EU adopted 15 sanctions packages in swift succession. The Council Decision setting out sanctions –adopted under Article 29 TEU – is to be implemented by further regulations, which are jointly proposed by the Commission and the High Representative, under Article 215 Treaty on the Functioning of the European Union (TFEU). So, collaboration of the European Commission with other institutions was vital. Due to the close alignment between the Commission, the Council and the High Representative, all sanctions measures have been adopted often on the very same day, showing a unity of response.

Thus, in response to Russian President Putin's unprecedented and unprovoked military attack against Ukraine, the EU has put in place a comprehensive and robust package of restrictive sanctions designed to undermine Russia's ability to finance the war, impose clear economic and political costs on Russia's political elite responsible for the invasion, and diminish Russia's economic base. These measures are proportionate and targeted.

As President Ursula von der Leyen pointed out in her State of the Union address on 14 September 2022:

> From day one, Europe has stood at Ukraine's side. With weapons. With funds. With hospitality for refugees. And with the toughest sanctions the world has ever seen. Russia's financial sector is on life-support. We have cut off three quarters of Russia's banking sector from international markets. Nearly one thousand international companies have left the country. The production of cars fell by three-quarters compared to last year. Aeroflot is grounding planes because there are no more spare parts. The Russian military is taking chips from dishwashers and refrigerators to fix their military hardware, because they ran out of semiconductors. Russia's industry is in tatters.

Some of the most important sanctions set by the EU to date include (but are not limited to) the following:

- Targeted sanctions against individuals: asset freezing (€21.5 billion in the EU so far) and travel bans, targeting primarily Russian officials, elites and propagandists, including Russian President Vladimir Putin and commanders of the Wagner Group, as well as associated entities. In total, considering as well earlier individual sanctions imposed after the annexation of Crimea in 2014, the EU has sanctioned 1,473 individuals and 205 entities.
- Disconnecting many leading Russian financial institutions, including Sberbank, Russia's largest bank, from the SWIFT international financial messaging system.
- Prohibiting exports to Russia (including transit) of dual-use goods/technology, drone engines, arms, civilian firearms, ammunition, military vehicles, paramilitary equipment. The total estimated value of export restrictions on goods and technologies to date is €32.5 billion. This represents 36 per cent of the EU's export before the invasion.

- Banning certain exports in the aviation, maritime and technology sectors (eg, semiconductors) and the export of luxury goods to Russia. Three-quarters of Russia's current commercial air fleet was built in the EU, the US and Canada. This means that Russia will not be able to maintain its fleet to international standards.
- Closing EU airspace, sea ports and roads to Russian aircraft, vessels and transport operators, respectively.
- Banning imports from Russia of coal and of crude oil and petroleum products, phased and with limited exceptions. 57 per cent of pre-war imports are covered by measures, representing €89.9 billion.
- Imposing a price cap on Russian crude oil and petroleum products exported to third countries, banning the provision of maritime transport, insurance and other assistance services for the transport of products sold above the cap (G7 oil price cap).

Last, but not least, speaking of the impact of the war on the Digital Single Market, let us not forget that, in another unprecedented step, the Union also suspended the broadcasting licences of propaganda media such as the state-owned Russia Today and Sputnik. And, when it comes to defend these restrictive measures, I would just refer to the 11-hour long court hearing in which I represented the European Commission, intervening in support of the Council, with many Member States, before the General Court in an action brought by Russia Today France. Russia Today challenged the restrictive measures which banned it from broadcasting its content in the EU. This case clearly shows that in the EU the Court always has the final word on the legality of our measures. Indeed, this is not an isolated case.

This wave of sanctions has led to a significant increase in litigation in this field. As the Court of Justice of the European Union has highlighted, one of the major developments in 2022 was the emergence of cases involving the restrictive measures adopted by the EU in the context of the war in Ukraine. More generally, cases involving restrictive measures, totalling 103 new cases, represented 11.4 per cent of all new cases brought in 2022 (as against 4.8 per cent in 2021 and 3 per cent in 2020).

17.2.2. Safe Haven

Yet, our work did not stop with adoption and defence of the sanctions. Without law enforcement, there is no law, and if there is no law, there can be no justice. Therefore, it is as equally important to formally adopt sanctions as it is to ensure their execution. Sanction effectiveness is determined by two concomitant factors: the degree of multilateral alignment around them; and the efficacy of their enforcement. After Russia's full-scale invasion of Ukraine in February 2022, the G7 countries decided to impose some degree of sanction against Russia. Russia is now the world's most sanctioned country, surpassing even North Korea.

However, while the 'sanctions coalition' countries represent over half the world's economy, two-thirds of the world's population live in neutral or Russia-leaning countries regarding the war in Ukraine. Key trading partners, such as the remaining BRICS countries (Brazil, India, China, South Africa) or Türkiye, do not currently impose sanctions, nor do Russia's neighbours, such as Armenia or Central Asian countries. As of today, sanctions against Russia are multilateral, but not global, which leaves ample room for manoeuvre to circumvent them via third-country imports, direct or indirect re-export, or false transit. Significantly, Russia's exports to Brazil, China, India and Türkiye have increased by at least 50 per cent since the 2022 war began, relative to the previous year, while Turkish exports to Russia grew 46 per cent in the six months after the imposition of sanctions.

That it is why the European Commission pays utmost attention to the proper enforcement of the existing sanctions and has taken various actions to this end. For example, to navigate this issue, the Commission decided on December 2022 to create the new role of International Special Envoy for the Implementation of EU Sanctions to ensure continuous and high-level discussions with third countries to avoid the evasion or even the circumvention of the unprecedented restrictive measures that have been imposed on Russia since the start of its war against Ukraine.

Furthermore, upon a proposal by the Commission, in November 2022, the Council adopted a decision to add the violation of restrictive measures (sanctions) to the list of areas of particularly serious crime ('EU crimes') under Article 83(1) TFEU. Shortly after, the Commission presented its proposal for a directive 'on the definition of criminal offences and penalties for the violation of Union restrictive measures', establishing harmonised minimum rules across the EU – a necessary step for implementing the above decision. The Directive (2024/1226), adopted in April 2024, is seen by experts as a 'major milestone in the harmonization of EU sanctions enforcement, as well as in the development of European criminal law more generally'.

We should not forget, of course, that the implementation and enforcement of EU sanctions is primarily the responsibility of EU Member States. While Council Decisions and Regulations imposing sanctions are directly applicable in the Member States, each of them has its own framework of national competent authorities and national legislation penalising sanctions breaches. In its role as guardian of the Treaties, the Commission oversees the application of Union law and ensures the uniform implementation of sanctions throughout the Union, also by facilitating a common understanding of the relevant legal provisions. It does so by means of opinions, public outreach and legal guidance addressed to authorities and operators.

So, in short, the European Commission is responsible for ensuring, through monitoring, that the regulations imposing restrictive measures adopted under Article 215 TFEU are implemented and enforced by the Member States, and for guiding their implementation. Yet, I trust that the necessary commitment on the part of the EU Member States for the proper implementation of sanctions is also present. In fact, the European Council underlined in its conclusions of March 2023: 'the importance and urgency of stepping up … efforts to ensure effective implementation of sanctions at European and national level' and its '[firm commitment] to effectively preventing and countering circumvention in and by third countries'.

17.3. Energy (and State Aid)

There is probably no better sector to demonstrate the impact of the war on the single market and competition law than the energy one. Since the outbreak of the war, Russian supplies of gas to the EU were disrupted as a deliberate attempt to use energy as a political weapon. Russia has been for many years the main gas supplier of the EU, the EU historically relying on Russia for more than 40 per cent of its gas supplies. However, the war quickly made apparent that Russia was no longer a reliable energy partner, and that EU energy policy had to be carefully reconsidered, to reduce its dependence.

As a clear vision and timely action was essential, in May 2022 the Commission presented it RePowerEU Plan – a €300 billion plan which sets out concrete measures to fast-forward the green transition and make Europe independent from Russian fossil fuels well before 2030. Furthermore, in 2022, upon Commission proposals, the Council adopted five Regulations on the basis of Article 122 TFEU which set out urgent, proportionate and temporary measures aimed at addressing the energy crisis, in a spirit of solidarity between the Member States.

Let me recall that Article 122 is part of the TFEU's chapter on economic policy. It allows the Council, by way of a derogatory legislative procedure, to adopt economic policy 'measures' (including regulations) based on qualified majority voting (QMV) on the basis of a Commission proposal. The Council may amend the Commission proposal only by acting unanimously. The European Parliament is informed. As a result, regulations under Article 122 TFEU can generally be adopted much faster than regulations under the ordinary legislative procedure, and this speed of action has been essential in tacking the energy crisis. These regulations have tackled core aspects of the energy crisis.

17.3.1. Council Regulation 2022/1369 of 5 August 2022 on Coordinated Demand Reduction Measures for Gas

This Regulation was adopted to increase the EU's security of energy supply. The Regulation: (1) sets a target for all Member States to reduce gas demand by 15 per cent between 1 August 2022 and 31 March 2023; and (2) gives the Commission the possibility to declare, after consulting Member States, a 'Union Alert' on security of supply, imposing a mandatory gas demand reduction on all Member States.

During the spring of 2023, Member States worked diligently and adopted measures aiming to reduce their respective gas demand by 15 per cent, as foreseen by the aforementioned Regulation. This resulted in effective gas demand reductions across the EU by 19 per cent between August 2022 and January 2023. As the heating season came to an end in late March 2023 levels of gas storage were historically high and new infrastructure has been built to help diversification. Moreover, Russia can no longer weaponise energy and introduce uncertainty in the system to the same extent as in 2022.

Despite the demand reduction achieved and diversification of supply, severe difficulties persisted in the supply of energy, which can affect the competitiveness of the EU and the general economic situation. The risks include a possible rebound of LNG demand in Asia, which can reduce the availability of gas on the global market; weather conditions, which can affect hydropower storage and nuclear production and require a higher recourse to gas-fired power generation; and some further gas supply disruptions, which could affect the filling of underground gas storage facilities required for a safer winter 2023–24. That is why the European Commission proposed on 20 March 2023 to prolong emergency legislation on measures to reduce gas demand (2022/1369) by 15 per cent for another 12 months (on the basis of Article 122 TFUE).

17.3.2. Council Regulation (EU) 2022/1854 of 6 October 2022 on an Emergency Intervention to Address High Energy Prices

This Regulation includes measures to reduce electricity demand especially during the expensive peak hours, to help lower electricity costs for consumers. It also contains a temporary revenue cap on electricity producers using technologies with lower costs, such as renewables, nuclear and lignite.

17.3.3. Council Regulation (EU) 2022/2576 of 19 December 2022 Enhancing Solidarity Through Better Coordination of Gas Purchases, Reliable Price Benchmarks and Exchanges of Gas across Borders

This Regulation addressed high energy prices and ensured security of supply for the 2023–24 winter. The main tools of the proposal are aggregation of demand and joint gas purchasing for gas to increase leverage.

17.3.4. Council Regulation (EU) 2022/2577 of 22 December 2022 Laying Down a Framework to Accelerate the Deployment of Renewable Energy

The Regulation accelerates permit-granting in the realm of renewables, particularly those capable of achieving short-term acceleration of the Union's renewable energy deployment.

17.3.5. Council Regulation (EU) 2022/2578 of 22 December 2022 Establishing a Market Correction Mechanism to Protect Union Citizens and the Economy against Excessively High Prices

This Regulation protects EU businesses and households from episodes of excessively high gas prices in the EU by introducing a market correction mechanism on virtual gas trading platforms in the EU.

In view of the seriousness of the situation, the EU continues to take key measures in the energy sector. The energy crisis spurred on by the war underlined the need to quickly adapt the electricity market to better support the green transition and offer energy consumers (both households and businesses) widespread access to affordable renewable and non-fossil electricity. So, on 14 March 2023, the Commission proposed to reform the EU's electricity market design to accelerate a surge in renewables and the phase-out of gas, make consumer bills less dependent on volatile fossil fuel prices, better protect consumers from future price spikes and potential market manipulation, and make the EU's industry clean and more competitive (the new rules – the amending Directive EU/2024/1711 and the amending Regulation EU/2024/1747 – were adopted on 21 May 2024 and entered into force on 16 July 2024). This was complemented on 16 March 2023 by plans on how to stimulate and support investment in sustainable hydrogen production through a European Hydrogen Bank (EHB).

Hydrogen can make a major contribution to the EU's ambitions to end imports of Russian fossil fuels in the next few years and help to achieve climate-neutrality by 2050. This initiative is aimed at accelerating investment and bridging the investment gap for the EU to reach its ambitious REPowerEU targets of producing domestically 10 million tonnes (mt) of renewable hydrogen by 2030, coupled with 10 mt of imports.

Let me note, however, that the Commission's response to the energy crisis has not been limited to the energy sector alone. The aim of the Temporary Crisis and Transition Framework, which the Commission adopted in 2022, is to enable Member States to support the economy in the context of Russia's invasion of Ukraine, particularly to counter increases in energy costs and accelerate the roll out of renewables. The Framework was subsequently amended several times, to better respond to the persistent challenges the Union was confronted with, and in March 2023, the Commission adopted the Temporary Crisis and Transition Framework (which was amended on 20 November 2023 and on 2 May 2024, in the light of the economic situation).

On 9 March 2023 the European Commission also endorsed a targeted amendment to the General Block Exemption Regulation (GBER) to further facilitate, simplify and speed up support for the EU's green and digital transitions. Together with the new Temporary Crisis and Transition Framework, this targeted amendment makes it easier for the Member States to grant necessary support for key sectors in line with the Green Deal Industrial Plan.

While there may be concerns that the relaxation of state aid controls in general may result in an uneven playing field and weaken the single market, the Commission has consistently acknowledged that the integrity of the internal market is important to withstand external pressure and to avoid subsidy races, where Member States with deeper pockets can outspend neighbours to the detriment of cohesion within the Union.

That is why the framework contains safeguards to preserve the EU level-playing field, including on proportionality and sustainability. In fact, Member States must therefore show that the state aid measures notified to the Commission and falling within the scope of the Commission Communication are necessary, appropriate and proportionate to remedy a serious disturbance in the economy of the Member State concerned and that all the requirements of this Communication are fulfilled.

17.4. Defence

Hand in hand with the work on sanctions, the EU has been taking measures to help Ukraine defend itself, as well as to improve the Union's own defence capabilities. More specifically, defence assistance to Ukraine has three elements. First, each Member State has directly and individually provided military assistance to Ukraine. Secondly, the Union has delivered so far under the European Peace Facility a total of €3.6 billion in military assistance, and the Commission has played its role in that regard. In fact, when in 2020, upon the Council's request, the Commission accepted the innovative task of administering the budget under assistance measures for the Facility, it was not known that it would be procuring equipment for a war in the very heart of Europe. Yet, this assistance has been vital in supporting Ukraine. Furthermore, the Council agreed on 20 March 2020 to provide one million ammunitions to Ukraine over the next 12 months, speeding up the delivery and joint procurement.

Thirdly, the war has made clear the need to reinforce the Union's own defence industrial base. More specifically, on 11 March 2022, the members of the European Council met at Versailles and committed, among other things, to boost European defence capabilities, increase defence budgets, close shortfalls and capability objectives, enhance innovation and strengthen and develop the European defence industrial and technological base (EDTIB).

On 19 July 2022, the Commission proposed a Regulation establishing the European Defence Industry Reinforcement through common Procurement Act for 2022–24 (EDIRPA). The Commission proposed to earmark €500 million of the EU budget in current prices for the 2022–24 period for this purpose. The Regulation (2023/2418) was adopted by the co-legislators on 13 October 2023. The instrument is intended to encourage Member States to procure defence products jointly and for the first time establishes a joint EU defence procurement fund. The legal basis for the EDIRPA is found in Article 173 TFEU (support for competitiveness of the European industry). The Regulation seeks to enhance the competitiveness of the EDTIB by supporting cooperation between Member States in the field of joint defence procurement.

This short-term instrument will serve as the basis for the more long-term EU framework for defence joint procurement, the so-called European Defence Investment Programme (EDIP). The Regulation will establish the 'conditions for Member States to form European Defence Capability Consortia (EDCC)'. Within an EDCC, Member States will jointly procure, for the use of participating Member States, defence capabilities that are developed in a collaborative way within the EU and will benefit from a VAT exemption.

Other example of the ongoing talks on defence investment and capabilities is the agreement reached on 20 March 2023 on the European Defence Agency (EDA) project for the collaborative procurement of ammunition to assist Ukraine and rebuild Member States' national stockpiles, which will involve an investment of €2 billion (drawing on the European Peace Fund). As stated by the High Representative of the Union for Foreign Affairs and Security Policy, Josep Borrell, Member States agreed to deliver one million rounds of artillery ammunition over the course of one year. The Commission will therefore work with Member States to increase defence industrial production in the EU to meet this target.

These initiatives show that the need for cooperation between Member States, in terms of defence policy, is greater than ever.

Cooperation with NATO is also very important. In this regard, a recent example of this cooperation is the EU–NATO Task Force on Resilience of Critical Infrastructure to reinforce our common security, announced jointly by President von der Leyen and

NATO Secretary General Stoltenberg on 11 January 2023. The EU and NATO will share best practices, enhance shared situational awareness, develop key principles to improve resilience including mitigating measures and remedial actions. The Task Force will cover four sectors at this stage: energy; digital infrastructure; transport; and space. Let us also not forget that Danish citizens decided in a referendum to abolish the defence opt-out. Finland and Sweden have applied to join NATO. These are just recent examples of the interest in the further progress on EU's security and defence and on strengthening NATO as a defensive alliance.

In fact, Russia's invasion of Ukraine has dramatically altered the geopolitical situation in Europe. The challenges to the EU's security are becoming increasingly complex and dynamic, as a range of actors constantly test its resilience, seeking to exploit the openness, interdependence and connectivity of its societies and economies.

In such a context, this crisis is a possibility to perfect possible further development of the Union defence policy under Article 42(2) TEU (which refers to the 'progressive framing of a common Union defence policy', which 'will lead to a common defence, when the European Council, acting unanimously, so decides'), fully compatible with the role of NATO (Article 42(2) TEU, second sentence).

17.5. Single Market

Since Russia's unprovoked and unjustified invasion of Ukraine and the blockade of Ukrainian seaports, Ukraine has been unable to export its produce to destinations around the world via the usual routes. This situation threatens global food security so alternative routes were needed urgently. In this sense, the Commission has made it a priority to preserve the free circulation of goods within the EU. After all, the free movement of goods is the linchpin of the European single market.

As part of the EU's response, the following initiatives were outlined by President von der Leyen in her opening remarks at the joint press conference with President Michel following the meeting of the European Council of 23 March 2023:

- On 18 March 2023, a deal allowing Ukrainian grain exports to pass through the blockaded Black Sea was extended. Initially brokered by the UN and Turkey in July 2022, after Russia's invasion of Ukraine in February 2022 fueled a global food crisis, the pact was extended in November for 120 days. A renewal of the deal was necessary to help stave off hunger in the most food insecure countries, as Ukraine and Russia produce a significant chunk of the world's grain and fertiliser, together supplying some 28 per cent of globally traded wheat and 75 per cent of sunflower oil during peacetime.
- The President also stressed 'the great success of the solidarity lanes in enabling Ukraine to export large quantities of grains and other agricultural products. This is besides the Black Sea Grain Initiative, the second big initiative on helping Ukraine to export its grain. In this context, it is important that we are helping our farmers in the European Union that have to deal with the market consequences. Because a lot of grain is now coming to the European market, and this has an influence on the

prices. And therefore, those front-line countries that are helping the most with the solidarity lanes should not suffer then from disadvantages.'

- In March 2022,the emergency synchronisation of the Continental European power system with the power systems of Ukraine and Moldova took place. This important milestone was accelerated by the TSOs of Continental Europe to support the power systems of Ukraine and Moldova following the invasion on 24 February 2022 and following a request from the TSOs, Ukrenergo and Moldelectrica. With the support of Continental European TSOs, Ukrenergo was able to increase the stability of the grid and maintain the security of its power system through the most difficult periods. In particular, it minimised the incidence of having to reduce or turn off the supply of electricity to its businesses and citizens during winter and to ensure a faster recovery time for system restoration following the significant attacks and damage to Ukrainian energy infrastructure. The synchronisation played an important role in managing the challenging winter. With the onset of Russian attacks on Ukraine's energy infrastructure, the synchronisation allowed Ukraine and Moldova to import electricity during the most difficult periods. By opening the possibility of Ukrainian electricity exports in June 2022, it demonstrated the significance of the interconnection for commercial exchanges between EU and Ukraine.

17.6. Concluding Remarks

As Commission President Ursula von der Leyen has stressed, this is not only a war unleashed by Russia against Ukraine. This is a war on the EU's energy, its economy, its security, its values and its future. Through timely and appropriate measures the Union shows it has the legal tools to reply quickly and effectively in such situations. The Commission, as the guardian of the Treaties will continue to play its role. But this will not be enough without the duty of loyal cooperation, enshrined in the Treaties. What is yet to come will be less no demanding, neither in political, economic, nor in legal terms. We must acknowledge that we are living in a reality that is increasingly challenging for all Member States, for EU citizens and for business. Thus, our thinking – including our legal thinking – must focus on how to respond to that reality and to the Union as it is today, which is not the Union we knew a decade ago.

Unity and solidarity are the two key principles at stake here. Staying united and working closely with the Member States is more essential than ever. In this regard, beyond the formal opportunities, we have to work together via legislative and Court legal procedures, and informal fora for legal dialogue are extremely valuable. To conclude, for 70 years, law has been the driving force behind the ever-deeper integration of Europe. Or as the EU President likes to say:

> The community of law is the foundation of everything we have achieved and everything we are still to do. The rule of law is amongst the founding values of the Union and at the core of our common identity. We must protect it all times as this is what keeps the Union together and allows it to move forward, whatever the challenges it has to face.

INDEX

www.ingramcontent.com/pod-product-compliance
Ingram Content Group UK Ltd.
Pitfield, Milton Keynes, MK11 3LW, UK
UKHW020845290926
15470UKWH00004B/1564

9 781509 986088